Doan Bui

D0012683

DANTE ALIGHIERI was born in Florence in 1265 and belonged to a noble but impoverished family. He followed a normal course of studies, possibly attending university in Bologna, and when he was about twenty he married Gemma Donati, by whom he had five children. He had first met Bice Portinari, whom he called Beatrice, in 1274, and when she died in 1290 he sought distraction by studying philosophy and theology and by writing *La Vita Nuova*. During this time he became involved in the strife between the Guelfs and the Ghibellines; he became a prominent White Guelf and when the Black Guelfs came to power in 1302 Dante, during an absence from Florence, was condemned to exile. He took refuge first in Verona and after wandering from place to place, as far as Paris and even, some have said, to Oxford, he settled in Ravenna. While there he completed the *Divine Comedy*, which he began in about 1308. Dante died in Ravenna in 1321.

DOROTHY LEIGH SAYERS translated *The Song of Roland*, in addition to Dante's *Divine Comedy*, for the Penguin Classics. She graduated with first class honours in medieval literature from Somerville College, Oxford, in 1915, having already published two volumes of poetry. Her first novel appeared in 1923 and she later wrote fifteen more books of detective fiction including *The Nine Tailors*, a fascinating novel about campanology. She also wrote religious plays, notably *The Man Born to Be King*. She died in 1957.

THE COMEDY

OF

DANTE ALIGHIERI

THE FLORENTINE

*

CANTICA I

HELL

⟨L'INFERNO⟩

*

TRANSLATED BY
DOROTHY L. SAYERS

*

PENGUIN BOOKS

Penguin Books Ltd, Harmondsworth, Middlesex, England
Penguin Books, 625 Madison Avenue, New York, New York 10022, U.S.A.
Penguin Books Australia Ltd, Ringwood, Victoria, Australia
Penguin Books Canada Ltd, 2801 John Street, Markham, Ontario, Canada L3R 1B4
Penguin Books (N.Z.) Ltd, 182–190 Wairau Road, Auckland 10, New Zealand

—

This translation of Dante's *Inferno* first published in 1949
Reprinted in 1950, 1951, 1953, 1954, 1955, 1957, 1959 (twice), 1960,
1961, 1962, 1963, 1964, 1965, 1966, 1967, 1968, 1969, 1971, 1972, 1973, 1974,
1975, 1976, 1977, 1978, 1979, 1980, 1981

—

—

Made and printed in Great Britain by
Hazell Watson & Viney Ltd,
Aylesbury, Bucks
Set in Monotype Bembo

Maps and diagrams
specially drawn for this edition by
C. W. Scott-Giles

CONTENTS

Introduction   9
The Greater Images   67
THE DIVINE COMEDY
    CANTICA I: HELL   71
Appendices:
    Dante's Universe   292
    Chronology   296
    Hour of the Earthquake   297
Glossary of Proper Names   299
Books to Read   346

DIAGRAMS

Section of the Earth   70
Map of Upper Hell (Circles i to v)   84
Map of Nether Hell 1 (Circles vi and vii)   122
Section-map of Hell   138
Map of the Po Basin   173
Map of Nether Hell 2 (Circle viii)   180
Bridge over Bowge iii   194
Font in Baptistery at Pisa   194
Diagram to illustrate Canto xxiv, 34–5   226
Map and Sketch of Nether Hell 3 (Circle ix)   264

INTRODUCTION

THE ideal way of reading *The Divine Comedy* would be to start at the first line and go straight through to the end, surrendering to the vigour of the story-telling and the swift movement of the verse, and not bothering about any historical allusions or theological explanations which do not occur in the text itself. That is how Dante himself tackles his subject. His opening words plunge us abruptly into the middle of a situation:

> *Midway this way of life we're bound upon*
> *I woke to find myself in a dark wood,*
> *Where the right road was wholly lost and gone.*

From that moment the pace of the narrative never slackens. Down the twenty-four great circles of Hell we go, through the world and out again under the Southern stars; up the two terraces and the seven cornices of Mount Purgatory, high over the sea, high over the clouds to the Earthly Paradise at its summit; up again, whirled from sphere to sphere of the singing Heavens, beyond the planets, beyond the stars, beyond the Primum Mobile, into the Empyrean, there to behold God as He is – the ultimate, the ineffable, yet, in a manner beyond all understanding, "marked with our image" – until, in that final ecstasy,

> *Power failed high fantasy here; yet, swift to move*
> *Even as a wheel moves equal, free from jars,*
> *Already my heart and will were wheeled by love,*
> *The Love that moves the sun and the other stars.*

Yet the twentieth-century reader who starts out on this tremendous journey without any critical apparatus to assist him is liable to get bogged half-way unless he knows something of Dante's theological, political, and personal background. For not only is the poem a religious and political allegory – it is an allegory of a rather special kind. If we know how to read it, we shall find that it has an enormous relevance both to us as individuals and to the world situation of to-day. Dante's Europe – remote and strange as it seemed to the Liberals of the eighteenth and nineteenth centuries – had much in common with our own distracted times, and his vivid awareness of the deeps and heights within the soul comes home poignantly to us who have so recently rediscovered the problem of evil, the problem of power, and the ease with which our most God-like imaginings are "betrayed by what is false within". Moreover, Dante is a poet after our own hearts, possessed of a vivid personality, which flows into and steeps the whole texture of his work. Every line he ever wrote is the record of an intimate personal experience; few men have ever displayed their own strength and weakness so unreservedly, or interpreted the universe so consistently in terms of their own self-exploring. Nor, I suppose, have passionate flesh and passionate intellect ever been fused together in such a furnace of the passionate spirit. Browning's phrase for the *Comedy*:

> *the majestic mass*
> *Leavened as the sea whose fire is mixed with glass,*

comes nearer than any other to expressing Dante's miracle of burning clarity.

But if Dante is to "speak to our condition", as the Quakers so charmingly put it, we must take him seriously and ourselves seriously. We must forget a great deal of the nonsense that is talked about Dante – all the legends about his sourness, arrogance, and "obscurity", and especially that libel which, as Professor Vincent[1] has observed, "persists with the tenacity of an evil weed", namely, that he was a peevish political exile who indulged his petty spites and prejudices by putting his enemies in Hell and his friends in Paradise. We need not forget that Dante is sublime, intellectual, and, on occasion, grim; but we must also be prepared to find him simple, homely, humorous, tender, and bubbling over with ecstasy. Nor must we look to find in him only a poet of "period" interest; he is a universal poet, speaking prophetically of God and the Soul and the Society of Men in their universal relations.

We must also be prepared, while we are reading Dante, to accept the Christian and Catholic view of ourselves as responsible

1. E. R. Vincent, *On Re-Reading Dante.*

rational beings. We must abandon any idea that we are the slaves of chance, or environment, or our subconscious; any vague notion that good and evil are merely relative terms, or that conduct and opinion do not really matter; any comfortable persuasion that, however shiftlessly we muddle through life, it will somehow or other all come right on the night. We must try to believe that man's will is free, that he can consciously exercise choice, and that his choice can be decisive to all eternity. For *The Divine Comedy* is precisely the drama of the soul's choice. It is not a fairy-story, but a great Christian allegory, deriving its power from the terror and splendour of the Christian revelation. Clear, hard thought went to its making: its beauty is of that solid and indestructible sort that is built upon a framework of nobly proportioned bones. If we ignore the theological structure, and merely browse about in it for detached purple passages and poetic bits and pieces we shall be disappointed, and never see the architectural grandeur of the poem as a whole. People who tackle Dante in this superficial way seldom get beyond the picturesque squalors of the *Inferno*. This is as though we were to judge a great city after a few days spent underground among the cellars and sewers; it would not be surprising if we were to report only an impression of sordidness, suffocation, rats, fetor, and gloom. But the grim substructure is only there for the sake of the city whose walls and spires stand up and take the morning; it is for the vision of God in the *Paradiso* that all the rest of the allegory exists.

Allegory is the interpretation of experience by means of images. In its simplest form it is a kind of extended metaphor. Supposing we say: "John very much wanted to do so-and-so, but hesitated for fear of the consequences"; that is a plain statement. If we say: "In John's mind desire and fear contended for the mastery" we are already beginning to speak allegorically: John's mind has become a field of battle in which two personified emotions are carrying on a conflict. From this we can easily proceed to build up a full-blown allegory. We can represent the object of John's ambition as a lady imprisoned in a castle, which is attacked by a knight called Desire and defended by a giant called Fear, and we can put in as much description of the place and people as will serve to make the story exciting. We can show Desire so badly battered by Fear that he is discouraged and ready to give up, until rebuked by his squire, called Shame, who takes him to have his wounds dressed by a cheerful lady named Hope. Later, he is accosted by a plausible stranger called Suspicion, who says that the lady is much less virtuous and good-looking than she is made out to be. ... And so forth, introducing as many personifications of this kind as may be needed to express John's successive changes of mind. In this way we can work out quite a complicated psychological pattern, and at the same time entertain the reader with an exciting and colourful tale of adventure. In this purest kind of allegory, John himself never appears: his psyche is merely the landscape in which his personified feelings carry out their manoeuvres. But there is also a form in which John himself – or what we may perhaps call John's conscious self, or super-self – figures among the personages of the allegory, as a pilgrim or knight-errant, exploring the wildernesses of his own soul and fighting against opposition both from within and without. The earlier part of *The Romance of the Rose* is an example of the first kind of allegory and *The Pilgrim's Progress* of the second. In neither kind does the actual story pretend to be a relation of fact; in its *literal* meaning, the whole tale is fiction; the *allegorical* meaning is the true story.

Dante's allegory is more complex. It differs from the standard type in two ways: (1) in its *literal* meaning, the story is – up to a certain point and with a great many important qualifications – intended to be a true story; (2) the figures of the allegory, instead of being personified abstractions, are *symbolic personages*.

To take the second point first: In dealing with the vexed subject of symbolism, we shall save ourselves much bewilderment of mind by realizing that there are two kinds of symbols.

A *conventional* symbol is a sign, arbitrarily chosen to represent, or "stand for", something with which it has no integral connexion: thus the scrawl X may, by common agreement, stand, in mathematics, for an unknown quantity; in the alphabet, for a sound composed of a cluck and a hiss; at the end of a letter, for a fond embrace. The figure X *is* not, in itself, any of these things and tells us nothing about them. Any other sign would serve the same purpose if we agreed to accept it so, nor is there any reason why the same sign should not stand, if we agreed that it should, for quite different things: infinity, or a murmuring sound, or a threat. With this kind of symbol we need not now concern ourselves, except to distinguish it from the other.

A *natural* symbol is not an arbitrary sign, but a thing really existing which, by its very nature, stands for and images forth a greater reality of which it is itself an instance. Thus an arch, maintaining itself as it does by a balance of opposing strains, is a *natural symbol* of that stability in tension by which the whole universe maintains itself. Its significance is the same in all languages and in all circumstances, and may be applied indifferently to physical, psychical, or spiritual experience. Dante's symbolism is of this kind. To avoid confusion with the conventional or arbitrary symbol I shall follow the example of Charles Williams and others and refer to Dante's natural symbols as his "images".

We are now in a position to distinguish between a simple allegorical figure and a symbolic image. The allegorical figure is a personified abstraction. Thus, in an *allegorical masque*, Tyranny might be represented as a demon with a club in one hand and a set of fetters in the other, riding in a juggernaut chariot drawn by tigers over the bodies of Youth, Innocence, Happiness, and whatnot, and declaiming sentiments appropriate to tyrannical passions. In a play using *symbolic imagery*, the dramatist might bring in the figure of Nero or Hitler, wearing his ordinary clothes and simply talking like Nero or Hitler, and every one would understand that this personage was meant for the image of Tyranny.

In the *Comedy*, Dante uses the allegorical figure only occasionally; by far the greater number of his figures are symbolic images. Thus, he is accompanied through Hell, not by a personified abstraction called Reason or Wisdom, or Science, or Art, or Statecraft, but by Virgil the Poet, a real person, who is, by his own nature, qualified to symbolize all these abstractions. The characters encountered in the circles of Hell, Purgatory, and Paradise are similarly not personifications of Sin and Virtue, but the souls of real people, represented as remaining in, or purging off, their sins, or experiencing the fruition of their virtues.

Being thus real personages, the images of the *Divine Comedy* are set in a real environment: Hell, Purgatory, and Heaven are not a fiction invented to carry the allegory, but a true picture of the three states of the life after death. I do not, of course, mean by this that Dante's description of them is meant to be physically accurate. He did not really suppose that Hell was a pit extending from a little way below the foundations of Jerusalem to the centre of the earth, or that Purgatory was a mountainous island in the Antipodes, or that a person could go from one to the other in his mortal body in the space of two and a half days; nor did he really imagine that Heaven was located among the celestial spheres. He takes the utmost pains to make his geographical details plausible and scientifically correct; but that is just the novelist's method of giving verisimilitude to the story. Dante knew better, and from time to time he warns his readers against mistaking a work of the imagination for a bald statement of material fact. He did, however, share the belief of all Catholic Christians that every living soul in the world has to make the choice between accepting or rejecting God, and that at the moment of death it will discover what it has chosen: whether to remain in the outer darkness of the alien self, knowing God only as terror and judgment and pain, or to pass joyfully through the strenuous purgation which fits it to endure and enjoy eternally the unveiled presence of God.

But although the *literal story* of the *Comedy* is (with the qualification and within the limits I have mentioned) a true one, and the characters in it are real people, the poem is nevertheless an allegory. The literal meaning is the least important part of it: the story with its images is only there for the sake of the truth which it symbolizes, and the real environment within which all the events take place is the human soul. Since Dante has suffered a good deal at the hands of readers who suppose him to be interested only in the post-mortal destination of his friends and enemies, let us hear what he himself has to say on the subject. We have a letter, written to his patron, Can Grande della Scala, in which he explains the nature of allegory and the way in which he intended his book to be read:

The meaning of this work is not simple ... for we obtain one meaning from the letter of it, and another from that which the letter signifies; and the first is called literal, *but the other* allegorical *or* mystical. *And to make this matter of treatment clearer, it may be studied in the verse:*

Introduction

"*When Israel came out of Egypt and the House of Jacob from among a strange people, Judah was his sanctuary and Israel his dominion*". *For if we regard the letter alone, what is set before us is the exodus of the Children of Israel from Egypt in the days of Moses; if the allegory, our redemption wrought by Christ; if the moral sense, we are shown the conversion of the soul from the grief and wretchedness of sin to the state of grace; if the anagogical, we are shown the departure of the holy soul from the thraldom of this corruption to the liberty of eternal glory. And although these mystical meanings are called by various names, they may all be called in general allegorical, since they differ from the literal and historical.*

The subject of the whole work, then, taken merely in the literal sense is "the state of the soul after death straightforwardly affirmed", for the development of the whole work hinges on and about that. But if, indeed, the work is taken allegorically, its subject is: "Man, as by good or ill deserts, in the exercise of his free choice, he becomes liable to rewarding or punishing Justice".

It will be seen that Dante has chosen as his illustrative example a text which, taken literally, asserts a historical fact, but which can be interpreted allegorically on three different levels. This suggests that the allegory of the *Commedia* also may, and should, find various levels of interpretation; and this is true, both of it and of all great allegories which convey universal truths.

Two other consequences follow. In the first place, because the personages are symbolic images in an allegory, we need not trouble too much about the accuracy of Dante's information and judgment, or waste our time in exclaiming over his arrogance in adjudicating eternal awards and punishments. He may have erred in supposing that Guido da Montefeltro had committed the fraud for which he suffers in the eighth pit of Malbowges, or that the notorious Cunizza repented her sins and attained beatitude: for the allegory it is immaterial. Historians are fallible, and God alone knows the secrets of the heart; for all we know a Marquis de Sade may have been much maligned and a Julius Streicher may have died penitent and at peace with his Maker. But that need not, and does not, prevent us – as it did not prevent Dante – from saying: "If his deeds do not belie him, then in that man we behold some-

15

thing that is an embodied damnation". Literally, we may or may not believe that such a man has cut himself off from redemption; but in any case, we can scarcely be mistaken in saying: "That man presents the image of something in civilization which will corrupt and ruin civilization; of something in myself which (if I do not recognize and repent it) will assuredly corrupt and ruin me".

In the second place, by using for his images real people, rather than personified abstractions, Dante gains an enormous artistic advantage over the simple allegorist. Except in the hands of the greatest masters, such as Bunyan, personified virtues and vices are apt to seem frigid and artificial. Dante's mastery was equal to anything: in his early book, *The New Life*, he had already handled personification beautifully, and no doubt he could have done it again, and on the grand scale, if he had tried. But he did not try: he looked at the great bristling difficulty of allegory, over which so many writers, before and since, have come a cropper, and, with his infallible poetic tact, quietly by-passed it. Instead of endeavouring to interest us in personages labelled "Counsel" or "Divine Grace" or "Simony" or "Theology" he gave us portraits of Virgil, Beatrice, Pope Nicholas III, and Thomas Aquinas, in whom, since they are human, we are predisposed to be interested. In this way he saved himself pages of elaborate description and made room in his poem for the discussion of a great many subjects of the utmost importance, thus widening its range and increasing its variety.

We are apt to be astonished at first, in reading (say) the *Inferno*, to find how little is actually said about the particular sin of which Dante and we are witnessing the retribution. Sometimes the souls relate their histories (as do Francesca da Rimini,[1] for instance, and Guido da Montefeltro[2]), but even then there is little or no moralizing on the subject. More often there is merely a description of the conditions in which the sinners find themselves, after which a character is introduced and talks with Dante upon some apparently extraneous matter which is closely related, indeed, to the subject of the *Comedy* taken as a whole, but has no special relevancy to the immediate circumstances. In showing us his images, Dante has already told us all we need to know about the sin. He has intro-

1. *Inf.* v. 97 *sqq.*   2. *Inf.* xxvii. 67 *sqq.*

duced us, for example, to Ciacco – a rich and amiable Florentine gentleman, well known and much ridiculed by his contemporaries for his monstrous self-indulgence: the familiar name is enough to remind contemporary readers of what Gluttony looks like to the world; he has also shown us the conditions of Ciacco's part of Hell – a cold wallowing in mud under the fangs and claws of Cerberus: that, stripped of all glamour, is what Gluttony *is*, seen in its true and eternal nature. Why waste more words upon it? Let Ciacco and Dante converse upon the state of Florence.[1]

We now begin to see the necessity for all the notes and explanations with which editors feel obliged to encumber the pages of Dante. To the fourteenth-century Italian, the personages of the *Comedy* were familiar. To identify them, and to appreciate the positions they occupy in the Three Kingdoms of the After-world, was to combine an understanding of the allegorical significance with the excitement of a *chronique scandaleuse* and the intellectual entertainment of solving one of the more enigmatical varieties of crossword puzzle. For us it is different. We do not know these people; nor indeed are we to-day quite so familiar with our classical authors, or even with our Bible, as a medieval poet might reasonably expect his public to be. Let us suppose that an Englishman were to write a contemporary *Divine Comedy* on Dante's model, and that in it, mixed up with a number of scriptural and mythological characters, we were to find, assigned to various circles of Hell, Purgatory, and Paradise, according to the religious and political convictions of the author, the following assortment of people – some referred to by their full names, some by Christian name or surname alone, and some indicated only by a witty or allusive phrase: Chamberlain ("him of the orchid"), Chamberlain ("him of the umbrella"), [Stewart Houston] Chamberlain, "Brides-in-the-Bath" Smith, "Galloper" Smith, Horatio Bottomley, Horatio [Lord Nelson], Fox [Charles or George to be inferred from the context], the Man who picked up the Bomb in Jermyn Street, Oscar Wilde, Oscar Slater, Oscar Browning, Spencer, Spenser, Lord Castlereagh, Lord Castlerosse, Lawrence [of Arabia], [D. H.] Lawrence, "Butcher" Heydrich, W. G. Grace, Grace Darling, the Captain of the *Jarvis Bay*, the Sisters of

1. *Inf.* vi. 38 *sqq.*

17

Haworth, the Woodcutter of Hawarden, the Ladies of Llangollen, the Lady with the Lamp, the Lady-with-the-Lampshade-made-of-Human-Skin, Titus Oates, Captain Oates, Quisling, the Owner of "Hermit", the French Bluebeard, Bacon, Roger Bacon, Roger Fry, the Claimant, the Bishop of Zanzibar, Clarence Hatry, the Tolpuddle Martyrs, Brown and Kennedy, the Dean of St Patrick's, the Dean of St Paul's, Dean Farrar, Fred Archer, Mrs Dyer, Lord George Sanger, Lord George Gordon, General Gordon, Ouida, William Joyce, James Joyce, "the Officer in the Tower", Peter the Painter, Jenkins "of the Ear", Dick Sheppard, Jack Sheppard, and "the Widow at Windsor". Let us further suppose that the writer holds strong views on Trade Unionism, the constitution of UNO, the "theology of crisis", Freudian psychology, Einsteinian astronomy, and the art of Mr Jacob Epstein. Let us then suppose that the book is to be read, six hundred years hence, by an intelligent Portuguese with no particular knowledge of English social history. Would he not require a few notes, in order to savour the full pungency of the poet's pronouncements and thoroughly understand his attitude to the cosmic set-up?

We need to know what Dante's characters stood for in his eyes, and therefore we need to know who they were. But that is as much as we need. The purely historical approach to a work of art can easily be overdone by the general reader. Just because it puts the thing away into a "period", it tends to limit its relevance to that period. So long as we can amuse ourselves with antiquarian details about Alessio Interminei,[1] or with the entertaining circumstance that Dante confused the historical Thaïs[2] with a character in a play, so long are we likely to refrain from asking ourselves whether there is anything in our own public or private lives which places us, spiritually, in the stinking ditch where the corruptors of language wallow in their own excreted filth. Valuable as the historian's researches are, Dante has become such a quarry for the amateur of medieval fossils that I have thought it well, even at the cost of seeming heavily didactic, to add to the necessary historical Notes another series of Notes, called "The Images", which aim at suggesting the lines along which the allegory may be inter-

1. *Inf.* xviii. 115 *sqq.*   2. *Inf.* xviii. 127 *sqq.*

preted so as to bring out its universal relevance. Needless to say, these suggestions do not exhaust the possible meanings of the poem: a great poetical image is much more than the sum of its interpretations, and the more closely we meditate upon it the richer does it grow in significance.

The poem is an allegory of the Way to God – to that union of our wills with the Universal Will in which every creature finds its true self and its true being. But, as Dante himself has shown, it may be interpreted at various levels. It may be seen, for example, as the way of the artist, or as the way of the lover[1] – both these ways are specifically included in the imagery. Since there is not room for everything in one small volume, I have concentrated chiefly upon two levels of interpretation: the way of the Community ("the City") and the way of the individual Soul. The latter is, perhaps, in the long run, the more important; but both loomed large in Dante's mind, and they interpenetrate and complete one another. For many of us it may be easier to understand Hell as the picture of a corrupt society than as that of a corrupt self. Whichever we start with, it is likely to lead to the other; and it does not much matter by which road we come to Dante so long as we get to him in the end.

We cannot, of course, do without the historical approach altogether, for the poem is largely concerned with historical events. Neither can we do altogether without the biographical approach, since the poem is so closely concerned with the poet's personal experience. The allegory is universal, but it is so precisely because it is a man's answer to a situation – a particular man and a particular situation in time and place. The man is Dante; the time is the beginning of the fourteenth century; the place is Florence. All Heaven and Earth and Hell are, in a sense, included within that narrow compass.

Even so, the compass is not really so narrow as we are apt to imagine, accustomed as we are to thinking in terms of continents and myriads and supersonic speeds, and supposing nothing to be of importance unless it is very large indeed. Because of our habitual snobbery about size, Dante has sometimes been reproached for his absorbing interest in "local politics". But this

1. See Charles Williams: *The Figure of Beatrice.*

is a very misleading way of putting the thing. The Italian cities in the thirteenth and fourteenth centuries were not places like Little-Hugley-in-the-Hole, nor were their politics the politics of the parish pump. They were sovereign states, and some of them (Venice is the outstanding example) had the status of world powers. In the Western civilization of that day, whose centre was the Mediterranean, they were as important as the Balkan States in the larger world of to-day; their internal dissensions might exercise upon the European history of the time an influence comparable to that of the recent Spanish Civil War upon our own, and might involve equally wide issues.

The unifying power in the Ancient World had been that of the Roman Empire; it held all Europe as far East as the Danube, together with Asia Minor, and the African coast of the Mediterranean, in a complicated nexus of tributary states, of which those of Italy were, naturally, the most closely united to the central government.

When Constantine was converted, and established Christianity as the official Imperial religion, he moved his seat of Empire from Rome to Byzantium,[1] which, under its new name of Constantinople, became the centre of a strong and flourishing civilization, capable of resisting the barbarians for a thousand years. The Western half of the Empire, though still administered from Rome by the "Emperor of the West", was exposed to those innumerable invasions by Germanic tribes from the North which make the period called the Dark Ages so chaotic a tale of devastation and bloodshed. Rome was five times taken and three times sacked; the government fled to Ravenna; unity in the West was broken and lost. In the gloom of five confused centuries, the lights of culture and civilization were kept alive in the West only by the exertions of the Church. Unlike the Eastern Church which, being closely fused into the Imperial power at Constantinople, never lost its strong consciousness of the coinherence of the functions of Church and State, whether in spiritual or secular matters, the Western Church developed independently, and the See of St Peter at Rome rose to a position of unchallenged spiritual authority, from which it proceeded to lay claim to the temporal

1. *Para.* vi. 1 *sqq.*

power also. When the Eastern Empire finally succumbed to attack from without and disintegration from within, it was at the hands of Pope Leo III that, in the year 800, the Frankish prince, Charlemagne, received his consecration and the crown of that Empire – presently to be called Holy and still called Roman – whose title indeed descended from the Empire of the Caesars, but which no longer had its geographical centre at Rome.

By this time, however, the power of the Papacy was no longer purely spiritual. A forged document ("the Donation of Constantine") purporting to show that the Emperor Constantine had made a gift of Italy and the West to Pope Sylvester, was produced in justification, and was for many years accepted as the legal basis of a claim to complete temporal jurisdiction over the whole of Western Christendom.[1] Further, by a political bargain concluded in 753 between Pope Stephen and the Frankish King Pépin the Short, a number of cities which the Lombard invaders had seized from the Empire had been retaken and handed over, not to the Emperor but to the See of Rome. This transaction was the origin of the Papal States, and of the Pope's appearance as a *territorial* power among the secular European powers, over all of which he claimed to exercise a general *temporal* power as Head of the Church.

Italy, her political unity thus disintegrated by the upheavals of the Dark Ages, remained, then, at the beginning of the thirteenth century, a loose bundle of independent city-republics,[2] which had no formal centre of government, and were only held together after a fashion by (a) a common spiritual allegiance to Rome, (b) a nominal connexion with the Empire, (c) the tradition of the ancient Roman Law, which was supposed to regulate the internal constitution of all these various states. Between one city and another there was constant feud and rivalry, accompanied

1. This claim meant, among other things, that in every country, ecclesiastical wealth and appointments, as well as the ecclesiastical courts of law, were wholly independent of control by the lay state, and that all secular princes, from the Emperor downwards, derived their authority from the Pope, who could, if they were recalcitrant, not only excommunicate but depose them and absolve their subjects from their allegiance.

2. These were not the survivals of the ancient Roman provinces, but new units which had risen spontaneously during the years of the Germanic invasions.

by continual shifting alliances for mutual defence or for combined aggression. Across the whole country there raged a perpetual series of territorial and ideological quarrels, whose lines of cleavage sometimes coincided with political frontiers and sometimes cut across them. We may imagine the situation as being something like that in the Balkan States to-day. We must further imagine the whole population to be divided, like that of England after the Conquest, into two racial groups: an aristocracy descended from invaders of an alien blood and culture, and a native stock, comprising most of the burgess and peasant classes, still obstinately clinging to their ancient laws and privileges. But whereas in England the constitution tended to become centralized and stabilized under the Crown, in Italy there was no such focus of national self-consciousness. Moreover, the Italian nobility was violently divided by internecine clan feuds like those of the Campbells and MacGregors, so that each great family was a law unto itself and its followers, overriding the native constitution, bearing rule according to its own tribal custom, and indulging in perpetual raids and vendettas against its rivals.

At the bottom, therefore, of all this confusion there lay an ideological conflict of a sort very familiar to us at present: that between government by law and arbitrary government by a military clique. On the surface, however, it appeared rather as a conflict between two political parties: the Guelfs and the Ghibellines.[1] On the whole, and very roughly speaking, the Ghibellines were the aristocratic party; they upheld the authority of the Emperor and looked for support to him, and were opposed to the growing territorial power of the Papacy. The Guelfs, again very roughly speaking, may be called the "democratic" party – not, of course, in the modern sense that they stood for class-equality, but in the sense that they wanted constitutional government. On the whole they represented the indigenous Italian stock, and included many of the minor nobility together with the mercantile middle-class, who were now rising into importance. Their slogan was "Civic Liberty"; they wanted to shake off the

1. The names, inherited from the ancient rivalry of the Welf and Weiblingen families for the Imperial crown, had by now lost their original significance, and become mere party labels, like "Whig" and "Tory".

yoke of the Empire, and looked to the Pope for support against the domination of the aristocratic Ghibelline clans.[1]

One must not regard any of these lines of division as clear-cut or permanent. Territorial rivalry between two adjacent Guelf cities might throw the weaker into temporary alliance with a Ghibelline neighbour, or vice versa. Or a Guelf-Ghibelline clash within a city might lead to a "purge" and the expulsion of the defeated party, who would promptly seek allies among the surrounding cities, in the hope of staging a return from exile and banishing the victors in their turn. In each city "the Party", whichever it was, formed a separate state within the state, distinct from the legal constitution, and administering the affairs of the republic by its own officers – much as we have recently seen the Communist or the Fascist party doing, on a larger scale, in various states of Europe.

Behind all this complex of ideological, territorial, party, and family feuds stood the great European powers, who often found it advantageous to fish in the troubled waters of Italy. The Germanic Imperial states might be expected to support the claims of the Emperor and so of the Ghibelline party; France was called in by the Pope to support the Guelfs against Imperial encroachment. We saw a somewhat similar situation in the Spanish Civil War.

So that, if we make a kind of composite picture of the Balkans to-day, and the Spain of the nineteen-thirties, with a flavour of post-Conquest England and a dash of the Scottish Highlands before the Union, we shall be in a fair way to imagine the complications of medieval Italy. But we must remember also that all this political unrest was, nevertheless, accompanied by a tremendous flowering of wealth and culture. The Dark Ages were over; the Early Renaissance was beginning. Trade was vigorous, the great guilds of the craftsmen and merchants were rising to power; the old classical learning was being rediscovered, and a civilized and cultured society was eagerly patronizing music and the arts, while scholars, both clerical and lay, were founding

1. In Florence especially, powerful support for the Papacy came from the great Guelf banking houses, of which – notwithstanding the Church's official condemnation of usury – the Popes were by far the most important and influential customers.

schools and universities for the encouragement of education and the study of philosophy and science. And finally, we must remember that with all these multifarious dissensions, there was no clear-cut schism in the Western Church, of the kind to which we have grown accustomed since the Reformation. The great Dualist heresy,[1] which had been brought into Europe from the East, and which, in the preceding century, had flourished exceedingly in Languedoc and the South, had been driven underground, partly by persecution and the Inquisition, and partly by the missionary efforts of the Franciscan and Dominican orders. The Waldensian sects in the North, which were to become the ancestors of Protestantism, were as yet rather a movement for reform within the Church than a separatist body. It was still possible to be anti-clerical without being anti-Catholic, or to denounce ecclesiastical corruption and the abuse of the Temporal Power without abating one's reverence for the Chair of Peter. Neither did religious disputes necessarily take on a political colour. In Italy, many of the Ghibelline nobles were indeed suspected of heresy, and even of atheism; yet, generally speaking, it remained true that Pope's man and Emperor's man believed the same doctrine, and took the Sacrament at the same altar. Those, however, who, like Dante, were aware of the underground rumblings which foreboded the earthquake to come might well be anxious, for the Church's own sake, to see on the one hand the reform of her interior discipline and, on the other, the removal of the secular state from ecclesiastical control and its union under a central authority.[2]

1. The Dualist churches, of which there were many varieties – e.g. Albigensian, Patarene, Catharist, etc. – were what we should call Gnostic or, more loosely, Manichean. They agreed in believing that matter was created by the Devil and in itself irredeemably evil, and consequently in rejecting the doctrines of the perfect God-Manhood of Christ, the Fall and the Atonement, the sanctity and resurrection of the body and other central tenets of the Christian faith. An excellent short account of them is available in Steven Runciman's *The Mediaeval Manichee*.

2. I am acquainted with the theory, first put forward by G. P. G. Rossetti and since sporadically revived, that the *Comedy* (like every other work of Dante) is nothing but an anti-Roman tract, preaching in cryptogrammatic form the Manichean heresy of the Cathar and Patarene sects. I need only say here that the arguments adduced are scarcely such as to commend themselves to sober scholarship or critical judgment.

Introduction

Towards the middle of the thirteenth century, a chance of Italian, if not of European, unity offered itself, under that astonishing Emperor of the Hohenstaufen dynasty, Frederick II, King of Sicily, called by his contemporaries "Stupor Mundi" (the "Wonder of the World"), for his multifarious and eccentric brilliance. "The object of Frederick was to make of Italy and Sicily a united kingdom within the Empire. The settled purpose of the Papacy, supported by a revived and enlarged league of Lombard towns, was to frustrate this design. In the end the Papacy won the battle. The man was defeated by the institution, and with him passed away the last chance of an effective Roman Empire in central Europe or for many centuries of an united Italian kingdom."[1]

Thus the hind-sight of the historian. To contemporary political foresight that conclusion was not so evident. Long after Frederick's death in 1250, the partisans of the Empire still had good hopes of their cause. In desperation, the French Popes Urban IV and Clement IV offered the crown of Sicily to Charles of Anjou and so called in foreign arms to decide the affairs of Italy. In February 1266 – or 1265 by the Old Calendar – Charles of Anjou crushingly defeated the Sicilian army under Frederick's bastard son, Manfred, at the Battle of Benevento;[2] three years later, the line of Hohenstaufen was extinguished by the brutal murder of Frederick's grandson, Conradin, after the Battle of Tagliacozzo.

In that same momentous year of Benevento, in 1265, "under the sign of Gemini" – that is, some time between the middle of May and the middle of June[3] – Dante Alighieri was born at Florence. He was of gentle blood, though not of the great nobility. His family were Guelfs and prided themselves on their pure Florentine descent; they owned a certain amount of land and house property and were apparently of good standing and reasonably well-to-do. His mother died when he was five or six years old, and his father when he was twelve, leaving him and his brothers to the care of a stepmother.

It was while he was still a child that he underwent a personal experience which, trivial as it might appear at first sight, was yet to prove the most important and the most enduring influence upon

1. H. A. L. Fisher: *History of Europe.*   2. *Purg.* iii. 103–45.
3. There is some evidence that it was 30 May.

25

his life and genius, and to provide, as it were, the mirror in which, at the height of his powers and to the end of his days, he beheld all heaven and earth reflected. We must, for a moment, forget Pope and Emperor, Guelf and Ghibelline, and hold up the course of history while we trace out the story of that experience, and discover, if we can, just what it was that happened to him.

He was nearly nine when his father took him to a May-Day party at the house of one Folco Portinari, a wealthy Florentine citizen, and here he met his host's little daughter, a child about a year younger than himself. "She appeared to me dressed in a most noble colour, a rich and subdued red, girded and adorned in a manner becoming to her very tender age." And he "declares most truly" that at that very moment his heart trembled and said, "Behold a god stronger than I that is come to bear rule over me";[1] that his soul and intellect began to marvel and said to his eyes: "Now is your bliss made manifest";[2] and that his senses lamenting replied: "Alas! how often henceforth shall we be troubled."[3]

So Dante told the story,[4] twenty years later, and the poetic manner of the telling need not make us doubt the essential truth of the story. These things happen. "It is", says Sir Osbert Sitwell,[5] recounting a similar experience which befel him when he was not very much older than Dante, "as though you had been hitherto colour-blind, and now, by looking for a moment at the face of a stranger, had been made whole and given the entire world of vision. ... Why ... should this single glimpse of a stranger raise life to a level I had never hitherto known, and why should the memory of it remain with me now, albeit I have long forgotten the child's name, to persist, no doubt, until the hour of my dying?" Dante's whole life-work is, in a manner, the answer to that question. His case, however, was in one point a little different. He never forgot the child's name, neither has he allowed the world to forget it. The name was Beatrice.

Dante himself has told us nearly all that we know about this

1. Ecce Deus fortior me qui veniens dominabitur mihi.
2. Apparuit jam beatitudo vestra.
3. Heu miser! quia frequenter impeditus ero deinceps.
4. In the *Vita Nuova*, from which these quotations are taken.
5. *The Scarlet Tree*, p. 208.

strange and memorable love-affair. It is a history without sensational incident; the one event which to modern eyes might appear important – Beatrice's marriage in 1287 to the banker Simone dei Bardi – he does not so much as mention. When he assures us that his love was "most chaste", we may believe him; it was not directed to marriage (in his day a matter, for the most part, of politic alliance), nor indeed to any kind of possession. He sought, he says, to go where he might look upon Beatrice, because the mere sight of her gracious beauty was to him a revelation, as of something divine walking the earth bodily. He was eighteen when, "of her ineffable courtesy", she first acknowledged him and spoke to him in the street, giving him "a salutation of such virtue that I seemed to behold the uttermost bounds of bliss". On a subsequent occasion, having heard some scandalous rumours about him, she "refused him her salutation"; and he learned that love could be an initiation into suffering as well as into ecstasy. A little later he saw her at a party in somebody's house, and was so much overcome by his feelings that the friend who was with him thought he had been taken ill; Beatrice made fun of him (or so he thought), and he was cut to the quick. In 1289, Folco Portinari died, and Dante grieved in sympathy for his lady's grief. In 1290, Beatrice herself died, and it seemed to him that the light had gone out of life, and that the whole city of Florence was widowed by her death.

From these slender and shining strands of experience he wove his vision of love, singing it out as he went in that "sweet new style – *il dolce stil nuovo*" which was already revivifying the conventional lyric of "courtly love" with a springtime freshness of personal feeling. Young poets were plentiful in thirteenth-century Florence, but his contemporaries recognized in Dante Alighieri a new voice of unusual quality. Some time after Beatrice's death he collected his verses into a book, which he called *La Vita Nuova* – *The New Life*, adding a running commentary in prose, in which, with a candid and eager sincerity, he tried to explain just what it was that had happened to him, and to communicate the quickening influence of his love upon his life. And he ended by telling how he had had a "marvellous vision" of the dead and glorified Beatrice, "in which I beheld things that determined me to speak no more of that blessed one until such time as I could treat of her more worthily. And to this end I study as much as I can, as she well knows. So that, if it please Him by whom all things live to prolong my life for a few years, I hope to write of her what never yet was written of any woman." All this programme he fulfilled to the letter. But earlier than that he had written of himself as "one who in Hell shall say to the damned, *I have seen the hope of the blessed*". The words were prophetic; but he had first to behold himself as one of the damned, in a hell of his own making.

The significance of Beatrice in the *Divine Comedy* is briefly summed up on p. 67, and will be better discussed in detail when we come to consider the *Purgatorio* and *Paradiso*. All we need for the moment is to understand how it was that this Florentine girl came to be for Dante the "God-bearing image", the vehicle of the Glory, and type of all other such communications of Grace. The clue is best sought in a passage of the *Vita Nuova*, in which lovers will recognize an experience which is universal, however the illuminating moment may afterwards become dimmed and lost amid the familiar contacts and disillusionments of daily life. Dante is describing the effect upon him of Beatrice's" salutation"; and it should be remembered that the Italian word *salute* means not only "salutation" but also "salvation":

> *I say that when she appeared from any direction, then, in the hope of her wondrous salutation, there was no enemy left to me; rather there smote into me a flame of charity, which made me forgive every person who had ever injured me; and if at that moment anybody had put a question to me about anything whatsoever, my answer would have been simply "Love", with a countenance clothed in humility.*

Not lovers alone, but also all those who have undergone the experience known as conversion, will recognize that frame of mind. In the language of religion, Dante, when he stood in the presence of Beatrice, knew himself to be in a state of grace; he had found salvation.

Although the *Vita Nuova* is autobiographical, it is not an auto-biography. Dante is not concerned to display himself in all his attitudes, but only in his attitude to Beatrice; and if we had only that book to go upon we might suppose that from his tenth to his twenty-fifth year he did nothing except circulate sonnets among the intelligentsia of Florence, and moon his tearful way from one emotional crisis to another. It is with a faint surprise that we find him, at the age of eighteen, engaged in prosaic business transactions as head of his house, and, in his twenty-fifth year, fighting at the Battle of Campaldino, being then, as he wrote to a friend, "no novice in arms". The Florence of Dante's day was Guelf. The historic schism, by which Florence had, till then, remained comparatively untouched, was imported into the city in 1215, as the result of a blood-feud between two great Florentine houses. A nobleman called Buondelmonte dei Buondelmonti, who was engaged to a lady of the Amidei family, jilted her for the daughter of one of the Donati – an insult which the Amidei naturally resented.

And as they were in council among themselves as to how they should retaliate on him ... Mosca de' Lamberti spoke the evil word: What's done is ended – that is, that he should be killed. And so it was done; for on the morning of Easter Day they gathered together in the house of the Amidei of Santo Stefano, and Messer Buondelmonte coming from the other side of the Arno, bravely dressed in new garments white all over, and riding a white palfrey, when he reached the foot of the Ponte Vecchio on this side, just at the base of the pillar where stood the statue of Mars, the said Messer Buondelmonte was thrown from his horse on to the ground by Schiatta degli Uberti, and set on and stabbed by Mosca Lamberti and Lambertuccio degli Amidei, and his throat cut by Oderigo Fifanti, and an end made of him. ... Whereupon the city rushed to arms in an uproar; and the death of Messer Buondelmonte was the cause and beginning of the accursed Guelf and Ghibelline parties in Florence ... [for] all the families of the nobles and other citizens of Florence took sides, and some held with the Buondelmonti, who joined the Guelf party and became its leaders, and some with the Uberti, who became the leaders of the Ghibellines.[1]

Once begun, the conflict raged on in Florence for fifty-two years, now one side and now another gaining a temporary

---

1. Villani, v. 38. Maurice Hewlett was retold the tale vividly in his short story *Buondelmonte's Saga* in *Fond Adventures*. Readers of the *Comedy* will meet with Mosca dei Lamberti in Canto XXVIII of the *Inferno*.

advantage. In 1248, the Ghibellines, with the help of Frederick II, expelled the Guelfs from the city and razed their houses to the ground. In 1250, Frederick died; the Guelfs came back, incited the Florentines to make war upon the Ghibelline town of Pistoia and, returning victorious, threw out the more obstructive of the Ghibellines and changed the arms of the city from a white lily on a red field to a red lily on a white field. The remaining Ghibellines clung to the white lily and to their hopes of revenge; in 1258 they conspired with Manfred to overthrow the Guelf government. The people rose in arms against them, drove them from the city and demolished their houses. The Ghibellines took refuge in Siena and, under the leadership of the great captain, Farinata degli Uberti,[1] bided their time. In 1260, Farinata jockeyed the Florentines into making an ill-advised assault upon Siena; they were cut to pieces, memorably and terribly, at the Battle of Montaperti on the banks of the Arbia.[2] It was the turn of the Guelfs to flee, and before very long, says the chronicler, "there remained neither town nor castle, little or great, throughout Tuscany, but was subject to the Ghibellines". But with the fall of the Hohenstaufens the position was reversed, and the Ghibelline cause was everywhere in eclipse. After an attempt at a coalition government, which ended only in an abortive Ghibelline insurrection, and a fresh peace-treaty which went the way of others of their kind, the Florentine Guelfs, "feeling themselves powerful", applied for help to Charles of Anjou. He sent them eight hundred French horsemen, under Count Guy de Montfort, the son of our own Simon. He arrived in Florence on Easter Day, 1267, "and when the Ghibellines heard of his coming … they departed out of Florence without stroke of sword". They never again came back.

But there was a moment, twenty years later, when it looked as though they might come back. Arezzo, refuge of many of the banished Florentines, had become a powerful Ghibelline stronghold, and in 1287 a number of Tuscan cities leagued together to declare war upon her. At first, the Aretines had some success, but eventually a strong force was dispatched against them – sixteen hundred horsemen and ten thousand foot, from Florence, Lucca, Prato, Pistoia, Siena, Volterra, Bologna, and other Guelf cities.

1. *Inf.* x. 22 *sqq.*   2. *Inf.* x. 85 *sqq.*; xxxii. 80–81.

The Florentine contingent was the largest, including, besides a number of French mercenaries, "six hundred horsemen ... the best armed and the best mounted that ever went out from Florence"; and in the first rank of these, on 2 June 1289, rode young Dante Alighieri. So they went, the red lily of Florence and the golden lilies of France floating overhead, and all the bells of the war-chariots sounding; "and the field of battle was on the plain at the foot of Poppi, in the district called Certamondo ... and the plain is called Campaldino".[1]

Dante wrote to a friend that he was at first much alarmed, but afterwards joyful, because of the varying fortunes of the battle. He had good reason; for in the first shock the Florentine horse were broken and thrown back by the weight of the Aretine charge. But they rallied and stood firm; the allies closed in on the flanks of the pursuers; and so in the end "the Florentines had the victory and the Aretines were defeated", losing over seventeen hundred killed and two thousand taken.

The rest of the campaign was fought out on Aretine soil, Dante being present at the siege and capture of Caprona. Florence remained Guelf; but for the moment it had been touch-and-go. Dante lived through these exciting events, and wrote about them later in his *Comedy*.[2] But in the *Vita Nuova*, the year of Campaldino is marked only as that of the death of Folco Portinari. By the next year, military triumphs had lost their savour; Beatrice was dead.

During the next ten years we find Dante faithfully carrying out his intention to "study as much as he could". His people had given him a good education as a boy, under the guidance and encouragement of old Bruno Latini – the elderly statesman and man of letters whom he was later to grieve over in his vision of Hell.[3] As a young man, he had made himself familiar with the language and literature of Provence, on which all fashionable Italian verse was modelled. He now set himself to improve his Latin and extend his range. He read philosophy, theology,[4] science (especially astro-

1. Villani, vii. 131. 2. See *Inf.* xxi. 94–6; *Purg.* v. 88 *sqq.* 3. *Inf.* xv. 22 *sqq.*
4. Dante's philosophical and theological studies, and in particular the immense influence of St Thomas Aquinas, will be more conveniently discussed in detail in connexion with the *Purgatory* and *Paradise*. As much as is necessary for understanding the *Inferno* will be found in the "Images" and "Notes" attached to each canto.

nomy), and classical poetry, nosing his own way into contemporary learning, as his eager, inquisitive mind led him. He was a voracious reader, with an invaluable gift of concentration; there is a story of how, becoming immersed in a new book outside an apothecary's shop, he browsed on oblivious for five or six hours, totally unaware of an uproarious city festival that was going on in the street behind him. According to his own account, he nearly read his eyes out and had for a time to fall back on darkness and applications of cold water. It is however, pleasant to know that "he nevertheless maintained all his social and civic intercourse; and it was wonderful how, though he studied without cessation, no one would have supposed from his style and youthful company that he was studying at all".[1] He was, after all, a young man and a poet; and he could not only make verses and write them in his "tall, fine and accurate"[2] hand; he could also draw and sing, and delighted in the society of artists and musicians.

About this time – certainly not later than 1298, and probably a year or two earlier – his family arranged a marriage for him; to console him (says the sentimental Boccaccio) for the death of Beatrice, but also and chiefly, no doubt, because, as head of his house, he could scarcely be allowed to neglect his obvious social duty. His wife was Gemma, of the noble and ancient Guelf family of the Donati, and he had by her at least four children. That his marriage was unhappy is as strenuously denied by some biographers as it is positively asserted by others: there is little reliable evidence either way. We may, however, accept the witness of Boccaccio that Dante was given to sitting up late over his books and his business, "in so much that many a time both his household and his wife were grieved thereat, until they grew used to his ways and took no further notice of it". There is a ring of truth about that. Probably, like some other men of genius, he was imperfectly house-trained; possibly Gemma was a trifle conventional, and rather put up with genius than ecstatically served it.

Art and learning, and the responsibilities of a householder, were not all: there were also the claims of the republic; and as soon as he had attained the age of full citizenship, Dante threw himself energetically into politics. In order to qualify for the higher posts

1. Lionardo Bruni.   2. Boccaccio.

in the government, it was necessary, under the new "democratic" constitution set up by the Guelfs in 1284, to be a member of one of the great city guilds. Accordingly, in 1295 or 1296, Dante enrolled himself in the Guild of the Physicians and Apothecaries, which included not only the merchants of spices and drugs, but also the jewellers, painters, and booksellers – books being, in fact, sold in those days at the apothecaries' shops. Florence was governed by a Standard-Bearer of Justice and six Priors, elected every two months from members of the city guilds, assisted by various councils and administrative officers. From time to time the name of Dante Alighieri crops up in the city archives – recording a vote, offering an opinion in committee, making a speech in the Council. In the spring of 1300 he was chosen to go as ambassador to the town of San Gemignano, to invite representatives to come and take part in the election of a new Captain for the Guelf League of Tuscany. Whether or not much diplomacy was required, or only a dignified presence and a polished manner of speech, he apparently acquitted himself satisfactorily, for we still have the minute which records that, after debate, the proposal of the Florentine ambassador was adopted. When, a few months later, Messer Dante Alighieri was elected to the Priorate, to serve from 15 June to 15 August, it looked as though he was marked out for an honourable and distinguished career in his own city, which had never yet been so flourishing, so important, so well-found in men and resources.

And indeed there seemed no reason why the Florentine Guelfs, having got rid of their Ghibellines and established civil order, should not settle down in peace to develop their liberal institutions. Unhappily for themselves, for Florence, and above all for Dante, they chose this moment to develop a disastrous party split. As usual, the occasion of it was a family feud, imported this time from Pistoia. There, a quarrel between two branches of the Cancellieri family, the Whites and the Blacks,[1] was exasperated into open hostilities by a peculiarly disgusting murder perpetrated by a youth called Foccaccia.[2] This led to so much uproar

1. The two branches were descended respectively from the two wives of the original Cancelliere. The first wife being named Bianca (Blanche), her descendants called themselves the Bianchi (Whites), the descendants of the second wife calling themselves the Neri (Blacks) in a spirit of opposition.
2. *Inf.* XXXII. 63.

that the Florentine Guelfs intervened, summoned the ringleaders to Florence, and imprisoned them there, in the hope of putting an end to the feud. The effect, as might have been expected, was merely to extend the quarrel to Florence, where it found a rich and fertile seed-bed in the jealousy of the Cerchi and Donati families. The Cerchi, who were rich, self-made, and vulgar, espoused the cause of the Whites; the Donati, less ostentatiously wealthy but much better bred than their rivals, took the part of the Blacks. An accidental collision in the street during the May Festival of 1300 led to a brawl, the brawl to a riot, and the riot to a whole series of disturbances, so that the city was divided into two armed camps.

It was at this unpropitious juncture that Dante entered upon his priorate. The Blacks, feeling that something must be done in this state of emergency, held a secret meeting, and determined to send to the Pope and request him to dispatch Charles of Valois, the French king's brother, "to Florence, as pacificator and re-organizer of the city". The Whites, getting wind of this, were alarmed; for though, as Guelfs, they may have preferred the Pope to the Emperor, they were suspicious of Papal interference in home politics, and certainly did not want Charles of Valois. They appealed to the Priors, protesting that the Blacks' secret meeting was unconstitutional; the Blacks appealed in their turn, affirming that the Whites were trumping up charges against them and con-spiring to get them all banished. The Priors made a decree, banish-ing the leaders of both sides impartially; Dante, who was himself a White, though his wife's family were Black, thus setting his hand to the exile both of his own friend and fellow-poet, Guido Cavalcanti, and also of his wife's kinsman, Corso Donati.[1]

In October of the following year, the Whites, more and more disturbed by the menace to Florentine independence, determined to send an embassy to the Pope, in the hope of averting the visi-tation of Charles of Valois. The Pope was Boniface VIII, that

---

1. The White exiles were soon after permitted to return, having pleaded that the place to which they were sent was malarial and unhealthy. This discrimination was afterwards made the foundation for a charge of corrup-tion against Dante, though he was no longer prior when it took place, and though the plea was shown to be justified by the fact that Guido Cavalcanti died in August 1300 of an illness contracted during his banishment.

brilliant and ambitious statesman who was to become for Dante a symbol of everything that was wrong with the Church. Born at Anagni (Alagna) *c.* 1217, and made cardinal in 1281, in 1294 he procured the abdication of the aged Pope Celestine V and, through the influence of Charles II of Naples, to whom he promised assistance in his campaign to recover Sicily, got himself elected to the Papal Chair. We shall meet him many times in the *Comedy* – consigned to Hell for his simony,[1] denounced for his usurpation, for his avarice, for his vigorous assertion of the Papal claim to the temporal power, for his prostitution of his holy office to political expediency,[2] and for various other offences. In the *Paradiso*, the saints of the Eighth Heaven blush red for the crimes of Boniface, and the last word spoken by Beatrice in the height of the Empyrean is a condemnation upon "him of Alagna". In the end, his political ambitions had tragic consequences both for himself and for the Church. In 1303 Philip the Fair of France, exasperated by Papal interference in French affairs, had Boniface seized and imprisoned at Anagni, by Sciarra Cologna and William de Nogaret, who treated the old man with such indignity that he died shortly after his release; so that all Christendom beheld, as Dante said, "Christ led captive and crucified in the person of his Vicar".[3]

All this was in the near future; but the figure of Boniface VIII looms so large in Dante's mind and forms so important a part of the imagery of the *Comedy* that it is well to form some picture of him in our own minds. Perhaps the description given of him by the fourteenth-century chronicler Villani – himself a Guelf, and therefore the less swayed by anti-Papal prejudice – shows best how he appeared in the eyes of his contemporaries:

He was very learned in the Scriptures and of great natural parts, and a very prudent and able man, and of great knowledge and memory; he was very proud and haughty and cruel to his foes and adversaries, and of a high stomach, and greatly feared by all, and he greatly exalted and magnified the state and counsels of Holy Church. ... He was magnanimous and generous to those who pleased him, and to all valorous men; very avid of worldly pomps according to his degree, and very covetous,

1. *Inf.* XIX. 52.   2. *Inf.* XXVII. 70 *sqq.*   3. *Purg.* XX. 85 *sqq.*

not looking closely nor keeping a strict conscience when it was a question of gain, in order to aggrandize the Church and his own family. ... He as more worldly than befitted his dignity, and he did many things which were displeasing to God.

Such was the man who, in the year 1301, held the fate of Florence – and, as it turned out, of Dante – in his hands. It appears that Dante was one of the envoys chosen by the Whites to carry their message to the Pope; and it is naturally attractive to think that the great Pontiff and the still greater Poet who was to give him so terrible a posthumous fame did once confront one another face to face. Unfortunately, there is considerable doubt about whether the envoys ever actually went; the traditional story is that they did – too late, however, to prevent an issue that was already decided against them – and that it was during their absence that, on All Saints' Day, 1301, Charles of Valois presented himself at the Gates of Florence. He was let in, on the security of his promise to arbitrate peacefully and impartially; whereupon he instantly put himself on the side of the Blacks, armed his followers, and held the ring while Corso Donati,[1] returning in triumph with the rest of the Black exiles, held a five-day carnival of fire and pillage among the houses of the Whites.

The next step was a foregone conclusion. Dante Alighieri and four other prominent Whites were summoned to appear before the Podestà, on charges of fraud and corruption while in office, and of conspiracy against the Pope, Charles, the Guelf party, and the peace of Florence. The story goes that Dante, hearing at Rome of the November affair, rode back hotfoot, and was met at Siena by the news of his own ruin. On 27 January 1302, sentence was passed: a fine of 5000 florins, to be paid within three days on pain of total confiscation; exile for two years; perpetual deprivation of office. On 10 March, a second and severer decree was proclaimed against the original five and ten others; it ended with the ominous words: "and if any of the aforesaid should come into the hands of the said commonwealth, such an one shall be burned with fire till he be dead".

Knowing what we do nowadays of the machinery and methods of "party purges", we need not waste time seriously considering

1. See *Purg.* xxiv. 82–4.

the charge of barratry, from which Dante was later to extract so much grim fun in his *Inferno*.[1] His real crime was that of belonging to a disaffected group within the party in power. He said himself afterwards that he had been lacking in prudence; and he had, indeed, three gifts hampering to the career of the practical politician: an unaccommodating temper, a blistering tongue, and an indecent superfluity of brains. But the fatal defect, which clung to him all his life, was that of being insufficiently party-minded. He was born and brought up Guelf, and he liked the sturdy native quality of the Guelfs, their tang of the soil, as of an old-fashioned squirearchy, their rooted republican constitutionalism and their modern liberal outlook, their underlying puritanism in conduct and religion. But he did not like the commercialism and vulgarity of the self-made middle-class plutocracy that was growing up among them, and he came more and more to loathe and fear the temporal power of the Papacy which their policy supported and encouraged; the avarice and corruption of a wealthy church, the appalling prevalence of simony in every ecclesiastical office, and the undignified spectacle of the Vicar of Christ manoeuvring, like a bishop on a chess-board, through that game of European politics in which kings and queens set the pace. By many of his strongest sympathies he was drawn to the Ghibellines, and indeed he has often been called "the Ghibelline", both in his own time and afterwards. He liked their princeliness – the large mind, the magnificent aristocratic gesture; the patronage of art and learning, which was the heritage and reflection of the Imperial house of Swabia; the public spirit of some of their great leaders; and later, he came to be passionately of their mind in desiring to see a united Italy as part of a united Empire, free from Papal interference in the political sphere. But he could not but dislike their irreligion, their lack of principle and contempt of law, their tyranny, their Gothic clannishness overriding the claims of the commonwealth; and he could not but know that their régime of despotic privilege was a thing outmoded and doomed, eventually, to disappear. It is easy to see why he was a White Guelf, and equally easy to see why the Whites, in the manner of other moderate and disaffected minorities, found themselves helpless between the upper and nether

1. Cantos XXI and XXII.

millstones. To be merely anti-Pope and anti-Emperor was a policy too negative to sustain itself in a world where Pope and Empire were the effective sources of military power. And it may as well be admitted that Dante was not fitted for the rôle of practical politician; it is true that, under the pressure of world events, he became a profound political thinker, but in 1302 his political theory was not yet formed.

The ejected Whites, after the manner of disaffected minorities, next turned for support to their opposite numbers of the other party, and entered into an alliance with the exiled Ghibellines, in the hope of forcing a return to Florence. Dante, whom we know to have been present at a party meeting in June 1302, later spoke bitterly of the "vile and worthless company"[1] in which he found himself. In the summer of 1304, all efforts at peaceful negotiation having failed, the exiles made an unsuccessful attack upon Florence, and it seems that round about that time Dante separated himself from them and entered upon his twenty years of roving and solitary exile. His family was safe in Florence – it was not then customary to make reprisals upon the dependents of political victims – and Gemma, after all, was a Donati. She scraped together what money she could from the wreck of her husband's fortunes, and brought up the children carefully and well. It has been held against both her and Dante that she never joined him, nor, so far as is known, held any direct communication with him – but perhaps that is not unnatural. It would have been impossible to subject four small children to the hazards of a wandering and impoverished life; her relatives, on whom she must have been largely dependent, are not likely to have encouraged any such idea; and, as time passed, and the habit of a separated life became established, the gap of estrangement probably became too wide to be easily bridged. During the second world war, we came to understand how these things happen to the uprooted and the disfranchised.

From now on, indeed, Dante's life passes almost into the mist of legend. Now and again the curtain lifts – it is certain that he found refuge for some time with Bartolommeo della Scala, head of the great Scaliger family at Verona. Later on, we hear of him as the

1. *Para.* xvii. 62.

guest of the Malaspini in Lunigiana. Here and there, in towns scattered over Italy, a document, a tradition, bears witness to his passing. From time to time we find him conducting a small diplomatic negotiation for a wealthy patron, acting as secretary to a great lady who wants a letter written in the best Latin, addressing petitions to members of the Florentine government and appeals to the people in the hope of getting his sentence annulled. There are hints of a violent and unhappy love-affair[1] – a tale (it is perhaps no more) of a tired and desperate traveller arriving at a monastery gate, and saying: "I want peace." Perhaps he taught, in private or in public: certainly, before 1308, he had written part of a book, *The Banquet* (*il Convivio*), which bears some signs of having originally been delivered as a set of lectures. It is a popular exposition of philosophy – the first of its kind in the vulgar tongue – and takes the form of a commentary upon fourteen of his own Odes. Only four of the fifteen projected treatises of the *Convivio* were ever completed. In the Introductory treatise he says of himself: "Wandering as a stranger through almost every region to which our language reaches, I have gone about as a beggar, showing against my will the wound of fortune. ... Verily I have been as a ship without sails and without rudder, driven to various harbours and shores by the dry wind which blows from pinching poverty." There is a reasonable amount of evidence that, at some time or other, he visited Bologna, and that he journeyed to Paris and studied at the University; it is alleged that he even went as far as Oxford, but that is probably fable. Somehow he contrived to live; somehow he contrived to obtain books and to write – an unfinished Latin discourse on *Writing in the Vulgar Tongue* (*De Vulgari Eloquentia*) probably belongs to the early years of his exile. Later, in the *Paradiso*, he was to put into the mouth of one of his own ancestors words which have found an echo in the heart of every refugee from his day to ours: "Thou shalt leave everything beloved most dearly; this is the first shaft which the bow of exile lets fly. Thou shalt prove how salt is the taste of other men's bread, and how hard a path it is to go up and down upon another's stairs."[2]

1. See the poems known as the *Pietra* group in Dante's *Canzoniere*.
2. *Para.* xvii. 55–60.

The minds of political exiles are apt to turn to the theory of government; nor was Dante's mind any exception to the rule. What is perhaps exceptional is that he approached the subject rather slowly and tentatively, dealing with it at first almost incidentally while working out a general philosophy of the good life. His theory was adumbrated in the *Convivio*, defined on the political side in the *De Monarchia*, and only fitted into place in the universal scheme of things when he finally built up the immense theological structure of the *Comedy*. It explains so many things which, without it, seem to us disconcerting and queer that it is necessary to say a little about it.

The *Convivio* is in many ways an odd book. After some preliminary matter about the use of the vulgar tongue, it begins the main argument by referring to an episode at the end of the *Vita Nuova*. There, Dante had told how, at one moment, he was distracted from his mourning for Beatrice by a strong attachment to a lady who looked at him compassionately from a window; and how, after a time, he repented of this unfaithfulness, and was rewarded by that wonderful vision of Beatrice which made him resolve to write no more of her until – and so forth. He now says that there never was any flesh-and-blood lady at a window; that his "second love", to whom his Odes were written, was "the Lady Philosophy, daughter of the Emperor of the Universe"; that the *Vita* (though, of course, he abides by everything he said in it) was, after all, rather a juvenile performance, whereas the new book is to be more adult and masculine altogether; and that, having said so much, he now proposes to leave the Lady Beatrice out of it altogether. In short, he "will write no more of her, until ... "; but we are aware of a very great change in the tone, and also of a certain disingenuousness. For the extreme awkwardness he experiences in interpreting his first Ode allegorically as an address to the Lady Philosophy persuades us that, whatever he may say, it was originally written to a quite substantial lady at a quite substantial window. Controversy has raged about this. The truth, I think, is that there really was a lady, and that in the consolation he found in her presence for the loss of Beatrice he could not but see an analogue of the consolation he was beginning to find in philosophy for the loss of that first incomparable radiance which had been withdrawn from him when Beatrice departed and took his youth with her. If so, why could he not have said so? Well, because, for one thing, his political misfortunes had filled him with that self-conscious defensiveness and morbid sensitiveness to criticism which makes the path of the refugee harder even than it need be; because he was irritably aware that scandalous things were being said about him and his love-poetry; and because there were four or five poems looming in the background, which were obviously not addressed to Beatrice or to the Lady at the Window either, and to which – if he were to sustain his dignity as a professor of philosophy – it might be well to give an allegorical turn. Because, also, when one has turned forty, and is not particularly happy, one is apt to feel a false shame about one's earlier intimations of immortality. And, finally, because, whether he quite realized it at the time or not, he was in the Dark Wood, and standing on the brink of the Pit. It was not only that he was exiled, disappointed, imperilled, impoverished, and disillusioned; there was more to it than that. When later he came to write his spiritual pilgrimage, he dated his descent into Hell, not from the crash of all his hopes in 1301, but from the spring of 1300 – the moment when his confidence stood highest and his career seemed most assured; and he said that he had then been going astray for some time, wandering from the path like a man half asleep. In the poem, the descent takes thirty-six hours; in fact, it took something like twelve years before he passed through the lowest point of the spiritual abyss and struggled out "to look once more upon the stars".

In the meantime, then, he laid the "blessed and glorious Beatrice" – with the utmost reverence – on the shelf, and with her, that peculiar sense of revealed ecstasy, "of something far more deeply interfused", which his young heart had experienced without fully understanding. Now, with an almost mystical devotion, he worships, and calls others to worship, the Lady Philosophy. It would seem that she had taken the place of Beatrice and outgone her; for he equates her with the *Sophia* – the Divine Wisdom of the Jewish theologians, and with the Logos of St John. Yet, for all this, the book is somehow not altogether Christian. In its tone, though not of course in its technique, it suggests the Renaissance rather than the Middle Ages, in the sense that, although it springs from a Christian background and although its basic assumptions are Christian, the passion of the writer seems to be aroused rather by classical than by Christian exemplars. There is passion in it, but it is the passion of the eager scientific intellect – it is, so to speak, a cold passion. And the Dante who reveals himself in it has nobility, but without charm. The youthful bloom has gone – and something more than bloom. The shortest way of putting it is perhaps to say that one cannot imagine the Dante of the *Convivio* answering to any question "simply *Love*, with a countenance clothed in humility".

The book is tentative; it is unfinished. Dante is concerned, as he will be again later, with the nature of true happiness, and with the pre-eminence of the speculative over the active life; though he has not yet made the Christian distinction between the spheres of reason and of revelation, and is concerned rather with temporal than with eternal happiness. Revelation – once manifest to him incarnate in the image of Beatrice – has now been taken up and merged into the image of Philosophy. He will not see it directly, and transcending its own first image, till he has climbed Mount Purgatory, when we shall have to deal with it more fully. But meanwhile, towards the end of the finished part of the *Convivio*, while he is sketching out his ideas about the necessary conditions of happiness in *this* world, we find his mind occupied with the sanctions of secular monarchy, and in especial with the significance of the Roman Empire and the Roman Law.

Man, according to Aristotle, is a "social animal"; and so, in order to "live in felicity" in this world, and realize all his natural potentialities, he needs a civilization and a settled background of social order. But, because of the greed of the "Haves" and the envy of the "Have-nots", this social order is continually disturbed by the wars of rival states. What is needed, therefore, is a "monarchy" – that is to say, a single centre of world-government, to maintain peace and execute justice under a reign of universal law. That, briefly, is Dante's thesis; and we have heard something not unlike it of late years. "He imagined", says Dean Church, writing in 1849, "a single authority, unselfish, inflexible, irresistible, which would make all smaller tyrannies to cease and enable every man to live in peace and liberty so that he lived in justice. It is simply", concludes the good Dean, "what each separate state of Christendom has by this time more or less perfectly achieved."[1] We might, perhaps, hesitate to add that comment to-day.

The authority to which Dante looked for the unification of the civilized world was the Roman Empire, which had, in fact, once gone near to achieving that very thing. A study of its history persuaded him that the Roman people had been divinely called and miraculously guided to this great secular destiny, and that the establishment of the Empire represented the triumph, not of force, nor yet of "racial superiority" in the modern sense, but of the Roman conception of government by law. To him, it seemed providentially ordained that the World-Monarchy should be Roman, Imperial, and Holy; just as to our political idealists it seems axiomatic that it should be international and equalitarian, and should derive its sanction from the will of the peoples. The form changes, but the substance of Dante's theory is one for which the twentieth-century reader, living in the collapse of the liberal experiment, can feel an intelligent sympathy.

It was from Virgil, whose great epic is an apologia for and glorification of the pacifying and unificatory mission of Rome, that Dante derived this conception which redeemed secular history from chaos and put order and purpose into the political development of mankind. In the *Convivio*, this "design for living" is only briefly sketched, as part of an argument about the nature of human felicity. But in 1308 something happened which promised to remove it from the realm of theory and bring it within the range of practical politics. This was the election to the Imperial throne of Prince Henry of Luxemburg. "He was a man of noble character and great enthusiasm, and he took exactly the same ideal views of his office that Dante did. He hated the very names of Guelf and Ghibelline, and would not allow them to be uttered in his presence. His duty, he would often declare, was not to Italian or Frenchman or German, but to his Brother-Man; and it was well known that he cherished exalted hopes of ending the prolonged agony of Italy's internecine feuds, of restoring

1. Dean Church: *Essay on Dante.*

exiles, of reconciling factions, and of establishing the reign of peace and law".[1]

In June 1309, Henry was crowned at Aix-la-Chapelle, and in the following year he crossed the Alps and entered Italy by way of Turin, in order to make war upon King Robert of Sicily. Dante, filled with high hopes, ecstatically proclaimed his coming in an open letter (or, as we might call it to-day, a pamphlet) written in Latin and addressed to the rulers of Italy:

Lo, now is the acceptable time wherein arise the signs of consolation and peace. For a new day beginneth to glow, showing forth the dawn which is even now dissipating the darkness of our long calamity. ... And we, too, shall see the unlooked-for joy, we who have kept vigil through the long night in the desert. For peace-bringing Titan shall arise, and Justice, which, without the sun, hath languished like the heliotrope, will revive again so soon as he shall brandish his first rays, and they who love iniquity shall be confounded before his shining face. ... O Italy! henceforth rejoice; though now to be pitied by the very Saracens, yet soon to be envied throughout the world! because thy bridegroom, the solace of the world and the glory of thy people, the most clement Henry, Divus and Augustus and Caesar, is hastening to the bridal. ... Will he not have compassion on any? Yea, he will pardon all who implore his mercy, since he is Caesar and his majesty floweth from the fount of compassion. His judgment abhorreth all severity, and, smiting ever on this side of the mean, planteth itself beyond the mean in rewarding. Will he then applaud the audacities of worthless men, and drink to the undertakings of presumption? Far be it! for he is Augustus.[2]

He calls upon the oppressors to receive the Emperor with fear and trembling and with submission to authority; and upon the oppressed to show mercy and generosity in the day of their coming triumph.

Be merciful, be merciful, even henceforth, O dearest ones who have suffered wrong with me, that the Hectorean [Trojan – i.e. Roman and Imperial] *pastor may recognize you as sheep of his fold. For though temporal punishment be divinely committed to him, yet (that he may savour of the goodness of Him from whom, as from a single point, the*

---

1. P. 4, Wicksteed: *From Vita Nuova to Paradiso.*
2. Dante: *Epist. V* (T. C. trans.).

power of Peter and of Caesar brancheth) he delicately correcteth his household, and yet more gladly doth take compassion on it.[1]

It seems probable that it was in honour of this same occasion that Dante wrote the Latin treatise known as *De Monarchia – Concerning Monarchy*, in which he develops the idea underlying the phrase "him from whom, as from a single point, the power of Peter and of Caesar brancheth". His argument is that the temporal power (Caesar), like the spiritual power (Peter), derives its mandate directly from God, and not intermediately through the Church. As the Jews were a chosen people appointed to be the seed of the Church, so the Romans were likewise a chosen people appointed to be the seed of the Empire. Both powers, temporal and spiritual, have their proper seat at Rome, but they exercise their functions independently and in parallel. The authority of the Empire does not rest upon force, but upon law, and laws are made for the good of the people and not the people for the laws; consequently, kings and governments are to be considered the servants, not the masters, of the people. Nevertheless (says Dante, herein more realistic than the framers of the Covenant of the League of Nations) the monarch must be armed with power, "for law (*jus*, which in Latin means not only 'law' but 'right') does not extend beyond power" (i.e. it is no good having laws if you cannot enforce them). Accordingly, lest the universal monarchy should become a universal tyranny, a check is needed upon the Empire. This, in Dante's scheme, is provided by the Church, which at every point interfuses and penetrates the secular order, not by directly intervening in politics (since this can only corrupt the spiritual power by worldly greed and ambition), but by forming men of such a character that they will produce a temporal society in which it is possible to live a full and a Christian life.

It is at this point that we find Dante clearly distinguishing between the proper functions of Reason and Revelation. The secular order is founded upon Reason, and its task is to lead to happiness in *this* world; the spiritual order is founded upon Revelation, and its task is to lead men to eternal beatitude. While making this distinction, Dante adds the warning that this truth

1. *Ibid.*

"is not to be received in such narrow sense as that the Roman prince is subordinate in nothing to the Roman pontiffs; in as much as mortal felicity is in a certain sense ordained with reference to immortal felicity". This point is one which he will, later on, develop in the grand scheme of the *Comedy*, where Revelation (Beatrice) is seen at all points directing, guiding, and finally superseding Reason (Virgil), as Man proceeds through self-knowledge to the Earthly and thence to the Heavenly Paradise. But as far as the affairs of this world are concerned, Dante never ceased to protest against that drive towards theocracy which a great modern Catholic philosopher has called "the temptation, the evil spirit of medieval Christendom"[1] – the attempt to establish the Kingdom of God here and now as an ecclesiastical-political structure. This theory by which "all power, temporal as well as spiritual, belonged to the Pope, who delegated to the Emperor, and through him to the other monarchs, temporal power for the perfect unification of the world in the reign of Christ",[2] located the "Kingdom", not in eternity but in time, and so, like much modern socialistic theory, had the effect of shutting up God inside history, and making the Church an instrument for building the perfect secular state. Dante's theory, while seeking to provide for the establishment of a just social order in history, avoids involving the Church in the secular order, and leaves her free to function in the sphere of eternity to which the true "Kingdom of God" belongs. For "Christ Himself, when He had become man for the revealing of the Spirit, and was preaching the Gospel upon earth, as though partitioning the two kingdoms and distributing the universe between Himself and Caesar, 'Render', He said, 'to either the things that are his own'."[3]

Although we may think Dante's political theory fundamentally wrong, it no longer appears so pathetically out of touch with reality as it did in the nineteenth century. It is interesting to compare it, on the one hand, with schemes for world-government put forward under the menace of the atom bomb, and, on the other, with modern Catholic theories of the relations of Church and State, such as that outlined by, for example, Jacques Maritain in the work just quoted. It is, however, certain that in Dante's own

1. Jacques Maritain: *True Humanism.*   2. *Ibid.*   3. Dante: *Epist. V.*

time it was not practical politics. The Empire was dying on its feet, and the states of Europe, already moving towards national self-consciousness and centralized constitutions of their own, had not the slightest desire to find themselves under the control of a really effective Imperial power. The Church, clinging to the temporalities, was already set on the path that was to lead inevitably, in the long run, to the rejection of the Papal claims and the schisms of the Reformation. But we must have Dante's theory in our minds while reading the *Comedy*, if we are to follow the unfolding of its great twofold pattern of temporal and eternal salvation, and understand the passion and bitterness with which he assails those who have undermined the Empire and corrupted the Church.[1]

In January 1311, Henry VII was crowned at Milan. Next month, the Florentines, who had already declined to receive his ambassadors, prepared to resist him in arms, thus calling forth from Dante a letter of the bitterest reproach. The Florentines, unmoved, again refused to enter into negotiations with Henry. In 1311, while the Emperor was besieging Cremona, Dante addressed to him a letter, upbraiding him for his delay in entering Tuscany. Cremona and Brescia fell, and Henry, after retiring to Genoa, moved on to make his headquarters at Pisa. In April 1312, he advanced upon Rome, and, after fighting his way through the streets, was crowned at St John Lateran, since St Peter's was in the hands of King Robert. In the autumn he at last undertook the siege of Florence. Dante, it is said, though approving and urging the action, refused to join him in person, being unwilling to bear arms against his own city, or to make his longed-for return from exile in blood and conquest. After about six weeks, the Emperor was compelled to raise the siege and retired once more on Pisa. After lingering there inactively for six months, he at length moved south again, and, on 24 August 1313, died of fever, with a sinister suddenness, at Buonconvento near Siena. The campaign, which had been doomed from the start, ended in futility; the Imperial Crown, disputed by rival claimants, lay to all intents vacant for nearly ten years; and Dante's dream of a just Empire was over,

---

1. It explains much, for instance, of Dante's hatred of Pope Boniface VIII whose famous bull, *Unam Sanctam* (1302), asserted the temporal claims of the papacy in no uncertain manner.

together with all hope of his ever returning from exile. "For", says the chronicler Lionardo Bruni, "he had cut himself off from the way of pardon by his violent speech and writings against the citizens who were directing the Commonwealth. So, relinquishing all hope, he passed the rest of his life, in great poverty, in various places up and down Lombardy, Tuscany, and Romagna, under the protection of various Seigneurs, till at last he withdrew to Ravenna, where he ended his life."

In 1314, the Florentine decrees against the exiles were renewed. Dante's sons, Pietro and Jacopo, who had now reached the age of legal manhood (14 years), were branded with him as Ghibellines and rebels, and condemned, if captured within the city, to be publicly beheaded. They had, however, already fled to join their father. In the next year, King Robert of Sicily proclaimed an amnesty, and permission was granted to certain of the exiles to return, on condition of paying a heavy fine and performing a humiliating public penance in the Baptistery. Dante's friends seem to have hoped that he might take advantage of these terms, for we find him writing to a correspondent in Florence –

This, then, is the gracious recall by which Dante Alighieri may be brought back to his native land, after enduring almost fifteen years of exile! This is the reward of an innocence known to all men! of the sweat and labour of unceasing study! Can a man who is anything of a philosopher stoop to such humiliation? ... Shall one who has preached justice and suffered injustice pay money to those who have injured him, as though they had been his benefactors? That, Father, is not the way to return to my country. If any other way can be found ... that may not be derogatory to Dante's reputation and honour, I shall not be slow to accept it. But if I cannot enter Florence by such a way, then I will never enter Florence. What then? Can I not everywhere gaze upon the mirror of the sun and stars? Can I not everywhere under heaven mirror forth the most precious truths, without first making myself inglorious, nay, ignominious in the sight of the city of Florence? I shall not want for bread.

To gaze upon the mirror of the sun and stars and in himself to mirror forth the truth. This was the task which Dante had set himself – as Milton was to do some three hundred years later – in the wreck of all his earthly hopes. He had lost love and youth and earthly goods and household peace and citizenship and active political usefulness and the dream of a decent world and a reign of justice. He was stripped bare. He looked outwards upon the corruption of Church and Empire, and he looked inwards into the corruption of the human heart; and what he saw was the vision of Hell. And, having seen it, he set himself down to write the great Comedy of Redemption and of the return of all things by the Way of Self-Knowledge and Purification, to the beatitude of the Presence of God.

We do not know exactly when he began the *Commedia*. Possibly it was something like this that he already had in mind when his vision came to him after the death of Beatrice. There is a tradition that he had written the first seven cantos of the *Inferno* before the exile – probably in Latin, and almost certainly not as we have them to-day. It seems likely that the completed *Inferno* as we know it was first "published" – that is, circulated in manuscript form and made available to copyists and purchasers – about the year 1314. It was written – to the scandal of Dante's more academic admirers, who thought Latin the only proper medium for dignified verse – in the vulgar tongue, "in which", as Dante observed later, "even women can exchange ideas". He meant no disrespect to women – far from it; he meant merely that he wanted every intelligent person in Italy to read it, for, as he had pointed out some time before in the *Convivio*, "there are many people with excellent minds who, owing to the grievous decay of good custom in the world, are not educated in letters: princes, barons, and knights, and many other gentlefolk, not only men but women, of which men and women alike there are many of this [i.e. the Italian] tongue, who can use the vernacular but have no Latin". He wrote his *Comedy*, then, for the "common reader", and, taking as its basis two popular types of story which everybody knew and loved – the story of a vision of Hell, Purgatory, and Paradise, and the story of the Lover who has to adventure through the Underworld to find his lost Lady – he combined them into a great allegory of the soul's search for God. He made it as swift and exciting and topical as he could; he lavished upon it all his learning and wit, all his tenderness, humour, and enthusiasm, and all his poetry. And he built it all closely about his own personal experience; for the redemption he tells of is first and foremost his own. Anybody who doubts this has only to read the *Vita Nuova*, the *Convivio*, and the *Commedia* in the order in which they were written and see how, with the return to Beatrice, Dante has come back to his earlier self. It is the return to love and humility, and, with humility, to joy. For Dante (so often called "bitter", "grim", and "gloomy" by those who have never got further than the *Inferno* is the supreme poet of joy. No one has ever sung the rapture of eternal fulfilment like him who had first "gone down quick into Hell" and looked upon the face of eternal loss. "The Church militant", says Beatrice of him in the *Paradiso*,[1] "has no son more full of hope than he"; and that claim was justified, although, by his own confession, he had once got to the point where the voices of the three theological virtues were inaudible to him, and was saved only because, by the grace of God, his reason did not give way. It is right that our study of the *Comedy* should begin with the *Inferno*; Dante wrote it in that order because he experienced it in that order. But, while reading it we must always remember that the experience, and the story, lead through that realm to the Earthly Paradise and beyond it to that dancing Heaven of light which "seemed to me like a smile of the whole universe".

It is pleasant to know that the last years of Dante's life were passed in comparative peace and comfort. He stayed for some time at the court of the magnificent Can Grande della Scala,[2] Imperial Vicar of Verona, and younger brother of Dante's earlier patron Bartolommeo. Stories, highly picturesque and probably apocryphal, are told of his relations with this handsome, brilliant and imperious young Ghibelline nobleman – stories which include some (to our minds) ill-mannered practical joking on Can Grande's part and acid repartees from his distinguished guest. The account of the court of Verona given by a fellow-guest and exile is probably more reliable than these traditions:

> *Different apartments, according to their condition, were assigned to the exiles in the Scala palace; each had his own servants, and*

1. *Para.* xxv. 52–3.   2. *Para.* xvii. 70–76.

a well-appointed table served in private. The various apartments were distinguished by appropriate devices and figures, such as Victory for soldiers, Hope for exiles, Muses for poets, Mercury for artists, and Paradise for preachers. During meals musicians, jesters, and jugglers performed in these rooms. The halls were decorated with pictures representing the vicissitudes of fortune. On occasion Cane invited certain of his guests to his own table, notably Guido da Castello,[1] who on account of his single-mindedness was known as the Simple Lombard, and the poet Dante Alighieri.[2]

It sounds liberal, superb (in every sense of the word), and perhaps a trifle oppressive. That Dante was grateful – he who never forgot a benefit or an injury – is proved by his eulogy of the della Scala family and of Can Grande himself in the *Paradiso*. But he was still "going up and down another's stairs", and perhaps the atmosphere of the Scaliger palace was not wholly favourable to concentrated work.

At any rate, in 1317 or thereabouts, he shifted his quarters for the last time, accepting the invitation of Guido Novello, Count of Polenta, to come and live with him at Ravenna. Here at length he was given, what he had lacked so long, a house of his own. His sons Jacopo and Pietro went with him and he was joined by his daughter Beatrice. At Ravenna, it would appear, he wrote the last part at any rate of the *Purgatorio*[3] and the whole of the *Paradiso*, supporting himself at the same time by giving lectures and lessons in the art of poetry. He was still a poor man, as is evident from the letter in which he dedicates the *Paradiso* to Can Grande, but that he was happier and more independent at Ravenna than at any other time of his exile we may readily believe.

In the summer of 1321, a dispute arose between Venice and Ravenna, and Dante was one of the ambassadors sent by Guido to treat with the Doge. Tradition tells that the embassy was coldly

---

1. Mentioned by Dante, *Purg.* xvi. 125.
2. This account, given by Sagacio Mucio Gazata, a chronicler of Reggio, quoted by Sismondi (Paget Toynbee: *Dante Dictionary*, art. Can Grande).
3. The description of the Earthly Paradise in the concluding cantos of the *Purgatorio* is thought to be based upon the landscape of the Pineta at Ravenna, the beautiful pine-forest which was unhappily destroyed during the war of 1939–45.

received, and that, having failed in their mission, its members were refused a ship to carry them back to Ravenna and were thus obliged to make their way home by land along the malaria-infested seaboard. On the journey, Dante was taken with fever, and although he struggled back to Ravenna, he rapidly became worse, and (says Boccaccio)

in accordance with the Christian religion [he] received every sacrament of the Church humbly and devoutly, and reconciled himself with God by contrition for everything that, being but man, he had done against His pleasure; and in the month of September in the year of Christ one thousand three hundred and twenty-one, on the day whereon the exaltation of the Holy Cross is celebrated by the Church [14 September] ... he rendered up to his Creator his toil-worn spirit, the which I doubt not was received into the arms of his most noble Beatrice, with whom, in the sight of Him who is the supreme good, the miseries of this present life left behind, he now lives most joyously in that life the felicity of which expects no end.[1]

He was, according to a statement made by himself upon his deathbed, fifty-six years and four months old.

Dante was dead; he was laid to rest in the convent of the Friars Minor in Ravenna, robed in the scarlet robes of a doctor and crowned at last with laurel, and Guido Novello pronounced with his own lips a long and handsome oration over the body of his dead poet. But Boccaccio goes on to tell a story which – though it may be pure legend – has a charm of its own, suggesting as it does that even after death Dante was still Dante, and felt a certain concernment for his *Comedy* as he waited on Tiber's shore for the angel-pilot to come and ferry him across the world to Mount Purgatory.

It was his custom, when he had completed six or eight cantos, to send them, before anybody else had seen them, to Messer Can Grande della Scala, whom he reverenced more than any other man; and after he had seen them, he made copies available to whoever wanted them. And having in this way sent them all, except the last thirteen (though these

1. *Vita di Dante* (trans. Wicksteed).

*thirteen were already written), it came to pass that he died without having
made any memorandum about them, neither could his sons find them,
although they searched for them over and over again. The sons, therefore,
Jacopo and Pietro, who were both poets, being urged by their friends to
finish their father's work, set about it as best they could. But a marvel-
lous vision, appearing to Jacopo, who was the more eager in this business,
not only forbade this fatuous presumption, but showed them where to find
the thirteen cantos they had been so industriously searching for.*

*A worthy man of Ravenna, called Piero Giardino, who had been for
a long time a pupil of Dante's, a sober-minded and trustworthy man,
related that when eight months had elapsed from the day of his master's
death, Jacopo di Dante came to his house one night, close upon the hour
we call mattins, and said that, that very night and a little before that hour,
he had in his sleep seen his father Dante come to him, dressed in shining
white garments and his face resplendent with unwonted light. And it
seemed to him that he asked him whether he was alive, and heard him
answer: "Yes, but with the true life and not this of ours". Wherefore he
dreamed that he went on to ask, whether he had finished his work before
passing into the true life, and, if he had, where was the missing portion
which they had never been able to find. To this he seemed, as before, to
hear the answer: "Yes, I finished it". And then it seemed to him that he
took him by the hand and led him into the room where he used to sleep
when he lived in this life, and, touching one of the walls with his hand,
said: "Here is what you have been searching for so long". And as soon
as these words were spoken, it seemed to him that his sleep and Dante
departed from him together. And so, he said, he could not wait, but had
to come and tell what he had seen, so that they might go together to look
in the place shown to him (which remained very clearly impressed upon
his memory) so as to see whether that which had so pointed it out was a
true spirit or a false delusion. Accordingly, since a good part of the night
still remained, they set out together and came to the house in which Dante
was residing at the time of his death; and, having knocked up the present
tenant and been let in by him, they went to the place indicated, and there
found a mat fixed to the wall, which they had always seen hanging there
in the past. This they gently lifted, and found in the wall a tiny window,
which neither of them had ever seen before or known to be there; and in
it they found a quantity of written sheets, all mouldy with the dampness
of the wall and ready to rot away if they had been left there any longer.*

When they had cleaned off all the mould, they saw that the pages were numbered and, having placed them in order, they found they had recovered, all together, the thirteen cantos that were lacking of the Comedy. *Wherefore they copied them out rejoicing and, according to the custom of the author, sent them first of all to Messer Cane, and afterwards reunited them to the unfinished work where they belonged. And thus the work which had taken so many years in the making was completed.*[1]

We may or may not believe that Dante was in fact made uneasy, even in the true life, by the thought of what his offspring might make of the last three heavens – it would be like him, for, as he once remarked, he "trusted himself more than another". But the dream is not in itself incredible, and the details seem plausible. Curiously enough, the adventures of Dante's manuscript were repeated, many years later, with their author's own body, which became, literally as one may say, a bone of contention between Florence and Ravenna. Florence, who had exiled him and forbidden his return on pain of burning alive, laid claim to him when he was safely dead and famous. Ravenna, stoutly and with some indignation, rejected the claim, determined that he who had found peace with her should not be disturbed for the benefit of the city that had not known how to cherish her greatest son. Requests were made in 1396, in 1429, and in 1476, but were refused. In 1519 a resolute attempt was made, backed by the authority of Pope Leo X himself, to secure the body. This, it seemed impossible to resist; the Florentine envoys arrived and the tomb was opened; it contained nothing but a few small bones and some withered laurel leaves. The envoys made the best of this to the Pope, cautiously observing that they "found Dante neither in soul nor in body; and it is supposed that, as in his lifetime he journeyed in soul and in body through Hell, Purgatory, and Paradise, so in death he must have been received, body and soul, into one of those realms".

The matter was hushed up, both then, and again when in 1782 the tomb was opened on the occasion of its restoration. In 1865, when the sixth centenary of Dante's birth was being celebrated, and the Florentines had once again petitioned for the custody

[1]. Boccaccio: *Vita de Dante* (Compendium).

of the body and been for the fifth time refused, the opening of the tomb and verification of the remains was announced as part of the sexcentenary celebrations. The cat, it seemed, would be out of the bag at last. And so, indeed, it was – but it had another kind of surprise to spring. In the course of some repairs in the Bracciaforte Chapel, which backed upon the mausoleum, it became necessary to install a pump, and to make room for the pump-handle, it was decided to knock away a portion of the party-wall. The workman's pick struck upon wood; investigation disclosed a wooden chest. Within it was a skeleton; on the bottom of the chest was written in ink – *Dantis ossa denuper revisa die 3 Junii 1677;*[1] and on the lid: *Dantis ossa a me Fre Antonio Santi hic posita Ano 1677 die 18 Octobris.*[2]

Presumably it was in 1519 that the Franciscans, alarmed by Pope Leo's manoeuvre, had knocked a hole through party-wall and sarcophagus, extracted the bones and hidden Dante away out of reach of the Florentines. During the hundred and fifty years intervening before Fra Antonio Santi "revisited" the remains preparatory to "depositing" them in the new wall which was erected in 1677 to block up the former entrance to the Bracciaforte Chapel, they must have been hidden in the monastery. The secret was well kept; but it is said that until the time of the discovery in 1865, a tradition still lingered among the brethren that their chapel "held a great treasure"; an aged sacristan, who used to sleep in that part of the building, was accustomed to tell of seeing in dreams a figure clad in red, who issued from the wall and passed through the chapel and, being asked who he was, replied: "I am Dante". The old man did not live to see his dream interpreted.

The chest, with its inscription, is in the Bibliotheca Nazionale; the bones, after lying for three days in a glass coffin for the veneration of the people of Ravenna, were restored to the original sarcophagus, and Ravenna still remains guardian of her treasure.

THE TRANSLATION

I ought to say a few words about the translation. It is not, of

---

1. Dante's bones, revisited again 3 June 1677.
2. Dante's bones, deposited here by me, Fra Antonio Santi, 18 October 1677.

course, Dante; no translation could ever be Dante. He himself said in the *Convivio* that he detested translations – a fact which adds an acute feeling of compunction to the translator's other difficulties, and doubles the embarrassment of counting up the already existing translations with which any new version has to compete. (But since the Dante of the *Commedia* had re-learnt charity since writing the *Convivio*, and was eager above all things that his poem should bring as many people as possible to salvation, we must hope that he forgives us all.)

I have stuck to the *terza rima*, despite the alleged impossibility of finding sufficient rhymes in English – it is, after all, less exacting in this respect than the Spenserian stanza, which nobody dreams of calling impossible. In prose, a greater verbal accuracy would of course be attainable; but for the general reader this does not, I think, compensate for the loss of speed and rhythm and the "punch" of the rhyme.

The rhyme-scheme (aba, bcb, cdc, ded ... xyx, yzy, z) runs continuously from the beginning to the end of every canto, each three-line stanza (terzain) being rhyme-linked to the one before and the one after, until the sequence is neatly tied off by a single line rhyming with the middle line of the preceding stanza. By overrunning and light rhyming, the *terza rima* can be made to run almost continuously; or, by end-stopping and conspicuous rhyming, it can be broken at will into stanza-form; and it can be carried from the one rhythm to the other by the linked rhyme without for a moment losing the strong forward movement of the verse, which is like that of a flowing tide, each wave riding in on the back of the one before it. Blank verse, with its insidious temptation to be literal at the expense of the verse, has little advantage over prose and, though easier to write badly, is far more difficult to write well; while the rhymed couplet, or any stanza-form other than Dante's own, involves the placing of stanza-breaks at places where he did not choose to place them. I agree, therefore, with Maurice Hewlett that, for the translator, the choice is "*terza rima* or nothing". I have used all the licence which English poetic tradition allows in the way of half-rhyme, light "Cockney", identical, and (if necessary) eccentric rhyme – and indeed, without these aids, the heavy thump of the mascu-

Introduction

line rhymes (which predominate in English) would be tiresome.[1]

I have used a liberal admixture of feminine rhyme. This is the usual English custom, and I do not know why Dante's translators for the most part fight shy of it. A *preponderance* of feminine rhyme tends to produce special effects – of sonority (e.g. the inscription over Hell-Gate in Canto III, or the opening of Canto IV), of elegiac lamentation (Canto V), or of burlesque (the Gilbertian gallop at the beginning of Canto XXII); its *occasional* use is the practice of all English writers of *terza rima* or any other rhymed verse. (And Dante himself does not scruple to vary his feminine endings with masculine endings, when he wants to, rare as these latter are in Italian verse.)

As regards the metre, the translator is not faced with the same kind of difficulty which confronts him when trying to render into English the classical hexameter or the French alexandrine, whose rhythms are hopelessly alien to our native verse. We are fortunate in having a metrical unit which almost exactly corresponds to that of the *Commedia*. Like our own "heroic" line, the Italian hendecasyllable (line of eleven syllables) normally carries five accentual beats in rising duple rhythm, though it is distinguished from it in general effect by the fact that in Italian the "feminine" and in English the "masculine" ending predominates. Thus, if we take the opening lines of one of Shakespeare's sonnets:

Farewell! thou art too dear for my possessing

And like enough thou know'st thy estimate,

1. English is "poor in rhymes" because it is remarkably rich in vowel-sounds. Of these, Italian possesses seven only, all "pure" and unmodified by the succeeding consonants. For English, on the other hand, the Shorter O.E.D. lists no fewer than fifty-two native varieties, shading into one another by imperceptible degrees. This phenomenon results from the fact that most English vowels are diphthongs to start with and nearly all are subtly modified by a following consonant, particularly by a following "r". Indeed, in Southern English, this self-effacing consonant when it appears at the end of a word seems to exist for the sole purpose of performing this duty to its vowel, dying without a murmur when its work is done, after the manner of certain male spiders. (In Northern English and in the Celtic dialects the "r" is more tenacious of life.) In consequence of all this, "pure" rhymes are scarce in English; but "impure" rhymes are frequent and legitimate, producing many curious melodic effects which have no parallel in the verse of pure-vowelled languages.

the first faithfully represents the Italian, and the second the English, norm or basic line.

As in English, so too in Italian, the line can be varied in two principal ways: (1) by varying the regular fall of the beat, and (2) by crowding extra syllables into the line so as to produce, when desired, a triple instead of a duple rhythm. The former of these variations is executed in Italian exactly as in English, except that even bolder liberties may be taken with it; the latter is managed rather differently, though with much the same final result. Because the Italian line is scanned by syllables and not by accent, extra syllables can only be worked in where two vowel-sounds, coming together, can be elided, and not counted separately in the scansion; whereas the English line, being scanned by accent, will tolerate extra unaccented syllables of any kind and in any number, provided that the basic five-stress rhythm is not wholly lost to the ear. By either method, the line can be expanded, if desirable, from its "normal" ten or eleven syllables to accommodate as many as fifteen or sixteen.

A few examples will make this clear:

(1) The "normal" ten-syllable line of five rising accents:

> *Midway this way of life we're bound upon*
> (Basic in English and possible in Italian.)

(2) The "normal" eleven-syllable line of five rising accents:

> *And fife and drum and signal flares a-brandish*
> (Basic in Italian and frequent in English.)

(3) Variation by reversed stress:

> *Thousand and more, thronging the barbican*
> (Frequent in both languages.)

(4) Extra syllables introduced by elision of vowels:

> *Already across the water heaves in sight*
> (The normal Italian method, and frequent in English.)

(5) Extra unaccented syllables introduced without elision:

Then the terr or of alight ing seemed worse than the terror of soaring
(Perfectly possible in English; wholly impossible in Italian.)

Generally speaking, the syllable-scanned Italian metre can vary its stress-pattern more boldly *from line to line* than is possible in English, where the accentual pull is stronger. Attempts at direct imitation of the packed syllables and indeterminate beat of the Italian are apt to result in a cramped and waddling line, suggestive of a person walking in thin tight shoes over cobble-stones. Lines of monotonously regular normality, on the other hand, are not only intolerable in themselves but also far removed from Dante's inexhaustible metrical variety. The best plan is, I think, to let the verse run at its own pace, as the feeling of the passage demands, using to the full all such metrical variations as offer a native equivalent for the Italian play upon stress-shift and elision. It will be found that the natural tendency in English is for the rhythm to vary between duple and triple measure rather from terzain to terzain than from line to line.

One variation from the norm is so characteristic of Dante's verse and so startling at first to English ears that it deserves special mention. This is the occasional appearance – sometimes in single lines and sometimes extended over several successive stanzas – of the metre made familiar to us by the nursery jingle

Diddle-diddle dumpling, my son John

or, more decorously, and still more like the Italian, by Meredith's *Love in the Valley*:

When her mother tends her before the laughing mirror.

We are not accustomed to find this invigorating jog-trot mixed up with our "heroic" metre; and one trouble about it is that, though easy enough to drop into, it is (even, I am told, in Italian) difficult to get out of again; while to jerk into it and out again in the course of three consecutive lines[1] is, in English, very nearly

---

1. As, for instance, in the grotesque passage at the opening of *Inferno*, Canto XXII, where the single line

quando con trombe, e quando con campane

rattles suddenly across the metre with a clatter as of tin trays falling down an iron staircase.

impracticable. But the effect of it where it occurs is so entertaining that in one passage of the *Inferno* where it runs – like the creature whose movement it represents – over several terzains of the text, I have reproduced it as faithfully as I can:

> *And just as a lizard, with a quick, slick slither,*
> *Flicks across the highway from hedge to hedge, etc.*
>
> (xxv. 79 *sqq.*)

The only other metrical peculiarity which is likely to disconcert the reader is the frequent running-over of the lines in such a way as to leave, for example, the adjective at the end of one line and the noun which it qualifies at the beginning of the next. This is highly characteristic of the original, for Dante is a hardy over-runner, and will not hesitate, if it suits him, to separate subject from verb, verb from direct object, numeral or demonstrative adjective or even the definite article from its noun, or to chop a word in two bodily. This is, indeed, one of the devices by which the *terza rima* is made to flow. The reader will find that if he will read the verse continuously (and for preference aloud), letting the stress fall where it would fall in natural speech, and pausing only where the sense pauses without making any attempt to "end-stop" the lines, rhyme and rhythm will fall automatically into place; and he will then feel something of the elastic pulse – the cease-lessly vital thrust-and-pull – of the movement which makes *terza rima* one of the most flexible and satisfying measures ever devised for verse-narration.

As regards diction and syntax, I have interpreted liberally the phrase "in modern English" which applies to the present series of translations. The vocabulary and the sentence-rhythms of verse are not, and never can be, exactly the same as those of contemporary prose. I have considered the whole range of intelligible English speech to be open to me, excluding, however, at the one end of the scale, words and forms so archaic as to be incomprehensible, and, at the other, "nonce-words" and up-to-the-minute slang. I have tried, that is, to steer a discreet middle course between Wardour Street and Hollywood, and to eschew: "Marry, quotha!" without declining upon "Sez you!" I have tried to avoid, as far as possible, Latinized inversions (especially when they involve

ambiguity), poetic clichés, and sudden drops into slang or bathos –
bearing in mind, however, that Dante's own style moves continu-
ally from the grand manner to the colloquial, and that nothing
could be more unfair to him, or more unlike him, than to iron
out all his lively irregularities into one flat level of dignified
commonplace. Generally speaking, ancient and solemn words and
locutions appear most frequently in the "poetic" bits of the poem,
and modern ones in the colloquial bits – which is, I hope, where
one might expect to find them. Where some one particular word
seemed to be absolutely demanded by the necessity of strict
accuracy (particularly of theological accuracy) and no other word
would do, I have used that word, regardless of its age or origin.
Where sense, metre, and rhyme would accommodate themselves
indifferently to either an ancient or a modern phrase, I have
plumped for the modern, especially if the passage was humorous
or conversational. For example, in *Inf.* xxi. 127, where the candi-
dates for admission were:

> "*Sir, I don't like the look of this one bit*"

and

> "*Master, this prospect likes me not a whit*",

the context seemed to call for liveliness rather than for archaic
dignity.

After careful consideration, however, I decided to use the
ancient "thee and thou" throughout, rather than the modern
"you". For one thing, it is important to be able to distinguish in
certain passages between the singular and the plural, and in others,
between the intimate "*tu*" and the ceremonial "*voi*". And further,
the word "thou", which was commonly used in speech up to the
beginning of the nineteenth century and in verse to the beginning
of the twentieth – and which, indeed, is alive in North-country
speech to this day – provides, as it were, a kind of link between
the ancient and modern speech-forms, and a test of what forms can
be linked in the same phrase without a too-jarring anachronism.
"Thou art tired and weary" is poetic common form; an eighteenth-
century person might have said "th'art fagged"; it is conceivable
that a North-country airman might even to-day say, "th'art
brassed-off, lad"; what is inconceivable is that anybody should

say: "thou art brassed-off, methinks". In such matters, the ear and taste of the translator must be his guides; and if he gets into trouble with his critics, he must console himself by remembering that Dante himself used not only learned, obscure, and Latinized expressions, but also many provincial and dialect forms, and such an abundance of colloquialisms as to be severely censured by eighteenth-century pundits for his lowness, vulgarity, and lack of proper dignity.

He has been scolded also for his love of puns and conceits, and internal rhymes and chimes, such as were fashionable in his day. They are part of his style, and I have done my best to reproduce them where it was possible, as also to preserve some of his alliterations. Thus the play on the word "Salse" in *Inf.* xviii. 51 is represented by a playful evocation of the name of Wormwood Scrubs, and the complete alliterative scheme of the three great passages on the Last Judgment (*Inf.* vi. 95; x. 10-12; xiii. 108) is there in the English for those who care to look for it. I have also been particular not to lose, if I could help it, the effects made by the iteration of similar words in similar positions (as, for example, the iterated "love ... love ... love" at the beginnings of the three parallel terzains of *Inf.* v. 100-106). And I have also so far succeeded – though at the cost of some rather acrobatic rhyme – in keeping all Dante's Latin quotations in the original form and in the places where he put them (readers will find that they work in better if given the "old", or "English", pronunciation).[1] These things are, perhaps, no more than Dante's eccentricities; but the eccentricities are part of the man.

Two things remain to be mentioned. The first is Dante's humour. This, of all his qualities, has been the most hopelessly obscured by his translators and critics. Most of them (rather grudgingly) admit that the burlesque opening of Canto xxxi of the *Inferno* is meant to be funny, though his early translator Cary shrinks from allowing even that, and merges the whole passage into a stateliness of sober Miltonics. But the pervading flavour of Dante's humour is much more subtle: it is dry and delicate and satirical; in particular his portrait of himself is tinged throughout with a charming self-mockery which has no parallel that I

1. E.g. *Inf.* xxxiv. 1.

know of outside the pages of Jane Austen. In translating I have,
inevitably, coarsened what is, for the most part, something more
like a faintly ironic inflection in the voice than anything humorous
in the words themselves; but here again, it seemed better to err by
over-emphasis than by ignoring the change of tone. The easiest
way to show what I have done is to lay a few passages side by
side with other translations; for example:

Inf. xi. 76:

> *"What error has seduced thy reason, pray?"*
> *Said he; "thou art not wont to be so dull;*
> *Or are thy wits woolgathering miles away?"*

where Cary has:

> *He answer thus return'd:*
> *"Wherefore in dotage wanders thus thy mind,*
> *Not so accustomed? Or what other thoughts*
> *Possess it?"*

Inf. xvi. 124:

> *When truth looks like a lie, a man's to blame*
> *Not to sit still, if he can, and hold his tongue,*
> *Or he'll only cover his innocent head with shame.*

where Wright has:

> *That truth which bears the semblance of a lie*
> *To pass the lips man never should allow:*
> *Though crime be absent – still disgrace is nigh.*

Inf. xvii. 91:

> *So I climbed to those dread shoulders obediently;*
> *"Only do" (I meant to say, but my voice somehow*
> *Wouldn't come out right) "please catch hold of me."*

where Binyon has:

> *On those dread shoulders did I then get hold.*
> *I wished to say, only the voice came not*
> *As I had meant: "Thy arms about me fold."*

In this last case, it is a question, not only of translating, but of
choosing between two possible readings of the Italian; *which* one

chooses – the unbroken phrase or the broken, gasping one – will depend, precisely, on whether one thinks Dante is laughing at himself or not. I believe that he is, and that his treatment of his own character is suffused throughout with a delicate spirit of comedy, which no reverence should tempt the translator to obscure by dignified phrases.

The second thing, of course, is Dante's poetry. When Dante chooses to be sheerly beautiful, he writes not like a man but like an angel, and at that point the translator has to give up the chase after perfection

As, at his art's end, every artist must.[1]

The most that one can do with passages like the one about Benaco (*Inf.* xx. 61–78), or the Last Voyage of Ulysses (*Inf.* xxvi. 85–142), or the heart-breaking little vision of the brooks of the Casentino (*Inf.* xxx. 64–7), and *a fortiori* with the first eight cantos of the *Purgatorio* or the ecstatic glories of the *Paradiso*, is to erect, as best one can, a kind of sign-post to indicate: "Here is beauty; make haste to learn Italian, so that you may read it for yourselves". For when one has disposed of Dante the politician, Dante the moralist, Dante the theologian, and even of Dante "the most piercing intellect ever granted to the sons of men",[2] there remains Dante the poet, who walks equal with Homer and Aeschylus and Virgil and Shakespeare, and whose shoe's latchet none but the very greatest is worthy to unloose. Such beauties as can be partially detached from their poetic form we can, indeed, notice and reproduce, such as the wonderful series of similes – homely, vivid, observed with the swift accuracy of the painter's eye – which stud the whole complicated pattern of the *Comedy*. There are the fires drifting down upon the Abominable Sand "as Alpine snows in windless weather fall", and the shades squinnying at Dante "like an old tailor at the needle's eye"; the thief who is metamorphosed into a lizard, when

inside his head
He pulled his ears, as a snail pulls her horn,

and the lovely simile of the phoenix, which wafts a breath of

1. *Para.* xxx. 33.
2. Roden Buxton: *Prophets of Heaven and Hell.*

exotic perfume across the horrors of the seventh pit of Malbowges:

> *Living, nor herb nor grain is food for her,*
> *Only amomum, and dropping incense-gums,*
> *And her last swathings are of nard and myrrh.*

The whole of the Middle Ages moves before us in Dante's thumb-nail sketches: the shipbuilders in the Venice Arsenal, the cooks and scullions "prodding the stew" with long forks, the labourer resting on the hillside of an evening and watching the fireflies flickering down the valley, the shepherd despairing at the long-continued frost, the peasant-girl pursued into dreamland by her daily task of gleaning, the overworked ostler hurrying to get his horses groomed, the Romans inventing a system of traffic-control for the handling of holiday crowds, green logs sizzling on the hearth, a night alarm of fire and the mother fleeing naked with her child clutched in her arms, beggars in the street and the savage watch-dogs rushing out upon them, the sounds and smells of a medieval hospital; the pleasures of hawking, hunting, bathing, gambling; the bustle of tilt and tournament, the noise and vicissitudes of war.[1] These things we can appreciate, as we can appreciate the tremendous architectural grandeur of the *Comedy*, the vigour of the narrative, the brilliance of the characterization and the brisk cut-and-thrust of the dialogue. They are part of the poetry, but they are not the poetry itself: *that* is incommunicable in any other language than Dante's own. But Dante has so much and such varied greatness that even of its fragments one may take up twelve baskets full: and the translator may perhaps hope to have preserved enough of the essential Dante to explain why those who love him at all love him with a devouring passion, and will be content with no lesser titles for him than those which he bestowed upon Virgil: "Master, leader, and lord".

EXPLANATORY MATTER

I have tried to include in the *Images* or *Notes* to each canto all such, but only such, explanatory matter as the reader needs in order to understand the poem as he goes along. Other sorts of

---

1. These few examples are taken from the *Inferno* alone. A selection from the whole *Comedy* would, of course, cover a still wider field.

information have been relegated to the *Glossary of Names*, or to an *Appendix*, so as not to bury the text under a pile of commentary. Thus, while reading Canto v, it is sufficient to know, of most of the characters mentioned, that they are famous lovers; but to appreciate the passage about Paolo and Francesca we want to know a little about their history. Accordingly, Paolo and Francesca go into the *Notes* and their fellow-sufferers into the *Glossary*, where the reader may look them up or not as he likes.

There is an *Appendix* on p. 296 about the Chronology of the *Comedy*, and another on p. 292 about the Ptolemaic system of astronomy on which Dante's plan of the universe is founded.

TEXTS AND COMMENTARIES

While I have consulted from time to time most of the great critical texts from Lana to Vandelli, I have been somewhat eclectic in my choice of readings, not infrequently preferring the version which appeared to me to make the better sense or the better poetry to that supported by a greater numerical weight of manuscript authority. Many English renderings have been suggested by such prose versions as those of the Temple Classics edition, Warren Vernon's *Readings*, and John D. Sinclair's translation; where my rendering coincides with those of previous verse-translators, the resemblance is fortuitous, being dictated in many cases by the exigence of the rhyme.

The help received from the innumerable scholars and critics who have commented on Dante could scarcely be acknowledged otherwise than in an extensive bibliography; I must not, however, fail to acknowledge my debt to Charles Williams's study *The Figure of Beatrice*, which lays down the lines along which, I believe, the allegory can be most fruitfully interpreted to present-day readers.

My notes and comments make no pretence to original scholarship or research. Where scholars disagree, I have sometimes offered alternative versions and sometimes silently made my own choice; but I have never put forward a reading, and seldom an interpretation, without some good authority behind it. In the rare cases where I have ventured an unsupported conjecture of my own, I have tried to indicate as much.   D. L. S.

May 1948

THE GREATER IMAGES

DANTE in the *story* is always himself – the Florentine poet, philosopher, and politician, and the man who loved Beatrice. In the *allegory*, he is the image of every Christian sinner, and his pilgrimage is that which every soul must make, by one road or another, from the dark and solitary Wood of Error to the City of God.

VIRGIL is in the *story* the shade of the poet who, in the *Aeneid*, celebrated the origin and high destiny of the Roman Empire and its function in unifying the civilized world. In the Middle Ages he was looked upon as having been an unconscious prophet of Christianity and also (in popular tradition) as a great "White Magician", whose natural virtue gave him power among the dead. Dante's portrait of him has preserved traces of these medieval fancies, and also agrees very well with what we know of the gentle and charming characteristics of the real Virgil. In the *allegory*, Virgil is the image of Human Wisdom – the best that man can become in his own strength without the especial grace of God. He is the best of human philosophy, the best of human morality; he is also poetry and art, the best of human feeling and imagination. Virgil, as the image of these things, cannot himself enter Heaven or bring anyone else there (art and morality and philosophy cannot be made into substitutes for religion), but he can (and they can), under the direction of the Heavenly Wisdom, be used to awaken the soul to a realization of its own sinfulness, and can thereafter accompany and assist it towards that state of natural perfection in which it is again open to receive the immediate operation of Divine Grace.

BEATRICE remains in the *story* what she was in real life: the Florentine girl whom Dante loved from the first moment that he saw her, and in whom he seemed (as is sometimes the case with lovers) to see Heaven's glory walking the earth bodily. Because, for him, she was thus in fact the vehicle of the Glory – the earthly vessel in which the divine experience was carried – she is, in the *allegory*, from time to time likened to, or equated with, those other "God-bearers": the Church, and Divine Grace in the Church; the Blessed Virgin; even Christ Himself. She is the image by which Dante perceives all these, and her function in the poem is to bring him to that state in which he is able to perceive them directly; at the end of the *Paradiso* the image of Beatrice is – not replaced by, but – taken up into the images, successively, of the Church Triumphant; of Mary, the historic and universal God-bearer; and of God, in whom Image and Reality are one and the same. Beatrice thus represents for every man that person – or, more generally, that experience of the Not-self – which, by arousing his adoring love, has become for him the God-bearing image, the revelation of the presence of God.

HELL in the *story* is the place or condition of lost souls after death; it is pictured as a huge funnel-shaped pit, situated beneath the Northern Hemisphere and running down to the centre of the earth. In the *allegory*, it is the image of the deepening possibilities of evil within the soul. Similarly, the sinners who there remain fixed forever in the evil which they have obstinately chosen are also images of the perverted choice itself. For the *story*, they are historical or legendary personages, external to Dante (and to us); for the *allegory* they figure his (and our) disordered desires, seen and known to us as we plunge ever deeper into the hidden places of the self: every condemned sinner in the poem is thus the image of a self-condemned sin (actual or potential) in every man. Neither in the *story* nor in the *allegory* is Hell a place of punishment to which anybody is arbitrarily *sent*: it is the condition to which the soul reduces itself by a stubborn determination to evil, and in which it suffers the torment of its own perversions.

We must be careful to distinguish between Hell itself, taken literally, and the *vision of Hell* which is offered to Dante. Hell itself is not remedial; the dead who have chosen the "eternal exile" from God, and who thus experience the reality of their choice, cannot profit by that experience. In that sense, no living soul can enter Hell, since, however great the sin, repentance is always possible while there is life, even to the very moment of dying.[1] But the *vision of Hell*, which is remedial, is the soul's self-knowledge in all its evil potentialities – "the revelation of the nature of impenitent sin".[2]

PURGATORY in the *story*, as in Catholic theology, is the place or condition of redeemed souls after death, and is imagined by

---

1. Unless, indeed, the will is so hardened in sin that the power to repent is destroyed, in which case the condition of the soul, even in this world, is literally a "living hell". Dante deals with this possibility in Canto XXXIII.
2. See P. H. Wicksteed: *From Vita Nuova to Paradiso*, from which the last few words are quoted.

Dante as a lofty mountain on an island in the Southern Hemisphere. On its seven encircling cornices, the souls are purged successively of the taint of the seven deadly sins, and so made fit to ascend into the presence of God in Paradise. In the *allegory*, it is the image of repentance, by which the soul purges the guilt of sin in *this* life; and, similarly, the blessed spirits who willingly embrace its purifying pains figure the motions of the soul, eagerly confessing and making atonement for its sins.

PARADISE, in the same way, is, in the *story*, the place or condition, after death, of beatified souls in Heaven. Dante pictures it, first, under the figure of the ten Heavens of medieval astronomy and, secondly, under that of the Mystical Rose. He explains that, although the souls are shown as enjoying ascending degrees of bliss in the ten successive Heavens, all these are, in reality, one Heaven; nor is the bliss unequal, each soul being filled, according to its capacity, with all the joy it is able to experience. In the *allegory*, Paradise is the image of the soul in a state of grace, enjoying the foretaste of the Heaven which it knows to be its true home and city; and in the inhabitants of Paradise we may recognize the figure of the ascending stages by which it rises to the contemplation of the Beatific Vision.

THE EMPIRE AND THE CITY. Throughout the poem, we come across various images of the Empire of the City (Florence, Rome, and other cities of Italy, as well as the City and Empire of Dis in Hell, and the Eternal City or Heavenly Rome in Paradise). All these may be taken as expressing, in one way or another, what to-day we should perhaps more readily think of as the Community. Indeed, the whole *allegory* may be interpreted politically, in the widest sense of the word, as representing the way of salvation, not only for the individual man, but for Man-in-community. Civilizations, as well as persons, need to know the Hell within them and purge their sins before entering into a state of Grace, Justice, and Charity and so becoming the City of God on earth.

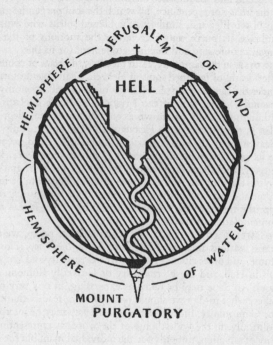

HEMISPHERE — JERUSALEM — OF LAND

HELL

HEMISPHERE — OF WATER

MOUNT
PURGATORY

CANTO I

THE STORY. *Dante finds that he has strayed from the right road and is
lost in a Dark Wood. He tries to escape by climbing a beautiful Mountain,
but is turned aside, first by a gambolling Leopard, then by a fierce Lion,
and finally by a ravenous She-Wolf. As he is fleeing back into the Wood,
he is stopped by the shade of Virgil, who tells him that he cannot hope to
pass the Wolf and ascend the Mountain by that road. One day a Grey-
hound will come and drive the Wolf back to Hell; but the only course
at present left open to Dante is to trust himself to Virgil, who will guide
him by a longer way, leading through Hell and Purgatory. From there, a
worthier spirit than Virgil (Beatrice) will lead him on to see the blessed
souls in Paradise. Dante accepts Virgil as his "master, leader, and lord",
and they set out together.*

Midway this way of life we're bound upon,
  I woke to find myself in a dark wood,
  Where the right road was wholly lost and gone.

Ay me! how hard to speak of it – that rude   4
  And rough and stubborn forest! the mere breath
  Of memory stirs the old fear in the blood;

It is so bitter, it goes nigh to death;   7
  Yet there I gained such good, that, to convey
  The tale, I'll write what else I found therewith.

How I got into it I cannot say,   10
  Because I was so heavy and full of sleep
  When first I stumbled from the narrow way;

But when at last I stood beneath a steep   13
  Hill's side, which closed that valley's wandering maze
  Whose dread had pierced me to the heart-root deep,

Then I looked up, and saw the morning rays   16
  Mantle its shoulder from that planet bright
  Which guides men's feet aright on all their ways;

And this a little quieted the affright   19
  That lurking in my bosom's lake had lain
  Through the long horror of that piteous night.

22   And as a swimmer, panting, from the main
            Heaves safe to shore, then turns to face the drive
            Of perilous seas, and looks, and looks again,

25   So, while my soul yet fled, did I contrive
            To turn and gaze on that dread pass once more
            Whence no man yet came ever out alive.

28   Weary of limb I rested a brief hour,
            Then rose and onward through the desert hied,
            So that the fixed foot always was the lower;

31   And see! not far from where the mountain-side
            First rose, a Leopard, nimble and light and fleet,
            Clothed in a fine furred pelt all dapple-dyed,

34   Came gambolling out, and skipped before my feet,
            Hindering me so, that from the forthright line
            Time and again I turned to beat retreat.

37   The morn was young, and in his native sign
            The Sun climbed with the stars whose glitterings
            Attended on him when the Love Divine

40   First moved those happy, prime-created things:
            So the sweet reason and the new-born day
            Filled me with hope and cheerful augurings

43   Of the bright beast so speckled and so gay;
            Yet not so much but that I fell to quaking
            At a fresh sight – a Lion in the way.

46   I saw him coming, swift and savage, making
            For me, head high, with ravenous hunger raving
            So that for dread the very air seemed shaking.

49   And next, a Wolf, gaunt with the famished craving
            Lodged ever in her horrible lean flank,
            The ancient cause of many men's enslaving; –

52   She was the worst – at that dread sight a blank
            Despair and whelming terror pinned me fast,
            Until all hope to scale the mountain sank.

55   Like one who loves the gains he has amassed,
            And meets the hour when he must lose his loot,
            Distracted in his mind and all aghast,

Even so was I, faced with that restless brute 58
   Which little by little edged and thrust me back,
   Back, to that place wherein the sun is mute.

Then, as I stumbled headlong down the track, 61
   Sudden a form was there, which dumbly crossed
   My path, as though grown voiceless from long lack

Of speech; and seeing it in that desert lost, 64
   "Have pity on me!" I hailed it as I ran,
   "Whate'er thou art – or very man, or ghost!"

It spoke: "No man, although I once was man; 67
   My parents' native land was Lombardy
   And both by citizenship were Mantuan.

Sub Julio born, though late in time, was I, 70
   And lived at Rome in good Augustus' days,
   When the false gods were worshipped ignorantly.

Poet was I, and tuned my verse to praise 73
   Anchises' righteous son, who sailed from Troy
   When Ilium's pride fell ruined down ablaze.

But thou – oh, why run back where fears destroy 76
   Peace? Why not climb the blissful mountain yonder,
   The cause and first beginning of all joy?"

"Canst thou be Virgil? thou that fount of splendour 79
   Whence poured so wide a stream of lordly speech?"
   Said I, and bowed my awe-struck head in wonder;

"Oh honour and light of poets all and each, 82
   Now let my great love stead me – the bent brow
   And long hours pondering all thy book can teach!

Thou art my master, and my author thou, 85
   From thee alone I learned the singing strain,
   The noble style, that does me honour now.

See there the beast that turned me back again – 88
   Save me from her, great sage – I fear her so,
   She shakes my blood through every pulse and vein."

"Nay, by another path thou needs must go 91
   If thou wilt ever leave this waste," he said,
   Looking upon me as I wept, "for lo!

94   The savage brute that makes thee cry for dread
     Lets no man pass this road of hers, but still
     Trammels him, till at last she lays him dead.

97   Vicious her nature is, and framed for ill;
     When crammed she craves more fiercely than before;
     Her raging greed can never gorge its fill.

100   With many a beast she mates, and shall with more,
     Until the Greyhound come, the Master-hound,
     And he shall slay her with a stroke right sore.

103   He'll not eat gold nor yet devour the ground;
     Wisdom and love and power his food shall be,
     His birthplace between Feltro and Feltro found;

106   Saviour he'll be to that low Italy
     For which Euryalus and Nisus died,
     Turnus and chaste Camilla, bloodily.

109   He'll hunt the Wolf through cities far and wide,
     Till in the end he hunt her back to Hell,
     Whence Envy first of all her leash untied.

112   But, as for thee, I think and deem it well
     Thou take me for thy guide, and pass with me
     Through an eternal place and terrible

115   Where thou shalt hear despairing cries, and see
     Long-parted souls that in their torments dire
     Howl for the second death perpetually.

118   Next, thou shalt gaze on those who in the fire
     Are happy, for they look to mount on high,
     In God's good time, up to the blissful quire;

121   To which glad place, a worthier spirit than I
     Must lead thy steps, if thou desire to come,
     With whom I'll leave thee then, and say good-bye;

124   For the Emperor of that high Imperium
     Wills not that I, once rebel to His crown,
     Into that city of His should lead men home.

127   Everywhere is His realm, but there His throne,
     There is His city and exalted seat:
     Thrice-blest whom there He chooses for His own!"

Then I to him: "Poet, I thee entreat,   130
  By that great God whom thou didst never know,
  Lead on, that I may free my wandering feet

From these snares and from worse; and I will go   133
  Along with thee, St Peter's Gate to find,
  And those whom thou portray'st as suffering so."

So he moved on; and I moved on behind.   136

THE IMAGES. *The Dark Wood* is the image of Sin or Error – not so
much of any specific act of sin or intellectual perversion as of that
spiritual condition called "hardness of heart", in which sinfulness
has so taken possession of the soul as to render it incapable of
turning to God, or even knowing which way to turn.

The Mountain, which on the mystical level is the image of the Soul's
Ascent to God, is thus on the moral level the image of Repent-
ance, by which the sinner returns to God. It can be ascended
directly from "the right road", but not from the Dark Wood,
because there the soul's cherished sins have become, as it were,
externalized, and appear to it like demons or "beasts" with a will
and power of their own, blocking all progress. Once lost in the
Dark Wood, a man can only escape by so descending into him-
self that he sees his sin, not as an external obstacle, but as the will
to chaos and death within him (Hell). Only when he has "died
to sin" can he repent and purge it. Mount Purgatory and the
Mountain of Canto I are, therefore, really one and the same
mountain, as seen on the far side, and on this side, of the "death
unto sin".

The Beasts. These are the images of sin. They may be identified with
Lust, Pride, and Avarice respectively, or with the sins of Youth,
Manhood, and Age; but they are perhaps best thought of as the
images of the three *types* of sin which, if not repented, land the
soul in one or other of the three main divisions of Hell (*v*. Canto
XI).

  The gay *Leopard* is the image of the self-indulgent sins – *Inconti-
nence*; the fierce *Lion*, of the violent sins – *Bestiality*; the *She-Wolf*
of the malicious sins, which involve *Fraud*.

The Greyhound has been much argued about. I think it has both an
historical and a spiritual significance. Historically, it is perhaps the

image of some hoped-for political saviour who should establish
the just World-Empire. Spiritually, the Greyhound, which has
the attributes of God ("wisdom, love, and power"), is prob-
ably the image of the reign of the Holy Ghost on earth – the
visible Kingdom of God for which we pray in the Lord's Prayer
(cf. *Purg*. xi. 7–9).

NOTES. l. 1: *midway*: i.e. at the age of 35, the middle point of man's
earthly pilgrimage of three-score and ten years.

l. 17: *that planet bright*: the Sun. In medieval astronomy, the Earth
was looked upon as being the centre of the universe, and the sun
counted as a planet. In the *Comedy*, the Sun is often used as a figure
for "the spiritual sun, which is God". (Dante: *Convivio*, iv. 12.)

l. 27: *whence no man yet came ever out alive*: Dante, as we shall see,
is by no means "out" as yet; nor will he be, until he has passed
through the "death unto sin".

l. 30: *so that the fixed foot always was the lower*: i.e. he was going up-
hill. In walking, there is always one fixed foot and one moving foot;
in going uphill, the moving foot is brought *above*, and in going
downhill *below*, the fixed foot.

l. 37: *in his native sign*: According to tradition, the Sun was in the
Zodiacal sign of Aries (the Ram) at the moment of the creation. The
Sun is in Aries from 21 March to 21 April: therefore the "sweet
season" is that of spring. Later, we shall discover that the day is Good
Friday, and that the moon was full on the previous night. These indi-
cations do not precisely correspond to the actual Easter sky of 1300;
Dante has merely described the astronomical phenomena typical of
Eastertide.

ll. 63–4: *as though grown voiceless from long lack of speech*: i.e. the form
is trying to speak to Dante, but cannot make itself heard. From the
point of view of the *story*, I think this means that, being in fact that of
a ghost, it cannot speak until Dante has established communication
by addressing it first. *Allegorically*, we may take it in two ways: (1) on
the historical level, it perhaps means that the wisdom and poetry of
the classical age had been long neglected; (2) on the spiritual level, it
undoubtedly means that Dante had sunk so deep into sin that the
voice of reason, and even of poetry itself, had become faint and
almost powerless to recall him.

l. 70: *sub Julio*: under Julius (Caesar). Virgil was born in 70 B.C. and
had published none of his great poems before the murder of Julius in
44 B.C., so that he never enjoyed his patronage.

l. 87: *the noble style*: Dante, in 1300, was already a poet of considerable reputation for his love-lyrics and philosophic odes, though he had not as yet composed any narrative verse directly modelled upon the *Aeneid*. When he says that he owes to Virgil the "*bello stilo* which has won him honour", he can scarcely be referring to the style of his own *prose* works, whether in Latin or Italian, still less to that of the as yet unwritten *Comedy*. Presumably he means that he had studied to imitate, in his poems written in the vernacular, the elegance, concise power, and melodious rhythms of the Virgilian line.

l. 105: *between Feltro and Feltro*: This is a much-debated line. If the Greyhound represents a political "saviour", it may mean that his birthplace lies between Feltre in Venetia and Montefeltro in Romagna (i.e. in the valley of the Po). But some commentators think that "feltro" is not a geographical name at all, but simply that of a coarse cloth (felt, or frieze); in which case Dante would be expecting salvation to come from among those who wear the robe of poverty, and have renounced "gold and ground" – i.e. earthly possessions. We should perhaps translate: "In cloth of frieze his people shall be found".

l. 106: *low Italy*: The Italian word is *umile*, humble, which may mean either "low-lying", as opposed to "high Italy" among the Alps, or "humiliated", with reference to the degradation to which the country had been brought. In either case, the classical allusions which follow show that Dante meant Rome.

l. 114: *an eternal place and terrible*: Hell.

l. 117: *the second death*: this might mean "cry for a second death to put an end to their misery", but more probably means "cry out because of the pains of hell", in allusion to *Rev.* xx. 14.

ll. 118–19: *those who in the fire are happy*: the redeemed in Purgatory.

l. 134: *St Peter's Gate*: the gate by which redeemed souls are admitted to Purgatory (*Purg.* ix. 76 *sqq.*); not the gate of Heaven.

CANTO II

THE STORY. *Dante's attempts to climb the Mountain have taken the whole day and it is now Good Friday evening. Dante has not gone far before he loses heart and "begins to make excuse". To his specious arguments Virgil replies flatly: "This is mere cowardice;" and then tells how Beatrice, prompted by St Lucy at the instance of the Virgin Mary herself, descended into Limbo to entreat him to go to Dante's rescue. Thus encouraged, Dante pulls himself together, and they start off again.*

> Day was departing and the dusk drew on,
>   Loosing from labour every living thing
>   Save me, in all the world; I – I alone –

4
> Must gird me to the wars – rough travelling,
>   And pity's sharp assault upon the heart –
>   Which memory shall record, unfaltering;

7
> Now, Muses, now, high Genius, do your part!
>   And Memory, faithful scrivener to the eyes,
>   Here show thy virtue, noble as thou art!

10
> I soon began: "Poet – dear guide – 'twere wise
>   Surely, to test my powers and weigh their worth
>   Ere trusting me to this great enterprise.

13
> Thou sayest, the author of young Silvius' birth,
>   Did to the world immortal, mortal go,
>   Clothed in the body of flesh he wore on earth –

16
> Granted; if Hell's great Foeman deigned to show
>   To *him* such favour, seeing the vast effect,
>   And what and who has destined issue – no,

19
> That need surprise no thoughtful intellect,
>   Since to Rome's fostering city and empery
>   High Heaven had sealed him as the father-elect;

22
> Both these were there established, verily,
>   To found that place, holy and dedicate,
>   Wherein great Peter's heir should hold his See;

So that the deed thy verses celebrate   25
   Taught him the road to victory, and bestowed
   The Papal Mantle in its high estate.

Thither the Chosen Vessel, in like mode,   28
   Went afterward, and much confirmed thereby
   The faith that sets us on salvation's road.

But how should *I* go there? Who says so? Why?   31
   I'm not Aeneas, and I am not Paul!
   Who thinks me fit? Not others. And not I.

Say I submit, and go – suppose I fall   34
   Into some folly? Though I speak but ill,
   Thy better wisdom will construe it all."

As one who wills, and then unwills his will,   37
   Changing his mind with every changing whim,
   Till all his best intentions come to nil,

So I stood havering in that moorland dim,   40
   While through fond rifts of fancy oozed away
   The first quick zest that filled me to the brim.

"If I have grasped what thou dost seem to say,"   43
   The shade of greatness answered, "these doubts breed
   From sheer black cowardice, which day by day

Lays ambushes for men, checking the speed   46
   Of honourable purpose in mid-flight,
   As shapes half-seen startle a shying steed.

Well then, to rid thee of this foolish fright,   49
   Hear why I came, and learn whose eloquence
   Urged me to take compassion on thy plight.

While I was with the spirits who dwell suspense,   52
   A Lady summoned me – so blest, so rare,
   I begged her to command my diligence.

Her eyes outshone the firmament by far   55
   As she began, in her own gracious tongue,
   Gentle and low, as tongues of angels are:

'O courteous Mantuan soul, whose skill in song   58
   Keeps green on earth a fame that shall not end
   While motion rolls the turning spheres along!

61   A friend of mine, who is not Fortune's friend,
        Is hard beset upon the shadowy coast;
        Terrors and snares his fearful steps attend,

64   Driving him back; yea, and I fear almost
        I have risen too late to help – for I was told
        Such news of him in Heaven – he's too far lost.

67   But thou – go thou! Lift up thy voice of gold;
        Try every needful means to find and reach
        And free him, that my heart may rest consoled.

70   Beatrice am I, who thy good speed beseech;
        Love that first moved me from the blissful place
        Whither I'd fain return, now moves my speech.

73   Lo! when I stand before my Lord's bright face
        I'll praise thee many a time to Him.' Thereon
        She fell on silence; I replied apace:

76   'Excellent lady, for whose sake alone
        The breed of men exceeds all things that dwell
        Closed in the heaven whose circles narrowest run

79   To do thy bidding pleases me so well
        That were't already done, I should seem slow;
        I know thy wish, and more needs not to tell.

82   Yet say – how can thy blest feet bear to know
        This dark road downward to the dreadful centre,
        From that wide room which thou dost yearn for so?'

85   'Few words will serve (if thou desire to enter
        Thus far into our mystery),' she said,
        'To tell thee why I have no fear to venture.

88   Of hurtful things we ought to be afraid,
        But of no others, truly, inasmuch
        As these have nothing to give cause for dread;

91   My nature, by God's mercy, is made such
        As your calamities can nowise shake,
        Nor these dark fires have any power to touch.

94   Heaven hath a noble Lady, who doth take
        Ruth of this man thou goest to disensnare
        Such that high doom is cancelled for her sake.

She summoned Lucy to her side, and there   97
   Exhorted her: "Thy faithful votary
   Needs thee, and I commend him to thy care."

Lucy, the foe to every cruelty,   100
   Ran quickly and came and found me in my place
   Beside ancestral Rachel, crying to me:

"How now, how now, Beatrice, God's true praise!   103
   No help for him who once thy liegeman was,
   Quitting the common herd to win thy grace?

Dost thou not hear his piteous cries, alas?   106
   Dost thou not see death grapple him, on the river
   Whose furious rage no ocean can surpass?"

When I heard that, no living wight was ever   109
   So swift to seek his good or flee his fear
   As I from that high resting-place to sever

And speed me down, trusting my purpose dear   112
   To thee, and to thy golden rhetoric
   Which honours thee, and honours all who hear.'

She spoke; and as she turned from me the quick   115
   Tears starred the lustre of her eyes, which still
   Spurred on my going with a keener prick.

Therefore I sought thee out, as was her will,   118
   And brought thee safe off from that beast of prey
   Which barred thee from the short road up the hill.

What ails thee then? Why, why this dull delay?   121
   Why bring so white a liver to the deed?
   Why canst thou find no manhood to display

When three such blessed ladies deign to plead   124
   Thy cause at that supreme assize of right,
   And when my words promise thee such good speed?"

As little flowers, which all the frosty night   127
   Hung pinched and drooping, lift their stalks and fan
   Their blossoms out, touched by the warm white light,

So did my fainting powers; and therewith ran   130
   Such good, strong courage round about my heart
   That I spoke boldly out like a free man:

133   "O blessed she that stooped to take my part!
          O courteous thou, to obey her true-discerning
          Speech, and thus promptly to my rescue start!

136   Fired by thy words, my spirit now is burning
          So to go on, and see this venture through.
          I find my former stout resolve returning.

139   Forward! henceforth there's but one will for two,
          Thou master, and thou leader, and thou lord."
          I spoke; he moved; so, setting out anew,

142   I entered on that savage path and froward.

THE IMAGES. *Mary, The Blessed Virgin*, whom the Church calls *Theotokos* (Mother of God), is the historical and universal God-bearer, of whom Beatrice, like any other God-bearing image, is a particular type. Mary is thus, in an especial and supreme manner, the vessel of Divine Grace, as experienced in, and mediated through, the redeemed creation. (Note that the name of Mary, like the name of Christ, is never spoken in Hell.)

Lucìa (St Lucy), a virgin martyr of the third century, is the patron saint of those with weak sight, and chosen here as the image of Illuminating Grace. Mary, Beatrice, and Lucia are a threefold image of Divine Grace in its various manifestations.

Virgil's Mission. Dante is so far gone in sin and error that Divine Grace can no longer move him directly; but there is still something left in him which is capable of responding to the voice of poetry and of human reason; and this, under Grace, may yet be used to lead him back to God. In this profound and beautiful image, Dante places Religion, on the one hand, and human Art and Philosophy, on the other, in their just relationship.

NOTES. l. 7: Canto I forms, as it were, a prologue to the whole *Divine Comedy*. The actual *Inferno* (Hell) begins with Canto II; and here we have the invocation which, in each of the three books, prefaces the journey to Hell, Purgatory, and Paradise respectively. It is addressed, in the classic manner, to the Muses, to Genius, and to Memory, the Mother of the Muses. (As the story proceeds, Dante will invoke higher, and still higher aid; till the final invocation towards the end of the *Paradiso*, is made to God, the "supreme light" Himself.)

Commentaries

l. 13: *the author of young Silvius' birth*: Aeneas; the allusion is to the sixth book of the *Aeneid*, which describes how Aeneas visits Hades and is told that he is to settle in Italy and so bring about the foundation of Rome, the seat both of the Empire and the Papacy.

l. 16: *Hell's great Foeman*: God.

l. 28: *the Chosen Vessel*: St Paul (*Acts* ix. 15). His vision of Hell is described in the fourth-century apocryphal book known as *The Apocalypse of Paul*, which Dante had evidently read. (See M. R. James: *The Apocryphal New Testament*.) There is probably also an allusion to 2 *Cor.* xii. 2.

l. 52: *the spirits who dwell suspense*: those of the virtuous pagans, who taste neither the bliss of salvation nor the pains of damnation, but dwell forever suspended between the two, in Limbo, the uppermost circle of Hell. (We shall meet them in Canto IV.)

l. 70: Of all this passage, Charles Williams says: "Beatrice has to ask [Virgil] to go; she cannot command him, though she puts her trust in his 'fair speech'. Religion itself cannot order poetry about; the grand art is wholly autonomous ... We should have been fortunate if the ministers of religion and poetry had always spoken to each other with such courtesy as these." (*The Figure of Beatrice*, p. 112.)

l. 78: *the heaven whose circles narrowest run*: The heaven of the Moon, the smallest and nearest to the Earth. (See note on *Dante's Universe*, p. 292.)

l. 91: *my nature, by God's mercy, is made such*: The souls of the blessed can still pity the self-inflicted misery of the wicked, but they can no longer be hurt or infected by it: "the action of pity will live for ever; the passion of pity will not". (C. S. Lewis: *The Great Divorce*, p. 111, where the subject is handled in a very illuminating way.)

l. 102: *ancestral Rachel*: Leah and Rachel, the two wives of Jacob, figure respectively the active and the contemplative life.

l. 107: *the river*: no literal river is intended; it is only a metaphor for human life.

l. 120: *the short road up the hill*: this line shows clearly that the "blissful Mountain" and Mount Purgatory are in reality one and the same; since the Beasts prevent Dante from taking "the short road", he is obliged to go by the long road – i.e. through Hell – to find the mountain again on the other side of the world.

UPPER HELL

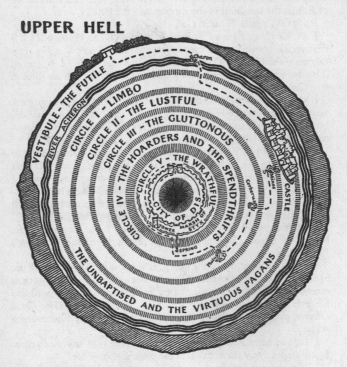

VESTIBULE - THE FUTILE
RIVER ACHERON
CIRCLE I - LIMBO
CIRCLE II - THE LUSTFUL
CIRCLE III - THE GLUTTONOUS
CIRCLE IV - THE HOARDERS AND THE SPENDTHRIFTS
CIRCLE V - THE WRATHFUL
CITY OF DIS
TOWER
MARSH OF STYX
SPRING
PHLEGYAS
CERBERUS
CASTLE
Charon
THE UNBAPTISED AND THE VIRTUOUS PAGANS

INCONTINENCE –
THE SINS OF THE LEOPARD

CANTO III

THE STORY. *Arriving at the gate of Hell, the Poets read the inscription upon its lintel. They enter and find themselves in the Vestibule of Hell, where the Futile run perpetually after a whirling standard. Passing quickly on, they reach the river Acheron. Here the souls of all the damned come at death to be ferried across by Charon, who refuses to take the living body of Dante till Virgil silences him with a word of power. While they are watching the departure of a boatload of souls the river banks are shaken by an earthquake so violent that Dante swoons away.*

THROUGH ME THE ROAD TO THE CITY OF DESOLATION,
   THROUGH ME THE ROAD TO SORROWS DIUTURNAL,
   THROUGH ME THE ROAD AMONG THE LOST CREATION.

JUSTICE MOVED MY GREAT MAKER; GOD ETERNAL   4
   WROUGHT ME: THE POWER, AND THE UNSEARCHABLY
   HIGH WISDOM, AND THE PRIMAL LOVE SUPERNAL.

NOTHING ERE I WAS MADE WAS MADE TO BE   7
   SAVE THINGS ETERNE, AND I ETERNE ABIDE;
   LAY DOWN ALL HOPE, YOU THAT GO IN BY ME.

These words, of sombre colour, I descried   10
   Writ on the lintel of a gateway; "Sir,
   This sentence is right hard for me," I cried.

And like a man of quick discernment: "Here   13
   Lay down all thy distrust," said he, "reject
   Dead from within thee every coward fear;

We've reached the place I told thee to expect,   16
   Where thou shouldst see the miserable race,
   Those who have lost the good of intellect."

He laid his hand on mine, and with a face   19
   So joyous that it comforted my quailing,
   Into the hidden things he led my ways.

Here sighing, and here crying, and loud railing   22
   Smote on the starless air, with lamentation,
   So that at first I wept to hear such wailing.

gate without bars [handwritten marginal note]

25   Tongues mixed and mingled, horrible execration,
          Shrill shrieks, hoarse groans, fierce yells and hideous blether
          And clapping of hands thereto, without cessation

28   Made tumult through the timeless night, that hither
          And thither drives in dizzying circles sped,
          As whirlwind whips the spinning sands together.

31   Whereat, with horror flapping round my head:
          "Master, what's this I hear? Who can they be,
          These people so distraught with grief?" I said.

34   And he replied: "The dismal company
          Of wretched spirits thus find their guerdon due
          Whose lives knew neither praise nor infamy;

37   They're mingled with that caitiff angel-crew
          Who against God rebelled not, nor to Him
          Were faithful, but to self alone were true;

40   Heaven cast them forth – their presence there would dim
          The light; deep Hell rejects so base a herd,
          Lest sin should boast itself because of them.

43   Then I: "But, Master, by what torment spurred
          Are they driven on to vent such bitter breath?"
          He answered: "I will tell thee in a word:

46   This dreary huddle has no hope of death,
          Yet its blind life trails on so low and crass
          That every other fate it envieth.

49   No reputation in the world it has,
          Mercy and doom hold it alike in scorn –
          Let us not speak of these; but look, and pass."

52   So I beheld, and lo! an ensign borne
          Whirling, that span and ran, as in disdain
          Of any rest; and there the folk forlorn

55   Rushed after it, in such an endless train,
          It never would have entered in my head
          There were so many men whom death had slain.

58   And when I'd noted here and there a shade
          Whose face I knew, I saw and recognized
          The coward spirit of the man who made

86

The great refusal; and that proof sufficed;   61
  Here was that rabble, here without a doubt,
  Whom God and whom His enemies despised.

This scum, who'd never lived, now fled about   64
  Naked and goaded, for a swarm of fierce
  Hornets and wasps stung all the wretched rout

Until their cheeks ran blood, whose slubbered smears,   67
  Mingled with brine, around their footsteps fell,
  Where loathly worms licked up their blood and tears.

Then I peered on ahead, and soon quite well   70
  Made out the hither bank of a wide stream,
  Where stood much people. "Sir," said I, "pray tell

Who these are, what their custom, why they seem   73
  So eager to pass over and be gone –
  If I may trust my sight in this pale gleam."

And he to me: "The whole shall be made known;   76
  Only have patience till we stay our feet
  On yonder sorrowful shore of Acheron."

Abashed, I dropped my eyes; and, lest unmeet   79
  Chatter should vex him, held my tongue, and so
  Paced on with him, in silence and discreet,

To the riverside. When from the far bank lo!   82
  A boat shot forth, whose white-haired boatman old
  Bawled as he came: "Woe to the wicked! Woe!

Never you hope to look on Heaven – behold!   85
  I come to ferry you hence across the tide
  To endless night, fierce fires and shramming cold.

And thou, the living man there! stand aside   88
  From these who are dead!" I budged not, but abode;
  So, when he saw me hold my ground, he cried:

"Away with thee! for by another road   91
  And other ferries thou shalt make the shore,
  Not here; a lighter skiff must bear thy load."

Then said my guide: "Charon, why wilt thou roar   94
  And chafe in vain? Thus it is willed where power
  And will are one; enough; ask thou no more."

97 This shut the shaggy mouth up of that sour
    Infernal ferryman of the livid wash,
    Only his flame-ringed eyeballs rolled a-glower.

100 But those outwearied, naked souls – how gash
     And pale they grew, chattering their teeth for dread,
     When first they felt his harsh tongue's cruel lash.

103 God they blaspheme, blaspheme their parents' bed,
     The human race, the place, the time, the blood,
     The seed that got them, and the womb that bred;

106 Then, huddling hugger-mugger, down they scud,
     Dismally wailing, to the accursed strand
     Which waits for every man that fears not God.

109 Charon, his eyes red like a burning brand,
     Thumps with his oar the lingerers that delay,
     And rounds them up, and beckons with his hand.

112 And as, by one and one, leaves drift away
     In autumn, till the bough from which they fall
     Sees the earth strewn with all its brave array,

115 So, from the bank there, one by one, drop all
     Adam's ill seed, when signalled off the mark,
     As drops the falcon to the falconer's call.

118 Away they're borne across the waters dark,
     And ere they land that side the stream, anon
     Fresh troops this side come flocking to embark.

121 Then said my courteous master: "See, my son,
     All those that die beneath God's righteous ire
     From every country come here every one.

124 They press to pass the river, for the fire
     Of heavenly justice stings and spurs them so
     That all their fear is changed into desire;

127 And by this passage, good souls never go;
     Therefore, if Charon chide thee, do thou look
     What this may mean – 'tis not so hard to know."

130 When he thus said, the dusky champaign shook
     So terribly that, thinking on the event,
     I feel the sweat pour off me like a brook.

The sodden ground belched wind, and through the rent   133
   Shot the red levin, with a flash and sweep
   That robbed me of my wits, incontinent;

And down I fell, as one that swoons on sleep.   136

THE IMAGES. *Hell-Gate*. High and wide and without bars (*Inf.* viii. 126), the door "whose threshold is denied to none" (*Inf.* xiv. 87) always waits to receive those who are astray in the Dark Wood. Anyone may enter if he so chooses, but if he does, he must abandon hope, since it leads nowhere but to the *Citta Dolente*, the City of Desolation. In the *story*, Hell is filled with the souls of those who died with their wills set to enter by that gate; in the *allegory*, these souls are the images of sin in the self or in society.

The Vestibule was presumably suggested to Dante by the description in *Aeneid* vi. where, however, it is tenanted by rather a different set of people). It does not, I think, occur in any previous Christian eschatology. Heaven and Hell being states in which choice is permanently fixed, there must also be a state in which the refusal of choice is itself fixed, since to refuse choice is in fact to choose indecision. The Vestibule is the abode of the weather-cock mind, the vague tolerance which will neither approve nor condemn, the cautious cowardice for which no decision is ever final. The spirits rush aimlessly after the aimlessly whirling banner, stung and goaded, as of old, by the thought that, in doing anything definite whatsoever, they are missing doing something else.

Acheron, "the joyless", first of the great rivers of Hell whose names Dante took from Virgil and Virgil from Homer. (See map, p. 84.)

Charon, the classical ferryman of the dead. Most of the monstrous organisms by which the functions of Hell are discharged are taken from Greek and Roman mythology. They are neither devils nor damned souls, but the images of perverted appetites, presiding over the circles appropriate to their natures.

NOTES. l. 1: *the City of Desolation* (*la citta dolente*; lit.: the sorrowful city). Hell, like Heaven, is represented under the figure sometimes of a city, and sometimes of an empire. Later on (Canto IX) we shall come to the actual city itself, which has its fortifications on the edge of the Sixth Circle, and comprises the whole of Nether Hell. At present we are only in Upper Hell, forming as it were the suburbs of the city and made up of the Vestibule and the first five circles. (See map, p. 84.)

ll. 4–6: *power ... wisdom supreme and primal love*: the attributes of the Trinity. "If there is God, if there is freewill, then man is able to choose the opposite of God. Power, Wisdom, Love, gave man freewill; therefore Power, Wisdom, Love, created the gate of hell and the possibility of hell." (Charles Williams: *The Figure of Beatrice*, p. 113.)

l. 8: *things eterne*: In Canto XXXIV Dante tells how Hell was made when Satan fell from Heaven: it was created "for the devil and his angels" (*Matt.* xxv. 41) and before it nothing was made except the "eternal things", i.e. the Angels and the Heavens.

l. 9: *lay down all hope*: For the soul that literally enters Hell there is no return, nor any passage to Purgatory and repentance. Dante is naturally disturbed (l. 12) by this warning. But what he is entering upon, while yet in this life, is not Hell but the vision of Hell, and for him there is a way out, provided he keeps his hope and faith. Accordingly, Virgil enjoins him (ll. 14–15) to reject doubt and fear.

l. 18: *the good of intellect*: In the *Convivio* Dante quotes Aristotle as saying: "truth is the good of the intellect". What the lost souls have lost is not the intellect itself, which still functions mechanically, but the *good* of the intellect: i.e. the knowledge of God, who is Truth. (For Dante, as for Aquinas, "intellect" does not mean what we call, colloquially, "braininess"; it means the whole "reasonable soul" of man.)

l. 16: *the great refusal*: Probably Celestine V, who, in 1294, at the age of 80, was made pope, but resigned the papacy five months later. His successor was Pope Boniface VIII, to whom Dante attributed many of the evils which had overtaken the Church. (See also Introd. p. 35.)

ll. 91–2: *another road and other ferries*: souls destined for Heaven never cross Acheron; they assemble at the mouth of Tiber and are taken in a boat piloted by an angel to Mount Purgatory at the Antipodes (*Purg.* ii). Charon recognizes that Dante is a soul in Grace. (See ll. 127–9.)

l. 126: *all their fear is changed into desire*: This is another of the important passages in which Dante emphasizes that Hell is the soul's choice. The damned fear it and long for it, as in this life a man may hate the sin which makes him miserable, and yet obstinately seek and wallow in it.

CANTO IV

THE STORY. *Recovering from his swoon, Dante finds himself across Acheron and on the edge of the actual Pit of Hell. He follows Virgil into the First Circle – the Limbo where the Unbaptized and the Virtuous Pagans dwell "suspended", knowing no torment save exclusion from the positive bliss of God's presence. Virgil tells him of Christ's Harrowing of Hell, and then shows him the habitation of the great men of antiquity – poets, heroes, and philosophers.*

A heavy peal of thunder came to waken me
　　Out of the stunning slumber that had bound me,
　　Startling me up as though rude hands had shaken me.

I rose, and cast my rested eyes around me,　　　　　　　4
　　Gazing intent to satisfy my wonder
　　Concerning the strange place wherein I found me.

Hear truth: I stood on the steep brink whereunder　　　7
　　Runs down the dolorous chasm of the Pit,
　　Ringing with infinite groans like gathered thunder.

Deep, dense, and by no faintest glimmer lit　　　　　　10
　　It lay, and though I strained my sight to find
　　Bottom, not one thing could I see in it.

"Down must we go, to that dark world and blind,"　　13
　　The poet said, turning on me a bleak
　　Blanched face; "I will go first – come thou behind."

Then I, who had marked the colour of his cheek:　　　16
　　"How can I go, when even thou art white
　　For fear, who art wont to cheer me when I'm weak?"

But he: "Not so; the anguish infinite　　　　　　　　19
　　They suffer yonder paints my countenance
　　With pity, which thou takest for affright;

Come, we have far to go; let us advance."　　　　　　22
　　So, entering, he made me enter, where
　　The Pit's first circle makes circumference.

25   We heard no loud complaint, no crying there,
         No sound of grief except the sound of sighing
         Quivering for ever through the eternal air;

28   Grief, not for torment, but for loss undying,
         By women, men, and children sighed for so,
         Sorrowers thick-thronged, their sorrows multiplying.

31   Then my good guide: "Thou dost not ask me who
         These spirits are," said he, "whom thou perceivest?
         Ere going further, I would have thee know

34   They sinned not; yet their merit lacked its chiefest
         Fulfilment, lacking baptism, which is
         The gateway to the faith which thou believest;

37   Or, living before Christendom, their knees
         Paid not aright those tributes that belong
         To God; and I myself am one of these.

40   For such defects alone – no other wrong –
         We are lost; yet only by this grief offended:
         That, without hope, we ever live, and long."

43   Grief smote my heart to think, as he thus ended,
         What souls I knew, of great and sovran
         Virtue, who in that Limbo dwelt suspended.

46   "Tell me, sir – tell me, Master," I began
         (In hope some fresh assurance to be gleaning
         Of our sin-conquering Faith), "did any man

49   By his self-merit, or on another leaning,
         Ever fare forth from hence and come to be
         Among the blest?" He took my hidden meaning.

52   "When I was newly in this state," said he,
         "I saw One come in majesty and awe,
         And on His head were crowns of victory.

55   Our great first father's spirit He did withdraw,
         And righteous Abel, Noah who built the ark,
         Moses who gave and who obeyed the Law,

58   King David, Abraham the Patriarch,
         Israel with his father and generation,
         Rachel, for whom he did such deeds of mark,

With many another of His chosen nation;   61
  These did He bless; and know, that ere that day
  No human soul had ever seen salvation."

While he thus spake, we still made no delay,   64
  But passed the wood – I mean, the wood (as 'twere)
  Of souls ranged thick as trees. Being now some way –

Not far – from where I'd slept, I saw appear   67
  A light, which overcame the shadowy face
  Of gloom, and made a glowing hemisphere.

'Twas yet some distance on, yet I could trace   70
  So much as brought conviction to my heart
  That persons of great honour held that place.

"O thou that honour'st every science and art,   73
  Say, who are these whose honour gives them claim
  To different customs and a sphere apart?"

And he to me: "Their honourable name,   76
  Still in thy world resounding as it does,
  Wins here from Heaven the favour due to fame."

Meanwhile I heard a voice that cried out thus: 79
  "Honour the most high poet! his great shade,
  Which was departed, is returned to us."

It paused there, and was still; and lo! there made   82
  Toward us, four mighty shadows of the dead,
  Who in their mien nor grief nor joy displayed.

"Mark well the first of these," my master said,   85
  "Who in his right hand bears a naked sword
  And goes before the three as chief and head;

Homer is he, the poets' sovran lord;   88
  Next, Horace comes, the keen satirical;
  Ovid the third; and Lucan afterward.

Because I share with these that honourable   91
  Grand title the sole voice was heard to cry
  They do me honour, and therein do well."

Thus in their school assembled I, even I,   94
  Looked on the lords of loftiest song, whose style
  O'er all the rest goes soaring eagle-high.

97   When they had talked together a short while
     They all with signs of welcome turned my way,
     Which moved my master to a kindly smile;

100   And greater honour yet they did me – yea,
     Into their fellowship they deigned invite
     And make me sixth among such minds as they.

103   So we moved slowly onward toward the light
     In talk 'twere as unfitting to repeat
     Here, as to speak there was both fit and right.

196   And presently we reached a noble seat –
     A castle, girt with seven high walls around,
     And moated with a goodly rivulet

109   O'er which we went as though upon dry ground;
     With those wise men I passed the sevenfold gate
     Into a fresh green meadow, where we found

112   Persons with grave and tranquil eyes, and great
     Authority in their carriage and attitude,
     Who spoke but seldom and in voice sedate.

115   So here we walked aside a little, and stood
     Upon an open eminence, lit serene
     And clear, whence one and all might well be viewed.

118   Plain in my sight on the enamelled green
     All those grand spirits were shown me one by one –
     It thrills my heart to think what I have seen!

121   I saw Electra, saw with her anon
     Hector, Aeneas, many a Trojan peer,
     And hawk-eyed Caesar in his habergeon;

124   I saw Camilla and bold Penthesilea,
     On the other hand; Latinus on his throne
     Beside Lavinia his daughter dear;

127   Brutus, by whom proud Tarquin was o'erthrown,
     Marcia, Cornelia, Julia, Lucrece – and
     I saw great Saladin, aloof, alone.

130   Higher I raised my brows and further scanned,
     And saw the Master of the men who know
     Seated amid the philosophic band;

All do him honour and deep reverence show;   133
   Socrates, Plato, in the nearest room
   To him; Diogenes, Thales and Zeno,

Democritus, who held that all things come   136
   By chance; Empedocles, Anaxagoras wise,
   And Heraclitus, him that wept for doom;

Dioscorides, who named the qualities,   139
   Tully and Orpheus, Linus, and thereby
   Good Seneca, well-skilled to moralize;

Euclid the geometrician, Ptolemy,   142
   Galen, Hippocrates, and Avicen,
   Averroës who made the commentary –

Nay, but I tell not all that I saw then;   145
   The long theme drives me hard, and everywhere
   The wondrous truth outstrips my staggering pen.

The group of six dwindles to two; we fare   148
   Forth a new way, I and my guide withal,
   Out from that quiet to the quivering air,

And reach a place where nothing shines at all.   151

THE IMAGES. After those who refused choice come those without
opportunity of choice. They could not, that is, choose Christ;
they could, and did, choose human virtue, and for that they have
their reward. (Pagans who chose evil by their own standards are
judged by these standards – cf. *Rom.* ii. 8–15 – and are found
lower down.) Here again, the souls "have what they chose";
they enjoy that kind of after-life which they themselves imagined
for the virtuous dead; their failure lay in not imagining better.
They are lost (as Virgil says later, *Purg.* vii. 8) because they "had
not faith" – primarily the Christian Faith, but also, more gener-
ally, faith in the nature of things. The *allegory* is clear: it is the
weakness of Humanism to fall short in the imagination of ecstasy;
at its best it is noble, reasonable, and cold, and however optimistic
about a balanced happiness in this world, pessimistic about a
rapturous eternity. Sometimes wistfully aware that others claim
the experience of this positive bliss, the Humanist can neither

accept it by faith, embrace it by hope, nor abandon himself to it in charity. Dante discusses the question further in the *Purgatory* (esp. Cantos VII and XXII) and makes his full doctrine explicit in *Paradise*, Cantos XIX–XX.

NOTES l. 7: *I stood on the steep brink*: It is disputed how Dante passed Acheron; the simplest explanation is that Charon, obedient to Virgil's "word of power", ferried him across during his swoon. Technically speaking, Dante had to describe a passage by boat in Canto VIII, and did not want to anticipate his effects; I think, however, he had also an allegorical reason for omitting the description here (see Canto VII. *Images: Path down Cliff*, p. 116). Note that the "peal of thunder" in l. 1 is not that which followed the lightning-flash at the end of Canto III, but (l. 9) the din issuing from the mouth of the Pit – an orchestra of discord, here blended into one confused roar, which, resolved into its component disharmonies, will accompany us to the bottom circle of Hell.

l. 53: *I saw One come*: The episode, based upon 1 Peter iii. 19, of Christ's descent into Limbo to rescue the souls of the patriarchs (the "Harrowing of Hell") was a favourite subject of medieval legend and drama. The crucifixion is reckoned as having occurred in A.D. 34, when Virgil had been dead fifty-three years. Note that the name of Christ is never spoken in Hell – He is always referred to by some periphrasis.

l. 55: *our great first father*: Adam; for the various Biblical and classical persons mentioned in this Canto, see Glossary.

l. 106: *a noble seat*: The scene is, I think, a medievalized version of the Elysian Fields, surrounded by "many-watered Eridanus". (*Aen.* vi. 659.) Detailed allegorical interpretations of the seven gates, walls, etc., have no great value.

l. 121: *Electra etc.*: Pride of place is given to the Trojans, founders of the Roman line; (Julius) Caesar is grouped with them as a descendant of Aeneas.

l. 129: *Saladin*: His inclusion here, along with Lucan, Averroës, and other A.D. personages who were not, strictly speaking, without opportunity of choice, perhaps tacitly indicates Dante's opinion about all those who, though living in touch with Christianity and practising all the moral virtues, find themselves sincerely unable to accept the Christian revelation.

l. 131: *the Master of the men who know*: Aristotle.

CANTO V

THE STORY. *Dante and Virgil descend from the First Circle to the Second (the first of the Circles of Incontinence). On the threshold sits Minos, the judge of Hell, assigning the souls to their appropriate places of torment. His opposition is overcome by Virgil's word of power, and the Poets enter the Circle, where the souls of the Lustful are tossed for ever upon a howling wind. After Virgil has pointed out a number of famous lovers, Dante speaks to the shade of Francesca da Rimini, who tells him her story.*

From the first circle thus I came descending
    To the second, which, in narrower compass turning,
    Holds greater woe, with outcry loud and rending.

There in the threshold, horrible and girning,   4
Grim Minos sits, holding his ghastly session,
    And, as he girds him, sentencing and spurning;

For when the ill soul faces him, confession   7
    Pours out of it till nothing's left to tell;
    Whereon that connoisseur of all transgression

Assigns it to its proper place in hell,   10
    As many grades as he would have it fall,
    So oft he belts him round with his own tail.

Before him stands a throng continual;   13
    Each comes in turn to abye the fell arraign;
    They speak – they hear – they're whirled down one and all.

"Ho! thou that comest to the house of pain,"   16
    Cried Minos when he saw me, the appliance
    Of his dread powers suspending, "think again

How thou dost go, in whom is thy reliance;   19
    Be not deceived by the wide open door!"
    Then said my guide: "Wherefore this loud defiance?

Hinder not thou his fated way; be sure   22
    Hindrance is vain; thus it is willed where will
    And power are one; enough; ask now no more."

25   And now the sounds of grief begin to fill
      My ear; I'm come where cries of anguish smite
      My shrinking sense, and lamentation shrill –

28   A place made dumb of every glimmer of light,
      Which bellows like tempestuous ocean birling
      In the batter of a two-way wind's buffet and fight.

31   The blast of hell that never rests from whirling
      Harries the spirits along in the sweep of its swath,
      And vexes them, for ever beating and hurling.

34   When they are borne to the rim of the ruinous path
      With cry and wail and shriek they are caught by the gust,
      Railing and cursing the power of the Lord's wrath.

37   Into this torment carnal sinners are thrust,
      So I was told – the sinners who make their reason
      Bond thrall under the yoke of their lust.

40   Like as the starlings wheel in the wintry season
      In wide and clustering flocks wing-borne, wind-borne,
      Even so they go, the souls who did this treason,

43   Hither and thither, and up and down, outworn,
      Hopeless of any rest – rest, did I say?
      Of the least minishing of their pangs forlorn.

46   And as the cranes go chanting their harsh lay,
      Across the sky in long procession trailing,
      So I beheld some shadows borne my way,

49   Driven on the blast and uttering wail on wailing;
      Wherefore I said: "O Master, art thou able
      To name these spirits thrashed by the black wind's flailing?"

52   "Among this band," said he, "whose name and fable
      Thou seek'st to know, the first who yonder flies
      Was empress of many tongues, mistress of Babel.

55   She was so broken to lascivious vice
      She licensed lust by law, in hopes to cover
      Her scandal of unnumbered harlotries.

58   This was Semiramis; 'tis written of her
      That she was wife to Ninus and heiress, too,
      Who reigned in the land the Soldan now rules over.

Lo! she that slew herself for love, untrue   61
   To Sychaeus' ashes. Lo! tost on the blast,
   Voluptuous Cleopatra, whom love slew.

Look, look on Helen, for whose sake rolled past   64
   Long evil years. See great Achilles yonder,
   Who warred with love, and that war was his last.

See Paris, Tristram see!" And many – oh, wonder   67
   Many – a thousand more, he showed by name
   And pointing hand, whose life love rent asunder.

And when I had heard my Doctor tell the fame   70
   Of all those knights and ladies of long ago,
   I was pierced through with pity, and my head swam.

"Poet," said I, "fain would I speak those two   73
   That seem to ride as light as any foam,
   And hand in hand on the dark wind drifting go."

And he replied: "Wait till they nearer roam,   76
   And thou shalt see; summon them to thy side
   By the power of the love that leads them, and they will come."

So, as they eddied past on the whirling tide,   79
   I raised my voice: "O souls that wearily rove,
   Come to us, speak to us – if it be not denied."

And as desire wafts homeward dove with dove   82
   To their sweet nest, on raised and steady wing
   Down-dropping through the air, impelled by love,

So these from Dido's flock came fluttering   85
   And dropping toward us down the cruel wind,
   Such power was in my affectionate summoning.

"O living creature, gracious and so kind,   88
   Coming through this black air to visit us,
   Us, who in death the globe incarnadined,

Were the world's King our friend and might we thus   91
   Entreat, we would entreat Him for thy peace,
   That pitiest so our pangs dispiteous!

Hear all thou wilt, and speak as thou shalt please,   94
   And we will gladly speak with thee and hear,
   While the winds cease to howl, as they now cease.

97 There is a town upon the sea-coast, near
  Where Po with all his streams comes down to rest
  In ocean; I was born and nurtured there.

100 Love, that so soon takes hold in the gentle breast,
  Took this lad with the lovely body they tore
  From me; the way of it leaves me still distrest.

103 Love, that to no loved heart remits love's score,
  Took me with such great joy of him, that see!
  It holds me yet and never shall leave me more.

106 Love to a single death brought him and me;
  Cain's place lies waiting for our murderer now."
  These words came wafted to us plaintively.

109 Hearing those wounded souls, I bent my brow
  Downward, and thus bemused I let time pass,
  Till the poet said at length: "What thinkest thou?"

112 When I could answer, I began: "Alas!
  Sweet thoughts how many, and desire how great,
  Brought down these twain unto the dolorous pass!"

115 And then I turned to them: "Thy dreadful fate,
  Francesca, makes me weep, it so inspires
  Pity," said I, "and grief compassionate.

118 Tell me – in that time of sighing-sweet desires,
  How, and by what, did love his power disclose
  And grant you knowledge of your hidden fires?"

121 Then she to me: "The bitterest woe of woes
  Is to remember in our wretchedness
  Old happy times; and this thy Doctor knows;

124 Yet, if so dear desire thy heart possess
  To know that root of love which wrought our fall,
  I'll be as those who weep and who confess.

127 One day we read for pastime how in thrall
  Lord Lancelot lay to love, who loved the Queen;
  We were alone – we thought no harm at all.

130 As we read on, our eyes met now and then,
  And to our cheeks the changing colour started,
  But just one moment overcame us – when

We read of the smile, desired of lips long-thwarted,   133
  Such smile, by such a lover kissed away,
  He that may never more from me be parted

Trembling all over, kissed my mouth. I say   136
  The book was Galleot, Galleot the complying
  Ribald who wrote; we read no more that day."

While the one spirit thus spoke, the other's crying   139
  Wailed on me with a sound so lamentable,
  I swooned for pity like as I were dying,

And, as a dead man falling, down I fell.   142

THE IMAGES. *The Circles of Incontinence.* This and the next three
  circles are devoted to those who sinned less by deliberate choice
  of evil than by failure to make resolute choice of the good. Here
  are the sins of self-indulgence, weakness of will, and easy yielding
  to appetite – the "Sins of the Leopard".
The Lustful. The image here is sexual, though we need not confine
  the *allegory* to the sin of unchastity. Lust is a type of *shared* sin; at
  its best, and so long as it remains a sin of incontinence only, there
  is mutuality in it and exchange: although, in fact, mutual indul-
  gence only serves to push both parties along the road to Hell, it is
  not, in intention, wholly selfish. For this reason Dante, with per-
  fect orthodoxy, rates it as the least hateful of the deadly sins.
  (Sexual sins in which love and mutuality have no part find their
  place far below.)
Minos, a medievalized version of the classical Judge of the Under-
  world (see *Aen.* vi. 432). He may image an accusing conscience.
  The souls are damned on their own confession, for, Hell being the
  place of self-knowledge in sin, there can be no more self-decep-
  tion here. (Similarly, even in the circles of Fraud, all the shades
  tell Dante the truth about themselves; this is poetically convenient,
  but, given this conception of Hell, it must be so.) The *literally*
  damned, having lost "the good of the intellect", cannot profit by
  their self-knowledge; *allegorically*, for the living soul, this vision
  of the Hell in the self is the preliminary to repentance and restora-
  tion.
The Black Wind. As the lovers drifted into self-indulgence and were
  carried away by their passions, so now they drift for ever. The

bright, voluptuous sin is now seen *as it is* – a howling darkness of helpless discomfort. (The "punishment" for sin is simply the sin itself, experienced without illusion – though Dante does not work this out with mathematical rigidity in every circle.)

NOTES. l. 6: *as he girds him, sentencing*: as Dante explains in ll. 11–12, Minos girds himself so many times with his tail to indicate the number of the circle to which each soul is to go (cf. Canto XXVII. 124 and note).

l. 28: *a place made dumb of every glimmer of light* – (cf. Canto I. 60, "wherein the sun is mute"): Nevertheless, Dante is able to see the spirits. This is only one of many passages in which the poet conveys to us that the things he perceives during his journey are not perceived altogether by the mortal senses, but after another mode. (In *Purg.* xxi. 29, Virgil explains to another spirit that Dante "could not come alone, because he does not see after our manner, wherefore I was brought forth from Hell to guide him".) So, in the present case, Dante recognizes that the darkness is total, although he can see in the dark.

l. 61: *she that slew herself for love*: Dido. (For the various lovers mentioned, see Glossary.)

l. 88: *O living creature*: The speaker is Francesca da Rimini. Like many of the personages in the *Comedy*, she does not directly name herself, but gives Dante particulars about her birthplace and history which enable him to recognize her. She was the daughter of Guido Vecchio di Polenta of Ravenna, and aunt to Guido Novello di Polenta, who was Dante's friend and host during the latter years of his life; so that her history was of topical interest to Dante's readers. For political reasons, she was married to the deformed Gianciotto, son of Malatesta da Verrucchio, lord of Rimini, but fell in love with his handsome younger brother Paolo, who became her lover. Her husband, having one day surprised them together, stabbed them both to death (1285).

l. 94: *hear all thou wilt*: Tender and beautiful as Dante's handling of Francesca is, he has sketched her with a deadly accuracy. All the good is there; the charm, the courtesy, the instant response to affection, the grateful eagerness to please; but also all the evil; the easy yielding, the inability to say No, the intense self-pity.

Of this, the most famous episode in the whole *Comedy*, Charles Williams writes: "It is always quoted as an example of Dante's tenderness. So, no doubt, it is, but it is not here for that reason. ... It has a much more important place; it presents the first tender, passionate, and half-excusable consent of the soul to sin. ... [Dante] so manages the description, he so heightens the excuse, that the excuse reveals itself as precisely the sin ... the persistent parleying with the occasion of sin, the sweet prolonged laziness of love, is the first surrender of the soul to Hell – small but certain. The formal sin here is the adultery of the two lovers; the poetic sin is their shrinking from the adult love demanded of them, and their refusal of the opportunity of glory." (*The Figure of Beatrice*, p. 118.)

l. 97: *a town upon the sea-coast*: Ravenna.

l. 102: *the way of it leaves me still distrest*: Either (1) the way of the murder, because the lovers were killed in the very act of sin and so had no time for repentance; or (2) the way in which their love came about. The story went that Paolo was sent to conduct the marriage negotiations, and that Francesca was tricked into consenting by being led to suppose that he, and not Gianciotto, was to be her bridegroom. In the same way, in the Arthurian romances, Queen Guinevere falls in love with Lancelot when he is sent to woo her on King Arthur's behalf; and it is this parallel which makes the tale of Lancelot so poignant for her and Paolo.

l. 107: *Cain's place*: Caina, so called after Cain; the first ring of the lowest circle in Hell, where lie those who were treacherous to their own kindred. (Canto XXXII.)

l. 123: *thy Doctor*: Virgil (see l. 70). Dante is probably thinking of Aeneas' words to Dido: *infandum, regina, jubes renovare dolorem* ... (O queen, thou dost bid me renew an unspeakable sorrow ...), *Aeneid* ii. 3.

l. 137: *the book was Galleot*: In the romance of *Lancelot du Lac*, Galleot (or Galehalt) acted as intermediary between Lancelot and Guinevere, and so in the Middle Ages his name, like that of Pandarus in the tale of *Troilus and Cressida*, became a synonym for a go-between. The sense of the passage is: "The book was a pander and so was he who wrote it".

CANTO VI

THE STORY. *Dante now finds himself in the Third Circle, where the Gluttonous lie wallowing in the mire, drenched by perpetual rain and mauled by the three-headed dog Cerberus. After Virgil has quieted Cerberus by throwing earth into his jaws, Dante talks to the shade of Ciacco, a Florentine, who prophesies some of the disasters which are about to befall Florence, and tells him where he will find certain other of their fellow-citizens. Virgil tells Dante what the condition of the spirits will be, after the Last Judgment.*

When consciousness returned, which had shut close
    The doors of sense, leaving me stupefied
    For pity of those sad kinsfolk and their woes,

4   New sufferings and new sufferers, far and wide,
    Where'er I move, or turn myself, or strain
    My curious eyes, are seen on every side.

7   I am now in the Third Circle: that of rain –
    One ceaseless, heavy, cold, accursed quench,
    Whose law and nature vary never a grain;

10   Huge hailstones, sleet and snow, and turbid drench
    Of water sluice down through the darkened air,
    And the soaked earth gives off a putrid stench.

13   Cerberus, the cruel, misshapen monster, there
    Bays in his triple gullet and doglike growls
    Over the wallowing shades; his eyeballs glare

16   A bloodshot crimson, and his bearded jowls
    Are greasy and black; pot-bellied, talon-heeled,
    He clutches and flays and rips and rends the souls.

19   They howl in the rain like hounds; they try to shield
    One flank with the other; with many a twist and squirm,
    The impious wretches writhe in the filthy field.

22   When Cerberus spied us coming, the great Worm,
    He gaped his mouths with all their fangs a-gloat,
    Bristling and quivering till no limb stood firm.

At once my guide, spreading both hands wide out,   25
  Scooped up whole fistfuls of the miry ground
  And shot them swiftly into each craving throat.

And as a ravenous and barking hound   28
  Falls dumb the moment he gets his teeth on food,
  And worries and bolts with never a thought beyond,

So did those beastly muzzles of the rude   31
  Fiend Cerberus, who so yells on the souls, they're all
  Half deafened – or they would be, if they could.

Then o'er the shades whom the rain's heavy fall   34
  Beats down, we forward went; and our feet trod
  Their nothingness, which seems corporeal.

These all lay grovelling flat upon the sod;   37
  Only, as we went by, a single shade
  Sat suddenly up, seeing us pass that road.

"O thou that through this Hell of ours art led,   40
  Look if thou know me, since thou wast, for sure,"
  Said he, "or ever I was unmade, made."

Then I to him: "Perchance thy torments sore   43
  Have changed thee out of knowledge – there's no trusting
  Sight, if I e'er set eyes on thee before.

But say, who are thou? brought by what ill lusting   46
  To such a pass and punishment as, meseems,
  Worse there may be, but nothing so disgusting?"

"Thy native city," said he, "where envy teems   49
  And swells so that already it brims the sack,
  Called me her own in the life where the light beams.

Ciacco you citizens nicknamed me – alack!   52
  Damnable gluttony was my soul's disease;
  See how I waste for it now in the rain's wrack.

And I, poor sinner, am not alone: all these   55
  Lie bound in the like penalty with me
  For the like offence." And there he held his peace,

And I at once began: "The misery   58
  Moves me to tears, Ciacco, and weighs me down.
  But tell me if thou canst, what end may be

61 In store for the people of our distracted town.
Is there one just man left? And from what source
To such foul head have these distempers grown?"

64 And he: "Long time their strife will run its course,
And come to bloodshed; the wood party thence
Will drive the other out with brutal force;

67 But within three brief suns their confidence
Will have a fall, and t'other faction rise
By help of one who now sits on the fence;

70 And these will lord it long with arrogant eyes,
Crushing their foes with heavy loads indeed,
For all their bitter shame and outraged cries.

73 Two righteous men there are, whom none will heed;
Three sparks from Hell – Avarice, Envy, Pride –
In all men's bosoms sowed the fiery seed."

76 His boding speech thus ended; so I cried:
"Speak on, I beg thee! More, much more reveal!
Tegghiaio, Farinata – how betide

79 Those worthy men? and Rusticucci's zeal?
Arrigo, Mosca, and the rest as well
Whose minds were still set on the public weal?

82 Where are they? Can I find them? Prithee tell –
I am consumed with my desire to know –
Feasting in Heaven, or poisoned here in Hell?"

85 He answered: "With the blacker spirits below,
Dragged to the depth by other crimes abhorred;
There shalt thou see them, if so deep thou go.

88 But when to the sweet world thou art restored,
Recall my name to living memory;
I'll tell no more, nor speak another word."

91 Therewith he squinted his straight gaze awry,
Eyed me awhile, then, dropping down his head,
Rolled over amid that sightless company.

94 Then spake my guide: "He'll rouse no more," he said,
"Till the last loud angelic trumpet's sounding;
For when the Enemy Power shall come arrayed

Each soul shall seek its own grave's mournful mounding,   97
  Put on once more its earthly flesh and feature,
  And hear the Doom eternally redounding."

Thus with slow steps I and my gentle teacher,   100
  Over that filthy sludge of souls and snow,
  Passed on, touching a little upon the nature

Of the life to come. "Master," said I, "this woe –   103
  Will it grow less, or still more fiercely burning
  With the Great Sentence, or remain just so?"

"Go to," said he, "hast thou forgot thy learning,   106
  Which hath it: The more perfect, the more keen,
  Whether for pleasure's or for pain's discerning?

Though true perfection never can be seen   109
  In these damned souls, they'll be more near complete
  After the Judgment than they yet have been."

So, with more talk which I need not repeat,   112
  We followed the road that rings that circle round,
  Till on the next descent we set our feet;

There Pluto, the great enemy, we found.   115

THE IMAGES. *The Gluttonous*: The surrender to sin which began with
    mutual indulgence leads by an imperceptible degradation to soli-
    tary self-indulgence. Of this kind of sin, the Gluttons are chosen
    as the image. Here is no reciprocity and no communication; each
    soul grovels alone in the mud, without heeding his neighbours –
    "a sightless company", Dante calls them.

The Rain. Gluttony (like the other self-indulgences it typifies) often
    masquerades on earth as a warm, cosy, and indeed jolly kind of
    sin; here it is seen as it is – a cold sensuality, a sodden and filthy
    spiritual wretchedness.

Cerberus. In the *story*, Cerberus is the three-headed dog familiar to us
    from Homer and Virgil and the tale of the Twelve Labours of
    Hercules, who guards the threshold of the classical Hades. For the
    allegory, he is the image of uncontrolled appetite; the Glutton,
    whose appetite preyed upon people and things, is seen to be, in
    fact, the helpless prey on which that appetite gluts itself.

NOTES. l. 7: *I am now in the Third Circle*: Once again, Dante does not say how he got here: we may suppose that Virgil carried or assisted him down before he had wholly recovered his senses.

l. 22: *Worm*: This, in Old English as in Italian (*vermo*), is simply a word for a monster, cf. the fairy-tale of "The Laidly Worm of Spindleston Heugh", where it denotes a dragon.

l. 26: *whole fistfuls of the miry ground*: To throw something into his mouth was the traditional way of appeasing this particular guardian of Hell – hence the phrase "to give a sop to Cerberus". In *Aeneid* vi, the Sibyl who guides Aeneas through Hades brings a number of cakes for the purpose. Here Virgil, not having made this provision, makes use of the first substitute that comes to hand.

l. 49: *thy native city*: Florence.

l. 52: *Ciacco you citizens nicknamed me*: The word means "pig", and, according to Boccacio, was the nickname of a Florentine gentleman notorious for his gluttony.

l. 61: *our distracted town:* i.e. Florence.

l. 64: *long time their strife will run its course*: This is the first of a number of passages dealing (under the guise of prophecy) with political events in Italy, and especially in Florence, which took place after the supposed date of the Vision (1300). It refers to the struggle between the two Guelf parties (the Blacks and the Whites), and to the final expulsion of the Whites (including Dante) from Florence. (See Introduction, p. 33 *sqq.*)

l. 65: *the wood party*: the Whites. The adjective *selvaggia* means either the "woodland" party (because certain of its leaders had come into Florence from the surrounding country) or the "savage" (i.e. un-cultivated party) (as opposed to the more aristocratic Blacks). The English word "wood", which formerly had the meaning "mad, wild, savage", is thus a fairly exact equivalent of the ambiguous Italian.

The two parties "came to bloodshed" at the May-Day Festival of 1300, and the expulsion of the Black leaders took place shortly after. The Blacks returned in November 1301, with the help of Boniface VIII (the "sitter on the fence", l. 69), who till then had shown no de-cided preference for either party. The first decree banishing the Whites was published in January 1302, and the last in the latter half of the same year – all "within three suns" of the time at which Ciacco is supposed to be speaking.

l. 73: *two righteous men*: Dante is usually credited with meaning himself and his friend Guido Cavalcanti; but he does not say so, and we need not found a charge of self-righteousness on what he has not said.

ll. 78–80: *Tegghiaio … Mosca*: The persons named are all distinguished Florentines. We shall meet Farinata in Canto x, Tegghiaio and Rusticucci in Canto xvi, and Mosca in Canto xxviii. Arrigo (see Glossary) is not mentioned again.

l. 96: *the Enemy Power*: This is the strangest and most terrible periphrasis used for Christ in these circles of the damned, who have chosen to know all goodness as antagonism and judgment.

l. 106: *thy learning*: the philosophy of Aristotle, as incorporated in the theology of St Thomas Aquinas. The souls will be "more perfect" after the Last Judgment because they will then be reunited to their bodies.

l. 115: *Pluto*: god of the wealth that springs from the soil, naturally came to be regarded as an "underground" deity, and from early times was apt to be identified with Hades (Dis). Dante, however, distinguishes him from Dis (Satan), and while making him an infernal power, retains his primitive character as a symbol of riches. There is perhaps also a fusion with Plutus, the "god of wealth" mentioned by Phaedrus. "The great enemy" is probably an allusion to 1 *Tim*. vi. 10.

CANTO VII

THE STORY. *At the entrance to the Fourth Circle, the poets are opposed by Pluto, and Virgil is again obliged to use a "word of power". In this circle, the Hoarders and the Spendthrifts roll huge rocks against one another, and here Virgil explains the nature and working of Luck (or Fortune). Then, crossing the circle, they descend the cliff to the Marsh of Styx, which forms the Fifth Circle and contains the Wrathful. Skirting its edge, they reach the foot of a tower.*

"*Papè Satan, papè Satan aleppe,*"
   Pluto 'gan gabble with his clucking tongue;
   My all-wise, gentle guide, to me unhappy

4   Said hearteningly: "Let no fears do thee wrong;
   He shall not stay thy journey down this steep;
   His powers, whate'er they be, are not so strong."

7   Then, turning him, and letting his glance sweep
   O'er that bloat face: "Peace, thou damned wolf!" said he,
   "Go, choke in thine own venom! To the deep,

10   Not without cause, we go. I say to thee,
   Thus it is willed on high, where Michaël
   Took vengeance on the proud adultery."

13   Then, as the sails bellying in the wind's swell
   Tumble a-tangle at crack of the snapping mast,
   Even so to earth the savage monster fell;

16   And we to the Fourth Circle downward passed,
   Skirting a new stretch of the grim abyss
   Where all the ills of all the world are cast.

19   God's justice! Who shall tell the agonies,
   Heaped thick and new before my shuddering glance?
   Why must our guilt smite us with strokes like this?

22   As waves against the encountering waves advance
   Above Charybdis, clashing with toppling crest,
   So must the folk here dance and counter-dance.

More than elsewhere, I saw them thronged and pressed   25
    This side and that, yelling with all their might,
    And shoving each a great weight with his chest.

They bump together, and where they bump, wheel right   28
    Round, and return, trundling their loads again,
    Shouting: "Why chuck away?" "Why grab so tight?"

Then round the dismal ring they pant and strain   31
    Back on both sides to where they first began
    Still as they go bawling their rude refrain;

And when they meet, then each re-treads his span,   34
    Half round the ring to joust in the other list;
    I felt quite shocked, and like a stricken man.

"Pray tell me, sir," said I, "all this – what is't?   37
    Who are these people? On our left I find
    Numberless tonsured heads; was each a priest?"

"In life," said he, "these were so squint of mind   40
    As in the handling of their wealth to use
    No moderation – none, in either kind;

That's plain, from their shrill yelpings of abuse   43
    At the ring's turn, where opposite degrees
    Of crime divide them into rival crews.

They whose pates boast no hairy canopies   46
    Are clerks – yea, popes and cardinals, in whom
    Covetousness hath made its masterpiece."

"Why, sir," said I, "surely there must be some   49
    Faces I know in all this gang, thus brought
    By these defilements to a common doom."

"Nay," he replied, "that is an empty thought;   52
    Living, their minds distinguished nothing; dead,
    They cannot be distinguished. In this sort

They'll butt and brawl for ever; when from bed   55
    The Last Trump wakes the body, these will be
    Raised with tight fists, and those stripped, hide and head.

Hoarding and squandering filched the bright world's glee   58
    Away, and set them to this tourney's shock,
    Whose charms need no embroidered words from me.

61   See now, my son, the fine and fleeting mock
         Of all those goods men wrangle for – the boon
         That is delivered into the hand of Luck;

64   For all the gold that is beneath the moon,
         Or ever was, could not avail to buy
         Repose for one of these weary souls – not one."

67   "Master, I would hear more of this," said I;
         "What is this Luck, whose talons take in hand
         All life's good things that go so pleasantly?"

70   Then he: "Ah, witless world! Behold the grand
         Folly of ignorance! Make thine ear attendant
         Now on my judgment of her, and understand.

73   He whose high wisdom's over all transcendent
         Stretched forth the Heavens, and guiding spirits supplied,
         So that each part to each part shines resplendent,

76   Spreading the light equal on every side;
         Likewise for earthly splendours He saw fit
         To ordain a general minister and guide,

79   By whom vain wealth, as time grew ripe for it,
         From race to race, from blood to blood, should pass,
         Far beyond hindrance of all human wit.

82   Wherefore some nations minish, some amass
         Great power, obedient to her subtle codes,
         Which are hidden, like the snake beneath the grass.

85   For her your science finds no measuring-rods;
         She in her realm provides, maintains, makes laws,
         And judges, as do in theirs the other gods.

88   Her permutations never know truce nor pause;
         Necessity lends her speed, so swift in fame
         Men come and go, and cause succeeds to cause.

91   Lo! this is she that hath so curst a name
         Even from those that should give praise to her –
         Luck, whom men senselessly revile and blame;

94   But she is blissful and she does not hear;
         She, with the other primal creatures gay,
         Tastes her own blessedness, and turns her sphere.

Come! to more piteous woes we must away;　　　　97
　　All stars that rose when I set out now sink,
　　And the High Powers permit us no long stay."

So to the further edge we crossed the rink,　　　　100
　　Hard by a bubbling spring which, rising there,
　　Cuts its own cleft and pours on down the brink.

Darker than any perse its waters were, ·　　　　103
　　And keeping company with the ripples dim
　　We made our way down by that eerie stair.

A marsh there is called Styx, which the sad stream　　106
　　Forms when it finds the end of its descent
　　Under the grey, malignant rock-foot grim;

And I, staring about with eyes intent,　　　　109
　　Saw mud-stained figures in the mire beneath,
　　Naked, with looks of savage discontent,

At fisticuffs – not with fists alone, but with　　112
　　Their heads and heels, and with their bodies too,
　　And tearing each other piecemeal with their teeth.

"Son," the kind master said, "here may'st thou view　　115
　　The souls of those who yielded them to wrath;
　　Further, I'd have thee know and hold for true

That others lie plunged deep in this vile broth,　　118
　　Whose sighs – see there, wherever one may look –
　　Come bubbling up to the top and make it froth.

Bogged there they say: 'Sullen were we – we took　　121
　　No joy of the pleasant air, no joy of the good
　　Sun; our hearts smouldered with a sulky smoke;

Sullen we lie here now in the black mud.'　　　124
　　This hymn they gurgle in their throats, for whole
　　Words they can nowise frame." Thus we pursued

Our path round a wide arc of that ghast pool,　　127
　　Between the soggy marsh and arid shore,
　　Still eyeing those who gulp the marish foul,

And reached at length the foot of a tall tower.　　130

THE IMAGES. *The Hoarders and the Spendthrifts.* Mutual indulgence has already declined into selfish appetite; now, that appetite becomes aware of the incompatible and equally selfish appetites of other people. Indifference becomes mutual antagonism, imaged here by the antagonism between hoarding and squandering.

The Joust. Note the reappearance of community in a perverted form: these irrational appetites are united, after a fashion, by a common hatred, for the waging of a futile war. So nations, political parties, business combines, classes, gangs, etc., sometimes display a spurious comradeship in opposition.

The Wrathful. Community in sin is unstable: it soon disintegrates into an anarchy of hatred, all against all. Dante distinguishes two kinds of Wrath. The one is active and ferocious; it vents itself in sheer lust for inflicting pain and destruction – on other people, on itself, on anything and everything it meets. The other is passive and sullen, the withdrawal into a black sulkiness which can find no joy in God or man or the universe.

The Marsh. Both kinds of Wrath are figured as a muddy slough; on its surface, the active hatreds rend and snarl at one another; at the bottom, the sullen hatreds lie gurgling, unable even to express themselves for the rage that chokes them. This is the last of the Circles of Incontinence. This savage self-frustration is the end of that which had its tender and romantic beginnings in the dalliance of indulged passion.

The Path down the Cliff. For the first time, Dante's passage from one circle to the other is described in detail. We are not told at what precise point in the wilderness he found Hell-gate; one may encounter it at any moment. The crossing of Acheron – the image of the assent to sin – is made unconsciously. From Limbo to the Second Circle – from the lack of imagination that inhibits the will to the false imagination that saps it – the passage is easy and, as it were, unnoticed. From the Second Circle to the Third – from mutuality to separateness – the soul is carried as though in a dream. From the Third to the Fourth Circle the way is a little plainer – for as one continues in sin one becomes uneasily aware of inner antagonisms and resentments, though without any clear notion how they arise. But as antagonism turns to hatred, the steps of the downward path begin to be fearfully apparent. From this point on the descent is mapped out with inexorable clarity.

Styx – the name means "hateful" – is the second of the four chief rivers of Hell. It economically does double duty as the Fifth Circle and as the boundary between Upper and Nether Hell.

Commentaries

NOTES. l. 1: *Papè Satan aleppe*: Various attempts have been made to interpret this cryptic remark, but none of them is very convincing. One may safely conjecture that it is meant as an invocation to the Devil, and it is as well to leave it at that. Cf. Nimrod's jargon in Canto xxxi.

l. 12: *where Michaël took vengeance on the proud adultery*: The reference is to the Archangel Michael's war upon the rebellious angels (*Rev.* xii. 7–9). "Adultery" is used in the Biblical sense of unfaithfulness to God – as in "whoring after strange gods" (*Deut.* xxxi. 16, etc., and similar passages). "Proud", because Satan and his angels fell through pride.

l. 23: *Charybdis*: famous whirlpool near Messina. (See Glossary.)

l. 73 sqq.: *He whose high wisdom*: This is the first of the series of great discourses in which Dante gradually unfolds the plan of the spiritual and physical universe. The "guiding spirits" mentioned here are the celestial intelligences (angels) who control the heavenly spheres. *Luck* or *Fortune* is here conceived as a similar ministering spirit, whose function it is to control and distribute wealth and opportunity upon the earth. Virgil describes her under the familiar classical figure of a goddess with a wheel, or sphere, whose turning brings about the ups-and-downs of disaster and prosperity. By this figure Dante does not deny free will, or ascribe the course of history to blind chance: he says (*De Monarchia*, xii. 70): " … fortune, which agency we better and more rightly call the divine providence".

l. 87: *the other gods*: i.e. the angels. Dante several times uses this name for them, and not only when Virgil is speaking.

l. 89: *necessity lends her speed*: Here again Dante does not mean that, in the pagan phrase, "the gods themselves are subject to necessity", but merely that, such is the brevity of human life, the changes of fortune must needs be swift.

l. 95: *primal creatures*: the celestial Intelligences, who were created, with the heavens themselves, directly by God, and not through secondary agencies (i.e. they were not evolved or generated).

l. 98: *all stars that rose … now sink*: All the stars that were rising when Virgil first met Dante on Good Friday evening have passed the zenith and begun to set; i.e. it is now past midnight. (So long as the poets are descending into Hell the time is never indicated by the sun, but always by the changes of the night sky.)

l. 101: *a bubbling spring*: This is the water of the river Acheron, which, after forming a complete circle about Hell, runs underground beneath the first four circles, and now emerges again to pour down the cliff and form the river and marsh of Styx. (See map, p. 138).

CANTO VIII

THE STORY. *From the watch-tower on the edge of the marsh a beacon signals to the garrison of the City of Dis that Dante and Virgil are approaching, and a boat is sent to fetch them. Phlegyas ferries them across Styx. On the way they encounter Filippo Argenti, one of the Wrathful, who is recognized by Dante and tries to attack him. They draw near to the red-hot walls of the City and after a long circuit disembark at the gate. Virgil parleys with the Fallen Angels who are on guard there, but they slam the gate in his face. The two poets are obliged to wait for Divine assistance.*

I say, continuing, that ere we came
   To the tower's foot, our eyes had long been led
   To its summit, by two twinkling points of flame

4   Which we saw kindled there; while, far ahead,
   And almost out of eyeshot, we espied
   An answering beacon's flicker. So I said,

7   Turning to the well of wisdom at my side:
   "What does it say? What does that other light
   Wink back? Who make these signals?" He replied:

10   "Already across the water heaves in sight
   What's to be looked for from the signal's waft,
   So it be not veiled from thee by the blight

13   Of these marsh mists." I looked; and never shaft
   So swift from bowstring sped through the thin air
   As through those turbid waves a little craft

16   Came skimming toward us; one sole mariner
   Guided its course, who shouted from the prow:
   "Oho, thou wicked spirit! So thou art there!"

19   'Nay, Phlegyas, Phlegyas," said my lord, "peace now!
   This time thou criest in vain; we are no meat
   For thee – thou hast but to ferry us o'er the slough."

22   As one who hears of some outrageous cheat
   Practised on him, and fumes and chokes with gall,
   So Phlegyas, thwarted, fumed at his defeat.

So then my guide embarked, and at his call   25
  I followed him; and not till I was in
  Did the boat seem to bear a load at all.

When we were set, the ancient vessel then   28
  Put forth at once, cleaving the water's grime
  Deeper than her wont, our voyage to begin;

And as we ran the channel of the dead slime   32
  There started up at me a mud-soaked head,
  Crying: "Who are thou, come here before thy time?"

"Tho' I come," said I, "I stay not; thou who art made   34
  So rank and beastly, who art thou?" "Go to;
  Thou seest that I am one who weep," he said.

And I: "Amid the weeping and the woe,   37
  Accursed spirit, do thou remain and rot!
  I know thee, filthy as thou art – I know."

Then he stretched out both hands to clutch the boat,   40
  But the master was on his guard and thrust him back,
  Crying: "Hence to the other dogs! Trouble him not!"

And after, laid his arms about my neck   43
  And kissed my face and said: "Indignant soul,
  Blessed is the womb that bare thee! This bold jack

Was an arrogant brute in the world, nor in his whole   46
  Life can remembrance find one sweetening touch;
  So must his raging spirit writhe here and roll.

Many who strut like kings up there are such   49
  As here shall wallow hog-like in the mud,
  Leaving behind nothing but foul reproach."

"Master," said I, "I tell thee, it were good   52
  If I might see this villain soused in the swill
  Before we have passed the lake – Oh, that I could!"

And he made answer: "Thou shalt gaze thy fill   55
  Or ever thou set eyes on the far shore;
  Herein 'tis fitting thou shouldst have thy will."

And soon I saw him set upon so sore   58
  By the muddy gang, with such a pulling and hauling,
  That I still praise and thank my God therefor.

61 "Have at Filippo Argenti!" they were bawling;
   "Loo! loo!" The shade of the fierce Florentine
   Turned on himself, biting with his teeth and mauling.

64 There left we him, as doth this tale of mine;
   For on my ears there smote a wailing cry,
   And I craned forward, eager to divine

67 Its meaning. "See, my son! it now draws nigh,"
   Said my good lord, "the city named of Dis,
   With its sad citizens, its great company."

70 And I: "Already I see its mosques arise
   Clear from the valley yonder – a red shell,
   As though drawn out of glowing furnaces."

73 And he replied: "The flames unquenchable
   That fire them from within thus make them burn
   Ruddy, as thou seest, in this, the nether Hell."

76 We now were come to the deep moats, which turn
   To gird that city all disconsolate,
   Whose walls appeared as they were made of iron.

79 A long way round we had to navigate
   Before we came to where the ferryman
   Roared: "Out with you now, for here's the gate!"

82 Thousand and more, thronging the barbican,
   I saw, of spirits fallen from Heaven, who cried
   Angrily: "Who goes there? why walks this man,

85 Undead, the kingdom of the dead?" My guide,
   Wary and wise, made signs to them, to show
   He sought a secret parley. Then, their pride

88 Abating somewhat, they called out: "Why, so!
   Come thou within, and bid that fellow begone –
   That rash intruder on our realm below.

91 Let him wend back his foolish way alone;
   See if he can; for thou with us shalt stay
   That through this nighted land hast led him on."

94 Reader, do but conceive of my dismay,
   Hearing these dreadful words! It seemed quite plain
   I nevermore should see the light of day.

"O Master dear, that seven times over again   97
  Hast brought me safely through," said I, "and freed
  From all the perils that in my path have lain,

Leave me not utterly undone! Indeed,   100
  If we may not go forward, pray let's quit,
  And hasten back together with all good speed!"

Then said my lord and leader: "Fear no whit;   103
  There's none at all can stay our steps, nor make thee
  Forbear the pass: such Power hath granted it.

Wait for me here; to cheerful thoughts betake thee;   106
  Feed thy faint heart with hope, and calm thy breast,
  For in this underworld I'll not forsake thee."

My gentle father's gone! I'm left distrest,   109
  Abandoned here! Horrid perhapses throng
  My doubtful mind, where yeas and noes contest.

His proffered terms I could not hear. Not long   112
  He'd stood in talk with them, when suddenly
  They all rushed jostling in again headlong,

Leaving him outside. So the enemy   115
  Slammed the gate in my master's face; who thus
  Turned him, and came with slow steps back to me.

His eyes were downcast, and his anxious brows   118
  Shorn of all boldness. Sighing he said: "What's here?
  Who dares forbid me the Mansions Dolorous?"

And then aloud to me: "Have thou no fear   121
  Though I be wroth; I'll win this trial of power,
  Whatever hindrance they contrive in there.

Their truculence is no new thing; once before   124
  'Twas tried at a less secret gate, whereon
  No bars remain for ever. Above that door

Thou sawest the dead title. And now comes one,   127
  This side already treading the steep abyss
  And guardless passing all the circles down,

That shall unbar to us the gates of Dis."   130

THE IMAGES. *Phlegyas* in Greek mythology was a king of Boeotia, son of Ares the war-god by a human mother. His daughter Coronis was loved by Apollo; whereupon Phlegyas in his rage set fire to Apollo's temple. Apollo killed him with his arrows, and he was condemned to torment in Hades. (See *Aen.* vi. 618.) He is thus an appropriate ferryman to ply between the Circle of the Wrathful and the City of the Impious.

The City of Dis. This comprises the whole of Nether Hell, and its ramparts, moated by the Styx, form a complete circle about the Pit. (See map, p. 122.) The sins tormented within the City are those in which the will is actively involved (the sins of Violence and Fraud), and its iron walls are the image of a rigid and determined obstinacy in ill-doing.

Virgil's Repulse at the Gate. Humanism is always apt to underestimate, and to be baffled by, the deliberate will to evil. Neither is it any sure protection against Heresy. The *allegory* is further developed in the next canto.

NOTES. l. 3: *two twinkling points of flame*: to signal the approach of two passengers.

l. 18: *thou wicked spirit*: Phlegyas addresses only one of the poets; presumably because he (*a*) sees that Dante is not a shade, and (*b*) suspects Virgil of having brought him there for a felonious purpose (cf. Cantos IX. 54 and XII. 90).

l. 26: *not till I was in*: because of Dante's mortal weight.

l. 45: *blessed is the womb that bare thee*: It is important to understand this passage, since otherwise we may feel that Virgil is blasphemously encouraging Dante in very cruel and unchristian behaviour. We must distinguish here between the *literal* and *allegorical* meanings, which the poem fuses into a single image.

1. *Literally.* In Hell the soul is fixed eternally in that which it has chosen; it cannot, that is, enjoy there the good which it has rejected. Therefore, the reaction it calls forth from Dante can be no more than the reflection of what it has in itself. Thus Francesca calls forth that same easy pity which betrayed her to lust; Ciacco, the perfunctory pity which is all that the egotist can spare for his neighbours; the Hoarders and Spendthrifts, *because* they made no distinctions in life, are indistinguishable in eternity (Canto VII. 53, 54). But the Wrathful have rejected pity and chosen cruelty; therefore they can receive no pity, and goodness

Commentaries

can only manifest itself to them as wrath, since they have chosen to know it so.

2. *Allegorically*. In the *vision* of Hell, the soul knows itself in a state of sin. Up to this moment Dante has only wondered, grieved, pitied, or trembled; now, for the first time, he sees (in the image of the damned soul) sin as it is – vile, degraded, and dangerous – and turns indignantly against it. For whatever inadequate and unworthy reasons, he accepts judgment and places himself on God's side. It is the first feeble stirring of the birth of Christ within the soul, and Virgil accordingly hails it with words that were used of Christ Himself. (*Luke* xi. 27.)

l. 61: *Filippo Argenti*: a Florentine knight of the Adimari family, of very violent temper, and so purse-proud that he is said to have had his horse shod with silver (hence the nickname "Argenti"). The Adimari were of the opposite faction to Dante and bitterly opposed his recall from banishment.

l. 68: *the city named of Dis*: i.e. named after Dis or Pluto, the King of Hell. Virgil uses the classical name; Dante, as a Christian, calls him Beelzebub, Satan, or Lucifer.

l. 70: *mosques*: Mohammedanism was looked on – correctly enough – by the Middle Ages as being a Christian heresy (see Canto XXVIII), and immediately inside the walls of Dis we shall, in fact, find the Circle of the Heretics. More generally, the "mosques" indicate that the City is devoted to a perverse and infidel cult.

l. 72: *glowing furnaces*: It is only in Nether Hell, below the walls of Dis, that we encounter any torment by fire.

l. 83: *spirits fallen from Heaven*: These are the rebel angels of Christian tradition; the classical monsters continue right down to the bottom of Hell, but here, in the Circles of the perverted will, we find also the more malignant spirits who knew the true God and opposed Him.

l. 125: *a less secret gate*: the gate of Hell, when the devils sought to oppose Christ's entrance into Limbo.

l. 127: *the dead title*: the inscription over Hell-gate. (Canto III. 1–6.)

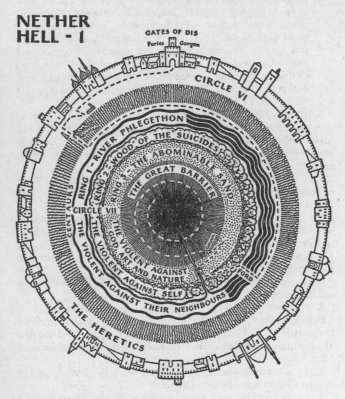

NETHER
HELL - 1

GATES OF DIS
Furies · Gorgon

CIRCLE VI

RING 1 · RIVER PHLEGETHON
RING 2 · WOOD OF THE SUICIDES
RING 3 · THE ABOMINABLE SAND
THE GREAT BARRIER

CENTAURS

CIRCLE VII

THE VIOLENT AGAINST
GOD ART AND NATURE

THE VIOLENT AGAINST SELF

THE VIOLENT AGAINST THEIR NEIGHBOURS

FORD

THE HERETICS

HERESY : VIOLENCE —
THE SINS OF THE LION

CANTO IX

THE STORY. *Dante, alarmed by Virgil's anxiety, tactfully inquires of him whether he really knows the way through Hell, and gets a reassuring answer. The Furies appear and threaten to unloose Medusa. A noise like thunder announces the arrival of a Heavenly Messenger, who opens the gates of Dis and rebukes the demons. When he has departed, the Poets enter the City and find themselves in a great plain covered with the burning tombs of the Heretics.*

Seeing my face, and what a coward colour
   It turned when he came back, my guide was quick
   To put away his own unwonted pallor.

He stood and leaned intent, as who should prick   4
   His ear to hear, for far one could not see,
   So black the air was, and the fog so thick.

"Nay, somehow we must win this fight," said he;   7
   "If not ... That great self-proffered aid is lent;
   But oh! how long his coming seems to be!"

I saw too clearly how his first intent   10
   Was cloaked by what came after; what he said
   Was not what he'd designed, but different.

But none the less his speech increased my dread –   13
   For maybe I pieced out the broken phrase
   To a worse ending than was in his head.

"Did any ever, descending from that place   16
   Where loss of hope remains their only woe,
   Thread to its depth this hollow's dreary maze?"

I put this question. He replied: "Although   19
   'Tis rare that one of us should come this way
   Or undertake the journey I now go,

Yet once before I made it, truth to say,   22
   Conjured by cruel Erichtho, she whose spell
   Wont to call back the shades to their dead clay.

I was not long stripped of my mortal shell   25
   When she compelled me pass within yon wall
   To fetch a spirit from Judas' circle of Hell;

28   That is the deepest, darkest place of all,
         And farthest from high Heaven's all-moving gyre;
         I know the way; take heart – no ill shall fall.

31   On every side, the vast and reeking mire
         Surrounds this city of the woe-begot,
         Where now's no entering, save with wrath and ire ..."

34   And he went on, saying I know not what,
         For my whole being was drawn up with my eyes
         To where the tower's high battlements burned red-hot:

37   For there of a sudden I saw three shapes arise,
         Three hellish Furies, boltered all with blood;
         Their form and bearing were made woman-wise;

40   Vivid green hydras girt them, and a brood
         Of asps and adders, each a living tress,
         Writhed round the brows of that fell sisterhood.

43   And, knowing well those handmaids pitiless
         Who serve the Queen of everlasting woe:
         "Behold," said he, "the fierce Erinyes.

46   There on the right Alecto howls, and lo!
         Megaera on the left; betwixt them wails
         Tisiphone." And he was silent so.

49   They beat their breasts, and tore them with their nails,
         Shrieking so loud that, faint and tremulous,
         I clutched the poet; and they, with fiercer yells,

52   Cried: "Fetch Medusa!", glaring down on us,
         "Turn him to stone! Why did we not requite –
         Woe worth the day! – the assault of Theseus?"

55   "Turn thee about, and shut thine eyelids tight;
         If Gorgon show her face and thou thereon
         Look once, there's no returning to the light."

58   Thus cried the master; nor to my hands alone
         Would trust, but turned me himself, and urgently
         Pressed my palms close and covered them with his own.

61   O you whose intellects keep their sanity,
         Do you mark well the doctrine shrouded o'er
         By the strange verses with their mystery.

Then o'er that dull tide came the crash and roar　64
　Of an enormous and appalling sound,
　So that the ground shuddered from shore to shore;

A sound like the sound of a violent wind, around　67
　The time of opposing heats and the parched weather,
　When it sweeps on the forest and leaps with a sudden bound,

Shattering and scattering the boughs hither and thither;　70
　Superb with a tower of dust for harbinger
　It goes, while the wolves and herdsmen flee together.

He loosed my eyes: "Now look", said he, "see there,　73
　Yonder, beyond the foam of the ancient lake,
　Where the harsh marsh mist hangs thickest upon the air."

And as the frogs, spying the foeman snake,　76
　Go squattering over the pond, and dive, and sit
　Huddled in the mud, even so I saw them break

Apart, whole shoals of ruined spirits, and flit　79
　Scudding from the path of one who came to us,
　Walking the water of Styx with unwet feet.

His left hand, moving, fanned away the gross　82
　Air from his face, nor elsewise did he seem
　At all to find the way laborious.

And when I saw him, right well did I deem　85
　Him sent from Heaven, and turned me to my guide,
　Who signed me to be still and bow to him.

What scorn was in his look! He stood beside　88
　The gate, and touched it with a wand; it flew
　Open; there was no resistance; all stood wide.

"Outcasts of Heaven, despicable crew,"　91
　Said he, his feet set on the dreadful sill,
　"Why dwells this foolish insolence in you?

Why kick against the pricks of that great Will　94
　Whose purpose never can be overborne,
　And which hath oft increased your sorrows still?

Or say, what boots it at the Fates to spurn?　97
　Think how your Cerberus tried it, and yet bears
　The marks of it on jowl and throttle torn."

100   Then back he went by those foul thoroughfares,
           And unto us said nothing, but appeared
           Like one much pressed with weightier affairs

103   Than the cares of those before him. So we stirred
           Our footsteps citywards, with hearts reposed,
           Safely protected by the heavenly word.

106   Through the great ward we entered unopposed,
           And I, being all agog to learn what state
           Of things these huge defensive works enclosed,

109   Gazed round, the moment I had passed the gate,
           And saw a plain, stretched spacious on both sides,
           Filled with ill woes and torments desolate.

112   For as at Arles, where soft the slow Rhone slides,
           Or as at Pola, near Quarnaro's bay,
           That fences Italy with its washing tides,

115   The ground is all uneven with the array,
           On every hand, of countless sepulchres,
           So here; but in a far more bitter way:

118   For strewn among the tombs tall flames flared fierce,
           Heating them so white-hot as never burned
           Iron in the forge of any artificers.

121   The grave-slabs all were thrown back and upturned,
           And from within came forth such fearful crying,
           'Twas plain that here sad tortured spirits mourned.

124   "O Sir," said I, "who are the people lying
           In these grim coffers, whose sharp pains disclose
           Their presence to the ear by their sad sighing?"

127   And he: "The great heresiarchs, with all those,
           Of every sect, their followers; and much more
           The tombs lie laden than thou wouldst suppose.

130   Here like with like is laid; and their flames roar
           More and less hot within their monuments."
           Then we moved onward, and right-handed bore

133   Between those fires and the high battlements.

THE IMAGES. *The Furies* (*Erinyes*) in Greek mythology were the avenging goddesses who haunted those who had committed great crimes. In the *allegory*, they are the image of the fruitless remorse which does not lead to penitence.

Medusa was a *Gorgon* (see Glossary) whose face was so terrible that anyone who looked upon it was turned to stone. In the *allegory*, she is the image of the despair which so hardens the heart that it becomes powerless to repent.

The Heavenly Messenger. He is, I think, the image of Divine revelation, (*a*) stirring the conscience, (*b*) safeguarding the mind against false doctrine.

The Heretics. See next canto.

NOTES. l. 8: *that great self-proffered aid is lent*: How Virgil summons this aid or knows of its coming is not stated; presumably he is aware that the help of Him who harrowed Hell is always available for a Christian soul in need.

l. 16: *descending from that place*, etc.: i.e. from Limbo.

l. 29: *high Heaven's all-moving gyre*: i.e. the *Primum Mobile*, the highest of the revolving heavens, which imparts motion to all the rest (see appendix on *Dante's Universe*, p. 292).

l. 44: *the Queen of everlasting woe*: Proserpine, or Persephone, queen of the classical underworld.

l. 54: *the assault of Theseus*: Theseus, king of Athens, tried to carry off Persephone from Hell; he failed, but was rescued by Hercules. The Furies mean that, if they had succeeded in punishing Theseus, other living men would have been deterred from venturing into the underworld, and they had better make an example of Dante.

l. 88: *what scorn was in his look!* In Hell, God's power is experienced only as judgment, alien and terrible.

l. 97: *what boots it at the Fates to spurn?* The Angel uses two forms of speech – one Christian, "that great Will", the other classical, "the Fates" – to denote the Divine power. The evil powers which he is addressing belong both to the Christian and to the pre-Christian mythology.

l. 98: *Cerberus*: As the last of his labours, Hercules brought Cerberus out of Hell, mauling his throat in the process.

l. 112: *Arles*: where in Dante's time the Rhone spread into a stagnant lake, contains many ancient tombs, said to be those of Charlemagne's soldiers slain in battle against the Saracens at Aleschans. *Pola* (on the Adriatic) is said to have formerly contained about 700 tombs of Slavonians, buried on the seashore.

CANTO X

THE STORY. *As the Poets are passing along beneath the city walls, Dante is hailed by Farinata from one of the burning tombs, and goes to speak to him. Their conversation is interrupted by Cavalcante dei Cavalcanti with a question about his son. Farinata prophesies Dante's exile and explains how the souls in Hell know nothing of the present, though they can remember the past and dimly foresee the future.*

Thus onward still, following a hidden track
   Between the city's ramparts and the fires,
   My master goes, and I go at his back.

4   "O sovran power, that through the impious gyres,"
   Said I, "dost wheel me as thou deemest well,
   Speak to me, satisfy my keen desires.

7   Those that find here their fiery burial,
   May they be seen? for nothing seems concealed;
   The lids are raised, and none stands sentinel."

10   And he: "All these shall be shut fast and sealed
   When from Jehoshaphat they come anew,
   Bringing their bodies now left far afield.

13   And hereabouts lie buried, close in view,
   Epicure and his followers – they who hold
   That when the body dies the soul dies too.

16   Hence that demand thou choosest to unfold
   May here and now be fully satisfied,
   Likewise thy hidden wish, to me untold."

19   "Alas," said I, "from thee I'd never hide
   One single thought, save that short speech is sweet,
   As thou hast warned me once or twice, dear guide."

22   "O Tuscan, walking thus with words discreet
   Alive through the city of fire, be it good to thee
   To turn thee hither awhile, and stay thy feet.

25   Thy native accent proves thee manifestly
   Born of the land I vexed with so great harm –
   A noble land, and too much vext, maybe."

This summons threw me into such alarm,   28
  Coming suddenly from a tomb, that in my dread
  I shrank up close against my escort's arm.

"Come, come, what art thou doing? Turn round," he said;   31
  "That's Farinata – look! he's risen to sight,
  And thou canst view him all, from waist to head."

Already my eyes were fixed on his; upright   34
  He had lifted him, strong-breasted, stony-fronted,
  Seeming to hold all Hell in deep despite;

And my good guide, with ready hands undaunted   37
  Thrusting me toward him through the tombs apace,
  Said: "In thy speech precision is what's wanted."

I reached the vault's foot, and he scanned my face   40
  A little while, and then said, with an air
  Almost contemptuous: "What's thy name and race?"

Being anxious to obey, I did not care   43
  To make a mystery, but told all out;
  He raised his brows a trifle, saying: "They were

Foes to me always, stubborn, fierce to flout   46
  Me and my house and party; I was quick
  To chase them, twice I put them to the rout."

"Quite true; and by that same arithmetic,"   49
  Said I, "they rallied all round and came back twice;
  Your side, it seems, have not yet learnt the trick."

Just then, close by him, I saw slowly rise   52
  Another shadow, visible down to the chin;
  It had got to its knees, I think. It moved its eyes

Round about me, as though it sought to win   55
  Sight of some person in my company;
  At last, when all such hope lay quenched within,

It wept: "If thy grand art has made thee free   58
  To walk at large in this blind prison of pain,
  Where is my son? why comes he not with thee?"

"I come not of myself," I answered plain,   61
  "He that waits yonder leads me on this road,
  For whom, perhaps, your Guido felt disdain."

64   The words he used, together with his mode
      Of torment, were sufficient to betray
      His name, as thus my pointed answer showed.

67   He leapt upright, crying: "What? what dost thou say?
      He felt? why felt? are life and feeling o'er?
      Looks he no longer on the pleasant day?"

70   Then, seeing me hesitate awhile before
      I made reply, he let himself suddenly fall
      Backward again, and showed his face no more.

73   But that great-hearted spirit, at whose call
      I'd stayed my steps, his countenance did not move,
      Nor bent his neck, nor stirred his side at all.

76   "And if," he spoke straight on where we broke off,
      "If they have missed the trick of it, I burn
      Less in this bed than with the thought thereof.

79   But thou, ere fifty times the light return
      To that queen's face who reigneth here below,
      Shalt find out just what that trick costs to learn.

82   But tell me why, as thou dost hope to go
      Back to the light, thy people make decrees
      So harsh against our house, and hate us so."

85   "That field of havoc and bloody butcheries,"
      I answered him, "when Arbia's stream ran red,
      Have filled our temple with these litanies."

88   He sighed before he spoke, and shook his head:
      "'Faith, I was not alone there, nor had gone
      In with the rest without good cause," he said;

91   "But when they made agreement, every one,
      To wipe out Florence, and I stood to plead
      Boldly for her – ay, there I was alone."

94   "Now, so may rest come some time to your seed,"
      Said I, "pray solve me this perplexity,
      Which ties my brains in a tight knot indeed.

97   It seems you can foresee and prophesy
      Events that time will bring, if I hear right,
      But with things present, you deal differently."

"We see," said he, "like men who are dim of sight,   100
   Things that are distant from us; just so far
   We still have gleams of the All-Guider's light.

But when these things draw near, or when they are,   103
   Our intellect is void, and your world's state
   Unknown, save some one bring us news from there.

Hence thou wilt see that all we can await   106
   Is the stark death of knowledge in us, then
   When time's last hour shall shut the future's gate."

At this my conscience smote me; I again   109
   Addressed him: "Tell that fallen shade, I pray,
   His son still walks the world of living men;

If I was silent when he asked me, say   112
   'Twas only that my wits were in a worry,
   Snared by that error which you've swept away."

And now my guide was calling me to hurry,   115
   Wherefore I urged the shade, with greater haste,
   To say who else was in that cemetery.

"I lie," said he, "with thousands; in this chest   118
   The second Frederick lies; our ranks include
   The Cardinal; I will not name the rest."

He spoke, and sank; returning to where stood   121
   The ancient poet, I pondered what they meant,
   Those words which seemed to bode me little good.

Then he moved on, and later, as we went,   124
   "Why so distraught?" said he. I set to work
   Answering his question to his full content.

Sagely he bade me: "See thou mind and mark   127
   Those adverse warnings; now to what I say – "
   And here he raised his finger – "prithee, hark!

When thou shalt stand bathed in the glorious ray   130
   Of her whose blest eyes see all things complete
   Thou'lt learn the meaning of thy life's whole way."

With that, leaving the wall, we turned our feet   133
   Towards the centre, by a path that ran
   Down to a vale, whose fumes rose high to greet

Our nostrils, even where the descent began.   136

THE IMAGES. *The Heretics.* "It is necessary to remember what Dante meant by heresy. He meant an obduracy of the mind; a spiritual state which defied, consciously, 'a power to which trust and obedience are due'; an intellectual obstinacy. A heretic, strictly, was a man who knew what he was doing; he accepted the Church, but at the same time he preferred his own judgment to that of the Church. This would seem to be impossible, except that it is apt to happen in all of us after our manner." (Charles Williams: *The Figure of Beatrice*, p. 125.)

　　The tombs of the intellectually obdurate – iron without and fire within – thus fittingly open the circles of Nether Hell: the circles of deliberately willed sin.

NOTES. l. 11: *Jehoshaphat*: The belief that the Valley of Jehoshaphat would be the scene of the Last Judgment was derived from *Joel* iii. 2, 12.

　　l. 18: *thy hidden wish, to me untold*: Virgil can often read Dante's thoughts, and sometimes seems to take a Sherlock-Holmes-like pleasure in surprising him by doing so. He knows that Dante's question covers an unspoken wish to see certain distinguished Florentines who had been followers of the school of Epicurus. (See Gloss.)

　　ll. 22–7: *O Tuscan ... thy native accent*: Dante is recognized as a Tuscan by his idiom and as a Florentine by his accent.

　　l. 32: *Farinata*: This is Farinata degli Uberti, the famous leader of the Ghibellines in Florence, about whom Dante had already inquired of Ciacco (Canto VI. 78). After he and his party were banished in 1250, they allied themselves with the Siennese and, in 1260, lured the Florentine Guelfs into an ambush and defeated them with appalling slaughter at Montaperti, near the river Arbia (see Introduction, p. 30). The Guelfs, among whom were Dante's ancestors, fled from Florence. They never forgave Farinata, and when they returned to power, they razed the Uberti palaces to the ground and pronounced relentless decrees of exile against the whole family. Farinata was condemned for heresy in 1283.

　　ll. 48–51: *twice ... to the rout ... they came back twice*: The first rout of the Guelfs was in 1248 and their first return in 1251. The second rout was at Montaperti in 1260, and the second and final return in 1266, after the Battle of Benevento, which extinguished the Ghibellines' hope of ever regaining power in Florence. (Note how Farinata's pride instantly evokes a corresponding pride in Dante.)

　　l. 53: *another shadow*: Cavalcante dei Cavalcanti, a Guelf knight, noted, like Farinata, for his Epicureanism. His son, Guido Cavalcanti, was a fellow-poet and friend of Dante and son-in-law to Farinata.

l. 58: *thy grand art* (lit.: "genius"): Cavalcante thinks that if poetical genius has enabled Dante to visit Hell in the flesh, his own poet-son should have been able to accompany his friend.

l. 63: *your Guido felt disdain*: either because Guido, as a modern, despised classical poetry; or because, as a Guelf, he disliked Virgil's imperialism; or because, as a sceptic, he had no use for Virgil's religious piety: or all three. The passage has been much disputed. Note that, in speaking to Farinata and Cavalcante, Dante shows his respect by using the formal "you" in place of the familiar "thou".

l. 70: *seeing me hesitate*: Dante is taken aback at finding that Cavalcante does not know whether Guido is alive or dead, and so does not answer immediately.

l. 80: *queen ... here below*: Proserpine, also identified with Hecate and Diana; the Moon (see Glossary). Fifty lunar months from the date of the vision (April 1300) bring us to the summer of 1304. Dante was banished in 1302, and the efforts of the White Guelfs to return to Florence were finally frustrated in July 1304.

l. 87: *these litanies*: This may mean that prayers were offered in church for the downfall of the Ghibellines, or else that, when the Guelfs were in power, the decrees of exile were formally signed and published in the church of St John.

l. 93: *to wipe out Florence*: After Montaperti, the wholesale destruction of Florence was voted by all the Ghibelline leaders except Farinata, who, drawing his sword, cried out that if they attempted it he was ready to lay down a thousand lives, if he had them, in defence of his native city; and Florence was accordingly spared.

l. 108: *when time's last hour shall shut the future's gate*: "When earthly time ceases there will be nothing to know – nothing but the sin of the past and that sin in the present. ... Charity has already failed here; presently prophecies and tongues and knowledge are to cease too." (Charles Williams: *The Figure of Beatrice*, p. 127.) Farinata's explanation clears up Dante's perplexity, and he hastens to convey to Cavalcante that his son is still alive. Guido's death (August 1300, see Introd. p. 34, note 1) was, however, so near in time that it had become veiled (l. 103) from the knowledge of the damned.

l. 119: *the second Frederick*: the Emperor Frederick II (1194–1250). (See Introduction, p. 25.)

l. 120: *the Cardinal*: Ottaviano degli Ubaldini. (See Glossary.)

l. 131: *her whose blest eyes*: Beatrice, under whose guidance Dante, in the Heaven of Mars, has the course of his life revealed to him by his ancestor Cacciaguida. (*Para.* xvi.)

CANTO XI

THE STORY. *While the Poets pause for a little on the brink of the descent to the Seventh Circle, Virgil explains to Dante the arrangement of Hell.*

Where a great cliff fell sheer, its beetling brow
    Ringed with huge jagged rocks, we reached the brink
    O'erhanging the still ghastlier dens below;

4   And here so overpowering was the stink
    The deep Abyss threw off, that we withdrew
    Staggered, and for a screen were forced to shrink

7   Behind a massive vault where, plain to view,
    Stood writ: "I hold Pope Anastasius,
    Lured by Photinus from the pathway true."

10 "We'll wait awhile," the master said, "that thus
    Our senses may grow used to this vile scent,
    And after that, it will not trouble us."

13 And I: "But let's not lose the time so spent;
    Think now what compensation thou canst find."
    "Surely," he answered, "such was my intent.

16 See now, my son: three narrowing circles wind
    Within these cliffs," thus he took up the tale,
    "Each under each, like those we've left behind.

19 Damned spirits fill them all; thou canst not fail
    To know them at a glance, though, if I state
    How and for what they're here pent up in jail.

22 Of all malicious wrong that earns Heaven's hate
    The end is injury; all such ends are won
    Either by force or fraud. Both perpetrate

25 Evil to others; but since man alone
    Is capable of fraud, God hates that worst;
    The fraudulent lie lowest, then, and groan

28 Deepest. Of these three circles, all the first
    Holds violent men; but as threefold may be
    Their victims, in three rings they are dispersed.

God, self, and neighbour – against all these three   31
   Force may be used; either to injure them
   Or theirs, as I shall show convincingly.

Man on his neighbour may bring death or mayhem   34
   By force; or damage his chattels, house, and lands
   By harsh extortions, pillage, or fire and flame;

So murderers, men who are violent of their hands,   37
   Robbers and plunderers, all find chastisement
   In the first ring, disposed in various bands.

Against themselves men may be violent,   40
   And their own lives or their own goods destroy;
   So they in the second ring in vain repent

Who rob themselves of your world, or make a toy   43
   Of fortune, gambling and wasting away their purse,
   And turn to weeping what was meant for joy.

Those men do violence to God, who curse   46
   And in their hearts deny Him, or defame
   His bounty and His Natural Universe;

So the third ring sets its seal on the double shame   49
   Of Sodom and of Cahors, and on the speech
   Of the froward heart, dishonouring God's great name.

Fraud, which gnaws every conscience, may be a breach   52
   Of trust against the confiding, or deceive
   Such as repose no confidence; though each

Is fraud, the latter sort seems but to cleave   55
   The general bond of love and Nature's tie;
   So the second circle opens to receive

Hypocrites, flatterers, dealers in sorcery,   58
   Panders and cheats, and all such filthy stuff,
   With theft, and simony and barratry.

Fraud of the other sort forgets both love   61
   Of kind, and that love too whence is begot
   The special trust that's over and above;

So, in the smallest circle, that dark spot,   64
   Core of the universe and throne of Dis,
   The traitors lie; and their worm dieth not."

67   "Master," said I, "how clear thy discourse is!
         It makes this gulf's arrangement plain as plain,
         With all its inmates; I quite follow this;

70   But tell me: all those others, whom the rain
         Beats, and the wind drives, and the sticky mire
         Bogs, and those brawlers with their shrill campaign –

73   Why dwell not they in the city red with fire
         If to God's wrath they too are fallen a prey?
         Or if not, wherefore is their plight so dire?"

76   "What error has seduced thy reason, pray?"
         Said he, "thou art not wont to be so dull;
         Or are thy wits woolgathering miles away?

79   Dost thou not mind the doctrine of thy school –
         Those pages where the *Ethics* tells of three
         Conditions contrary to Heaven's will and rule,

82   Incontinence, vice, and brute bestiality?
         And how incontinence offends God less
         Than the other two, and is less blameworthy?

85   If thou wilt think on what this teaching says,
         Bearing in mind what sort of sinners dwell
         Outside the city, and there endure distress,

88   Thou'lt see why they lie separate from these fell
         Spirits within, and why God's hammer-blow
         Of doom smites them with weight less terrible."

91   "O Sun that healest all dim sight, thou so
         Dost charm me in resolving of my doubt,
         To be perplexed is pleasant as to know.

94   Just once again," said I, "turn thee about
         To where thou spak'st of usury as a crime
         Against God's bounty – ravel me that knot out."

97   "Not in one place," said he, "but many a time
         Philosophy points out to who will learn,
         How Nature takes her course from the Sublime

100 Intellect and Its Art; note that; then turn
         The pages of thy *Physics*, and not far
         From the beginning, there shalt thou discern

How your Art, as it best can, follows her   103
   Like a pupil with his master; we may call
   This art of yours God's grandchild, as it were.

By Art and Nature, if thou well recall   106
   How Genesis begins, man ought to get
   His bread, and make prosperity for all.

But the usurer contrives a third way yet,   109
   And in herself and in her follower, Art,
   Scorns Nature, for his hope is elsewhere set.

Follow me now; I think we should depart;   112
   Horizon-high the twinkling Fishes swim,
   And the Wain's right over Caurus; we must start

Onward and downward, over the chasm's rim."   115

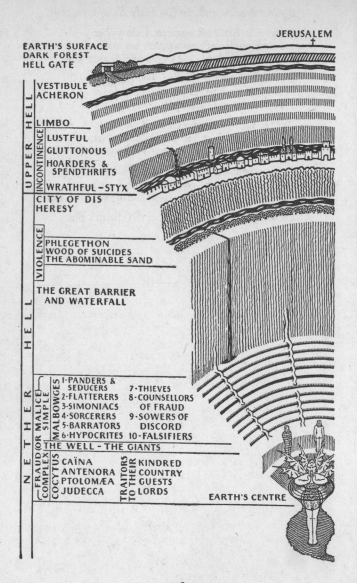

JERUSALEM

EARTH'S SURFACE
DARK FOREST
HELL GATE

UPPER HELL

VESTIBULE
ACHERON

LIMBO

INCONTINENCE

LUSTFUL
GLUTTONOUS
HOARDERS &
SPENDTHRIFTS
WRATHFUL ~ STYX

CITY OF DIS
HERESY

VIOLENCE

PHLEGETHON
WOOD OF SUICIDES
THE ABOMINABLE SAND

THE GREAT BARRIER
AND WATERFALL

NETHER HELL

FRAUD (OR MALICE)

SIMPLE

MALBOWGES

1·PANDERS &
  SEDUCERS
2·FLATTERERS
3·SIMONIACS
4·SORCERERS
5·BARRATORS
6·HYPOCRITES

7·THIEVES
8·COUNSELLORS
  OF FRAUD
9·SOWERS OF
  DISCORD
10·FALSIFIERS

THE WELL ~ THE GIANTS

COMPLEX

COCYTUS

CAÏNA
ANTENORA
PTOLOMÆA
JUDECCA

TRAITORS TO THEIR

KINDRED
COUNTRY
GUESTS
LORDS

EARTH'S CENTRE

Commentaries

THE IMAGES. The only image here is that of Hell itself. Dante's classification of sins is based chiefly on Aristotle, with a little assistance from Cicero. Aristotle divided wrong behaviour into three main kinds: (A) *Incontinence* (uncontrolled appetite); (B) *Bestiality* (perverted appetite); (C) *Malice* or *Vice* (abuse of the specifically human faculty of reason). Cicero declared that all injurious conduct acted by either (a) *Violence* or (b) *Fraud*. Combining these two classifications, Dante obtains three classes of sins: I. *Incontinence*; II *Violence* (or *Bestiality*); III. *Fraud* (or *Malice*). These he subdivides and arranges in 7 Circles: 4 of Incontinence, 1 of Violence, and 2 of Fraud.

To these purely ethical categories of wrong *behaviour* he, as a Christian, adds 2 Circles of wrong *belief*: 1 of *Unbelief* (Limbo) and 1 of *Mischief* (the Heretics), making 9 Circles in all. Finally, he adds the Vestibule of the Futile, who have neither faith nor works; this, not being a Circle, bears no number.

Thus we get the 10 main divisions of Hell. In the other books of the *Comedy* we shall find the same numerical scheme of 3, made up by subdivision to 7; plus 2 (=9); plus 1 (= 10). Hell, however, is complicated by still further subdivision. The Circle of *Violence* is again divided into 3 Rings; the Circle of Fraud Simple into 10 Bowges; and the Circle of Fraud Complex into 4 Regions. So that Hell contains a grand total of 24 divisions. (See section map on opposite page.)

NOTES. l. 8: *Pope Anastasius*: Anastasius II (Pope 496–8); incurred the imputation of heresy by giving communion to Photinus, a deacon of Thessalonica in communion with the Church of Constantinople, which was at this time at odds with the Western Church over the definition of the union of the two natures in Christ's one person. Dante probably got his information directly or indirectly from the *Liber Pontificalis*, a source hostile to Anastasius. (See Duchesne's edition, vol. i, p. 258.)

l. 16: *three narrowing circles*: i.e. the Circle of *Violence* (Circle 7) and the two Circles of *Fraud* (Circles 8 and 9). Virgil begins by describing that part of Nether Hell which still lies ahead. The circles get narrower as the Pit deepens.

l. 22: *malicious wrong*: the phrase "malicious" is here used generally to cover both Violence and Fraud; i.e. all deliberately injurious behaviour.

ll. 28–51: These lines describe the Circle of *Violence* (Circle 7), with its three component Rings devoted respectively to violence against (i) others, (ii) self, (iii) God.

l. 41: *their own lives or their own goods*: Property is regarded, in accordance with Roman law, as an extension of the personality. Consequently, to damage or destroy one's own or one's neighbour's goods is a sin of the same type as the damage and destruction of one's own or one's neighbour's body. Similarly (ll. 46–8), blasphemy against God's creation is blasphemy against God, for the creation belongs to Him.

l. 49: *the double shame of Sodom and of Cahors*: Sodomy (homosexual vice) is so named from Genesis xix. The "shame of Cahors" is Usury – so called from Cahors in the South of France, notorious for its many usurers in Dante's time. Ring iii thus punishes three sorts of violence against God: Sodomy, Usury, and Blasphemy.

ll. 52–66: Virgil now goes on to describe, successively, the two Circles of *Fraud*. There are two kinds of Fraud: the one (Fraud Simple, Circle 8) only betrays the confidence of humanity in general; the other (Fraud Complex, Circle 9) in addition betrays the confidence of those who had special reason to trust, and is, therefore, not merely fraudulent but treacherous.

l. 57: *the second circle*: i.e. the *second* in Nether Hell; the *first* Circle of *Fraud*; Circle 8 in the general scheme.

l. 61: *fraud of the other sort*: i.e. the treacherous sort – Circle 9.

l. 65: *Dis*: the classical king of Hades: i.e. Satan.

ll. 68 sqq.: *this gulf*: i.e. Nether Hell. Dante now asks about the people whom he had already seen in Upper Hell, and why they are not punished within the City of Dis. Virgil reminds him of the seventh chapter of Aristotle's *Ethics*, where incontinence is said to be less reprehensible than bestiality or malice, and treachery the worst conduct of all.

ll. 95 sqq.: *usury as a crime against God's bounty*: Dante's thought in this passage (which is that of the Medieval Church) is of such urgent relevance to-day that it is worth while to disentangle it from his (to us) rather odd and unfamiliar phraseology. What he is saying is that there are only two sources of real wealth: Nature and Art – or, as we should put it, Natural Resources and the Labour of Man. The buying and selling of Money as though it were a commodity creates only a spurious wealth, and results in injury to the earth (Nature) and the exploitation of labour (Art). The attitude to men and things which this implies is a kind of blasphemy; since Art derives from Nature, as Nature derives from God, so that contempt of them is contempt of Him.

l. 101: *thy Physics*: i.e. the *Physics* of Aristotle (ii. 2).

l. 107: *how Genesis begins*: "And the Lord God took the man, and

Commentaries

put him into the garden of Eden" [put the resources of Nature at his disposal] "to dress it and to keep it" [that he might preserve and cultivate them by his art and labour]. (*Gen.* ii. 15.)

l. 113: *the twinkling Fishes*, etc.: Virgil again indicates the time by describing the position of the unseen stars. The Wain (the Plough, or Great Bear) is lying right over the abode of Caurus, the north-west wind, and the constellation of Pisces (the Fishes) is just rising over the horizon. This is the zodiacal sign which immediately precedes Aries (the Ram); and since the signs rise at two-hourly intervals, and the Sun is in Aries (Canto I. 37), it is now two hours before sunrise on Holy Saturday – i.e. about 4 A.M.

CANTO XII

THE STORY. *At the point where the sheer precipice leading down to the Seventh Circle is made negotiable by a pile of tumbled rock, Virgil and Dante are faced by the Minotaur. A taunt from Virgil throws him into a fit of blind fury, and while he is thrashing wildly about, the Poets slip past him. Virgil tells Dante how the rocks were dislodged by the earthquake which took place at the hour of Christ's descent into Limbo. At the foot of the cliff they come to Phlegethon, the river of boiling blood, in which the Violent against their Neighbours are immersed, and whose banks are guarded by Centaurs. At Virgil's request, Chiron, the chief Centaur, sends Nessus to guide them to the ford and carry Dante over on his back. On the way, Nessus points out a number of notable tyrants and robbers.*

The place we came to, to descend the brink from,
 Was sheer crag; and there was a Thing there – making,
 All told, a prospect any eye would shrink from.

4 Like the great landslide that rushed downward, shaking
 The bank of Adige on this side Trent,
 (Whether through faulty shoring or the earth's quaking)

7 So that the rock, down from the summit rent
 Far as the plain, lies strewn, and one might crawl
 From top to bottom by that unsure descent,

10 Such was the precipice; and there we spied,
 Topping the cleft that split the rocky wall,
 That which was wombed in the false heifer's side,

13 The infamy of Crete, stretched out a-sprawl;
 And seeing us, he gnawed himself, like one
 Inly devoured with spite and burning gall.

16 Then cried my Wisdom: "How now, hellion!
 Thinkst thou the Duke of Athens comes anew,
 That slew thee in the upper world? Begone,

19 Monster! not guided by thy sister's clue
 Has this man come; only to see and know
 Your punishments, he threads the circle through."

Then, as a bull pierced by the mortal blow   22
  Breaks loose, and cannot go straight, but reels in the ring
  Plunging wildly and staggering to and fro,

I saw the Minotaur fall a-floundering,   25
  And my wary guide called: "Run! run for the pass!
  Make good thy going now, while his rage has its fling."

So down we clambered by that steep crevasse   28
  Of tumbled rock; and oft beneath my tread
  The stones slipped shifting with my unwonted mass.

I went bemused; wherefore: "Perchance thy head   31
  Puzzles at this great fissure here, watched o'er
  By the furious brute I quelled just now," he said.

"I'd have thee know, when I went down before,   34
  That other time, into Deep Hell this way,
  The rock had not yet fallen; but now for sure

'Twas thus, if I judge rightly: on the day   37
  When that great Prince to the First Circle above
  Entered, and seized from Dis the mighty prey,

Shortly ere He came, the deep foul gulf did move   40
  On all sides down to the centre, till I thought
  The universe trembled in the throes of love,

Whereby, as some believe, the world's been brought   43
  Oft-times to chaos; in that moment, here
  And elsewhere, was these old rocks' ruin wrought.

But now look to the vale, for we draw near   46
  The river of blood, where all those wretches boil
  Whose violence filled the earth with pain and fear."

O blind, O rash and wicked lust of spoil,   49
  That drives our short life with so keen a goad,
  And steeps our life eternal in such broil!

I saw a river, curving full and broad   52
  Arcwise, as though the whole plain's girth embracing.
  Just as my guide had told me on the road;

And 'twixt the bank and it came centaurs racing   55
  By one and one, their bows and quivers bearing
  As when through the woods of the world they went a-chasing.

58   They checked their flight to watch us downward faring,
          And three of the band wheeled out and stood a-row,
          Their bows and chosen arrows first preparing;

61   And one cried out from far: "Hey! whither go
          You on the cliff there? What's your penalty?
          Speak where you stand; if not, I draw the bow."

64   The master shouted back: "That word shall be
      For Chiron there; headstrong thou dost remain,
          And so thou ever wast – the worse for thee."

67   Then, nudging me: "That's Nessus, who was slain
      For fair Deïanira, and in the aftermath
          With his own blood avenged his blood again.

70   Gazing upon his breast, betwixt them both,
          Achilles' tutor, the great Chiron, stands;
          The third is Pholus, once so full of wrath.

73   All round the fosse they speed in myriad bands,
          Shooting at every soul that tries to lift
          Higher out of the blood than doom demands."

76   We were near them now, those creatures snell and swift,
          And Chiron took an arrow, and with the notch
          Put back upon his jaws his snowy drift

79   Of beard, and having freed his great mouth: "Watch,"
          Said he to those who stood with him; "mark you
          How the feet of the one behind move what they touch?

82   Those of the dead are not used so to do,"
          And my good guide, now standing at his breast
          Where the two natures join, replied: "Quite true,

85   He is alive; so, on his lonely quest,
          Needs must I lead him through the vales of night;
          Necessity brings him here, not sport nor jest;

88   From the singing of alleluias in the light
          Came she who laid on me this novel charge;
          The man's no poacher, I'm no thievish sprite

91   Now by the power that moves my steps at large
          On this wild way, lend us a courier
          Whom we may follow by the river's marge,

To show us where the ford is, and to bear   94
  This other upon his back across the tide,
  For he's no spirit to walk the empty air."

Then Chiron turned on his right flank, and cried: 97
  "Wheel round and guide them, Nessus; if you're met
  By another patrol, see that it stands aside."

So with this trusty escort, off we set   100
  Along the bank of the bubbling crimson flood,
  Whence the shrieks of the boiled rose shrill and desperate.

There saw I some – plunged eyebrow-deep they stood;   103
  And the great centaur said to me: "Behold
  Tyrants, who gave themselves to ravin and blood.

Here they bewail oppressions manifold;   106
  Alexander's here; Dionysius too, whose brute
  Fury long years vexed Sicily uncontrolled.

That forehead there, with locks as black as soot,   109
  Is Azzolino, and that fair-haired one
  Obizzo d' Este, he whose light was put

Out, up above there, by his stepson son."   112
  I turned here to the poet, who said, "Why, yes,
  He first, I second now, must guide thee on."

Further along, the centaur checked his pace   115
  Beside a second gang, who seemed to start
  Far as the throat from the stream's boiling race.

He showed one shade set by itself apart,   118
  Saying: "There stands the man who dared to smite,
  Even in the very bosom of God, the heart

They venerate still on Thames." Next, reared upright   121
  Both head and chest from the stream, another horde
  Appeared, full many known to me by sight.

Thus shallow and shallower still the red blood poured   124
  Till it was only deep enough to cook
  The feet; and here it was we passed the ford.

And the centaur said to me: "Now, prithee, look: 127
  Just as, this side, it ever grows less deep,
  On that, I'd have thee know, the boiling brook

130   Lowers its rocky bed, down-shelving steep,
             Until it comes full circle, and joins its ring
             There where the tyrants are condemned to weep.

133   Here doth the heavenly justice rack and wring
             Pyrrhus and Sextus; here it overbears
             That scourge of earth called Attila the King;

136   And here for ever it milks the trickling tears
             Squeezed by the scald from those rough highwaymen
             The Pazzian and Cornetan Riniers."

139   With this he turned and crossed the ford again.

THE IMAGES. *The Circle of Violence*. From now to the end of Canto
    XVII we are in the circle devoted to *Violence* or *Bestiality* (the "sins
    of the Lion") which, together with the Circle of the Heretics,
    makes up the first division of Nether Hell.

The Minotaur and The Centaurs. In this and the next ring we find
    demon-guardians compounded of man and brute. They are the
    types of perverted appetite – the human reason subdued to animal
    passion. The Minotaur had the body of a man and the head of a
    bull; the Centaurs were half-man, half-horse.

Phlegethon – "the fiery" – is the third chief river of Hell. Like Acheron
    and Styx, it forms a complete circuit about the abyss, and it is deep
    at one side and shallow at the other. The sinners whose fiery
    passions caused them to shed man's blood are here plunged in that
    blood-bath for ever.

NOTES. l. 5: *the bank of Adige*: Dante likens the fall of rock to the
    Slavini di Marco on the Adige between Trent and Verona. An early
    commentator (Benvenuto da Imola) says that the comparison is very
    apt, since before the landslide the bank was as sheer as the wall of a
    house and absolutely unscalable; but afterwards it was just possible
    to scramble down it.

    l. 13: *the infamy of Crete*: the Minotaur was the offspring of Pasi-
    phaë (wife of Minos, king of Crete), who became enamoured of a
    beautiful bull, and was brought to him in the effigy of a cow ("the
    false heifer") made for her by the cunning artificer Daedalus. Minos
    kept the Minotaur in the labyrinth at Cnossos. Later, having waged
    a successful war against Athens, he compelled the Athenians to send

Commentaries

him a yearly tribute of seven youths and seven maidens to be devoured by the monster. The Minotaur was slain by Theseus, "the Duke of Athens", who made his way back from the labyrinth by the aid of a clue of thread given to him by Ariadne, daughter of Minos and Pasiphaë.

l. 34: *when I went down before*: Virgil's previous journey (Canto IX. 22) was made before the death of Christ.

l. 39: *the mighty prey*: i.e. the souls of the patriarchs (Canto IV. 55 *sqq.*).

l. 42: *the universe trembled in the throes of love*, etc.: Empedocles taught that the universe was held together in tension by discord among the elements; but that from time to time the motions of the heavens brought about a state of harmony (love). When this happened, like matter flew to like, and the universe was once more resolved into its original elements and so reduced to chaos.

l. 47: *river of blood*: Phlegethon.

l. 62: *what's your penalty?* The Centaurs mistake Dante and Virgil for damned souls going to their allotted place of torment.

l. 65: *Chiron*: the great Centaur to whom Achilles, Peleus, Theseus, and other Greek heroes went to be tutored. He was famous for his skill in hunting, gymnastics, medicine, music, and prophecy, and was accounted the wisest and most just of the Centaurs. Accordingly, though placing him among the guardians of Phlegethon, Dante has given him the most amiable character of all the inhabitants of Hell.

l. 67: *Nessus*: This Centaur attempted to carry off Deïanira, the wife of Hercules, while taking her over a river on his back. Hercules killed him with an arrow, and the dying Nessus told Deïanira to take some of his blood, since it would act upon Hercules as a love-charm. Deïanira did so, and later, fearing that Hercules was falling in love with another woman, put on him a shirt steeped in the blood of Nessus. The blood was poisonous and, after suffering intolerable agonies, Hercules placed himself on a pyre of wood and had himself burned to death.

l. 72: *Pholus*: Little is known of him except that he also was killed by Hercules. The three Centaurs possibly typify three passions which may lead to violence: wrath, lust, and the will to dominate.

l. 88: *from the singing of alleluias ... came she*: i.e. Beatrice.

l. 90: *no poacher, and ... no thievish sprite*: Virgil means that he and Dante have not come, like Theseus or Orpheus, to try and rob Hell of any of its victims.

ll. 105 *sqq.*: *tyrants*: Particulars of the various tyrants will be found in the Glossary.

l. 112: *stepson son*: Actually his son; Dante calls him "stepson" because of his unnatural behaviour.

l. 120: *the heart they venerate still on Thames*: Prince Henry, son of Richard, Duke of Cornwall, and nephew to Henry III of England, was killed in the Cathedral at Viterbo, during High Mass ("in the very bosom of God"), by Guy, son of Simon de Montfort (1270). A statue of him, holding in its right hand the casket containing his heart, is said to have been placed on London Bridge.

l. 131: *until it comes full circle*: Apparently Dante and Virgil have made the full half-circle of Phlegethon, from the deep side where the tyrants stand to the shallow ford.

CANTO XIII

THE STORY. *The Poets enter a pathless Wood. Here Harpies sit shriek-ing among the withered trees, which enclose the souls of Suicides. Pier delle Vigne tells Dante his story, and also explains how these shades come to be changed into trees and what will happen to their bodies at the Last Day. The shades of two Profligates rush through the wood, pursued and torn by black hounds. Dante speaks to a bush containing the soul of a Florentine.*

Ere Nessus had regained the bank beyond
   We'd pushed into a forest, where no mark
   Of any beaten path was to be found.

No green here, but discoloured leaves and dark,   4
   No tender shoots, but writhen and gnarled and tough,
   No fruit, but poison-galls on the withered bark.

Wild beasts, from tilth and pasture slinking off   7
   'Twixt Cecina and Corveto, never come
   To lurk in scrub so tangled or so rough.

There the foul Harpies nest and are at home,   10
   Who chased the Trojans from the Strophades
   With dismal outcry ominous of doom.

Wide-winged like birds and lady-faced are these,   13
   With feathered belly broad and claws of steel;
   And there they sit and shriek on the strange trees.

And the good master thus began: "'Twere well,   16
   Ere going further, thou shouldst understand,
   Thou'rt now in the second ring, and shalt be, till

Thou comest to the abominable sand.   19
   But now, look well, and see a thing whose telling
   Might kill my credit with thee out of hand."

Already all round I heard a mournful wailing,   22
   But, seeing none to wail, I stopped short, blinking
   Bewilderedly, as though my wits were failing.

I think he must have thought that I was thinking   25
   That all these voices through the boles resounding
   Were those of folk who from our gaze hid shrinking,

28   Because he said: "If from these boughs abounding
        Thou wilt pluck off one small and single spray,
        Thy thoughts will stagger at their own dumbfounding."

31   So I put forth my hand a little way,
        And broke a branchlet from a thorn-tree tall;
        And the trunk cried out: "Why tear my limbs away?"

34   Then it grew dark with blood, and therewithal
        Cried out again: "Why dost thou rend my bones?
        Breathes there no pity in thy breast at all?

37   We that are turned to trees were human once;
        Nay, thou shouldst tender a more pious hand
        Though we had been the souls of scorpions."

40   As, when you burn one end of a green brand,
        Sap at the other oozes from the wood,
        Sizzling as the imprisoned airs expand,

43   So from that broken splint came words and blood
        At once: I dropped the twig, and like to one
        Rooted to the ground with terror, there I stood.

46   "O wounded soul," my sage replied anon,
        "Might I have brought him straightway to believe
        The thing he'd read of in my verse alone,

49   Never had he lifted finger to mischieve
        Thee thus; but 'twas incredible; so I
        Prompted his deed, for which myself must grieve.

52   But tell him who thou wast, that he may try
        For some amends, to right thee with mankind
        When, by permission, he returns on high."

55   To this the trunk made answer: "Words so kind
        Tempt me to speech; nor take it in ill part
        If at some length I'm lured to speak my mind.

58   I am he that held both keys of Frederick's heart,
        To lock and to unlock; and well I knew
        To turn them with so exquisite an art,

61   I kept his counsel and let few men through;
        Loyal to my glorious charge did I remain,
        And sacrificed my sleep and my strength too.

But that great harlot which can ne'er refrain 64
    From Caesar's household her adulterous eyes,
    The vice of kings' courts and their common bane,

Inflamed all hearts against me, and these likewise, 67
    Flaming, inflamed Augustus to distrust,
    Till my glad honours turned to obloquies.

So, in a scornful spirit of disgust, 70
    And thinking to escape from scorn by death,
    To my just self I made myself unjust;

But by these strange new roots my trunk beneath, 73
    Never to my most honourworthy lord,
    I swear to you, was I found false of faith;

And if to that bright world indeed restored 76
    One of you goes, oh, heal my memory,
    Which lies and bleeds from envy's venomed sword."

He paused there; and the poet said to me: 79
    "While he is mute, let not this moment go,
    But speak, and ask what more seems good to thee."

And I: "Ask thou, whate'er thou think'st will do 82
    My hunger good and satisfy me well;
    I cannot ask, pity unhearts me so."

Wherefore: "So may this man prove liberal," 85
    Thus he resumed, "thine errand to perform,
    Imprisoned spirit, do thou be pleased to tell

How souls get cramped into this knotty form, 88
    And, if thou canst, if any shall do off
    These limbs one day and find release therefrom."

At this the trunk blew hard, and the windy puff 91
    After this wise soon whistled into speech:
    "You shall be answered with brief words enough.

When the wild soul leaps from the body, which 94
    Its own mad violence forces it to quit,
    Minos dispatches it down to the seventh ditch.

It falls in the wood; no place is picked for it, 97
    But as chance carries it, there it falls to be,
    And where it falls, it sprouts like a corn of wheat,

100 And grows to a sapling, and thence to a wild tree;
　　　Then the Harpies feed on its leaves, and the sharp bite
　　　Gives agony, and a vent to agony.

103 We shall take our flight, when all souls take their flight,
　　　To seek our spoils, but not to be rearrayed,
　　　For the spoils of the spoiler cannot be his by right;

106 Here shall we drag them, to this gloomy glade;
　　　Here shall they hang, each body evermore
　　　Borne on the thorn of its own self-slaughtering shade."

109 Thinking the trunk might wish to tell us more,
　　　We stood intent, when suddenly there came crashing
　　　On our astonished ears a wild uproar,

112 As the huntsman hears the boar and the chase dashing
　　　Down on his post like the noise of a hurricane,
　　　With trampling of beasts and all the branches smashing.

115 And lo! on the left of us came two that ran
　　　Naked and torn, with such a furious burst
　　　As snapped to flinders every forest fan.

118 "O death, come now, come quickly!" thus the first;
　　　And the second, finding himself outstripped in the rush,
　　　Cried: "Lano, thy legs were not so nimble erst

121 At the jousts of Toppo." So in the last push,
　　　His breath failing perhaps, he shot sidelong
　　　And made one group of himself and a thick bush.

124 And filling the woods behind them came a throng
　　　Of great black braches, fleet of foot and grim,
　　　And keen as greyhounds fresh-slipped from the thong;

127 They seized the skulker, and set their teeth in him,
　　　And rent him piecemeal, and away they went
　　　Carrying the wretched fragments limb by limb.

130 Then my guide drew me by the hand, and bent
　　　His steps to the poor bush, left mangled there,
　　　Gasping vain protests through each bleeding rent.

133 "O Jacomo," it cried, "of Sant' Andrea,
　　　Why make a screen of me? What was the good?
　　　Am I to blame for thy misspent career?"

Then said my gentle master when he stood   136
  Beside it: "Who wast thou, that through such tattered
  Wounds sighest out thy grief mingled with blood?"

"O spirits, who come in time to see me battered   139
  Thus shamefully, and all my foliage torn,"
  It said, "bring back the leaves that lie there scattered,

Gather them close beneath the shrub forlorn.   142
  My city was she that for the Baptist changed
  Her ancient patron, wherefore on her scorn

Still by his art he makes himself avenged;   145
  Yea, did not Arno's bridge even now retain
  Some image of the guardian she estranged,

Those citizens who built her walls again   148
  On the ashes left by Attila, had been baffled
  Wholly, and all their labour spent in vain;

I am one that made my own roof-tree my scaffold."   151

THE IMAGES. *The Wood.* This forms the Second Ring of the Circle of the Violent, and contains the souls of those who wantonly destroyed their own lives or their own goods, "turning to weeping what was meant for joy" (Canto XI. 45).

The Harpies. Here again we have a mixture of brute and human. The Harpies had the bodies of birds, long claws, and the faces of women pale with hunger. When Aeneas and his companions came to the Islands of the Strophades, the Harpies swooped down upon their food, devouring and defiling it (*Aen.* iii. 209 *sqq.*). They are the image of the "will to destruction".

The Bleeding Trees. The sin of Suicide is, in an especial manner, an insult to the body; so, here, the shades are deprived of even the semblance of the human form. As they refused life, they remain fixed in a dead and withered sterility. They are the image of the self-hatred which dries up the very sap of energy and makes all life infertile.

The Profligates. These are very different from the "Spendthrifts" of Canto VII, who were merely guilty of extravagance. The profligates here were men possessed by a depraved passion, who dissipated their goods for the sheer wanton lust of wreckage and disorder. They may be called the image of "gambling-fever" – or, more generally, the itch to destroy civilization, order, and reputation.

NOTES. l. 2: *we'd pushed into a forest*: Note that the three rings of Circle 7 are all on the same level.

l. 8: '*twixt Cecina and Corveto*: Cecina (a river in the province of Volterra) and Corveto (a small town on the river Marta) mark the boundaries of the Tuscan Maremma, where, in Dante's time, there were many dense forests full of wild animals.

l. 19: *the abominable sand*: Ring iii. (See Canto XIV.)

l. 48: *the thing he had read of in my verse alone:* i.e. in the *Aeneid* (iii. 22 *sqq.*). (This famous episode of the bleeding tree has been frequently imitated, not only by Dante, but notably also by Ariosto, Tasso, and Spenser.)

l. 58: *he that held both keys of Frederick's heart*: Pier delle Vigne, for many years chief counsellor to the Emperor Frederick II (mentioned in Canto X). Accused of conspiring against his master, he was disgraced, imprisoned, and blinded, and in despair took his own life.

l. 64: *that great harlot*: i.e. Envy. (See l. 78.)

l. 68: *Augustus*: i.e. Caesar = the Emperor.

l. 77: *heal my memory*: The fact that Dante places Pier in the Wood of the Suicides, and not among the traitors at the bottom of the Pit, shows that he believed him to have been falsely accused.

l. 102: *a vent to agony*: The trees can only utter when broken and bleeding. The Harpies, by tearing the leaves, make wounds from which issue the wails that puzzled Dante (ll. 22–7).

l. 105: *the spoils of the spoiler cannot be his by right*: (lit.: "it is not just that a man should have what he takes from himself") – Dante treats suicide as a kind of self-robbery (Canto XI. 43). Here he means, I think, that a robber cannot have a just title to the goods he has plundered.

l. 107: *here shall they hang*: Nowhere, perhaps, does Dante assert more clearly than in this moving and terrible image his conviction of the intimate and unbreakable bond between spirit and flesh. The Suicides willed the death of the flesh, but they cannot be rid of it: their eternity is an eternity of that death. (The absurd charge of heretically denying the resurrection of the body was brought against Dante on the strength of these lines, but only by those to whom the language of poetic imagery is a sealed book.)

l. 115: *two that ran*: "The first" is Lano of Siena; he belonged to a club of young rakes (referred to again in Canto xxix), who sold up all their estates and "blued" the proceeds within twenty months. Lano then threw away his life in an encounter between the Sienese and Aretines at a ford called Pieve del Toppo (1288). "The second" is a Paduan, Jacomo di Sant' Andrea, who, not content with such pranks as playing ducks and drakes with gold pieces on the Lagoon at Venice, had a pleasant way of burning down his own and other people's houses for the fun of it. He is said to have been put to death in 1239 by Ezzelino.

l. 143: *my city*: Florence. Her "ancient patron" was Mars. When the Florentines were converted to Christianity they built the Church of St John Baptist on the site of the temple of Mars, and stowed the heathen statue away in a tower near the Arno. After the burning of the city by Totila (whom Dante, misled by some of the chroniclers, seems to have confused with Attila), the mutilated remains of the god were recovered from the river and set up on the Ponte Vecchio; and but for this, so the superstition ran, Florence could never have been rebuilt. Even so, it was said, Mars continued to vex the faithless city with continued internecine strife. But Dante may be covertly reproaching the Florentines with abandoning martial pursuits and concentrating on amassing the florins stamped with the Baptist's image.

l. 151: *one that made my own roof-tree my scaffold*: The speaker has been variously identified. Florence seems to have had a kind of "suicide-wave" about Dante's time; his son Jacopo observes that it is a special vice of the Florentines to hang themselves, "just as the people of Arezzo are given to throwing themselves down wells".

CANTO XIV

THE STORY. *In a desert of Burning Sand, under a rain of perpetual fire, Dante finds the Violent against God, Nature, and Art. The Violent against God lie supine, facing the Heaven which they insulted; among these is Capaneus, blasphemous and defiant in death as in life. The Poets pick their way carefully between the forest and the hot sand till they come to the edge of a boiling, red stream. Here Virgil explains the origin of all the rivers of Hell.*

Love of my native place with kind constraint
    Moving me, I brought back the scattered leaves
    To him whose voice already was grown faint;

4   Then on we went, to reach the bound which cleaves
    The second ring from the third, and saw appear
    A terrible art which justice here conceives.

7   I say, to make all this new matter clear,
    We reached a plain which spurns all foliage
    And every live plant from its surface sere.

10   The doleful wood garlands it like a hedge,
    As the sad moat garlands the wood around;
    And here we stayed our steps 'twixt edge and edge.

13   An arid, close-packed sand, in fashion found
    Not otherwise than that which once was trod
    By Cato's marching feet, such was the ground.

16   Fearful indeed art thou, vengeance of God!
    He that now reads what mine own eyes with awe
    Plainly beheld, well may he dread thy rod!

19   Great herds of naked spirits here I saw,
    Who all most wretchedly bewailed their lot,
    Seeming subjected to a diverse law.

22   Some on the ground lay supine in one spot,
    And some upon their hunkers squatted low,
    Others roamed ceaselessly and rested not;

25   Most numerous were the rovers to-and-fro;
    Of those that lay, the numbers were more small,
    But much the loudest were their cries of woe.

And slowly, slowly dropping over all
   The sand, there drifted down huge flakes of fire,
   As Alpine snows in windless weather fall.
  28

Like as Alexander, in those torrider
   Regions of Ind, saw flaming fireballs shed
   Over his host, floating to earth entire,
  31

So that his men and he took pains to tread
   The soil, trampling the blaze out with their feet,
   Since it was easier quenched before it spread,
  34

Even so rained down the everlasting heat,
   And, as steel kindles tinder, kindled the sands,
   Redoubling pain; nor ever ceased the beat
  37

And restless dance of miserable hands,
   Flapping away, now this side and now that,
   The raw smart of the still-fresh-biting brands.
  40

I thus began: "Master, strong to frustrate
   All hostile things, save only indeed those grim
   Fiends who opposed our entrance at the gate,
  43

Who is the shade that lies, mighty of limb,
   Contorted and contemptuous, scorning the flame,
   So that the rain seems not to ripen him?"
  46

But he himself, soon as he heard me frame
   This question to my guide about him, cried:
   "That which in life I was, in death I am.
  49

Though Jove tire out his armourer, who supplied
   His wrathful hand with the sharp thunder-stone
   That in my last day smote me through the side;
  52

Though he tire all the rest out, one by one,
   In Mongibel's black stithy, and break them quite,
   Crying, 'To aid! Vulcan, lay on, lay on!'
  55

As once before he cried at Phlegra's fight;
   Yea, though he crush me with his omnipotence,
   No merry vengeance shall his heart delight."
  58

Then my guide spoke out with a vehemence
   Such as I never had heard him use before:
   "O Capaneus, since thy proud insolence
  61

64 Will not be quenched, thy pains shall be the more;
  No torment save thine own hot rage could be
  A fitting cautery to thy rabid sore."

67 Then said with milder mouth, turning to me:
  "This was one of the seven kings who pressed
  The siege of Thebes; he held, and seemingly

70 Still holds, God light, and flouts Him with a jest;
  Yet, as I told him, his mad mouthings make
  A proper brooch for such a brazen breast.

73 Now follow me, and look to it that thou take
  No step upon the burning sand, but keep
  Thy feet close back against the woodland brake."

76 Silent we came where, from that forest deep,
  A little brook poured forth a bubbling jet
  Whose horrid redness makes my flesh still creep.

79 It was like that stream of the Bulicame, set
  Apart and shared by the women of the town;
  And straight out over the sand ran the rivulet.

82 Its bed, and both its shelving banks, and the crown
  Of the margins left and right, were turned to stone;
  Which made me think that here our path led down.

85 "Of all the marvels I as yet have shown
  Thine eyes, since first we entered by that door
  Of which the threshold is denied to none,

88 Nothing we've seen deserves thy wonder more
  Than this small stream which, flowing centreward,
  Puts out all flames above its either shore."

91 Thus said my guide; whom I at once implore
  Since he'd so whet my appetite to taste
  His food, immediately to spread the board.

94 "Far off amid the sea there lies a waste
  Country," said he, "called Crete, beneath whose king,
  Once on a long-lost time, the world was chaste.

97 A mount is there, named Ida; many a spring
  Laughed through its ferns of yore and the valleys smiled –
  Forsaken now, like some old, mouldering thing.

There Rhea once found safe cradling for her child,   100
    And to hide his cries, lest danger come to pass,
    Let fill the hills with Corybant clamours wild.

A great old man stands under the mountain's mass;   103
    Toward Damietta he keeps his shoulders holden,
    And he looks on Rome as though on a looking-glass.

He towers erect, and his head is purely golden,   106
    Of the silver fine his breast and arms and hands,
    Of brass down to the cleft his trunk is moulden,

And thence to the ground his legs are iron bands,   109
    Save that the right foot's baked of the earthen clay,
    And that is the foot upon which he chiefly stands.

All but the gold is cracked, and from the splay   112
    Of that great rift run tears gathering and dripping,
    Till out through the cavern floor they wear their way

Into this vale, from rock to rock down-dipping,   115
    Making Acheron, Styx and Phlegethon; then they take
    Their downward course, by this strait conduit slipping,

To where there is no more downward; there they make   118
    Cocytus; and what that's like I need not tell;
    For thine own eyes shall look on Cocytus lake."

Then I to him: "But, Master, if this rill   121
    Flows from our world, why is it only found
    Here on this bank, nor elsewhere visible?"

And he to me: "Thou knowest, the place is round;   124
    Though thou hast come a good long way, 'tis true,
    Still wheeling leftward toward the Pit's profound,

Thou hast not yet turned the full circle through;   127
    So why put on such a bewildered air
    If now and then we come upon something new?"

And I again: "Where's Lethe, sir? and where   130
    Is Phlegethon? The first thou leav'st aside,
    Tracing the second to that water there."

"Thy questions all delight me," he replied,   133
    "But for the one – thyself canst answer it:
    Think of the boiling of the blood-red tide.

136   And Lethe thou shalt see, far from this Pit,
            Where go the souls to wash them in its flood,
            Their guilt purged off, their penitence complete."

139   He added: "Come; it's time to leave the wood;
            See that thou follow closely where I tread;
            The margins burn not, they shall make our road,

142   And all the fires are quenched there overhead."

THE IMAGES. *The Sand.* "In these circles of the Violent the reader is peculiarly conscious of a sense of sterility. The bloody river, the dreary wood, the harsh sand, which compose them, to some extent are there as symbols of unfruitfulness" (Charles Williams: *The Figure of Beatrice*, p. 129). The images of the sand and burning rain are derived from the doom of Sodom and Gomorrah. (*Gen.* xix. 24.)

The Blasphemers. Capaneus the Blasphemer is chosen as the particular image of Violence against God: he is an image of Pride, which makes the soul obdurate under judgment. The arrangement of Hell, being classical, allots no special place to Pride (held by Christianity to be the root of all sin), but it offers a whole series of examples of Pride, each worse than the last, as the Pit deepens. Farinata's pride is dark and silent; that of Capaneus is loud and defiant, but not yet so wholly ignoble as that of Vanni Fucci (Canto XXV. 1), far down in the Eighth Circle.

NOTES. l. 3: *whose voice already was grown faint:* The small broken twigs were already clotted with blood, and the bush had no voice left.

l. 15: *Cato's marching feet:* The march of Cato of Utica (see Glossary) through the Libyan desert in 47 B.C. is described in Lucan's *Pharsalia* ix. 411 *sqq.*

ll. 22 *sqq.:* *some lay ... some squatted ... others roamed:* the Violent against God, Art, and Nature respectively.

l. 31: *like as Alexander:* Dante seems to have taken this story about Alexander the Great from Albertus Magnus (*De Meteoris*), who in turn took it, with certain alterations, from the spurious *Letter of Alexander to Aristotle about the Marvels of the Indies.*

ll. 51 *sqq.:* *that which in life I was,* etc.: This is Capaneus, who took part in the war of the "Seven against Thebes" (see Glossary). While scaling the city wall, he boasted that not even Jove could stop him, and was struck with a thunder-bolt. Dante read about him in the

Thebaïd of Statius (the poet whom he afterwards meets in Purgatory).

l. 52: *his armourer*: Vulcan, the blacksmith of the gods, who had his forge in Mongibello (Mount Etna).

l. 58: *Phlegra's fight*: the battle in which the rebellious Titans were overthrown by the gods. (See Canto XXXI. 91 *sqq.*)

l. 70: *still holds God light*: Note again the double vocabulary (as in Canto IX. 94–9). Capaneus says "Jove"; Virgil says "God", meaning the same thing. The heathen are judged by their own standards.

l. 77: *a small brook*: This is the effluent of Phlegethon, which, after crossing the Wood of the Suicides, now runs across the Third Ring to plunge over the edge of the Pit. It has the property of petrifying the sand which forms its bed.

l. 79: *the Bulicame*: a hot sulphur-spring of reddish colour near Viterbo, part of whose waters were specially portioned off for use in the prostitutes' quarter.

l. 90: *puts out all flames*: The steam from the boiling river forms a cloud above the banks and quenches the flames. (Canto XV. 1.)

ll. 95–6: *beneath whose king, ... the world was chaste*: i.e. in the fabled "Golden Age" of Saturn, the mythical king of Crete. (See Glossary: *Saturn*).

l. 100: *Rhea*: wife of Saturn and mother by him of Jupiter. It had been prophesied to Saturn that he would be dethroned by his own son, and he therefore devoured all his children as soon as they were born. Rhea deceived him by wrapping a stone in swaddling-clothes, and fled with Jupiter to Mount Ida; when the child cried, she caused the Corybants (Bacchantes) to make a wild clamour so that Saturn should not hear him.

ll. 103 *sqq.*: *a great old man*, etc.: This *allegory* of the successively degenerating periods of history is founded in *Daniel* ii. 32 *sqq.*; the four ages of man (gold, silver, brass, iron) are taken from Ovid: *Metamorphoses* i. 89 *sqq.* Only the Golden Age gave no cause for tears. The feet of iron and clay may be respectively the Empire and the Church. The statue stands in the middle of the Mediterranean (the centre of civilization), looking from the old civilization of the East (Damietta) to the new civilization of the West (Rome).

l. 118: *no more downward*: the centre of the earth and of gravity. Cocytus (Canto XXXIV) is the last of the infernal rivers.

ll. 130 *sqq.*: *Lethe and ... Phlegethon*: Virgil explains that Dante has already seen Phlegethon – it is the river of the tyrants, though its name was not mentioned in Canto XII. *Lethe* (the river of forgetfulness) flows to the Centre from the Earthly Paradise on Mount Purgatory on the other side of the world.

CANTO XV

THE STORY. *While crossing the Sand upon the dyke banking Phlegethon, Dante sees the Violent against Nature, who run perpetually, looking towards the human body against which they offended. He meets his old teacher, Brunetto Latini, whom he addresses with affectionate regret and deep gratitude for past benefits. Brunetto predicts Dante's ill-treatment at the hands of the Florentines.*

Now the hard margin bears us on, while steam
   From off the water makes a canopy
   Above, to fend the fire from bank and stream.

4   Just as the men of Flanders anxiously
   'Twixt Bruges and Wissant build their bulwarks wide
   Fearing the thrust and onset of the sea;

7   Or as the Paduans dyke up Brenta's tide
   To guard their towns and castles, ere the heat
   Loose down the snows from Chiarentana's side,

10   Such fashion were the brinks that banked the leat,
   Save that, whoe'er he was, their engineer
   In breadth and height had builded them less great.

13   Already we'd left the wood behind so far
   That I, had I turned back to view those glades,
   Could not have told their whereabouts; and here,

16   Hurrying close to the bank, a troop of shades
   Met us, who eyed us much as passers-by
   Eye one another when the daylight fades

19   To dusk and a new moon is in the sky,
   And knitting up their brows they squinnied at us
   Like an old tailor at the needle's eye.

22   Then, while the whole group peered upon me thus,
   One of them recognized me, who caught hard
   At my gown's hem, and cried: "O marvellous!"

25   When he put out his hand to me, I stared
   At his scorched face, searching him through and through,
   So that the shrivelled skin and features scarred

Might not mislead my memory: then I knew: 28
    And, stooping down to bring my face near his,
    I said: "What, you here, Ser Brunetto? you!"

And he: "My son, pray take it not amiss   31
    If now Brunetto Latini at thy side
    Turn back awhile, letting this troop dismiss."

"With all my heart I beg you to," I cried;   34
    "Or I'll sit down with you, as you like best,
    If he there will permit – for he's my guide."

"Oh, son," said he, "should one of our lot rest   37
    One second, a hundred years he must lie low,
    Nor even beat the flames back from his breast.

Therefore go on; I at thy skirts will go,   40
    And then rejoin my household, who thus race
    Forever lost, and weeping for their woe."

I durst not venture from the road to pace   43
    Beside him, so I walked with down-bent head,
    Like some devout soul in a holy place.

He thus began: "What chance or fate has led   46
    Thy footsteps here before thy final day?
    And who is this that guides thee?" So I said:

"Up in the sunlit life I lost my way   49
    In a dark vale, before my years had come
    To their full number. Only yesterday

At morn I turned my back upon its gloom;   52
    This other came, found me returning there,
    Stopped me, and by this path now leads me home."

And he made answer: "Follow but thy star;   55
    Thou canst not fail to win the glorious haven,
    If in glad life my judgment did not err.

Had I not died so soon, I would have given   58
    Counsel and aid to cheer thee in thy work,
    Seeing how favoured thou hast been by heaven.

But that ungrateful, that malignant folk   61
    Which formerly came down from Fiesole,
    And still is grained of mountain and hewn rock,

64   For thy good deeds will be thine enemy –
        With cause; for where the bitter sloes are rooted
        Is no fit orchard for the sweet fig-tree.

67   A blind people, and always so reputed,
        Proud, envious, covetous, since times remote;
        Cleanse off their customs lest thou be polluted.

70   Fortune has honours for thee – of such note,
        Both sides will seek to snatch thee and devour;
        But yet the good grass shall escape the goat.

73   Let Fiesole's wild beasts scratch up their sour
        Litter themselves from their rank native weed,
        Nor touch the plant, if any such can flower

76   Upon their midden, in whose sacred seed
        Survives the Roman line left there to dwell
        When this huge nest of vice began to breed."

79   I answered him: "Might I have had my will,
        Believe me, you'd not yet been thrust apart
        From human life; for I keep with me still,

82   Stamped on my mind, and now stabbing my heart,
        The dear, benign, paternal image of you,
        You living, you hourly teaching me the art

85   By which men grow immortal; know this too:
        I am so grateful, that while I breathe air
        My tongue shall speak the thanks which are your due.

88   Your words about my future I'll write fair,
        With other texts, to show to a wise lady
        Who'll gloss them, if I ever get to her.

91   This much I'd have you know: I can stand steady,
        So conscience chide not, facing unafraid
        Whatever Fortune brings, for I am ready.

94   Time and again I've heard these forecasts made;
        The whims of Luck shall find me undeterred,
        So let her ply her wheel, the churl his spade."

97   And when my master's ear had caught that word
        He turned right-face-about, and looked me straight
        In the eyes and said: "Well-heeded is well-heard."

Yet none the less I move on in debate   100
  With Ser Brunetto, asking him whose fame
  In all his band is widest and most great.

"Some," he replies, "it will be well to name;   103
  The rest we must pass over, for sheer dearth
  Of time – 'twould take too long to mention them.

All these, in brief, were clerks and men of worth   106
  In letters and in scholarship – none more so;
  And all defiled by one same taint on earth.

In that sad throng goes Francis of Accorso,   109
  And Priscian; could thy hunger have been sated
  By such scabbed meat, thou mightest have seen also

Him whom the Servant of servants once translated   112
  From Arno to Bacchiglione, where he left
  The body he'd unstrung and enervated.

I would say more, but must not; for a drift   115
  Of fresh dust rising from the sandy ground
  Warns me to cease and make my going swift;

Here come some folk with whom I mayn't be found;   118
  Keep handy my *Thesaurus*, where I yet
  Live on; I ask no more." Then he turned round,

And seemed like one of those who over the flat   121
  And open course in the fields beside Verona
  Run for the green cloth; and he seemed, at that,

Not like a loser, but the winning runner.   124

THE IMAGES. *The Sodomites* are chosen as the image of all pervese vices which damage and corrupt the natural powers of the body. (It is here, for instance, that Dante would probably place drug-takers and the vicious type of alcoholics.) Their perpetual fruit-less running forms a parallel, on a lower level, to the aimless drifting of the Lustful in Canto v.

NOTES. ll. 4 *sqq.*: Dante compares the dykes to those built in the Low Countries to keep out the sea, and to the embankments made by the Paduans along the river Brenta to prevent flooding in spring, when the river is swollen by melted snow from Chiarentana (probably Carenzana, a mountain in the Trentino).

l. 11: *their engineer*: God is, of course, the supreme Architect of Hell (Canto III. 4–6); but the constructional details would be supposed to be carried out by some one of the "Intelligences" who are His ministers. As we see from l. 23, the top of the dyke was about a man's height from the sand.

l. 29: *to bring my face near his*: another reading, perhaps even more attractive, has: "And reached my hand down to that face of his, Saying ..."

l. 30: *Ser Brunetto*: Messer Brunetto Latini (*c.* 1220–94) was a Florentine Guelf, a man of considerable learning. An early commentator says "that he was a neighbour of Dante and taught him a great many things; that he did not care for the soul, as he was altogether worldly; that he sinned greatly in unnatural crime, and scoffed much at the things of God and Holy Church" (Vernon). He wrote in French a prose encyclopedia called *Le Livre dou Tresor* or *Thesaurus* (see l. 119), and an abridged version in Italian verse, *Il Tesoretto*. Though he was an influence in Dante's early life, he was not a "tutor" or "schoolmaster", but a man holding public office in the state, till he was banished with other Guelfs after the Battle of Montaperti.

l. 56: *the glorious haven*: Brunetto seems to mistake Dante, and think that he is only aspiring to lasting fame on earth, and says that, if he himself had not died too soon, he would have helped him to achieve perfection of knowledge.

ll. 61–79: According to Florentine tradition, Julius Caesar besieged Catiline in Fiesole; when the city fell, the Romans built a new one – Florence – on the Arno, to be peopled half by Fiesolans and half by Romans. Dante attributes much of the strife and disorder in Florence to this adulteration of the Roman stock by families from Fiesole and the surrounding country (see *Para.* xvi. 67–9). "Blind Florentines" was a proverbial reproach, whose origin is now lost in mists of legend (cf. our "wise fools of Gotham").

l. 71: *both sides will seek to snatch thee*: i.e. Dante will be persecuted by both parties.

l. 87: *my tongue shall speak the thanks which are your due:* The episode of Brunetto Latini gives the lie to the common assertion that Dante put only his enemies in Hell. But while maintaining, on the one hand, that personal feelings cannot remove the difference in God's sight between right and wrong, he asserts, on the other, that, as between man and man, nothing can ever remove the obligation to acknowledge benefits received. "For ever and ever (derivation) must be remembered, willingly praised, and ardently published before earth and heaven. ... Such a loyalty is necessary to the life of the City." (Charles Williams: *The Figure of Beatrice*, p. 130.)

l. 89: *to show to a wise lady*: Dante, remembering Virgil's words (Canto x. 130–32), says he will ask Beatrice to explain all these prophecies about himself.

l. 96: *the churl his spade*: Let Luck turn her wheel, and the labourer turn the soil – Dante shall remain as unmoved by the one as by the other. Virgil seems not altogether to approve this parade of indifference, and warns Dante that he will do well to heed what is said to him.

l. 112: *him whom the Servant of servants once translated*: Andrea dei Mozzi (see Glossary for him and the other persons mentioned). The title "Servant of the servants of God" is one of the official titles of the Pope.

l. 121: *and seemed like one of those who ... run*: This foot-race, whose prize was a piece of green cloth, was instituted to celebrate a Veronese victory, and was run on the First Sunday in Lent.

CANTO XVI

THE STORY. *Dante is already within earshot of the waterfall at the end of the path, when he meets the shades of three distinguished Florentine noblemen and gives them news of their city. At the edge of the cliff, Virgil throws Dante's girdle into the gulf below, and in answer to this signal a strange form comes swimming up towards them.*

> Already I'd reached a place where the dull thrumming
>   Of the water tumbling down to the circle below
>   Was heard ahead like the sound of a beehive's humming,
>
> 4 When lo! three shadows, running all in a row,
>   Broke from a company that across the sand
>   Was passing under the rain of the burning woe.
>
> 7 They came towards us, crying with one voice: "Stand,
>   Thou there, the fashion of whose dress would seem
>   To make thee a native of our perverted land!"
>
> 10 O me! the marks I saw upon every limb,
>   Branded in by the flames, old scars and new –
>   It makes me heartsick only to think of them.
>
> 13 Heedful, my teacher heard those spirits through,
>   Then turned his face my way: "Now wait," said he;
>   "To those the utmost courtesy is due.
>
> 16 Were not this place by nature arrowy
>   With fire, I'd say it was far more suitable
>   That thou shouldst hurry to them than they to thee."
>
> 19 They raised their voices again when we stood still,
>   Renewing their ancient wail; then, coming close,
>   The three of them formed themselves into a wheel.
>
> 22 Like old-time champions, stript, oiled, on their toes
>   Circling, and spying for vantage of hold and place
>   Before getting down to clinches and to blows,
>
> 25 Just so they wheeled; but each one kept his gaze
>   So fixed on me that all the time one way
>   The feet went, and another way the face.

"Eh, though scorn prompt thee," one began to say,   28
   "Seeing our squalor, and scorched, filthy state,
   From us and from our prayers to turn away,

Let our great fame yet move thee to relate   31
   What man thou art, that free and dangerless
   Thus through deep Hell dost move thy living feet.

He in whose tracks I tread here, nevertheless,   34
   For all he now goes naked and peeled and scored,
   Was nobler in degree than thou couldst guess.

Grandson to good Gualdrada was this lord,   37
   He was called Guido Guerra, and his fame
   In life stood high with counsel and with sword.

He that behind me treads the sand and flame   40
   Was Tegghiai' Aldobrandi once; applause
   Up in your world should surely greet that name.

Here, partner in their pain, am I, who was   43
   Jacopo Rusticucci; of this woe
   My bestial wife's the first and foremost cause."

Could I have kept the fire off, there below,   46
   I'd have leapt down to them, and I declare
   I think my tutor would have let me go;

But I'd have burnt and baked me so, that fear   49
   Quite vanquished the good-will which made me yearn
   To clasp them to my bosom then and there.

So I began: "Indeed, indeed, not scorn   52
   But heartfelt grief to see your tribulation
   Pierced me, too deeply to be soon outworn,

When this my lord gave me an intimation   55
   Which made me think that I might look to gaze
   On men like you, and of such reputation.

Truly, your city's mine; I've heard your praise –   58
   Your deeds, your honoured names – rehearsed by all,
   And have with love rehearsed them all my days.

I'm one who, turning from the bitter gall,   61
   Seek the sweet fruit promised by my sure guide;
   But to the Centre I have first to fall."

64   "So may thy soul these many years abide
       Housed in thy body, and the after-light
       Of fame shine long behind thee," he replied,

67   "Tell us if in our city still burn bright
       Courage and courtesy, as they did of old,
       Or are their embers now extinguished quite?

70   For Guillim Borsier', but late enrolled
       With us, who runs in yon tormented train,
       Has much distressed us by the tales he's told."

73   "A glut of self-made men and quick-got gain
       Have bred excess in thee and pride, forsooth,
       O Florence! till e'en now thou criest for pain."

76   Thus I proclaimed aloud with lifted mouth;
       The three knew they were answered, each on each
       Looking, as men look when they hear the truth.

79   "If thou at other times canst thus enrich
       Men's ears," they all replied, "scot-free, as thus,
       Happy art thou, that hast the gift of speech!

82   Wherefore, if thou escape this place of loss
       And come to see the lovely stars again,
       Then, when thou shalt rejoice to say, 'I was,'

85   Look that thou speak of us to living men."
       Thereon they broke their wheel, and fled so fast,
       Their legs seemed wings; you could not say *Amen*

88   So quickly as across the sandy vast
       They vanished; only then my master stirred,
       Choosing to go. I followed. On we passed,

91   And went but a short way before we heard
       The sound of the water thundering down so close
       That had we spoken we'd scarce have heard a word.

94   As that first river that to the eastward flows
       From Monte Veso down to a mouth of its own,
       On the left slope of the Apennines (where it goes

97   By the name of Acquacheta, ere running down
       To its lower bed, and after that becomes
       Known by another name at Forlì town)

Resounds from the mountain-side as it drops and drums   100
  At the fall above St Benedict's, near the ground
  Where a thousand people should settle and have their homes,

So plunging over a steep chasm we found   103
  That dark-dyed water, bellowing with a din
  Such that the ear would soon be stunned with sound.

I was wearing a rope girdle, the same wherein   106
  I once, indeed, had nursed a fleeting hope
  To catch the leopard with the painted skin;

Now, at my guide's command, I loosed the rope   109
  And took it off, and held it out to him
  All neatly wound together and coiled up.

He took it, and leaning right-hand from the brim   112
  Of the Pit, he tossed it over the precipice,
  So that it dropped well out from the rocky rim.

"Surely some strange and novel thing will rise,"   115
  Said I to myself, "to answer this strange sign
  Which thus my master's following with his eyes."

Dear me! when one's with people who divine   118
  More than they see, and read one's thoughts right through,
  How careful one should be! My guide read mine:

"Oh, it will come," said he, "and quickly too,   121
  The thing I look for; what thy fancies frame
  There in thy head will soon be in thy view."

When truth looks like a lie, a man's to blame   124
  Not to sit still, if he can, and hold his tongue,
  Or he'll only cover his innocent head with shame;

But here I can't be silent; and by the song   127
  Of this my Comedy, Reader, hear me swear,
  So may my work find favour and live long,

That I beheld through that thick murky air   130
  Come swimming up a shape most marvellously
  Strange for even the stedfast heart to bear;

As he returns, that has gone down to free   133
  The anchor from whatever's fouling it,
  Or rock or other thing hid undersea,

Spreading his arms and gathering up his feet.   136

THE IMAGES. *The Rope Girdle*. Much controversy has raged about this. For the *story*, it is perhaps enough to say that something was needed to serve as a signal, and that the story-teller pitched upon this as one of the few detachable objects which his characters might be supposed to have about them. Dante, however, goes out of his way to tell us (for the first time and rather surprisingly) that he had once hoped to catch the Leopard of Canto I with the rope. The Leopard is the image of the sins of Youth, or Incontinence; and it seems likely that the girdle has something to do with Chastity – it may, e.g., symbolize some vow of chastity which failed in its object. The Circles of Incontinence are now left behind, and the girdle is therefore available for another purpose. This time it does "catch" something – a thing variegated and gay like the Leopard, but infinitely more dangerous, brought up from the Circles of Fraud. *Allegorically*, this may suggest that when the earlier and more obvious temptations seem to have departed, they may recur, disguised and more insidious, provoked by the very safeguards originally erected against them.

NOTES. l. 2: *the water tumbling down*: The effluent of all the upper rivers pours over the precipice, and runs either under or above ground across the Eighth Circle, to reappear as Cocytus in the Ninth.

l. 8: *the fashion of whose dress*: The characteristic Florentine costume – the straight gown (*lucco*) and hood (*capocchio*) – are familiar in all the pictures of Dante.

l. 21: *formed themselves into a wheel*: These shades may not stop running even for a moment (see Canto XV. 37–9) under a dire penalty, so they adopt this method of remaining abreast of Dante.

ll. 37–45: The three persons named are all noble Florentine Guelfs. Tegghiaio and Rusticucci are among the "worthy men" after whom Dante inquired so anxiously of Ciacco (Canto VI. 78–80).

Just as the shades in Brunetto's group were all men of letters, these are all persons of political importance; it appears from Canto XV. 118 that the various groups were not allowed to mix.

l. 76: *with lifted mouth*: Here, as again in Canto XIX, Dante marks the difference between his private speech and his prophetic speech: he lifts his head as though to proclaim the doom of Florence.

ll. 79–80: The shades acclaim Dante's powers of poetic inspiration, but hint that his eloquence may some day cost him dear.

l. 84: *when thou shalt rejoice to say*, *"I was"*: i.e. when he will be glad to remember that he once had this terrible experience.

l. 95: *down to a mouth of its own*: The Acquacheta, which from Forlì

onwards is called the Montone, was in Dante's time the first river ris-
ing in the Etruscan Alps to fall direct into the Adriatic, instead of into
the Po. (See map below.)

l. 102: *where a thousand people could settle*: This may refer to a
scheme of the Conti Guidi for settling a number of their vassals in
this district. (Some commentators think Dante means that the founda-
tion of St Benedict's could have supported many more monks than
it actually did.)

l. 118: *people who divine ... one's thoughts*: cf. Cantos x. 18, xiii. 25,
etc.

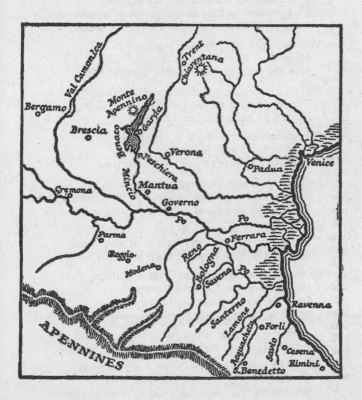

CANTO XVII

THE STORY. *Geryon, the monster called up from the Circles of Fraud, alights on the edge of the precipice. While Virgil talks to him, Dante goes to look at the shades of Usurers seated on the Burning Sand. The Poets then mount on Geryon's shoulders and are carried down over the Great Barrier to the Eighth Circle.*

"Behold the beast with stinging tail unfurled,
    That passes mountains and breaks weapon and wall;
    Behold him that pollutes the whole wide world."

4   Thus said my lord to me, and therewithal
    Made him a sign to bring him to aboard
    Near the path's end, but farther from the fall.

7   And on he came, that unclean image of Fraud,
    To ground upon the hard with head and chest,
    But not his tail, which still he left abroad.

10   His face was a just man's, it so expressed
    In every line a mild benignity;
    And like a wyvern's trunk was all the rest.

13   He had two fore-paws, shaggy arm-pit high,
    Whence breast and back and both flanks shimmered off,
    Painted with ring-knots and whorled tracery.

16   Nor Turk nor Tartar ever wrought coloured stuff
    So rainbow-trammed and broidered; never wore
    Arachne's web such dyes in warp and woof.

19   And as wherries many a time lie drawn ashore,
    Half in the water, half upon the strand,
    Or as the beaver plants him to wage war

22   At home there, in the guzzling Germans' land,
    So that worst beast of beastly kind hung clipped
    To the cliff whose curb of stone girdles the sand;

25   And all his tail quivered in the void and whipped
    Upward, twisting the venomed fork in air
    Wherewith, like a scorpion's tail, its point was tipped.

"Now," said my guide, "we must a little bear   28
    Aside, and make our way towards this same
    Malevolent brute that clings and crouches there."

So we descended on our right, and came   31
    Ten paces onward, skirting the cliff's face,
    To give a wide berth to the sand and flame,

And joined him thus; and when we reached the place,   34
    I saw some folk a little way ahead
    Sitting on the sand, near the empty edge of space;

Wherefore: "That thou mayst know," my master said,   37
    "All that there is to know about this ring,
    Go forward, view those shades and learn their state;

But do not linger too long parleying;   40
    While thou art gone I'll speak the beast, and borrow
    His sturdy back to speed our journeying."

So I went, all by myself, along the narrow   43
    Outermost brink of the seventh circle, and so
    Came where those people sat to dree their sorrow,

Which gushed from their eyes and made the sad tears flow;   46
    While this way and that they flapped their hands, for ease
    From the hot soil now, and now from the burning snow,

Behaving, in fact, exactly as one sees   49
    Dogs in the summer, scuffing with snout and paw,
    When they're eaten up with breeses and flies and fleas.

I looked at many thus scorched by the fiery flaw,   52
    And though I scanned their faces with utmost heed,
    There was no one there I recognized; but I saw

How, stamped with charge and tincture plain to read,   55
    About the neck of each a great purse hung,
    Whereon their eyes seemed still to fix and feed.

So as I went gazing upon the throng,   58
    I saw a purse display, azure on or,
    The gesture and form of a lion; further along

My eye pursued, and fell on one that bore   61
    A purse of blood-red gules, which had on it
    A goose whiter than curd; and yet one more

64   Beside him sat, who on his wallet white
        Showed a blue sow in farrow; this one cried
        To me: "What art thou doing in this pit?

67   Away! and learn (since thou hast not yet died),
        My neighbour Vitaliano shall come here
        To sit with me upon my left-hand side.

70   These Florentines keep bawling in my ear –
        I'm Paduan myself – all day they shout:
        'Let come, let come that knight without a peer

73   Who bears three goats upon his satchel stout!'"
        With that he writhed his mouth awry, and made
        A gross grimace, thrusting his tongue right out

76   Like an ox licking its nose. Then I, afraid
        To anger him who bade me make short stay
        By staying longer, left that sad brigade

79   And went to seek my guide without delay,
        And found him already mounted on the croup
        Of the fearsome beast. "Courage!" I heard him say,

82   "Such is the stair by which we have to stoop;
        I'll sit behind lest thou take harm from the tail,
        So do thou mount before; be bold now – up!"

85   Like one with the quartan fit on him, leaden-pale
        At the finger-nails already, and quaking faster
        At the mere sight of the shade, so did I quail

88   Hearing him; yet his hintings of disaster
        Shamed me to valour, as a hind may be
        Bold in the presence of an honoured master.

91   So I climbed to those dread shoulders obediently;
        "Only do" (I meant to say, but my voice somehow
        Wouldn't come out right) "please catch hold of me."

94   But he that at other times had not been slow
        In other straits to aid me, gripped me fast
        In his arms the moment I mounted, and held me now

97   Secure; and said: "Now move thee, Geryon! cast
        Thy circle wide, and wheel down gradually,
        Think of the strange new burden that thou hast."

And as a ship slips from her berth to sea   100
  Backing and backing, so did the beast begin
  To leave the bank; and when he felt quite free

He turned his tail to where his breast had been,   103
  Stretching it forth and wriggling like an eel,
  And with his paws gathered the thick air in.

No greater fear, methinks, did any feel   106
  When Phaeton dropped the chariot-reins of the sun,
  Firing the sky – we see the mark there still –

Nor when poor Icarus felt the hot wax run,   109
  Unfeathering him, and heard his father calling,
  "Alack! alack! thou fliest too high, my son!" –

Than I felt, finding myself in the void falling   112
  With nothing but air all round, nothing to show,
  No light, no sight but the sight of the beast appalling.

And on he goes, swimming and swimming slow,   115
  Round and down, though I only know it by feeling
  The wind come up and beat on my face from below.

And now I hear on the right as we spin wheeling   118
  The noise of the cataract under us horribly roaring,
  And I crane my head and look down with my senses reeling.

Then the terror of alighting seemed worse than the terror of soaring; 121
  For I heard the wails and I saw the tall fires leap,
  So that for fear I shrank back trembling and cowering.

And I saw – what before I could not see – the sweep   124
  And swoop of our downward flight through the grand woes,
  Which now drew near on every side of the deep.

And now, as a hawk that has long hung waiting does –   127
  When, without any sight at all of lure or prey,
  She makes the falconer cry: "She stoops!" and goes

Dropping down weary, then suddenly wheels away   130
  In a hundred circlings, and sets her far aloof
  From her master, sullen and scornful – so, I say,

133   Geryon set us down on the bottom rough,
            A-foot at the foot of the cliff-face that surrounded
            The chasm; and having shogged our burden off,

136   Brisker than bolt from bow away he bounded.

THE IMAGES. *Geryon*. In Greek mythology, Geryon was a monster
who was killed by Hercules. He was usually represented as hav-
ing a human form with three heads, or three conjoined bodies;
but Dante has given him a shape compounded of three natures –
human, bestial, and reptile. In the *allegory*, he is the image of
Fraud, with "the face of a just man" and an iridescence of beautiful
colour, but with the paws of a beast and a poisonous sting in his
serpent's tail – an image which scarcely calls for interpretation.
The Usurers. These, as we have seen, are the image of the Violent
against Nature and the Art derived from Nature; they sit looking
upon the ground, because they have sinned against that and against
the labour that should have cultivated its resources. The old com-
mentator Gelli observes brilliantly that the Sodomites and Usurers
are classed together because the first make sterile the natural in-
stincts which result in fertility, while the second make fertile that
which by its nature is sterile – i.e. they "make money breed".
More generally, the Usurers may be taken as types of all economic
and mechanical civilizations which multiply material luxuries at
the expense of vital necessities and have no roots in the earth or
in humanity.

NOTES. l. 12: *a wyvern's trunk*: Dante's word is *serpente*, which means
any kind of reptile, with or without legs. I have rendered it here by
"wyvern" – a fabulous creature with one pair of legs and a serpent's
tail.

l. 18: *Arachne's web*: See Glossary.

l. 21: *as the beaver plants him*: The beaver was popularly supposed
to angle for fish by sitting on the shore and dropping its tail into the
water by way of bait. In Dante's time it was commonly found further
south than it is to-day.

l. 31: *we descended on our right*: i.e. they descended from the dyke
and went along at the extreme edge of the precipice, which was of
stone (l. 24) and presumably outside the limits assigned by Providence
to the fiery rain.

ll. 55 *sqq.*: *stamped with charge and tincture*: The various devices
upon the Usurers' purses are the arms of men and families notorious

for their usury. The Paduan who speaks in ll. 64–76 is Rinaldo dei Scrovegni, and Vitaliano dei Vitaliani, whom he mentions, is also a Paduan. The rest are Florentines: one of the Gianfigliazzi family, one of the Ubbriachi, and Giovanni Buiamonte dei Becchi (the "knight without a peer").

l. 75: *a gross grimace*: to taunt Dante with the number of Florentines among the Usurers.

l. 85: *the quartan fit*: i.e. the cold fit of the quartan ague, announcing itself by premonitory shiverings.

l. 107: *Phaeton*: the son of Phoebus; he asked his father to allow him to drive the chariot of the Sun, but was unable to control the horses, so that they started out of their course, burning the track of the Milky Way across the sky, and would have set fire to the earth, but that Jupiter intervened by killing Phaeton with a thunderbolt.

l. 109: *Icarus*: was the son of Daedalus. His father made him wings, which were fastened to his shoulders with wax. Icarus flew too near the sun, so that the wax melted and he fell into the Aegean Sea and was drowned.

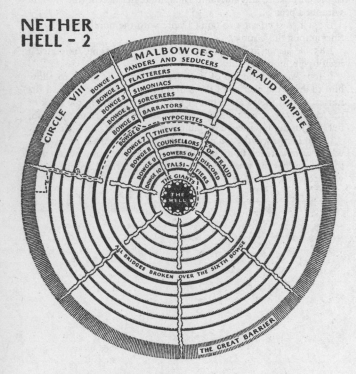

NETHER
HELL - 2

THE SINS OF THE WOLF

CANTO XVIII

THE STORY. *Dante now finds himself in the Eighth Circle (Mal-bowges), which is divided into ten trenches (bowges) containing those who committed Malicious Frauds upon mankind in general. The Poets walk along the edge of Bowge i, where Panders and Seducers run, in opposite directions, scourged by demons; and here Dante talks with Vene-dico Caccianemico of Bologna. As they cross the bridge over the bowge, they see the shade of Jason. Then they go on to the bridge over Bowge ii, where they see Thaïs, and Dante converses with another of the Flatterers who are here plunged in filth.*

There is in Hell a region that is called
   Malbowges; it is all of iron-grey stone,
   Like the huge barrier-rock with which it's walled.

Plumb in the middle of the dreadful cone   4
   There yawns a well, exceeding deep and wide,
   Whose form and fashion shall be told anon.

That which remains, then, of the foul Pit's side,   7
   Between the well and the foot of the craggy steep,
   Is a narrowing round, which ten great chasms divide.

As one may see the girding fosses deep   10
   Dug to defend a stronghold from the foe,
   Trench within trench about the castle-keep,

Such was the image here; and as men throw   13
   Their bridges outward from the fortress-wall,
   Crossing each moat to the far bank, just so

From the rock's base spring cliffs, spanning the fall   16
   Of dyke and ditch, to the central well, whose rim
   Cuts short their passage and unites them all.

When Geryon shook us off, 'twas in this grim   19
   Place that we found us; and the poet then
   Turned to the left, and I moved after him.

There, on our right, more anguished shades of men,   22
   New tortures and new torturers, I espied,
   Cramming the depth of this first bowge of ten.

25 In the bottom were naked sinners, who, our side
   The middle, moved to face us; on the other,
   Along with us, though with a swifter stride.

28 Just as the Romans, because of the great smother
   Of the Jubilee crowds, have thought of a good device
   For controlling the bridge, to make the traffic smoother,

31 So that on one side all must have their eyes
   On the Castle, and go to St Peter's; while all the throng
   On the other, towards the Mount moves contrariwise.

34 I saw horned fiends with heavy whips and strong
   Posted each side along the dismal rock,
   Who scourged their backs, and drove them on headlong.

37 Hey! how they made them skip at the first shock!
   How brisk they were to lift their legs and prance!
   Nobody stayed for the second or third stroke.

40 And as I was going, one of them caught my glance,
   And I promptly said to myself: "How now! who's he?
   Somewhere or other I've seen that countenance."

43 I stopped short, figuring out who this might be;
   And my good lord stopped too; then let me go
   Back a short way, to follow him and see.

46 The whipped shade hung his head, trying not to show
   His face; but little good he got thereby,
   For: "Hey, there! thou whose eyes are bent so low,

49 Thy name's Venedico – or thy features lie –
   Caccianemico, and I know thee well;
   What wormwood pickled such a rod," said I,

52 "To scrub thy back?" And he: "I would not tell,
   But for that voice of thine; those accents clear
   Remind me of the old life, and compel

55 My answer. I am the man who sold the fair
   Ghisola to the Marchese's lust; that's fact,
   However they tell the ugly tale up there.

58 I'm not alone here from Bologna; packed
   The place is with us; one could scarcely find
   More tongues saying 'Yep' for 'Yes' in all the tract

'Twixt Reno and Savena. Art inclined   61
   To call for proof? What witness need I join
   To the known witness of our covetous mind?"

And one of the fiends caught him a crack on the loin   64
   With the lash, even as he spoke, crying: "Away,
   Pander! there are no women here to coin!"

So to my escort I retraced my way,   67
   And soon we came, a few steps further wending,
   To where a great spur sprang from the barrier grey.

This we climbed lightly, and, right-handed bending,   70
   Crossed its rough crest, departing from that rout
   Of shades who run their circuits never-ending.

But, coming above the part that's tunnelled out   73
   To let the flogged pass under, "Stay" said he;
   "Let those who go the other way about

Strike on thine eyes; just now thou couldst not see   76
   Their faces, as we passed along the verge,
   For they were travelling the same road as we."

So from that ancient bridge we watched the surge   79
   Sweep on towards us of the wretched train
   On the farther side, chased likewise by the scourge.

"Look who comes here," my good guide said again   82
   Without my asking, "that great spirit of old,
   Who will not shed one tear for all his pain.

Is he not still right royal to behold?   85
   That's Jason, who by valour and by guile
   Bore from the Colchian strand the fleece of gold.

He took his way past Lemnos, where, short while   88
   Before, the pitiless bold women achieved
   The death of all the menfolk of their isle;

And there the young Hypsipyle received   91
   Tokens and fair false words, till, snared and shaken,
   She who deceived her fellows was deceived;

And there he left her, childing and forsaken;   94
   For those deceits he's sentenced to these woes,
   And for Medea too revenge is taken.

97   And with him every like deceiver goes.
        Suffice thee so much knowledge of this ditch
        And those whom its devouring jaws enclose."

100 Already we'd come to where the narrow ridge
        Crosses the second bank, and makes of it
        An abutment for the arch of the next bridge.

103 Here we heard people in the farther pit
        Make a loud whimpering noise, and heard them cough,
        And slap themselves with their hands, and snuffle and spit.

106 The banks were crusted with foul scum, thrown off
        By the fume, and caking there, till nose and eye
        Were vanquished with sight and reek of the noisome stuff.

109 So deep the trench, that one could not espy
        Its bed save from the topmost cliff, which makes
        The keystone of the arch. We climbed; and I,

112 Thence peering down, saw people in the lake's
        Foul bottom, plunged in dung, the which appeared
        Like human ordure running from a jakes.

115 Searching its depths, I there made out a smeared
        Head – whether clerk or lay was hard to tell,
        It was so thickly plastered with the merd.

118 "Why stand there gloating?" he began to yell,
        "Why stare at me more than the other scum?"
        "Because," said I, "if I remember well,

121 I've seen thy face, dry-headed, up at home;
        Thou art Alessio Interminei, late
        Of Lucca – so, more eagerly than on some,

124 I look on thee." He beat his pumpkin pate,
        And said: "The flatteries I spewed out apace
        With tireless tongue have sunk me to this state."

127 Then said my guide: "Before we leave the place,
        Lean out a little further, that with full
        And perfect clearness thou may'st see the face

130 Of that uncleanly and dishevelled trull
        Scratching with filthy nails, alternately
        Standing upright and crouching in the pool.

That is the harlot Thaïs. 'To what degree,'   133
   Her leman asked, 'have I earned thanks, my love?'
   'O, to a very miracle,' said she.

And having seen this, we have seen enough."   136

THE IMAGES. *The Eighth and Ninth Circles.* These are the Circles of
  Fraud or *Malice* – the "Sins of the Wolf".

Malbowges. The Eighth Circle is a huge funnel of rock, round which
run, at irregular intervals, a series of deep, narrow trenches called
"bowges" (*bolge*). From the foot of the Great Barrier at the top
to the Well which forms the neck of the funnel run immense
spurs of rock (like the ribs of an umbrella) raised above the general
contour of the slope and forming bridges over the bowges. The
maps on pp. 138 and 180 and the sketch on p. 194 show the
arrangement, except, of course, that the distances from bowge
to bowge are greater, and the rock-surfaces much steeper and
craggier, than it is possible to suggest in small diagrams.

    Malbowges is, I think, after a rather special manner, the image
of the City in corruption: the progressive disintegration of every
social relationship, personal and public. Sexuality, ecclesiastical
and civil office, language, ownership, counsel, authority, psychic
influence, and material interdependence – all the media of the
community's exchange are perverted and falsified, till nothing
remains but the descent into the final abyss where faith and trust
are wholly and for ever extinguished.

The Panders and Seducers. In the Circles of Fraud (the abuse of the
specifically human faculty of reason) the ministers of Hell are no
longer mere embodied *appetites*, but actual devils, images of the
perverted *intellect*. In the First Bowge, those who deliberately
exploited the passions of others and so drove them to serve their
own interests, are themselves driven and scourged. The image is a
sexual one; but the Panders and Seducers *allegorically* figure the
stimulation and exploitation of every kind of passion – e.g. rage
or greed – by which one may make tools of other people.

The Flatterers. These, too, exploit others by playing upon their de-
sires and fears; their especial weapon is that abuse and corruption
of language which destroys communication between mind and
mind. Here they are plunged in the slop and filth which they ex-
creted upon the world. Dante did not live to see the full develop-

ment of political propaganda, commercial advertisement, and sensational journalism, but he has prepared a place for them.

NOTES. l. 2: *Malbowges (Malebolge)*: The Italian word *bolgia* means (*a*) a trench in the ground; (*b*) a purse or pouch. *Malebolge* can thus be interpreted as either "evil pits" or "evil pouches"; and Dante puns on this double meaning (Canto XIX. 72). There is no English word which combines the two meanings; there is, however, an old word "bowge" meaning "pouch". This makes it possible to english *Malebolge* as "Malbowges" (which is, in all probability, the form which a medieval translator would have given it), and so to retain a suggestion of the pun about "pouching".

l. 6: *shall be told anon*: see Canto XXXI.

ll. 28–33: The fact that traffic control appears to Dante as a startling and ingenious novelty probably brings home to us, far more than his theology or his politics, the six hundred years which separate his times from ours. The year 1300 (the year of his vision) had been proclaimed by Pope Boniface VIII a Jubilee Year, and Rome was consequently crowded with pilgrims. For the better avoidance of congestion, the authorities (whose organization seems to have been remarkably efficient) adopted a rule of the road on the Bridge of Castello Sant' Angelo, so-called from the castle which stood at one end of it. The "Mount" at the other end was either the Janiculum or Monte Giordano. It will be noticed that in the First Bowge the rule is "keep to the right", as it is on the Continent to-day.

ll. 49–50: *Venedico Caccianemico*: a Bolognese Guelf. Ghisola was his own sister, and the Marchese was Obizzo d' Este (Canto XII. 111).

l. 51: *what wormwood*: lit.: "what has got thee into such a pickle (*pungenti salse*)?" The word *salse* means "*sauce*"; but it was also the name of a place near Bologna where criminals were flogged and executed, so that Dante's sauce is punning as well as pungent. I have done my best to supply a parallel allusion of a native and contemporary kind.

l. 57: *however they tell the ugly tale*: Presumably other, whitewashing, versions of the story, less disagreeable to the feelings of the powerful d' Este family, had been assiduously put about.

l. 60: "*yep*" (sipa) *for* "*yes*" (*sì*): an allusion to the Bolognese dialect. The Savena and Reno are rivers running west and east of Bologna.

l. 63: *the known witness of our covetous mind*: The Bolognese seem to have had a reputation for venality.

ll. 67 *sqq.*: *retraced my way*, etc.: The poets had turned left on entering Malbowges and walked along the edge of Bowge i. Then Dante

Commentaries

retraced his steps to go after Caccianemico. Now he returns to where Virgil is waiting for him, and they continue their original course till they come to where the first rock-spur runs across their path at right angles and forms a bridge over the bowge. To cross the bridge they have to *climb* on to this spur and turn right so as to walk *along* it till they are over the spot where the rock is tunnelled out to let the bowge pass below it. From this, the crest of the arch, they look down on the sinners passing below, as one would watch trains from the middle of a railway bridge (see illustration, p. 194). Once this procedure has been clearly visualized, the reader will have very little trouble with the geography of Malbowges.

l. 86: *Jason*: the Greek hero who led the Argonauts to fetch the Golden Fleece from the hands of Aietes, king of Colchis. He was helped by the king's daughter, Medea, whom he persuaded to accompany him home to Iolcus. He married her, but afterwards deserted her for Creusa.

l. 88: *Lemnos*: When the women of Lemnos killed all the men in the island because they had brought home some Thracian concubines, Hypsipyle, the daughter of King Thosa, saved her father by a ruse (l. 93). On their way to Colchis, the Argonauts landed at Lemnos and Jason seduced Hypsipyle.

ll. 100–101: *the narrow ridge*, etc.: The spur runs straight on, forming bridges over all the bowges in succession. (See map, p. 180.)

l. 122: *Alessio Interminei*: Little is known of him, except that he was a member of a White Guelf family, and was notorious for his oily manners.

l. 133: *Thaïs*: The fulsome reply here quoted really belongs, not to the historical Thaïs, the Athenian courtesan, but to a character in Terence's play, *Eunuchus*, of the same name and profession. It is mentioned by Cicero, and Dante presumably took it from him, under the impression that it was historical. Note that Thaïs is not here because she is personally a harlot; the sin which has plunged her far below the Lustful, and even below the traffickers in flesh, is the prostitution of words – the medium of *intellectual* intercourse.

CANTO XIX

THE STORY. *In the Third Bowge of Malbowges, Dante sees the Simoniacs, plunged head-downwards in holes of the rock, with flames playing upon their feet. He talks to the shade of Pope Nicholas III, who prophesies that two of his successors will come to the same bad end as himself. Dante rebukes the avarice of the Papacy.*

O Simon Magus! O disciples of his!
　　Miserable pimps and hucksters, that have sold
　　The things of God, troth-plight to righteousness,

4　Into adultery for silver and gold;
　　For you the trump must sound now – you are come
　　To the bag: the third bowge has you in its hold.

7　Already we'd mounted over the next tomb,
　　Scaling the cliff until we reached that part
　　Whence a dropped line would hit the centre plumb.

10　O most high Wisdom, how exact an art
　　Thou showest in heaven and earth and hell's profound;
　　How just thy judgments, righteous as thou art!

13　I saw the gulley, both its banks and ground,
　　Thickset with holes, all of the selfsame size,
　　Pierced through the livid stone; and each was round,

16　Seeming nor more nor less wide to mine eyes
　　Than those in my own beautiful St John,
　　Made for the priests to stand in, to baptize;

19　Whereof, not many years back, I broke up one,
　　To save a stifling youngster jammed in it;
　　And by these presents be the true facts known.

22　From each hole's mouth stuck out a sinner's feet
　　And legs up to the calf; but all the main
　　Part of the body was hid within the pit.

25　The soles of them were all on fire, whence pain
　　Made their joints quiver and thrash with such strong throes,
　　They'd have snapped withies and hempen ropes in twain.

And as on oily matter the flame flows 28
  On the outer surface only, in lambent flashes,
  So did it here, flickering from heels to toes.

"Master, who is that writhing wretch, who lashes 31
  Out harder than all the rest of his company,"
  Said I, "and whom a ruddier fire washes?"

"If thou wouldst have me carry thee down," said he, 34
  "By the lower bank, his own lips shall afford
  News of his guilt, and make him known to thee."

"Thy pleasure is my choice; for thou art lord," 37
  Said I, "and knowest I swerve not from thy will;
  Yea, knowest my heart, although I speak no word."

So to the fourth brink, and from thence downhill, 40
  Turning to the left, we clambered; and thus passed
  To the narrow and perforate bottom, my dear lord still

Loosing me not from his side, until at last 43
  He brought me close to the cleft, where he who made
  Such woeful play with his shanks was locked up fast.

"Oh thou, whoever thou art, unhappy shade, 46
  Heels over head thus planted like a stake,
  Speak if thou canst." This opening I essayed

And stood there like the friar who leans to take 49
  Confession from the treacherous murderer
  Quick-buried, who calls him back for respite's sake.

He cried aloud: "Already standing there? 52
  Art standing there already, Boniface?
  Why then, the writ has lied by many a year.

What! so soon sated with the gilded brass 55
  That nerved thee to betray and then to rape
  The Fairest among Women that ever was?"

Then I became like those who stand agape, 58
  Hearing remarks which seem to make no sense,
  Blank of retort for what seems jeer and jape.

But Virgil now broke in: "Tell him at once: 61
  'I am not who thou think'st, I am not he'";
  So I made answer in obedience.

64   At this the soul wrenched his feet furiously,
          Almost to spraining; then he sighed, and wept,
          Saying: "Why then, what dost thou ask of me?

67   Art so concerned to know my name, thou'st leapt
          These barriers just for that? Then truly know
          That the Great Mantle once my shoulders wrapped.

70   Son of the Bear was I, and thirsted so
          To advance the ursine litter that I pouched
          Coin up above, and pouched myself below.

73   Dragged down beneath my head lie others couched,
          My predecessors who simonized before,
          Now in the deep rock-fissures cowering crouched.

76   I too shall fall down thither and make one more
          When he shall come to stand here in my stead
          Whom my first sudden question took thee for.

79   But already have I been planted in this bed
          Longer with baked feet and thus topsy-turvy
          Than he shall stand flame-footed on his head;

82   For after him from the west comes one to serve ye
          With uglier acts, a lawless Shepherd indeed,
          Who'll cover us both – fit end for soul so scurvy;

85   He'll be another Jason, as we read
          The tale in Maccabees; as that controlled
          His king, so this shall bend France like a reed."

88   I know not whether I was here too bold,
          But in this strain my answer flowed out free:
          "Nay, tell me now how great a treasure of gold

91   Our Lord required of Peter, ere that He
          Committed the great Keys into his hand;
          Certes He nothing asked save 'Follow Me.'

94   Nor Peter nor the others made demand
          Of silver or gold when, in the lost soul's room,
          They chose Matthias to complete their band.

97   Then bide thou there; thou hast deserved thy doom;
          Do thou keep well those riches foully gained
          That against Charles made thee so venturesome.

And were it not that I am still constrained   100
  By veneration for the most high Keys
  Thou barest in glad life, I had not refrained

My tongue from yet more grievous words than these;   103
  Your avarice saddens the world, trampling on worth,
  Exalting the workers of iniquities.

Pastors like you the Evangelist shewed forth,   106
  Seeing her that sitteth on the floods committing
  Fornication with the kings of the earth;

Her, the seven-headed born, whose unremitting   109
  Witness uplifted in her ten horns thundered,
  While she yet pleased her Spouse with virtues fitting.

You deify silver and gold; how are you sundered   112
  In any fashion from the idolater,
  Save that he serves one god and you an hundred?

Ah, Constantine! what ills were gendered there –   115
  No, not from thy conversion, but the dower
  The first rich Pope received from thee as heir!"

While I thus chanted to him, such a sour   118
  Rage bit him – or perhaps his conscience stirred –
  He writhed and jerked his feet with all his power.

I think my guide approved of what he heard –   121
  I think so, since he patiently attended
  With a pleased smile to each outspoken word;

And after took me in both arms extended,   124
  And, when he had clasped me close upon his breast,
  Climbed back by the same road he had descended,

Nor wearied of the load that he embraced   127
  Till he had borne me to the arch's crown
  Linking the fourth and fifth banks; on that crest

He set at length his burden softly down,   130
  Soft on the steep, rough crag where even a goat
  Would find the way hard going; here was thrown

Open the view of yet another moat.   133

THE IMAGES. *The Simoniacs.* Simony is the sin of trafficking in holy things, e.g. the sale of sacraments or ecclesiastical offices. The sinners who thus made money for themselves out of what belongs to God are "pouched" in fiery pockets in the rock, head-downwards, because they reversed the proper order of things and subordinated the heavenly to the earthly. The image here is ecclesiastical: we need not, however, suppose that, *allegorically*, the traffic in holy things is confined to medieval people or even to modern clergymen. A mercenary marriage, for example, is also the sale of a sacrament.

NOTES. l. 1: *Simon Magus*: after whom the sin of Simony is named (*Acts* viii. 9–24).

l. 17: *my own beautiful St John*: The Church of St John Baptist at Florence, where Dante himself was baptized, and of which he always thinks, in his exile, with homesick affection (cf. *Para.* xvi. 25; xxv. 5). The font in the Baptistery was surrounded by holes in which the officiating priests stood, so as not to be jostled by the crowd on days when a great number of babies were being baptized at once. (There is a similar font to this day at Pisa: see sketch, p. 194.) A small boy who was playing round the font one day got jammed in one of these holes, and was extricated by Dante, who took the responsibility of breaking down the marble surround. A garbled account of this story was apparently circulated, in which Dante no doubt figured as a sacrilegious destroyer of Church property – hence his determination to put the facts on record.

l. 34: *if thou wouldst have me carry thee down*: In this bowge (as also in Bowge x) Dante is taken down on to the floor of the ditch in order to speak to the sinners. The banks are too steep for him to descend in his mortal body unassisted, so Virgil carries him. They go right over the bridge first, and then down on the *inner* and *lower* side of the bowge, which (as Dante explains in Canto XXIII) is shorter and less steep than the upper (see sketch, p. 194).

l. 46: *whoever thou art*: The shade is Nicholas III, Pope 1277–80.

l. 50: *the treacherous murderer*: By Florentine law, assassins were executed by being planted head-downwards in a hole, which was then filled up. Dante likens his own attitude to that of the attendant priest, stooping down to hear the wretch's last confession – prolonged, to postpone the fatal moment as long as possible.

l. 53: *Boniface*: The shade thinks he is being addressed by Pope Boniface VIII. There appears to have been only one hole allotted to popes, each of whom remained with his burning feet protruding till his successor arrived to thrust him down lower and take his place.

l. 54: *the writ has lied*: Nicholas, like the other damned souls, can foresee the distant future, and, knowing that Boniface is not due to die till 1303, is amazed to find him (as he supposes) there already.

l. 57: *the Fairest among Women*: i.e. the Church, the Bride of God, identified with the "Spouse of Lebanon" (*Song of Songs*, i. 8, etc.).

l. 69: *the Great Mantle*: i.e. the Papal Mantle.

l. 70: *son of the Bear*: Nicholas was one of the Orsini family – *orsa* is the Italian for "bear" – hence the pun on the "ursine" litter.

l. 83: *a lawless Shepherd*: Pope Clement V, who came from Gascony (the West). Nicholas will hold the uppermost place for twenty-three years (1280–1303), but Boniface only for eleven (from his death in 1303 to that of Clement in 1314).

l. 85: *Jason*: See 2 *Maccabees* iv. 7 *sqq*. He bribed Antiochus Epiphanes to make him High Priest and to connive at pagan practices; similarly Clement V will rise to the papacy by the influence of Philip the Fair of France.

l. 89: *in this strain* (lit.: metre): Dante is now about to speak (as in Canto XVI) in his own character of prophetic poet, and so uses this word, and again the word "chanted" (l. 118), to mark the difference between his private and his prophetic utterance.

ll. 92–3: *the great Keys ... follow Me*: *Matthew* iv. 19; *John* xxi. 19.

ll. 94–6: *nor Peter nor the others, etc.*: when the Apostles chose Matthias to fill the place of Judas (*Acts* i. 13–26).

ll. 98–9: *those riches foully gained*: Having been thwarted in his ambitious scheme to marry his niece to Charles of Anjou, king of Sicily, Nicholas joined a conspiracy against Charles, which eventually resulted in the notorious massacre known as the Sicilian Vespers.

ll. 106 *sqq*.: *the Evangelist, etc.*: see *Revelation* xvii: The figure here is of the Church corrupted by avarice: the "seven heads" and "ten horns" are usually interpreted as signifying the Seven Sacraments and the Ten Commandments. (The attribution of the seven heads to the Woman, instead of to the Beast she sits on, is probably due to a misreading of the Vulgate.)

l. 115: *Constantine*: The allusion is to the so-called "Donation of Constantine", by which the first Christian Emperor was alleged to have transferred to the Papal See his temporal sovereignty over Italy. The document is undoubtedly a forgery; it is, however, true that it was Constantine's adoption of Christianity as the official Imperial religion which made it possible for the Church to make those claims to temporal power which led, in Dante's opinion, to so many political and ecclesiastical evils.

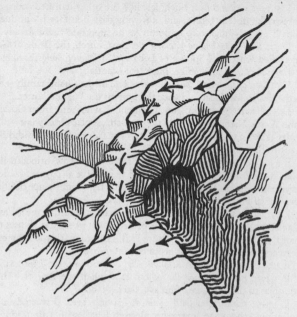

Bridge over Bowge iii, showing path taken by the poets
(Canto XIX. 34 sqq. and note)

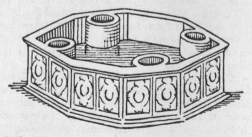

Font in the Baptistery at Pisa, showing the "holes" made for the priests
to stand in (Canto XIX. 17 sqq. and note)

CANTO XX

THE STORY. *In the Fourth Bowge of the Eighth Circle Dante sees the Sorcerers, whose heads are twisted so that they can only look behind them, and who are therefore compelled to walk backwards. Virgil tells him about the origin of Mantua. The moon is setting as the Poets leave the bowge.*

New punishments behoves me sing in this
    Twentieth canto of my first canticle,
    Which tells of spirits sunk in the Abyss.

I now stood ready to observe the full   4
    Extent of the new chasm thus laid bare,
    Drenched as it was in tears most miserable.

Through the round vale I saw folk drawing near,   7
    Weeping and silent, and at such slow pace
    As Litany processions keep, up here,

And presently, when I had dropped my gaze   10
    Lower than the head, I saw them strangely wried
    'Twixt collar-bone and chin, so that the face

Of each was turned towards his own backside,   13
    And backwards must they needs creep with their feet,
    All power of looking forward being denied.

Perhaps some kind of paralytic fit   16
    Could twist men so – such cases may have been;
    I never saw it, nor can I credit it;

And, Reader, so God give thee grace to glean   19
    Profit of my book, think if I could be left
    Dry-eyed, when close before me I had seen

Our image so distorted, so bereft   22
    Of dignity, that their eyes' brimming pools
    Spilled down to bathe the buttocks at the cleft.

Truly I wept, leaned on the pinnacles   25
    Of the hard rock; until my guide said, "Why!
    And art thou too like all the other fools?

28 Here pity, or here piety, must die
    If the other lives; who's wickeder than one
    That's agonized by God's high equity?

31 Lift up, lift up thy head, and look upon
    Him for whom once the earth gaped wide, before
    The Thebans' eyes: 'Whither wilt thou begone,

34 Amphiaraüs? Why leavest thou the war?'
    They cried; but he rushed down, and never stayed
    Till he reached Minos, that o'er such hath power.

37 See how he makes a breast of's shoulder-blade!
    Because he tried to see too far ahead,
    He now looks backward and goes retrograde.

40 And lo you there Tiresias, who shed
    His proper shape and altered every limb,
    Changing his manhood for a womanhead,

43 So that he needs must smite the second time
    His wand upon the twin and tangled snakes
    To get his cock-feathers restored to him.

46 Aruns behind his breast back-forward makes;
    In Luna's mountains, at whose foot the knave
    Who dwells down in Carrara hoes and rakes,

49 He 'mid the white bright marbles had his cave;
    There lived, and there looked out, with nought to screen
    His view of starry heaven and ocean wave.

52 And she that veils her breasts, by thee unseen,
    With her loose locks, and, viewed from where we stand,
    Has on the far side all her hairy skin

55 Was Manto, she that searched through many a land
    Ere settling in my birthplace; that's a tale
    I'd like to tell – brief patience, then, command.

58 After her father passed beyond life's pale,
    When Bacchus' city lay in bondage thralled,
    Long years she wandered up hill and down dale.

61 High in fair Italy, where Almayn's walled
    By the Alps above the Tyrol, lies and dreams
    At the mountain's foot a lake, Benaco called;

For the water here of over a thousand streams,
 Meseems, that lave Mount Apennine, running apace
 'Twixt Garda and Val Camonica, spreads and brims
64

To a mere; and there in the midst of it lies a place
 That the bishop of Verona, and those of Trent
 And Brescia, if they passed that way, might bless.
67

Peschiera sits at the circling shore's descent,
 'Gainst Bergamese and Brescians built for cover,
 A goodly keep; there all the effluent
70

Benaco's bosom cannot hold, spills over,
 Slipping and lipping down, and sliding so
 Through verdant meads, a river and a rover –
73

Benaco called no more, but Mincio,
 From where the water first sets head to run,
 Down to Governo, where it joins the Po.
76

It finds a level, ere half its course is done,
 And there stagnates and spreads to a marshy fen,
 Rank and unwholesome in the summer sun.
79

Passing that road, the cruel witch-maiden
 Found in the marsh firm tracts of land, which lay
 Untilled and uninhabited of men;
82

There, shunning human contact, did she stay
 With her familiar household; there she plied
 Her arts; there lived; there left her empty clay.
85

After, the scattered folk from far and wide
 Drew to the spot, which lay defensibly,
 Being girded by the swamp on every side.
88

O'er those dead bones they built their city, to be
 For her sake named that chose the place out thus,
 Mantua, with no further augury.
91

Far more than now it once was populous,
 Ere Casalodi's folly fell to the sword
 Of Pinamonte, who was treacherous.
94

I charge thee then, if stories go abroad,
 Other than this, of how my city grew,
 Let no such lying tales the truth defraud."
97

100 "Master, for me thy teaching is so true
And so compels belief, all other tales,"
Said I, "were dust and ash compared thereto.

103 But tell me of this great crowd that yonder trails,
If any worthy of note be now in sight;
My mind harks back to that before all else."

106 He answered: "He whose chin-beard shows so white
On his brown shoulders was a memorable
Augur in Greece, what time the land was quite

109 Emptied of males, so that you'd scarce be able
To find a cradling boy; he set the time,
With Calchas, for the cutting of the first cable;

112 Eurypylus his name; and my sublime
Tragedy sings him somewhere – thou'lt recall
The place, that hast by heart the whole long rhyme.

115 That other there, who looks so lean and small
In the flanks, was Michael Scott, who verily
Knew every trick of the art magical.

118 Lo! Guy Bonatti; lo! Asdente – he
May well wish now that he had stuck to his last,
But he repents too late; and yonder see

121 The witch-wives, miserable women who cast
Needle and spindle and shuttle away for skill
With mommets and philtres; there they all go past.

124 But come! Cain with his thorn-bush strides the sill
Of the two hemispheres; his lantern now
Already dips to the wave below Seville;

127 And yesternight the moon was full, as thou
Shouldst well remember, for throughout thy stay
In the deep wood she harmed thee not, I trow."

130 Thus he; and while he spake we went our way.

THE IMAGES. *The Sorcerers.* The primary image of sorcery here is
that of the fortune-tellers, who, having attempted to usurp God's
prerogative by prying into the future, are now so twisted that

eyes and feet face in opposite directions. More generally, there is
an image of the twisted nature of all magical art, which is a de-
formation of knowledge, and especially of the psychic powers, to
an end outside the unity of the creation in God. It is in especial
the misuse of knowledge so as to dominate environment (includ-
ing not only material things but the personalities of others) for
the benefit of the ego. Magic to-day takes many forms, ranging
from actual Satanism to attempts at "conditioning" other people
by manipulating their psyches; but even when it uses the legiti-
mate techniques of the scientist or the psychiatrist, it is distin-
guished from true science by the "twisted sight", which looks to
self instead of to God for the source and direction of its power.

NOTES. l. 22: *our image so distorted*: "Dante weeps, not now for any
personal discovery in Hell, but from sheer misery at the physical con-
tortion of the human form. ... All is gone awry; all is perverted –
and so much so that his pity has here no place." (Charles Williams:
The Figure of Beatrice, p. 136.)

l. 28: *here pity, or here piety, must die* (lit.: "Here *pietà* lives when
it is wholly dead"): the word *pietà* means both "pity" and "piety";
I have had to expand Dante's epigrammatic phrase to give the full
force of the equivoque.

ll. 29–30: *who's wickeder*, etc.: These two lines, again, have a double
significance: they may be rendered: "Who is more wicked than (the
sinner) who is (here) tormented by God's judgment?" or "Who is
more wicked than one who is tormented by (i.e. passionately pro-
tests against) God's judgment (as here exhibited)?" I have no doubt
that *both* meanings are intended. Pity and piety are here mutually
exclusive: it is necessary to acquiesce in judgment if one is not to
become (by sympathy) partaker in the sin.

The rebuke which Dante here puts into Virgil's mouth may have
been suggested by passages in the fourth-century *Apocalypse of Paul*:
"And I wept and said: Woe unto men! woe unto the sinners! ... And
the angel answered and said unto me: Wherefore weepest thou? Art
thou more merciful than the Lord God which is blessed for ever, who
hath established the judgment and left every man of his own will to
choose good and evil and to do as pleaseth him?" (M. R. James: *Apo-
cryphal New Testament*, p. 546; and see also p. 543.)

l. 34: *Amphiaraüs*: one of the "Seven against Thebes". Having
foreseen his own death, he tried to escape taking part in the war; but
his wife Eriphyle betrayed him, and while fleeing from the pursuit of
Polynices, he was swallowed up by an earthquake. (See Statius: *The-
baïd* viii. 147 *sqq.*)

l. 40: *Tiresias*: a Theban prophet. In his youth he found a pair of snakes twined together and struck them with his stick to separate them: whereupon he found himself changed into a woman, and so remained for seven years, until, having similarly separated another pair of snakes, he regained his manhood. (See Ovid: *Metam*. iii.)

l. 46: *Aruns*: an Etruscan augur (see Lucan: *Pharsalia* i. 584–8). Luna (Luni), near the mouth of the Macra, is called by Pliny the first city in Etruria. The mountains of Carrara, above Luna, are famous for their white marble.

l. 55: *Manto*: the daughter of Tiresias. The founding of Mantua by Manto is mentioned in *Aeneid* x. 198–200.

l. 59: *Bacchus' city*: Thebes, the legendary birthplace of Bacchus.

l. 61: *Almayn*: Germany.

l. 63: *Benaco*: now called Lake Garda.

l. 15: *Mount Apennine*: not the Apennine range, but a single mountain. (See map, p. 173.)

l. 68: *the bishop of Verona … Trent and Brescia*: the three dioceses met on an island in the lake.

l. 95: *Casalodi*: In 1272 the Brescian counts of Casalodi who were Guelfs, seized Mantua. Their rule was greatly resented; and Alberto di Casalodi foolishly let himself be persuaded by Pinamonte dei Buonaccorsi, a Mantuan, to appease the people by banishing all the unpopular nobles of his party. As soon as he had done so, Pinamonte put himself at the head of the citizens, and drove out the Casalodi with great slaughter.

l. 109: *emptied of males*: i.e. when all the Greeks had departed to the siege of Troy. Eurypylus is associated with Calchas in *Aen*. ii. 110 *sqq*. (See Glossary: "Eurypylus".)

l. 116: *Michael Scott*: the famous wizard of Balwearie mentioned in Scott's *Lay of the Last Minstrel*.

l. 118: *Bonatti … Asdente*: Bonatti of Forlì was an astrologer; Asdente, a shoemaker of Parma, who set up as a soothsayer.

l. 123: *mommets and philtres*: waxen images and magic potions made of herbs. Here Dante touches on magical arts even more dangerous than soothsaying; for the philtres were used to obtain power over the wills of others, and the waxen images were pierced with nails or melted before the fire to bring about the death of the victim.

l. 124: *Cain with his thorn-bush*: i.e. the Man in the Moon (cf. Shakespeare: *M.N.D.* iii. 1; v. 1, where Moon appears with a lantern and a thorn-bush). The Moon is now setting; i.e. it is about 6.52 A.M. on Saturday.

CANTO XXI

THE STORY. *In the Fifth Bowge, Barrators, who made money by trafficking in public offices, are plunged in Boiling Pitch, guarded by demons with sharp hooks. Virgil crosses the bridge and goes down to parley with the demons. Belzecue, the chief demon, says that the spur of rock which the Poets have been following was broken by an earthquake (at the moment of Christ's entry into Hell) and no longer bridges the Sixth Bowge; but he will give them an escort of ten demons to "see them safe as far as the bridge which is still unbroken". In this disagreeable company, Virgil and Dante set off along the lower brink of the Bowge.*

And so we passed along from bridge to bridge,
　　With other talk, whereof my Comedy
　Cares not to tell, until we topped the ridge;

And there we stayed our steps awhile, to see　　　　4
　　Malbowges' next ravine, and wailings all
　　Vain: and most marvellous dark it seemed to be.

For as at Venice, in the Arsenal　　　　　　　　7
　　In winter-time, they boil the gummy pitch
　　To caulk such ships as need an overhaul,

Now that they cannot sail – instead of which　　　10
　　One builds him a new boat, one toils to plug
　　Seams strained by many a voyage, others stitch

Canvas to patch a tattered jib or lug,　　　　　13
　　Hammer at the prow, hammer at the stern, or twine
　　Ropes, or shave oars, refit and make all snug –

So, not by fire, but by the art divine,　　　　16
　　A thick pitch boiled down there, spattering the brink
　　With viscous glue; I saw this, but therein

Nothing; only great bubbles black as ink　　　　19
　　Would rise and burst there; or the seething tide
　　Heave up all over, and settle again, and sink.

And while I stood intent to gaze, my guide,　　　22
　　Suddenly crying to me, "Look out! look out!"
　　Caught me where I stood, and pulled me to his side.

25 O then I turned, as one who turns about,
Longing to see the thing he has to shun,
Dares not, and dares, and, dashed with hideous doubt,

28 Casts a look back and still goes fleeing on;
And there behind us I beheld a grim
Black fiend come over the rock-ridge at a run.

31 Wow! what a grisly look he had on him!
How fierce his rush! And, skimming with spread wing,
How swift of foot he seemed! how light of limb!

34 On high-hunched shoulders he was carrying
A wretched sinner, hoist by haunch and hip,
Clutching each ankle by the sinew-string.

37 "Bridge ho!" he bawled, "Our own Hellrakership!
Here's an alderman of St Zita's coming down;
Go souse him, while I make another trip

40 For more; they're barrators all in that good town –
Except Bonturo, hey? – I've packed it stiff
With fellows who'd swear black's white for half-a-crown."

43 He tossed him in, and over the flinty cliff
Wheeled off; and never did mastiff run so hot
And hard on the trail, unleashed to follow a thief.

46 Down bobbed the sinner, then up in a writhing knot;
But the fiends beneath the archway yelled as he rose up:
"No Sacred Face will help thee here! it's not

49 A Serchio bathing-party! Now then, toes up
And dive!'Ware hooks! To save thyself a jabbing,
Stay in the pitch, nor dare to poke thy nose up!"

52 Then, with a hundred prongs clawing and stabbing:
"Go cut thy capers! Try down there to do
Subsurface deals and secret money-grabbing!"

55 Just so, cooks make their scullions prod the stew
With forks, to thrust the flesh well down within
The cauldron, lest it float above the brew.

58 Then the good master: "Better not be seen,"
Said he; "so crouch well down in some embrasure
Behind a crag, to serve thee for a screen;

And whatsoever outrage or displeasure   61
   They do to me, fear nothing; I have faced
   Frays of this sort before, and have their measure."

He passed the bridgehead then; but when he placed   64
   His foot on the sixth bank, good need had he
   Of a bold front; for with such furious haste

And concentrated venom of savagery   67
   As dogs rush out upon some harmless tramp
   Who stops, alarmed, to falter out his plea,

Out dashed the demons lurking under the ramp,   70
   Each flourishing in his face a hideous hook;
   But he: "Hands off! ere grappling-iron or cramp

Touch me, send one to hear me speak; then look   73
   You take good counsel, before any of you
   Try to dispose of me by hook or crook!"

This checked them; and they cried: "Send Belzecue!"   76
   And one moved forward, snarling as he went:
   "What good does he imagine this will do?"

"Dost thou think, Belzecue, that I had bent   79
   My footsteps thus far hither," the master said,
   "Safe against all your harms, were I not sent

By will divine, by fates propitious led?   82
   Let me pass on; 'tis willed in Heaven that I
   Should guide another by this pathway dread."

At this the fiend, crestfallen utterly,   85
   Let fall his grappling-iron at his feet,
   Crying to the rest: "Strike not! he must go by."

My guide called up: "Thou, cowering there discreet,   88
   Hid mousey-mouse among the splintery, cracked
   Crags of the bridge, come down! all's safe for it."

I rose and ran to him, and sure I slacked   91
   Not speed; for the fiends pressed forward, and grave doubt
   Seized me, for fear they might not keep the pact.

So I once saw the footmen, who marched out   94
   Under treaty from Caprona, look and feel
   Nervous, with all their foes ringed round about.

97 I pressed close to my guide from head to heel,
   Cringing, and keeping a sharp eye upon
   Their looks, which were by no means amiable.

100 They lowered their hooks to the ready, and, "Just for fun,"
   Says one, "shall I tickle his rump for him?" "Yes, try it,"
   Says another, "nick him and prick him, boy – go on!"

103 But the other devil, the one that stood in diet
   Still with my escort, turned him instant round,
   Saying: "Now Scaramallion! quiet, quiet!"

106 And then to us: "By this cliff 'twill be found
   Impossible to proceed, for the sixth arch
   Lies at the bottom, shattered to the ground.

109 If you're determined to pursue your march,
   Follow the bank; a span quite free from block
   Or fall, lies handy to reward your search;

112 But this – why, yesterday, five hours by the clock
   From now, 'twas just twelve hundred, sixty and six
   Years since the road was rent by earthquake shock.

115 I'm sending a squad your way, to fork and fix
   Any rash soul who may be taking the air;
   Why not go with them? They will play no tricks.

118 Stand forward, Hacklespur and Hellkin there!"
   He then began, "and Harrowhound as well,
   And your decurion shall be Barbiger;

121 Let Libbicock go too, and Dragonel,
   Guttlehog of the tusks, and Grabbersnitch
   And raving Rubicant and Farfarel

124 Take a good look all round the boiling pitch;
   See these two safe, as far as to the spit
   That runs unbroken on from ditch to ditch."

127 "Sir, I don't like the looks of this one bit,"
   Said I; "no escort, please; let's go alone,
   If thou know'st how – for I've no stomach to it!

130 Where is thy wonted caution? Ugh! they frown,
   They grind their teeth – dost thou not see them? Lo,
   How they threat mischief, with their brows drawn down!"

But he: "I'd have thee firmer-minded; no,   133
    Let them go grind and gnash their teeth to suit
    Their mood; 'tis the broiled souls they glare at so."

They by the left bank wheeling chose their route;   136
    But first in signal to their captain each
    Thrust out his tongue; and, taking the salute,

He promptly made a bugle of his breech.   139

THE IMAGES. *The Barrators and the Pitch.* The Barrators are to the
    City what the Simoniacs are to the Church: they make profit out
    of the trust reposed in them by the community; and what they
    sell is justice. As the Simoniacs are imbedded in the burning rock,
    so these are plunged beneath the black and boiling stream, for
    their dealings were secret. Money stuck to their fingers: so now
    the defilement of the pitch sticks fast to them.

NOTES. *Cantos XXI and XXII.* The mood of these two cantos – a mix-
    ture of savage satire and tearing high spirits – is unlike anything else
    in the *Comedy*, and is a little disconcerting to the more solemn-minded
    of Dante's admirers. Artistically, this grim burlesque is of great value
    as an interlude in the ever-deepening descent from horror to horror;
    but Dante had also personal reasons for letting his pen rip at this point,
    since an accusation of barratry was the pretext upon which he was
    banished from Florence. (I have translated rather more freely here
    than elsewhere, in order to keep up the pace of the original.)

    l. 7: *at Venice, in the Arsenal*: Venice, in the Middle Ages, was a
    great sea-power, and the old Arsenal, built in 1104, was one of the
    most important shipyards in Europe.

    l. 35: *a wretched sinner*: One old commentator identifies him as an
    alderman called Martino Bottaio, who died in 1300.

    l. 37: *our own Hellrakership* (lit.: *Malebranche* of our bridge): Dante
    calls the demons in this bowge *Malebranche* = Evil Claws, which I
    have rendered "Hellrakers".

    l. 38: *St Zita's*: i.e. Lucca, whose patron saint was St Zita.

    l. 41: *except Bonturo*: This is sarcasm, since Bonturo Dati was
    especially notorious for his barratry.

    l. 48: *Sacred Face*: an ancient wooden figure of Christ, revered at
    Lucca, and invoked in time of need.

l. 49: *Serchio*: a river near Lucca.

l. 65: *the sixth bank*: i.e. the lower bank of the Fifth Bowge, which is also the upper bank of the Sixth.

l. 76: *Belzecue*: In Italian, *Malacoda* = Evil Tail. The names of the demons in the Fifth Bowge are thought by some to contain allusions to various Florentine officials who were Dante's enemies; but even if they do, the average English reader cannot get much fun out of it at this time of day. I have therefore englished most of the names for the greater convenience of rhyme and metre. The original name of each devil will be found in the Glossary.

l. 82: *by will divine, by fates propitious*: Notice once again the double terminology, as in Canto IX. 94–7 and Canto XIV. 52 and 70.

l. 88: *cowering there*: Dante's comic terror in this bowge is, characteristically, a double-edged gibe at himself and his accusers.

l. 95: *Caprona*: This Pisan fortress was taken by the Tuscan Guelfs in 1289, and Dante, apparently, took part in the operation.

ll. 112–14: *five hours by the clock from now*, etc.: The earthquake is that which followed the Crucifixion and is mentioned by Virgil as having heralded Christ's entry into Hell and caused the landslide on the cliff between the Sixth and Seventh Circles (Canto XII. 34–45). According to the Synoptists, it took place at the ninth hour (3 P.M.); this would make the conversation with Belzecue take place five hours earlier, i.e. at 10 A.M. (But see Appendix p. 297.)

l. 113: *twelve hundred, sixty and six*: The Crucifixion is reckoned as having taken place A.D. 34.

l. 125–6: *safe, as far as to the spit that runs unbroken*: As will be seen later (Canto XXIII), the safe-conduct is less valuable than it might appear, and the malicious grimaces of the demons show that they have taken these instructions in the spirit in which they were meant.

CANTO XXII

THE STORY. *As the party proceeds along the bank of the bowge, the devils fork a Barrator up out of the pitch, who tells the Poets who he is and mentions the names of some of his fellow-sinners. By a trick he eludes the devils who are preparing to tear him to pieces; whereupon his captors quarrel among themselves and two of them fall into the pitch.*

I have seen horsemen moving camp, and beating
   The muster and assault, seen troops advancing,
   And sometimes with uncommon haste retreating,

Seen forays in your land, and coursers prancing,   4
   O Aretines! and I've beheld some grandish
   Tilts run and tourneys fought, with banners dancing,

And fife and drum, and signal-flares a-brandish   7
   From towers, and cars with tintinnabulation
   Of bells, and things both native and outlandish;

But to so strange a trumpet's proclamation   10
   I ne'er saw move or infantry or cavalry,
   Or ship by sea-mark or by constellation.

Well, off we started with that bunch of devilry;   13
   Queer company – but there! "with saints at church,
   And at the inn with roisterers and revelry".

Meanwhile, my eyes were wholly bent to search   16
   The pitch, to learn the custom of that moat
   And those who wallowed in the scald and smirch.

And very like the dolphins, when they float   19
   Hump-backed, to warn poor seamen of the heightening
   Storm, that they may prepare to save the boat,

So now and then, to get a little slightening   22
   Of pain, some miserable wretch would hulk
   His back up, and pop down again like lightning.

Others lay round about like frogs, that skulk   25
   At the stream's edge, just noses out of shelter,
   The water hiding all their limbs and bulk, –

28   Till Barbiger arrived; then, in a welter
        Of fear, with unanimity quite clannish,
        They shot into the hot-pot helter-skelter.

31   I saw – and from my memory cannot banish
        The horrid thrill – one soul remain a squatter,
        As one frog will at times, when others vanish;

34   And Grabbersnitch, the nearest truant-spotter,
        Hooked him by the clogged hair, and up he came,
        Looking to me exactly like an otter.

37   (I could pick all the fiends out now by name;
        I'd watched while they were chosen, noted how
        They called each other, and made sure of them.)

40   "Claws, claws there, Rubicant! we've got him now!
        Worry him, worry him, flay him high and low!"
        Yelled all the demon-guardians of the slough.

43   "O master, if thou canst, contrive to know
        Who is this wretched criminal," I said,
        "Thus fallen into the clutches of the foe."

46   My guide drew near to him thus hard-bested,
        And asked him whence he came; he said: "Navarre;
        In that same kingdom was I born and bred.

49   My mother placed me servant to a peer,
        For he that got me was a ribald knave,
        A spendthrift of himself and of his gear.

52   Next, I was good King Tibbald's man, and gave
        My mind to jobbery; now, I job no more,
        But foot the bill this hotter side the grave."

55   Here Guttlehog, who, like a savage boar,
        Carried great tushes either side his jaws,
        Let the wretch feel how deep the fangs could score.

58   'Twas cat and mouse – ten cats with cruel claws!
        But Barbiger, with both arms seizing him,
        Cried: "Back! I'll do the grabbing!" In the pause

61   He leered round at my lord, and said with grim
        Relish: "Any further questions? Ask away!
        Quick – before some one tears him limb from limb!"

So then my guide: "Name if thou canst, I pray,　　64
　　Some Latian rogues among these tarry throngs."
　　And he: "But now, I left one such – or, nay,

One that to a near-neighbouring isle belongs;　　67
　　Would I lay hid beside him still! – I'd mock
　　At threatening claws, and ugly tusks, and prongs."

"We've stood too much of this!" cried Libbicock,　　70
　　And from his arm, making a sudden snatch,
　　Ripped off a sinewy gobbet with his hook.

Then Dragonel was fain to have a catch　　73
　　At the dangling legs; which made their leader spin
　　Round with ferocious haste, and looks to match.

When they were somewhat calmer, and the din　　76
　　Died down, my guide, turning to him who still
　　Stared upon his own mangled flesh and skin,

Asked promptly: "Who was he, whom in an ill　　79
　　Hour thou didst quit, thou sayest, to seek the brink?"
　　"'Twas Fra Gomita, the ineffable

Scamp of Gallura, corruption's very sink,"　　82
　　Said he; "he held his lord's foes in his power,
　　And earned their praise – earned it right well, I think;

'The golden key,' says he, 'undid the door';　　85
　　But all his jobs were jobbed; no petty jobbery
　　For him – he was a sovereign barrator.

With him's Don Michael Zanche, artist in robbery　　88
　　From Logodor'; their tongues, going clack-clack-clack
　　About Sardinia, kick up a ceaseless bobbery.

O look! that fiend there grinning at me! alack,　　91
　　He frightens me! – I've plenty more to tell,
　　But sure he'll flay my scalp or skin my back!"

Then their huge prefect turned on Farfarel,　　94
　　Whose eyes were rolling in the act to pounce,
　　Crying: "Hop off, thou filthy bird of hell!"

"Are there no souls from other lands or towns,"　　97
　　The quivering wretch went on, "you'd like to see?
　　Tuscans? or Lombards? I'll get them here at once.

100   Let but the Hellrakers draw back a wee
          Bit from the shore, so that they need not fear
          Reprisals, and for one poor little me

103   I'll fetch up seven, just sitting quietly here
          And whistling, as it is our wont to do
          When one pops out and finds the coast is clear."

106   Harrowhound shook his head and scornful threw
          His snout up: "That's a dirty trick," said he,
          "He's thought of, to get back beneath the brew."

109   "Trickster I am, and what a trick 'twill be,"
          Said he who had every dodge at his command,
          "Luring my neighbours to worse misery!"

112   Here Hellkin got completely out of hand
          And burst out: "If thou stoop to hit the ditch
          I need not gallop after thee by land,

115   I have my wings to soar above the pitch;
          We'll leave the crest and hide behind the bank –
          Are ten heads best, or one? We'll show thee which!"

118   New sport, good Reader! hear this merry prank!
          The silly demons turned their eyes away –
          And he who first held back now led the rank.

121   The Navarrese chose well the time to play;
          He dug his toes in hard, then, quick as thought,
          Dived; and so baulked the sportsmen of their prey.

124   Then all were stung with guilt, and he who taught
          The rest to play the fool was angriest;
          He swooped off to pursue him, shouting: "Caught!"

127   But all in vain; no wings could fly so fast
          As fear; the quarry plunged; the hunter rose,
          Skimming the surface with uplifted breast.

130   Just as the wild-duck, with the falcon close
          Upon her, all of a sudden dives down quick,
          And up he skirrs again, foiled and morose.

133   Hacklespur, who was furious at the trick,
          Went rushing after, hoping very much
          The sinner would escape, that he might pick

A quarrel; so when he saw the jobber touch | 136
Surface and vanish, he turned his claws on his brother-
Fiend, and they grappled over the ditch in a clutch.

But Hellkin was a hawk as good as another | 139
To fight back tooth and nail; so, scratching and chewing,
They both dropped down plumb in the boiling smother.

The heat at once unlocked them; their undoing | 142
Came when they tried to rise; they struggled, fluttering
With helpless wings clogged stiff by the tarry glueing.

Barbiger, who with the others stood there spluttering | 145
With rage, sent four across to the farthermost
Bank with their draghooks; so the band flew scuttering

This side and that, each to some vantage-post | 148
Whence they could reach their drags to the pair half-strangled
And baked already beneath the scummy crust;

And there we left them, floundering and entangled. | 151

THE IMAGES. *The Tricked and Quarrelling Demons.* Though it may
present an appearance of solidarity, Satan's kingdom is divided
against itself and cannot stand, for it has no true order, and fear is
its only discipline. Moreover, in the long run, the devil is a fool:
trickery preys on trickery and cruelty on cruelty.

NOTES. ll. 1 *sqq.*: *I have seen horsemen*, etc.: The Battle of Campaldino
(1289) was fought between the Guelfs (headed by Florence) and the
Ghibellines (headed by Arezzo). The Florentine forces, among whom
Dante was, were thrown into confusion by the first charge of the
Aretines; but the Guelfs rallied and eventually defeated the Ghibellines
with great slaughter, and the rest of the campaign was fought on Are-
tine territory.

l. 6: *tilts run and tourneys fought*: A *tilt* was an encounter between
two knights across a barrier; a *tourney* or *tournament* was an "all-in"
encounter between equal parties of knights in open field.

l. 8: *cars with tintinnabulation of bells*: In Dante's time, each Italian
city had a car (*carroccio*), or war-chariot. It was gaily painted, drawn
by oxen, and furnished with a bell, and served as a rallying-point in
battle.

ll. 19–21: *dolphins*: This common belief about dolphins is mentioned in a popular Italian version of Brunetto Latini's *Thesaurus*, and elsewhere.

l. 44: *who is this wretched criminal*: Tradition says that this is a certain Spaniard, named Ciampolo, or Gian Polo.

l. 52: *King Tibbald*: Teobaldo II (Count Thibaut V of Champagne), king of Navarre (1253–70).

l. 65: *Latian*: a native of Lower Italy. (Dante never uses the word "Italian", but speaks only of Tuscans, Lombards, etc., in the north and Latians in the south.)

l. 67: *a near-neighbouring isle*: Sardinia.

l. 81: *Fra Gomita*: Sardinia at that time belonged to Pisa, and Gomita was judge of the province of Gallura, under Nino Visconti of Pisa, who put up with his peculations until he found that he had been bribed to let some prisoners escape, whereupon he had him hanged.

l. 88: *Michael Zanche*: Vicar of Logodoro under Enzo, king of Sardinia, who was a natural son of Frederick II. About 1290 he was murdered by his son-in-law, Branca d' Oria, whom we shall hear of in Canto XXXIII. 134–47.

CANTO XXIII

THE STORY. *The angry demons pursue the Poets, who are forced to escape by scrambling down the upper bank of Bowge vi. Here they find the Hypocrites, walking in Gilded Cloaks lined with lead. They talk to two Jovial Friars from Bologna, and see the shade of Caiaphas crucified upon the ground.*

Silent, apart, companionless we went,
   One going on before and one behind,
   Like Friars Minor on a journey bent.

And Aesop's fable came into my mind   4
   As I was pondering on the late affray –
   I mean the frog-and-mouse one; for you'll find

That if with an attentive mind you lay   6
   Their heads and tails together, the two things
   Are just as much alike as Yes and Yea.

And, as one fancy from another springs   10
   Sometimes, this started a new train of thought
   Which doubled my first fears and flutterings.

I argued thus: "These demons have been brought,   13
   Through us, to a most mortifying plight –
   Tricked, knocked about, made fools of, set at naught;

If rage be added to their natural spite   16
   They'll come for us, pursuing on our heel
   Like greyhounds on the hare, teeth bared to bite."

I kept on looking backward, and could feel   19
   My hair already bristling on my head;
   "Master," said I, "unless thou canst conceal

Thyself and me, I'm very much afraid   22
   Of the Hellrakers; they're after us; I see
   And imagine it so, I can hear them now," I said.

"If I were made of looking-glass," said he,   25
   "My outward image scarce could mirror thine
   So jump as I mirror thine image inwardly.

28   Even now thy mind came entering into mine,
          Its living likeness both in act and face;
          So to one single purpose we'll combine

31   The two; if on our right-hand side this place
          So slopes that we can manage to descend
          To the next bowge, we'll flee the imagined chase."

34   Thus he resolved. He'd hardly made an end,
          When lo! I saw them, close at hand, and making
          To seize us, swooping on wide wings careened.

37   Then my master caught me up, like a mother, waking
          To the roar and crackle of fire, who sees the flare,
          And snatches her child from the cradle and runs, taking

40   More thought for him than herself, and will not spare
          A moment even so much as to cast a shift
          About her body, but flees naked and bare;

43   And over the flinty ridge of the great rift
          He slithered and slid with his back to the hanging spill
          Of the rock that walls one side of the next cleft.

46   Never yet did water run to the mill
          So swift and sure, where the head-race rushes on
          Through the narrow sluice to hit the floats of the wheel,

49   As down that bank my master went at a run,
          Carrying me off, hugged closely to his breast,
          Truly not like a comrade, but a son.

52   And his foot had scarce touched bottom, when on the crest
          Above us, there they were! But he, at large
          In the other chasm, could set his fears at rest;

55   For that high provident Will which gave them charge
          Over the fifth moat, curbs them with constraint,
          So that they have no power to pass its verge.

58   And now we saw a people decked with paint,
          Who trod their circling way with tear and groan
          And slow, slow steps, seeming subdued and faint.

61   They all wore cloaks, with deep hoods forward thrown
          Over their eyes, and shaped in fashion quite
          Like the great cowls the monks wear at Cologne;

Outwardly they were gilded dazzling-bright,　　　　　64
　　But all within was lead, and, weighed thereby,
　　King Frederick's copes would have seemed feather-light.

O weary mantle for eternity!　　　　　67
　　Once more we turned to the left, and by their side
　　Paced on, intent upon their mournful cry.

But crushed 'neath that vast load those sad folk plied　　　70
　　Such slow feet that abreast of us we found
　　Fresh company with every changing stride.

Wherefore: "Try now to find some soul renowned　　　73
　　In name or deed, and as we forward fare,"
　　I begged my guide, "pray cast thine eyes around."

And, hearing the Tuscan tongue, some one, somewhere　　　76
　　Behind us cried: "Stay, stay now! slack your speed,
　　You two that run so fast through this dark air,

And I, maybe, can furnish what you need."　　　79
　　My guide looked round, and then to me said: "Good!
　　Wait here, and then at his own pace proceed."

I stopped, and saw two toiling on, who showed,　　　82
　　By looks, much haste of mind to get beside me,
　　Though cumbered by the great load and strait road.

But when at length they reached us, then they eyed me　　　85
　　Askance for a long time before they spoke;
　　Then turned to each other, saying, while still they spied me:

"That one seems living – his throat moves to the stroke　　　88
　　Of the breath and the blood; besides, if they are dead,
　　What favour exempts them from the heavy cloak?"

And then to me: "O Tuscan, strangely led　　　91
　　To the sad college of hypocrites, do not scorn
　　To tell us who thou art," the spirits said.

I answered them: "I was bred up and born　　　94
　　In the great city on Arno's lovely stream,
　　And wear the body that I've always worn.

But who are you, whose cheeks are seen to teem　　　97
　　Such distillation of grief? What comfortless
　　Garments of guilt upon your shoulders gleam?"

100 And one replied: "Our orange-gilded dress
Is leaden, and so heavy that its weight
Wrings out these creakings from the balances.

103 Two Jovial Friars were we; our city-state
Bologna; Catalano was my name,
His, Loderingo; we were designate

106 By thine own city, to keep peace and tame
Faction, as one sole judge is wont to do;
What peace we kept, Gardingo can proclaim."

109 "Friars," I began, "the miseries that you –"
But broke off short, seeing one lie crucified
There on the ground, with three stakes stricken through;

112 Who, when he saw me, writhed himself, and sighed
Most bitterly in his beard; and seeing me make
A questioning sign, Friar Catalan replied:

115 "He thou dost gaze on, pierced by the triple stake,
Counselled the Pharisees 'twas expedient
One man should suffer for the people's sake.

118 Naked, transverse, barring the road's extent,
He lies; and all who pass, with all their load
Must tread him down; such is his punishment.

121 In this same ditch lie stretched in this same mode
His father-in-law, and all the Sanhedrim
Whose counsel sowed for the Jews the seed of blood."

124 Then I saw Virgil stand and marvel at him
Thus racked for ever on the shameful cross
In the everlasting exile. He to them

127 Turning him, then addressed the Friars thus:
"May it so please you, if your rule permit,
To tell us if, on this right side the fosse,

130 Be any gap to take us out of it,
That we need not compel any of the Black
Angels to extricate us from this pit."

133 "Nearer than thou hop'st," the Friar answered back,
"There lies a rock, part of the mighty spur
That springs from the great wall, and makes a track

O'er all the cruel moats save this, for here   136
 The arch is down; but you could scale the rock,
 Whose ruins are piled from the floor to the barrier."

My guide stood with bent head and downward look   139
 Awhile; then said: "He gave us bad advice,
 Who spears the sinners yonder with his hook."

And the Friar: "I heard the devil's iniquities   142
 Much canvassed at Bologna; among the rest
 'Twas said, he was a liar and father of lies."

My guide with raking steps strode off in haste,   145
 Troubled in his looks, and showing some small heat
 Of anger; so I left those spirits oppressed,

Following in the prints of the belovèd feet.   148

THE IMAGES. *The Leaden Cloaks.* The image of Hypocrisy, present-
 ing a brilliant show and weighing like lead so as to make spiritual
 progress impossible, scarcely needs interpretation.

Caiaphas. This image lends itself peculiarly well to Dante's fourfold
 system of interpretation (see Introduction, p. 14). (1) *Literal:* the
 punishment of Caiaphas after death; (2) *Allegorical:* the condition
 of the Jews in this world, being identified with the Image they
 rejected and the suffering they inflicted – "crucified for ever in the
 eternal exile"; (3) *Moral:* the condition in this life of the man who
 sacrifices his inner truth to expediency (e.g. his true vocation to
 money-making, or his true love to a politic alliance), and to
 whom the rejected good becomes at once a heaven from which
 he is exiled and a rack on which he suffers; (4) *Anagogical:* the
 state, here and hereafter, of the soul which rejects God, and which
 can know God only as wrath and terror, while at the same time
 it suffers the agony of eternal separation from God, who is its only
 true good.

NOTES. l. 3: *Friars Minor:* the Franciscans.

 l. 4: *Aesop's fable:* A frog offers to carry a mouse across a pond, tied
to its leg. Half-way over, the frog treacherously dives, drowning the
mouse. A hawk swoops down and devours both. The fable is found
in most of the medieval collections attributed to Aesop. In one version
the mouse escapes, and this may have been the one Dante had in mind.

The mouse = Ciampolo; the frog = Hellkin; the hawk = Hacklespur.

l. 9: *Yes and Yea*: In the Italian *mo* and *issa*, two words both meaning "now".

l. 25: *looking-glass*: lit.: "leaded glass", mirrors being then made with a backing of lead. Virgil is saying that his own feelings are a perfect reflection of Dante's, both in face (appearance of alarm) and act (recoil from danger); so they will combine their fears and form a common resolution: viz. flight.

l. 31: *on our right-hand side*: They had already crossed the intervening space and were walking along the upper edge of Bowge vi.

l. 54: *the other chasm*: i.e. the Sixth Bowge.

l. 58: *decked with paint*: Some commentators think this means that the faces of the hypocrites were "made up"; but since this could hardly have been apparent to Dante at the first glance, because of the deep hoods they wore, it seems more likely that it refers to the brilliant colour of their cloaks (l. 64).

l. 63: *at Cologne*: Several old commentators relate a story that the monks of Cologne once grew so arrogant that they made formal request to the Pope to be allowed to wear scarlet robes, with silver girdles and spurs. To punish their pride, the Pope commanded, on the contrary, that they should wear especially ample robes of very common material. Some editors for "Cologne" read "Cluny".

l. 66: *King Frederick's copes*: Frederick II was said to have punished traitors by wrapping them in lead and throwing them into a hot cauldron.

l. 88: *his throat moves*: We may notice the various ways by which Dante's living body is distinguished from the apparent bodies of the shades: in the twilight of Hell his weight sinks Phlegyas' boat "deeper than her wont" (Canto VIII) and dislodges stones (Canto XII); his throat moves when he breathes and speaks, as here; a blow from his foot surprises the souls by its heaviness (Canto XXXII. 90); in Purgatory, where the sun shines, he alone casts a shadow (*Purg.* iii. 16 *sqq.*, etc.).

l. 92: *college of hypocrites*: The word "college" here means only "company".

l. 95: *the great city on Arno's lovely stream*: i.e. Florence.

l. 103: *Jovial Friars*: the nickname of the *Ordo militiae beatae Mariae*, a religious order of knights founded in 1261. Its objects were to promote reconciliation, protect widows and poor persons, etc.; but its rule was so lax that before long it became a scandal and was suppressed.

ll. 105–8: *designate by thine own city*: Catalano de' Malavolti (a Guelf)

Commentaries

and Loderingo di Landolo (a Ghibelline), both from Bologna, were in 1266 appointed jointly to the office of *podesta* of Florence, in the hope that they might keep the peace and administer justice impartially; but all that came of their administration was a particularly savage anti-Ghibelline rising, in which the palaces of the Uberti, in the Gardingo, were sacked and burned.

l. 116: *counselled the Pharisees: John* xi. 49, 50.

l. 122: *his father-in-law*: Annas. (*John* xviii. 13.)

l. 124: *I saw Virgil ... marvel at him*: Virgil had not, of course, seen Caiaphas on his previous journey through Hell (see Canto IX. 19–30), which was made before the time of Christ.

l. 140: *he gave us bad advise*: Belzecue (Canto XXI. 123–6) had bidden the demons see the poets safe "as far as the unbroken bridge", which, he implied, was near at hand. But the next bridge is broken also, and it now dawns on Virgil that no "unbroken bridge" exists, and that the devil was sending them under a worthless safeguard on a fool's errand. (N.B. In the map on p. 180, the poets are shown as having already passed another bridgehead unawares on their way between Bowges v and vi; this liberty being taken to gain a little more room for the lettering.)

CANTO XXIV

THE STORY. *After an arduous climb from the bottom of Bowge vi, the Poets gain the arch of the seventh bridge. They hear voices from below, but it is too dark to see anything, so they cross to the far side and go down. The Seventh Bowge is filled with monstrous reptiles, among whom are the shades of Thieves. A Thief is stung by a serpent, reduced to ashes, and then restored to his former shape. He reveals himself to be Vanni Fucci of Pistoia, tells his story, and predicts the overthrow of the Florentine Whites.*

What time the Sun, in the year's early youth,
    Beneath Aquarius rinses his bright hair,
    And nights begin to dwindle toward the south;

When on the ground the hoar-frost copies fair   4
    Her snow-white sister's image, though her pen,
    Soon losing temper, leaves brief traces there;

The hind, no fodder in his empty bin,   7
    Wakes and looks forth; he sees the countryside
    All white, slaps a despairing thigh, and then

Back to his cot; and nowhere can abide,   10
    Nothing begin, but roams about the place,
    Grieving, poor soul! Once more he peeps outside,

And hope revives – the world has changed its face   13
    In that short time; away, then, to the pasture
    He takes his crook, and drives his lambs to graze.

Just so I felt distressed, to see my master   16
    So much put out; in just so brief a while
    To salve my sore there came the healing plaster;

For when we reached the arch's broken pile   19
    He turned towards me with the look I knew
    First at the mountain's foot – his old, sweet smile.

Opening his arms – but seeming first to do   22
    Some careful planning, and scanning of the rock –
    He seized and lifted me; then, like a true

And conscientious workman, who takes stock, 25
   And thinks things out ahead, expending great
   Pains, he would hoist me over one big block,

And when I was up, choose out another straight, 28
   Saying: "Now climb this spike – now this – take heed
   To test it first; make sure 'twill bear thy weight."

No path was that for one in cloak of lead! 31
   For even we – he weightless, I pushed on –
   From crag to crag made arduous way indeed.

Had not the nether of those banks of stone 34
   Been shorter than the upper – I can't tell
   How he'd have fared, but I should have been done.

But since toward the mouth of the central well 37
   Malbowges' sides form one continuous slope,
   It follows that in each succeeding vale

One bank must rise and the other bank must drop; 40
   And howsoever, we clambered till we got
   To the last jag, level with the barrier-top.

My lungs were so pumped out, I just had not 43
   Breath to go on; nor did I try, but came
   Scramblingly up and sat down on the spot.

"Put off this sloth," the master said, "for shame! 46
   Sitting on feather-pillows, lying reclined
   Beneath the blanket is no way to fame –

Fame, without which man's life wastes out of mind, 49
   Leaving on earth no more memorial
   Than foam in water or smoke upon the wind.

Rise up; control thy panting breath, and call 52
   The soul to aid, that wins in every fight,
   Save the dull flesh should drag it to a fall.

More stairs remain to climb – a longer flight; 55
   Merely to quit that crew suffices not;
   Dost take my meaning? Act, and profit by it."

So up I scrambled, making myself out 58
   Less breathless than I really felt; wherefore:
   "Lead on," said I, "I'm resolute and stout."

61 And on we went, scaling the flinty scaur,
   Which was rugged, narrow, and awkward in the ascent,
   And very much steeper than the one before.

64 Not wishing to seem weak, I spoke as I went;
   Whereon a voice rose from the ditch below,
   Which sounded like a voice that was not meant

67 For speech; what it was saying I do not know,
   Though already I stood on the crown of the bridge across
   The moat; but whoever it was seemed angry; so

70 I craned to see; but the darkness was so gross
   No living eye could pierce its heavy pall.
   "Master," said I, "do please go over the fosse

73 To the other bank and let's descend the wall;
   From hence I hear, but cannot understand,
   And look below, but cannot see at all."

76 "My sole reply," said he, "to that demand
   Is action; when a fit request is made
   Silence and deeds should follow out of hand."

79 So over we went and down, where the bridge's head
   Stooping to the eighth barrier, hits the brink of it,
   And now at last the chasm lay displayed;

82 And the most loathsome welter filled the sink of it –
   A mass of serpents, so diverse and daunting,
   My blood still turns to water when I think of it.

85 Let the great Libyan desert cease from vaunting
   Her cenchrid and chalydra broods, nor boast
   The amphisbenes, pareas and jacules haunting

88 Her sands; she never spawned so vile a host
   Of plagues, nor all the land of Ethiope,
   Nor that which lies along the Red Sea coast.

91 Amid this cruel and repulsive crop
   Of monsters, naked men ran terrified,
   Hopeless of hiding-hole or heliotrope;

94 Their hands were held behind their backs and tied
   With snakes, whose head and tail transfixed the loin,
   Writhing in knots convolved on the hither side.

And lo! as one came running near our coign   97
  Of vantage on the bank, a snake in a flash
  Leapt up and stung him where neck and shoulder join.

Never did writer with a single dash   100
  Of the pen write "o" or "i" so swift as he
  Took fire, and burned, and crumbled away to ash.

But as he lay on the ground dispersedly,   103
  All by itself the dust gathered and stirred
  And grew to its former shape immediately.

So wise men say the sole Arabian bird,   106
  The phoenix, dies and is reborn from fire
  When her five-hundredth year is near expired;

Living, nor herb nor grain is food for her,   109
  Only amomum and dropping incense-gums,
  And her last swathings are of nard and myrrh.

As one who falls, nor knows how the fit comes,   112
  By diabolic power, or oppilation
  That chokes the brain with stupefying fumes,

Who, when he rises, stares in consternation   115
  All round, bewildered by his late hard throes,
  With rolling eyes and anguished suspiration,

So seemed that wretched sinner when he rose.   118
  Stern is thy hand, Divine omnipotence,
  That in thy vengeance rainest down such blows!

Then my guide asked him who he was, and whence;   121
  And he: "From Tuscany I came pelting in
  To this fierce gullet, and no long time since.

I loved to live as beasts live and not men,   124
  Mule that I was! – Vanni Fucci, absolute
  Beast; and Pistoia was my fitting den."

I told my guide: "Bid him not budge a foot,   127
  But say what brought him here; – I've only seen him
  An evil-tempered, bloody-minded brute."

The sinner heard; nor did he try to screen him,   130
  Nor feign, but turned on me his mind and face,
  Showing a dismal shame at work within him.

133   "That thou," said he, "shouldst catch me in this place
  And see me so, torments me worse than leaving
  The other life, and doubles my disgrace.

136   Yet answer thee I must, without deceiving:
  I'm thrust so low, because I stole the treasure
  Of the sacristy; for which fine piece of thieving

139   Others were falsely blamed and put in seizure;
  But lest, if ever thou escape these drear
  Abodes, this picture should afford thee pleasure,

142   I'll tell thee something; prick thine ears and hear:
  Pistoia shall purge out the party Black;
  New men, new laws in Florence shall appear;

145   From Valdimagra Mars shall bring a stack
  Of vapour rolled in clouds turbid as night,
  And with impetuous storm and tempest-wrack

148   Over Piceno's field all shall rage the fight,
  Whence he shall suddenly rend the mists apart
  Striking a blow to stagger every White;

151   And so I tell thee; may it break thy heart."

THE IMAGES. *The Thieves.* Two cantos are devoted to the Thieves, the full nature of whose punishment is not fully developed till we get to Canto xxv. The old commentators point out the likeness between the subtle serpent and the creeping thief; in this canto we can already see how, as in life the thief stole other men's goods, so here he is himself robbed of his very semblance. One must always remember that to the mind of the Middle Ages a man's lawful property was an extension of his personality (see Canto XI. 41, note) – an exterior body, as it were, and, like that body, a sacred trust to be used and not abused, either by himself or by others. This accounts for the severe view which Dante takes of offences against property.

NOTES. ll. 1–3: *the year's early youth*, etc.: The Sun is in Aquarius (the Water-Carrier) from 21 January to 21 February; the year is just passing out of "childhood" into early "youth" – i.e. from winter to spring. As the Sun moves daily higher into the north, the "nights" (the point of the heavens opposed to the sun) begin to pass away southward, and grow shorter.

ll. 5–6: *her pen, soon losing temper*: Hoar-frost melts more quickly than snow:

ll. 34–5: *the nether … shorter than the upper*: See diagram, p. 226.

l. 42: *level with the barrier-top*: They have climbed to the top of the lower wall of the bowge, and have still to climb up the side of the spur and reach the arch of the next bridge.

l. 55: *more stairs remain to climb*: primarily, the spur; but Virgil is probably hinting that, even when the whole descent into Hell is accomplished, there remains the steep ascent to Purgatory. To renounce sin is not all: the active work of purgation remains to be done before (if Dante takes his meaning) he can be reunited with Beatrice.

l. 63: *the one before*: i.e. the spur which they had been following from the First Bowge to the Fifth.

ll. 85 *sqq.*: *the great Libyan desert*, etc.: This list of reptilian monsters is taken from Lucan's *Pharsalia* (ix. 708–21); cf. Milton: *Paradise Lost*, x. 519–28.

l. 93: *heliotrope*: a kind of chalcedony, supposed to make the wearer invisible.

l. 94: *their hands were … tied*: because they had been used for "picking and stealing".

ll. 107 *sqq.*: *the phoenix*: Legend has it that there was only one phoenix in all the world. Every 500 years she built herself a nest of myrrh and spices. When this had been kindled by the heat of the Arabian sun, she fanned the flames with her wings till she was wholly consumed, and was afterwards reborn from the ashes.

l. 110: *amomum*: a genus of aromatic plants, which includes cardamoms, etc.

ll. 112 *sqq.*: *one who falls*: Dante is probably describing an epileptic fit.

l. 125: *Vanni Fucci*: This notorious ruffian was a Black Guelf from Pistoia. With two accomplices he stole the treasure of San Jacopo from the Church of San Zeno (1293). For this crime an innocent man (Rampino dei Foresi) was arrested, but Vanni Fucci (who had fled the city) laid an information against the person who had acted as receiver. The latter was hanged and Rampino set at liberty.

l. 126: *Pistoia was my fitting den*: Pistoia was infamous as the birthplace of the feud between Blacks and Whites.

l. 128: *say what brought him here*: i.e. to the Bowge of the Thieves; for Dante had only known him as a "man of blood", and might have expected to find him in the Marsh of the Wrathful or the Boiling River.

ll. 142 *sqq.*: In May 1301, the Florentine Whites assisted the Pistoian Whites to rid Pistoia of the Blacks, who then took refuge in Florence, joined the Black party there, and in November, when Charles of Valois entered the city, helped in their turn to expel the Whites from Florence. "Piceno's field" is probably the battle in which the Florentine and Lucchese Blacks, under the command of Moroëllo Malaspina (the "stack of vapour"), Lord of Lunigiana in the Valdimagra, captured the White stronghold of Serravalle.

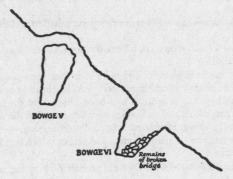

Diagram to illustrate Canto XXIV. 34–5

CANTO XXV

THE STORY. *Vanni Fucci defies God and flees, pursued by the monster Cacus. Three more spirits arrive, and the Poets watch while one of them becomes blended with the form of a reptile containing the spirit of a fourth, and the second exchanges shapes with yet another transformed Thief.*

This said, the thief lifted his hands on high,
    Making the figs with both his thumbs, and shrieking:
    "The fico for Thee, God! take that, say I!"

At once I liked the snakes; for one came sneaking   4
    About his throat, and wreathed itself around
    As though to say: "I will not have thee speaking";

Another wrapped his arms, and once more bound   7
    All fast in front, knotting the coils till he
    Could give no jog, they were so tightly wound.

Pistoia, O Pistoia! well were thee   10
    To burn thyself to ashes and perish all,
    Whose crimes outgo thy criminal ancestry!

Through all Hell's sable gyres funereal   13
    I saw no spirit so proud against the Lord –
    No, not that king who fell from the Theban wall –

As this; he fled without another word;   16
    And I saw a centaur galloping in a storm
    Of wrath: "Where, where's this insolent wretch?" he roared.

Maremma, methinks, breeds no such serpent-swarm   19
    As from his crupper writhed in hideous play
    To where horse-withers join with human form.

Behind his head, crouched on his shoulders, lay   22
    A dragon with spread wings, whose burning breath
    Set fire to all that crossed him on the way.

"Lo, Cacus!" said my guide, "who dwelt beneath   25
    Mount Aventine's high rock, and spilt abroad
    Full many a time a lake of blood and death.

28   He with his brethren goes not one same road,
          For when his knavish hand drew to his den
          His neighbour's kine, he wrought a theft by fraud,

31   Whereby his crooked courses ended, when
          Hercules with his club rained on him nigh
          One hundred blows, whereof he felt not ten."

34   While he thus spake, the centaur thundered by,
          And at the same time, close beneath us, three
          Spirits arrived, whom nor my guide nor I

37   Noticed, until they shouted: "Who are ye?"
          So we broke off the tale, to pay attention
          To them. Just who they were I could not see;

40   But, as so often haps, by intervention
          Of chance, or other such occasion-bringer,
          One of them, as they spoke, was moved to mention

43   Another, saying: "Why does Cianfa linger?
          Where is he?" So, to bid my guide give ear,
          From chin to nose I laid a warning finger.

46   Reader, if thou discredit what is here
          Set down, no wonder; for I hesitate
          Myself, who saw it all as clear as clear.

49   Lo! while I gazed, there darted up a great
          Six-leggèd worm, and leapt with all its claws
          On one of them from in front, and seized him straight;

52   Clasping his middle with its middle paws,
          Along his arms it made its fore-paws reach,
          And clenched its teeth tightly in both his jaws;

55   Hind-legs to thighs it fastened, each to each,
          And after, thrust its tail betwixt the two,
          Up-bent upon his loins behind the breech.

58   Ivy to oak so rooted never grew
          As limb by limb that monstrous beast obscene
          Cling him about, and close and closer drew,

61   Till like hot wax they stuck; and, melting in,
          Their tints began to mingle and to run,
          And neither seemed to be what it had been;

228

Just as when paper burns you see a dun   64
  Brown hue go creeping up before the flare,
  Not black as yet, although the white has gone.

The other two cried out, left gaping there: 67
  "O me, Agnel! how thou art changed!" they said;
  "Nor 'tother nor which! nor single nor a pair!"

Two heads already had become one head,   70
  We saw two faces fuse themselves, to weld
  One countenance whence both the first had fled;

Into two arms the four fore-quarters swelled;   73
  Legs and thighs, breast and belly, blent and knit
  Such nightmare limbs as never eye beheld;

All former forms wholly extinct in it,   76
  The perverse image – both at once and neither –
  Reeled slowly out of sight on languid feet.

And just as a lizard, with a quick, slick slither,   79
  Flicks across the highway from hedge to hedge,
  Fleeter than a flash, in the battering dog-day weather,

A fiery little monster, livid, in a rage,   82
  Black as any peppercorn, came and made a dart
  At the guts of the others, and leaping to engage

One of the pair, it pierced him at the part   85
  Through which we first draw food; then loosed its grip
  And fell before him, outstretched and apart.

The stung thief stared, but no word passed his lip;   88
  He stood, foot-fixed, rigid in every limb,
  Yawning, as though o'ercome by fever or sleep.

He eyed the monster and the monster him;   91
  From this one's mouth, from that one's wound, a trail
  Of smoke poured out: meeting, they merged their stream.

Let Lucan whisht now with his wondrous tale   94
  Of poor Sabellus and Nasidius,
  And wait to hear the wonder that befel;

Whisht Ovid! though he metamorphosed thus   97
  Cadmus and Arethusa to a snake
  And fountain, I need not be envious;

100 He never undertook in verse to make
 Two natures interchanging, eye to eye,
 Substance and form by mutual give-and-take

103 For with strange corresponding symmetry,
 The monster's tail forked to a double tine;
 The shade's feet clave together, till by and by

106 Legs, thighs and all so fused that never a sign
 Could be discerned of seam, or junction scarred,
 Or suture anywhere along the line;

109 The cloven tail put on the image marred
 And lost in the other, and the reptile's skin
 Softened all over, while the man's grew hard.

112 I saw the arms at the arm-pits shrivel in;
 And the brute's fore-feet, which were stubby and stout,
 As the other's shortened, lengthen and grow thin.

115 The hind-feet, intertwined, began to sprout
 Into the member which men keep concealed,
 Whence, in the thief, two nasty paws shot out.

118 The smoke with counter-change of colour wheeled
 Re-dyeing both; the hair was stript and sown
 So that one head grew shag, the other peeled.

121 One of them rose erect and one dropped down,
 Yet never shifting the fixed, evil stare
 Wherein each made the other's face his own.

124 The erect one's snout bulged temple-wards, and there
 Out of the superfluity of stuff,
 From each flat cheek-bone there emerged an ear;

127 Part went not back, but stayed in front, whereof
 The extra matter formed a nose to adorn
 The face, and proper lips made thick enough.

130 He that lay prostrate had his features drawn
 Forth to a muzzle, and inside his head
 He pulled his ears, as a snail pulls her horn;

133 The tongue once whole and apt for speech was splayed
 Into a fork; in the forked tongue the split
 Closed; and the smoke subsided. Then the shade

Now brutified, fled off with hiss and spit   136
    Along the valley; the other, in a crack,
    Chattering and sputtering, sped off after it;

Then suddenly turned on it his new-made back,   139
    Bawling to his fellow: "I'll see Buoso range,
    Crawling as I crawled, all around the track!"

Thus I saw change, re-change and interchange   142
    The seventh moat's ballast; if my pen has erred,
    Pray pardon me: 'twas all so new and strange.

And though my vision was perplexed and blurred,   145
    My mind distraught, the prompt celerity
    With which those flying sinners disappeared

Was no disguise for Limping Puccio – he   148
    Was the only one, in fact, who did not turn
    Into something else, of the original three;

The other was he that made Gaville mourn.   151

THE IMAGES. In this canto we see how the Thieves, who made no distinction between *meum* and *tuum* – between the "mine" and the "thine" – cannot call their forms or their personalities their own; for in Hell's horrible parody of exchange the "I" and the "thou" fluctuate and are lost.

NOTES. l. 2: *the figs*: an obscene and insulting gesture, made by thrusting the thumb between the first and second fingers.

l. 12: *thy criminal ancestry*: alluding to the tradition that Pistoia was founded by the remnants of Catiline's army.

l. 15: *that king who fell from the Theban wall*: Capaneus. (See Canto XIV. 51 and note.)

l. 25: *Cacus*: This giant was not really a Centaur; Dante was probably misled by Virgil's calling him "semi-human". He stole the oxen of Geryon, which Hercules was bringing from Spain as one of his Twelve Labours, and dragged them backwards into his cave so as to leave a misleading set of hoof-prints; but Hercules heard them bellowing, killed Cacus, and recovered his property.

l. 28: *his brethren*: the Centaurs of Circle 7, Ring i (Canto XII). Cacus added theft to his crimes of bloodshed, and is therefore placed in this lower circle.

l. 33: *whereof he felt not ten*: because he died after the first nine.

l. 35: *close beneath us*: It seems clear that the poets did not go right down to the floor of the bowge among the serpents. They either remained on the top of the bank or (as is perhaps more probable from Canto XXVI. 13–15) came part of the way down.

ll. 35–6: *three spirits*: Agnello dei Brunelleschi, Buoso degli Abati (or possibly the Buoso dei Donati mentioned in Canto XXX. 44), and Puccio dei Galigai. These, together with Cianfa dei Donati and Francesco Guercio dei Cavalcanti, who appear in the form of serpents, are the five Florentine nobles who, in this canto, confusingly exchange shapes.

ll. 49–50: *a great six-leggèd worm*: This is Cianfa dei Donati, the missing member of the party, who has been changed into a reptile.

l. 68: *Agnel*: This is Agnello dei Brunelleschi.

l. 82: *a little fiery monster*: This is Francesco Guercio dei Cavalcanti, whom Dante does not identify till the last line of the canto.

l. 85: *one of them*: This is Buoso degli Abati (or dei Donati).

ll. 85–6: *the part through which we first draw food*: the navel.

l. 94: *Lucan*: in his *Pharsalia* tells how, on Cato's march through the Libyan desert, two of his soldiers were stung by serpents. One, Sabellus, dissolved away into a puddle of liquid flesh; the other, Nasidius, swelled up into a shapeless mass that burst his coat of mail.

l. 97: *Ovid*: See *Metamorphoses* iv. 563 *sqq.*, and v. 572 *sqq.*

ll. 135–6: *the shade now brutified*: i.e Buoso.

l. 137: *the other*: i.e. Francesco dei Cavalcanti, now restored to human form.

l. 148: *Limping Puccio* (Puccio Sciancato): this is Puccio dei Galigai. Dante did not at first (l. 39) know him, but recognized him by his limp when he ran off.

l. 151: *that made Gaville mourn*: Francesco dei Cavalcanti was killed by the inhabitants of this village in the Arno Valley, and his kinsmen avenged his death on the villagers.

A summary of these various transformations may be a convenience:

(1) *Agnello:* appears as a man, and is blended with
(2) *Cianfa,* who appears as a six-legged monster.
(3) *Buoso:* appears first as a man, and changes shapes with
(4) *Francesco,* who appears first as a four-legged "lizard".
(5) *Puccio:* remains unchanged.

CANTO XXVI

THE STORY. *Dante, with bitter irony, reproaches Florence. The Poets climb up and along the rugged spur to the arch of the next bridge, from which they see the Counsellors of Fraud moving along the floor of the Eighth Bowge, each wrapped in a tall flame. Virgil stops the twin-flame which contains the souls of Ulysses and Diomede, and compels Ulysses to tell the story of his last voyage.*

Florence, rejoice, because thy soaring fame
　　Beats its broad wings across both land and sea,
　　And all the deep of Hell rings with thy name!

Five of thy noble townsmen did I see　　　　　　4
　　Among the thieves; which makes me blush anew,
　　And mighty little honour it does to thee.

But if toward the morning men dream true,　　　7
　　Thou must ere long abide the bitter boon
　　That Prato craves for thee, and others too;

Nay, were't already here, 'twere none too soon;　　10
　　Let come what must come, quickly – I shall find
　　The burden heavier as the years roll on.

We left that place; and by the stones that bind　　13
　　The brink, which made the stair for our descent,
　　My guide climbed back, and drew me up behind.

So on our solitary way we went,　　　　　　16
　　Up crags, up boulders, where the foot in vain
　　Might seek to speed, unless the hand were lent.

I sorrowed then; I sorrow now again,　　　　19
　　Pondering the things I saw, and curb my hot
　　Spirit with an unwontedly strong rein

For fear it run where virtue guide it not,　　　22
　　Lest, if kind star or greater grace have blest
　　Me with good gifts, I mar my own fair lot.

Now, thickly clustered, – as the peasant at rest　　25
　　On some hill-side, when he whose rays illume
　　The world conceals his burning countenance least,

233

28   What time the flies go and mosquitoes come,
            Looks down the vale and sees the fire-flies sprinkling
            Fields where he tills or brings the vintage home –

31   So thick and bright I saw the eighth moat twinkling
            With wandering fires, soon as the arching road
            Laid bare the bottom of the deep rock-wrinkling.

34   Such as the chariot of Elijah showed
            When he the bears avenged beheld it rise,
            And straight to Heaven the rearing steeds upstrode,

37   For he could not so follow it with his eyes
            But that at last it seemed a bodiless fire
            Like a little shining cloud high in the skies,

40   So through that gulf moved every flaming spire;
            For though none shows the theft, each, like a thief,
            Conceals a pilfered sinner. To admire,

43   I craned so tip-toe from the bridge, that if
            I had not clutched a rock I'd have gone over,
            Needing no push to send me down the cliff.

46   Seeing me thus intently lean and hover,
            My guide said: "In those flames the spirits go
            Shrouded, with their own torment for their cover."

49   "Now thou hast told me, sir," said I, "I know
            The truth for sure; but I'd already guessed,
            And meant to ask – thinking it must be so –

52   Who walks in that tall fire cleft at the crest
            As though it crowned the pyre where those great foes,
            His brother and Eteocles, were placed?"

55   "Tormented there," said he, "Ulysses goes
            With Diomede, for as they ran one course,
            Sharing their wrath, they share the avenging throes.

58   In fire they mourn the trickery of the horse,
            That opened up the gates through which the high
            Seed of the Romans issued forth perforce;

61   There mourn the cheat by which betrayed to die
            Deïdamia wails Achilles still;
            And the Palladium is avenged thereby."

234

Then I: "O Master! if these sparks have skill   64
  To speak, I pray, and re-pray that each prayer
  May count with thee for prayers innumerable,

Deny me not to tarry a moment here   67
  Until the horned flame come; how much I long
  And lean to it I think thee well aware."

And he to me: "That wish is nowise wrong,   70
  But worthy of high praise; gladly indeed
  I grant it; but do thou refrain thy tongue

And let me speak to them; for I can read   73
  The question in thy mind; and they, being Greek,
  Haply might scorn thy speech and pay no heed."

So, when by time and place the twin-fire peak,   76
  As to my guide seemed fitting, had come on,
  In this form conjuring it, I heard him speak:

"You that within one flame go two as one,   79
  By whatsoever I merited once of you,
  By whatsoever I merited under the sun

When I sang the high songs, whether little or great my due,   82
  Stand; and let one of you say what distant bourne,
  When he voyaged to loss and death, he voyaged unto."

Then of that age-old fire the loftier horn   85
  Began to mutter and move, as a wavering flame
  Wrestles against the wind and is over-worn;

And, like a speaking tongue vibrant to frame   88
  Language, the tip of it flickering to and fro
  Threw out a voice and answered: "When I came

From Circe at last, who would not let me go,   91
  But twelve months near Caieta hindered me
  Before Aeneas ever named it so,

No tenderness for my son, nor piety   94
  To my old father, nor the wedded love
  That should have comforted Penelope

Could conquer in me the restless itch to rove   97
  And rummage through the world exploring it,
  All human worth and wickedness to prove.

100 So on the deep and open sea I set
    Forth, with a single ship and that small band
    Of comrades that had never left me yet.

103 Far as Morocco, far as Spain I scanned
    Both shores; I saw the island of the Sardi,
    And all that sea, and every wave-girt land.

106 I and my fellows were grown old and tardy
    Or ere we made the straits where Hercules
    Set up his marks, that none should prove so hardy

109 To venture the uncharted distances;
    Ceuta I'd left to larboard, sailing by,
    Seville I now left in the starboard seas.

112 'Brothers,' said I, 'that have come valiantly
    Through hundred thousand jeopardies undergone
    To reach the West, you will not now deny

115 To this last little vigil left to run
    Of feeling life, the new experience
    Of the uninhabited world behind the sun.

118 Think of your breed; for brutish ignorance
    Your mettle was not made; you were made men,
    To follow after knowledge and excellence.'

121 My little speech made every one so keen
    To forge ahead, that even if I'd tried
    I hardly think I could have held them in.

124 So, with our poop shouldering the dawn, we plied,
    Making our oars wings to the witless flight,
    And steadily gaining on the larboard side.

127 Already the other pole was up by night
    With all its stars, and ours had sunk so low,
    It rose no more from the ocean-floor to sight;

130 Five times we had seen the light kindle and grow
    Beneath the moon, and five times wane away,
    Since to the deep we had set course to go,

133 When at long last hove up a mountain, grey
    With distance, and so lofty and so steep,
    I never had seen the like on any day.

Then we rejoiced; but soon we had to weep,   136
   For out of the unknown land there blew foul weather,
   And a whirlwind struck the forepart of the ship;

And three times round she went in a roaring smother   139
   With all the waters; at the fourth, the poop
   Rose, and the prow went down, as pleased Another,

And over our heads the hollow seas closed up."   142

THE IMAGES. *The Counsellors of Fraud.* The sinners in Bowge viii are not men who deceived those whom they counselled, but men who counselled others to practise fraud. The Thieves in the bowge above stole material goods; these are spiritual thieves, who rob other men of their integrity. This explains, I think, the name which Dante gives to their punishment.

The Thievish Fire: The fire which torments also conceals the Counsellors of Fraud, for theirs was a furtive sin (Lat.: *furtivus*, from *fur*, thief). And as they sinned with their tongues, so now speech has to pass through the tongue of the tormenting and thievish flame.

NOTES. l. 9: *Prato:* Cardinal Nicholas of Prato was sent to Florence in 1304 by Pope Benedict XI in hopes of reconciling the hostile factions. Finding all his efforts wasted, he said, "Since you refuse to be blessed, remain accursed," and laid the city under an interdict. Various disasters which happened shortly afterwards – the collapse of a bridge, killing a vast number of people, and a terrible fire in which over 2000 houses were destroyed and many great families ruined – were attributed to the curse of the Church.

ll. 20–24: Dante realizes that he, like the Counsellors, has been blessed by fate ("kind star") or Providence ("greater grace") with great intellectual gifts, and must, therefore, take particular care not to abuse them.

l. 26: *when he whose rays*, etc.: i.e. in summer, when the days are longest.

l. 28: *what time the flies go and mosquitoes come:* i.e. at dusk.

l. 35: *he the bears avenged:* Elisha. (2 Kings ii. 11–12, 23–4.)

l. 54: *Eteocles:* The war of the Seven against Thebes arose from the rival claims of Eteocles and his brother Polynices, the sons of Oedipus, to the throne. They killed each other in battle, and were placed on one pyre; but, even so, such was their mutual hatred that their very flames would not mingle. (Statius: *Thebaïd* xii, 429 *sqq.*)

ll. 55–6: *Ulysses ... Diomede*: the Greek heroes who fought against Troy. The "crafty Ulysses" (Odysseus) advised the stratagem of the Wooden Horse, by which Greek soldiers were smuggled into Troy to open the gates to the besiegers; and also the theft of the sacred statue of Pallas (the Palladium) on which the safety of Troy was held to depend. Thetis, the mother of Achilles, knowing that he would perish if he went to Troy, concealed him at the court of the king of Scyros, disguised as a woman; but he seduced the king's daughter, Deïdamia, who bore him a son. Ulysses discovered his hiding-place and persuaded him to go to Troy; whereupon Deïdamia died of grief.

ll. 74–5: *they: being Greek ... might scorn thy speech*: The great Greek heroes would despise Dante, as an Italian (i.e. a descendant of the defeated Trojans).

l. 78: *in this form*: Virgil is also an Italian; but he has the power, which Dante has not, of compelling the spirits. We must remember that Virgil, in the Middle Ages, was thought of as a "White Magician", and though the power he uses is not what we should nowadays call "magic" in any evil sense, what follows is in fact a *formal conjuration*. Notice that, since Virgil is here only gratifying Dante's laudable curiosity, he does not use any of those great "words of power" by which he overcame the ministers of Hell in the name of high Heaven (cf. Cantos III. 95; v. 23; VII. 11, etc.), but relies on his own power, which is twofold: (1) the native virtue of a good man who, though not in the Grace of Christ, is yet fulfilling a Divine commission "under the Protection"; (2) the claim of the Poet upon the souls who are indebted to him for their fame in the world.

ll. 80–83: "*By whatsoever ... stand and ... say*": This is the *forma* – the form, or formula – of conjuration: a twice-repeated obsecration, "by whatsoever ..." (naming the claim which constitutes the point of psychic contact between the master and the spirits), followed by a command: "stand ... speak". In the next canto we shall see that the spirits cannot depart until he dismisses them (Canto XXVII. 3) and a few lines later (Canto XXVII. 21) we shall be given the *forma* of the "licence to depart".

l. 83: *one of you*: i.e. Ulysses. Notice that, unlike the other spirits with whom the poets talk, Ulysses never addresses them personally. Compelled by the conjuration, his narrative reels off automatically like a gramophone record and then stops.

The voyage of Ulysses, perhaps the most beautiful thing in the whole *Inferno*, derives from no classical source, and appears to be

Dante's own invention. It may have been suggested to him by the Celtic voyages of Maelduin and St Brendan. It influenced Tasso (*Ger. Lib.* Canto xv), and furnished Tennyson with the theme for his poem *Ulysses*.

l. 91: *Circe*: the sorceress who detained Ulysses on his way from Troy to Ithaca, after turning several of his companions into swine. (See *Odyssey*, Bk. x.)

l. 92: *Caieta* (Gaeta): a town on the south coast of Italy, said to have been so named by Aeneas after his old nurse, who died and was buried there. (*Aen.* vii. 1–4.)

l. 96: *Penelope*: the faithful wife of Ulysses. (See Glossary: *Ulysses*.)

l. 104: *the island of the Sardi*: Sardinia.

l. 108: *his marks*: The Pillars of Hercules (see Glossary) were looked upon as the limit of the habitable globe, and the sun was imagined as setting close behind them.

ll. 127 *sqq.*: *the other pole*, etc.: The voyagers had crossed the equator and made so much leeway south that the Southern Celestial Pole stood high in the heavens with all its attendant constellations; consequently, not only was our Pole Star beneath the northern horizon, but the Arctic constellations (the Great and Little Bears, etc.), which in this hemisphere never set, there never rose.

l. 133: *a mountain*: This is the mountain of the Earthly Paradise, which, after Christ's Harrowing of Hell, becomes Mount Purgatory – the only land, according to Dante, in the Southern Hemisphere. (See Canto xxxiv. 122–3, note.)

l. 141: *as pleased Another*: i.e. as pleased God.

CANTO XXVII

THE STORY. *The spirit of Guido da Montefeltro asks for news of Romagna, and, being answered, tells his story.*

> Erect and quiet now, its utterance done,
>   The tall flame stood; and presently, dismissed
>   By the sweet poet's licence, it passed on;

4
> When lo! our eyes were drawn towards the crest
>   Of a new flame, coming behind its fellow,
>   By the strange muffled roarings it expressed.

7
> As the Sicilian bull, first made to bellow
>   (And that was justice) by his cries whose tool
>   Tuned the vile instrument and made it mellow,

10
> Bellowed with its victim's voice, until the bull,
>   Though brass throughout, appeared itself to roar,
>   Pierced through with torments unendurable,

13
> So, finding at the start no way nor door
>   Out of the fire, the sad words were translated
>   Into fire's native speech; but when they wore

16
> Their way up to the tip and had vibrated
>   That, with the same vibration given to them
>   By the tongue, as they passed out articulated,

19
> We heard it say: "O thou at whom I aim
>   My voice, who saidst in speech of Lombardy:
>   'Go now; I vex thee with no further claim';

22
> Though I have come a little late maybe,
>   Speak to me! let it not irk thee to be stayed,
>   For see! I burn, and yet it irks not me.

25
> If thou into this blind realm of the dead
>   Art fall'n but now from those sweet Latian shores
>   Whence I brought all my sins here on my head,

28
> Tell me, have the Romagnols peace or wars?
>   For I was of the mountains there, between
>   Urbino and the yoke whence Tiber pours."

Now as I leaned there still, intent and keen,   31
  My leader touched my side, and said: "Go to;
  This one is Latian, so do thou begin."

I had my answer all prepared, and so   34
  Made no delay but carried the talk on,
  Saying: "O spirit hidden there below,

Not now, nor ever, has thy Romagna known   37
  Times when her tyrants' hearts were free from feud,
  But open strife just now I there left none.

Ravenna stands as many a year she's stood;   40
  The Eagle of Polenta, with broad vans
  Stretched o'er Cervia, sits and guards his brood.

She that piled up the slaughtered hordes of France,   43
  Having endured such stubborn siege and strong,
  Is back beneath the Green Claws' governance.

The Mastiffs of Verrucchio old and young,   46
  That mauled Montagna with such murderous mouth,
  Flesh their keen teeth where they have fleshed them long.

Beside Lamone and Santerno both,   49
  The cities serve the white-laired Lioncel
  Who changes sides as he turns north or south.

The town where Savio bathes the city-wall,   52
  Lying betwixt the mountains and the plain,
  Like as she lies, so lives 'twixt free and thrall.

And now, pray tell, so may thy name remain   55
  Green upon earth, who wast thou? No deny
  Was made to thee; deny us not again."

So when the flame had roared confusedly   58
  After its wont awhile, it started quaking
  Its sharp point to and fro, and breathed reply

As follows: "If I thought that I were making   61
  Answer to one that might return to view
  The world, this flame should evermore cease shaking.

But since from this abyss, if I hear true,   64
  None ever came alive, I have no fear
  Of infamy, but give thee answer due.

67   A man of arms was I, turned Cordelier,
       Thinking, thus girt, to make amends for ill,
       And my whole hope had been fulfilled, I swear,

70   But for the High Priest – may he rot in Hell! –
       Who thrust me back in the old evil mesh;
       And how and why hearken! for I will tell.

73   While I was still that shape of bone and flesh
       In which my mother moulded me at birth
       My deeds were foxy and not lionish;

76   I knew each winding way, each covert earth,
       And used such art and cunning in deceit
       That to the ends of the world the sound went forth.

79   But when I reached the age when it is meet
       For every mariner, with his port in sight,
       To lower sail and gather in the sheet,

82   That which had pleased offended me; contrite,
       Confessed, I took the habit; O, and these
       Good means of grace had served to set me right.

85   But he, the Prince of the modern Pharisees,
       Having a war to wage by Lateran –
       Not against Jews, nor Moslem enemies,

88   For every foe he had was Christian,
       Not one had marched on Acre, none had bought
       Or sold within the realm of the Soldan –

91   Reckless of his High Office, setting at naught
       Both his own priesthood and that girdle of mine
       Which once made lean the wearer, – this man sought

94   Me out, as in Soracte Constantine
       Sought Silvester to cure his leprosy,
       Even so, as a skilled leech to medicine

97   The fever of his pride, he sent for me,
       Demanding counsel; I with dubious brow
       Sat mute – his words seemed drunken lunacy.

100   But then he said: 'Fear nothing; here and now
       I absolve thee in advance; therefore speak out,
       Teach me how to lay Palestrina low.

Thou knowest I have the power to open or shut   103
   The gates of Heaven, for those High Keys are twain,
   The Keys my predecessor cherished not.'

Then he showed weighty cause, till to refrain   106
   Seemed worse than speech. 'Father, since thou straightway,'
   Said I, 'dost cleanse me of the guilty stain

I must contract, why then, to hold thy sway   109
   Victor triumphant in the Holy See,
   Promise great things; promise, and do not pay.'

Later, I died, and Francis came for me;   112
   But one of the Black Cherubs cried, 'Beware
   Thou wrong me not! Hands off! He's not for thee;

He must go join my servitors down there;   115
   He counselled fraud – that was his contribution
   To Hell; since then I've had him by the hair.

Absolved uncontrite means no absolution;   118
   Nor can one will at once sin and contrition,
   The contradiction bars the false conclusion.'

O what a waking! when with fierce derision   121
   He seized on wretched me, saying: 'I'll be bound
   Thou didst not think that I was a logician.'

He haled me off to Minos; eight times round   124
   His scaly back the monster twined his tail,
   And in his rage he bit it; then he found

Against me, saying: 'Here's a criminal   127
   For the thievish fire.' So was I lost, so borne
   Where, as thou seest, thus clothed I walk and wail."

Its story told, the flame began to mourn   130
   Anew, and sorrowing passed away from us,
   Twisting and tossing with its pointed horn;

And we went on, my guide and I, to cross   133
   The bridge that o'er the following chasm lies,
   Where those who make division and purchase thus

A load of guilt, receive their merchandise.   136

NOTES. ll. 2–3: *dismissed by the sweet poet's licence*: These lines make it clear that the conjured spirits cannot move without the formal permission of the Master. (See note, Canto XXVI. 80–83.)

l. 7: *the Sicilian bull*: This instrument of torture was made by Perillus for Phalaris, the Sicilian tyrant. The victims were roasted alive in it, and their yells, issuing through the brazen mouth, were supposed to sound like the bull bellowing. Phalaris, with grisly humour, tried the invention out on Perillus. (Ovid: *Ars Amat.* i. 635–6.)

ll. 13–18: This rather complicated description becomes easily intelligible if one thinks how words spoken into a telephone are transmitted as electrical waves and retranslated into speech by vibrating the receiver at the other end of the line.

ll. 20–21: *who saidst in speech of Lombardy:* "*Go now*", etc.: This is the *forma* of the "licence to depart" – "*issa ten va, più non t' adizzo*" – "now go, I vex thee no further". (The fact that Virgil uses "speech of Lombardy" shows that it was not the difference of language that would have prevented the Greeks from paying attention to Dante).

l. 29: *I was of the mountains there*: The speaker is the great Ghibelline leader, Guido da Montefeltro (1223–98) of Romagna. (See Glossary.)

l. 40: *Ravenna*: The lords of Polenta, who bore an eagle on their coat of arms, ruled Ravenna from 1270 to 1441. In 1300 the head of the family was Guido Vecchio ("the elder"), uncle to Dante's friend Guido Novello ("the younger"); his territory had already been extended to cover Cervia, a town about twelve miles south of Ravenna.

l. 43: *She that piled up the ... hordes of France*: Forlì; its successful defence against French troops sent by Pope Martin IV (1282) was conducted by Guido da Montefeltro himself. In 1300 it was ruled by Sinibaldo degli Ordelaffi, whose arms were a lion, vert.

l. 46: *The Mastiffs of Verrucchio*: Malatesta and his son Malatestino of Rimini. They were Black Guelfs; Montagna dei Parcitati, whom they took prisoner (1295) and murdered, was a Ghibelline of the same city.

l. 48: *there*: in Verruchio, family seat of the lords of Rimini.

l. 50: *the white-haired Lioncel*: Mainardo Pagano (*d.* 1302), whose arms were a lion, azure, on a field, argent. He was lord of Faenza on the Lamone and of Imola on the Santerno (see map, p. 173); and is said to have behaved like a Ghibelline in Romagna (to the south) and a Guelf in Tuscany (to the north).

l. 52: *where Savio bathes the city-wall*: Cesna (between Forlì and Rimini) was continually changing its government, but was in 1300 comparatively free from tyranny, under the rule of its own officers.

ll. 56–7: *No deny ... deny us not*: i.e. "We have answered your question; now answer ours."

ll. 61–6: Guido cannot see that Dante is alive, and supposes him to be one of the damned souls on its way to its own place (*cf.* Cantos XII. 62; XXVIII. 42–5, etc.). Dante does not undeceive him, but leaves the Counsellor of Fraud to his self-deception (see note on Canto VIII. 45). Generally speaking, the shades in the Circles of Fraud, unlike those in the circles above, do not want to have their stories made known in the world.

l. 67: *Cordelier*: a friar, wearing the cord of the Franciscan Order, which Guido entered in 1296.

l. 70: *the High Priest*: i.e. the Pope (Boniface VIII).

l. 86: *a war to wage by Lateran*: The long and embittered feud between Boniface and the Colonna family (see Glossary) broke out into open warfare in 1297.

l. 89: *Acre*: the last stronghold that remained to the Christians in Palestine after the Crusades was retaken in 1291 by the Saracens, with the aid of renegade Jews and of Christian merchants who treacherously supplied them with contraband of war.

l. 94: *in Soracte*: The legend was that when the Emperor Constantine was stricken with leprosy for his persecution of Christians, he summoned Pope Silvester from his refuge in Soracte, and was converted and cured by him, making the alleged "Donation of Constantine" (see Canto XIX. 115, note) as a thank-offering. (See also Glossary: *Soracte, Silvester*.)

l. 102: *Palestrina* (or Penestrino): The forces of the Colonna had retired to this stronghold. On Guido's advice, the Pope offered them an amnesty, and when they had surrendered on those conditions, razed the place to the ground.

l. 105: *my predecessor*: Celestine V. (See Canto III, 60, note.)

l. 112: *Francis*: i.e. St Francis of Assisi, founder of the Franciscan Order.

ll. 118–20: "Contrition is necessary if the absolution is to be valid; but a man cannot be contrite for a sin at the same time that he is intending to commit it, since this involves a contradiction in logic (i.e. one cannot both will and not-will the same thing at the same time); therefore the absolution obtained in these circumstances is invalid".

l. 124: *eight times round*: indicating the Eighth Circle (see Canto V. 10–12), and adding "the Thievish Fire" to show which bowge of it.

CANTO XXVIII

THE STORY. *From the bridge over the Ninth Bowge the Poets look down upon the Sowers of Discord, who are continually smitten asunder by a Demon with a sword. Dante is addressed by Mahomet and Pier da Medicina, who send messages of warning to people on earth. He sees Curio and Mosca, and finally Bertrand de Born.*

Who, though with words unshackled from the rhymes,
   Could yet tell full the tale of wounds and blood
   Now shown me, let him try ten thousand times?

4 Truly all tongues would fail, for neither could
   The mind avail, nor any speech be found
   For things not to be named nor understood.

7 If in one single place were gathered round
   All those whose life-blood in the days of yore
   Made outcry from Apulia's fateful ground,

10 Victims of Trojan frays, and that long war
   Whose spoil was heaped so high with rings of gold,
   As Livy tells, who errs not; those that bore

13 The hammering brunt of battle, being bold
   'Gainst Robert Guiscard to make stand on stand;
   And they whose bones still whiten in the mould

16 Of Ceperan', where all the Apulian band
   Turned traitors, and on Tagliacozzo's field
   Won by old Alard, weaponless and outmanned;

19 If each should show his bleeding limbs unhealed,
   Pierced, lopt and maimed, 'twere nothing, nothing whatever
   To that ghast sight in the ninth bowge revealed.

22 No cask stove in by cant or middle ever
   So gaped as one I saw there, from the chin
   Down to the fart-hole split as by a cleaver.

25 His tripes hung by his heels; the pluck and spleen
   Showed with the liver and the sordid sack
   That turns to dung the food it swallows in.

I stood and stared; he saw me and stared back;   28
   Then with his hands wrenched open his own breast,
   Crying: "See how I rend myself! what rack

Mangles Mahomet! Weeping without rest   31
   Ali before me goes, his whole face slit
   By one great stroke upward from chin to crest.

All these whom thou beholdest in the pit   34
   Were sowers of scandal, sowers of schism abroad
   While they yet lived; therefore they now go split.

Back yonder stands a fiend, by whom we're scored   37
   Thus cruelly; and over and over again
   He puts us to the edge of the sharp sword

As we crawl through our bitter round of pain;   40
   For ere we come before him to be bruised
   Anew, the gashed flesh reunites its grain.

But who art thou that dalliest there bemused   43
   Up on the rock-spur – doubtless to delay
   Going to thy pangs self-judged and self-accused?"

"Nor dead as yet, nor brought here as a prey   46
   To torment by his guilt," my master said,
   "But to gain full experience of the Way

He comes; wherefore behoves him to be led –   49
   And this is true as that I speak to thee –
   Gyre after gyre through Hell, by me who am dead."

And, hearing him, stock-still to look on me   52
   Souls by the hundred stood in the valley of stone,
   And in amaze forgot their agony.

"Well, go then, thou that shalt behold the sun   55
   Belike ere long – let Fra Dolcino know,
   Unless he is in haste to follow me down,

He must well arm himself against the snow   58
   With victuals, lest the Novarese starve him out,
   Who else might find him hard to overthrow."

Thus unto me Mahomet, with one foot   61
   Lifted to leave us; having said, he straight
   Stretched it to earth and went his dreary route.

64   Then one with gullet pierced and nose shorn flat
            Off to the very eyebrows, and who bare
            Only a single ear upon his pate,

67   Having remained with all the rest to stare,
            Before the rest opened his weasand now,
            Which outwardly ran crimson everywhere,

70   And said: "O thou whom guilt condemns not, thou
            Whom I have seen up there in Italy
            Unless some likeness written in thy brow

73   Deceives me; if thou e'er return to see
            Once more the lovely plain that slopes between
            Vercelli and Marcabò, then think of me,

76   Of Pier da Medicina; and tell those twain,
            Ser Guido and Angiolello, Fano's best,
            That, if our foresight here be not all vain,

79   They'll be flung overboard and drowned, in the unblest
            Passage near La Cattolica, by the embargo
            Laid on their lives at a false lord's behest.

82   Neptune ne'er saw so foul a crime, such cargo
            Of wickedness 'twixt Cyprus and Majorca
            Ne'er passed, no pirate-crew, no men of Argo

85   Could show the like. That one-eyed mischief-worker
            Whose land there's one here with me in this vale
            Wishes he'd never seen, that smooth-tongued talker

88   Shall lure them to a parley, and when they sail
            Deal so with them that they shall have no need
            Of vow or prayer against Focara's gale."

91   Then I to him: "Tell me, so may I speed
            Thy message up to the world as thou dost seek,
            Who's he whose eyes brought him that bitter meed?"

94   At once he laid his hand upon the cheek
            Of a fellow-shade, and pulled his jaws apart,
            Saying: "Look! this is he; he cannot speak.

97   This outcast quenched the doubt in Caesar's heart:
            'To men prepared delays are dangerous';
            Thus he gave sign for civil strife to start."

O how deject to me, how dolorous   100
   Seemed Curio, with his tongue hacked from his throat,
   He that of speech was so adventurous!

And one that had both hands cut off upsmote   103
   The bloody stumps through the thick air and black,
   Sprinkling his face with many a filthy clot,

And cried: "Think, too, on Mosca, Mosca alack!   106
   Who said: 'What's done is ended,' and thereby
   For Tuscany sowed seed of ruin and wrack."

"And death to all thy kindred," added I;   109
   Whereat, heaping despair upon despair,
   He fled, like one made mad with misery.

But I remained to watch the throng, and there   112
   I saw a thing I'd hesitate to tell
   Without more proof – indeed, I should not dare,

Did not a blameless conscience stead me well –   115
   That trusty squire that harnesses a man
   In his own virtue like a coat of mail.

Truly I saw – it seems to me I can   118
   See still – I saw a headless trunk that sped
   Running towards me as the others ran;

And by the hair it held the severed head   121
   Swung, as one swings a lantern, in its hand;
   And that caught sight of us: "Ay me!" it said.

Itself was its own lamp, you understand,   124
   And two in one and one in two it was,
   But how – He only knows who thus ordained!

And when it reached our bridge, I saw it toss   127
   Arm up and head together, with design
   To bring the words it uttered near to us;

Which were: "O breathing soul, brought here to win   130
   Sight of the dead, behold this grievous thing,
   See if there be any sorrow like to mine.

And know, if news of me thou seek to bring   133
   Yonder, Bertrand de Born am I, whose fell
   Counsel, warping the mind of the Young King

136   Like Absalom with David, made rebel
           Son against father, father against son,
           Deadly as the malice of Achitophel.

139   Because I sundered those that should be one,
           I'm doomed, woe worth the day! to bear my brain
           Cleft from the trunk whence all its life should run;

142   Thus is my measure measured to me again."

THE IMAGES. *The Sowers of Discord.* Three types are shown: fomenters of (1) religious schism (Mahomet; Ali), (2) civil strife (de Medicina; Curio); (3) family disunion (Mosca; Bertrand).

   They appear in the Circle of Fraud because their sin is primarily of the intellect. They are the fanatics of party, seeing the world in a false perspective, and ready to rip up the whole fabric of society to gratify a sectional egotism.

The Sundering Sword. The image here is sufficiently obvious. Note how it is adapted to suit the various types of crime.

NOTES. l. 9: *Apulia's fatal ground*: The region in south-east Italy where all the wars and battles alluded to in this passage took place.

   l. 10: *Trojan frays*: Wars of the Romans (Trojans) against the Samnites (343–290 B.C.); *that long war*, etc.: the Punic Wars (264–146 B.C.).

   l. 11: *rings of gold*: According to Livy, so many Romans were killed at the Battle of Cannae, in the second Punic War, that three bushels of golden rings were collected from their bodies.

   l. 14: *Robert Guiscard*: combated Greeks and Saracens (1015–85).

   l. 16: *Ceperan(o)*: The Apulian barons, under Manfred, deserted at the pass of Ceperano, and let Charles of Anjou through to defeat Manfred at Benevento (1266).

   l. 17: *Tagliacozzo*: where Charles of Anjou defeated Manfred's nephew, Conradin; by the advice of Alard de Valéry, he allowed two-thirds of his army to retreat, and then, with his reserve troops, annihilated the enemy who had scattered in search of plunder.

   l. 31: *Mahomet*: classed as a Christian schismatic.

   l. 32: *Ali*: the nephew of Mahomet, was himself the figurehead of an internal schism within the following of the Prophet himself.

   l. 42: *the gashed flesh reunites*: We may suppose that in all cases where damned souls are mangled or mutilated (e.g. by Cerberus in the Third Circle or by the "black braches" in the Wood of the Suicides) the shadowy flesh is thus restored; but Dante, with great artistic tact, says nothing about it until, at this point, he can use it to make a ghastly and grotesque effect. He hints at it again in Canto xxxiv. 60.

l. 56: *Fra Dolcino*: Head of a sect, the "Apostolic Brethren", rightly or wrongly condemned as schismatic. In 1305 Pope Clement V ordered a crusade against the Brethren, and after holding out for a year and a day in the hills near Novara, they were forced to surrender. Dolcino was burnt at Vercelli in 1307.

l. 76: *Pier da Medicina*: whose intrigues were instrumental in fomenting the feud between the houses of Polenta and Malatesta in Romagna. His methods were to disseminate scandal and misrepresentation – hence he is shown mutilated in the eavesdropping ear, the lying throat, and the inquisitive nose.

l. 77: *Guido* (del Cassero) *and Angiolello* (da Calignano): two noblemen of Fano, were invited to a conference at La Cattolica, on the Adriatic, by Malatestino of Rimini, who had them treacherously drowned off the headland of Focara, notorious for its dangerous winds.

l. 84: *men of Argo*: lit.: the Argolican race, i.e. the Greeks, always famous for piracy. But there may be a specific reference to the crime of the Argonauts, who murdered Absyrtus and threw his body into the sea on their return from Colchis.

l. 85: *that one-eyed mischief-worker*: Malatestino of Rimini.

l. 93: *that bitter meed*: referring back to ll. 86–7. It was by Curio's advice that Julius Caesar crossed the Rubicon (near Rimini), which at that time (49 B.C.) was the frontier between Italy and Cis-Alpine Gaul, and so declared war on the Republic.

l. 98: *to men prepared*, etc.: Quoted from Lucan: *Pharsalia* (i. 281).

l. 106: *Mosca*: The great Guelf-Ghibelline feud in Florence flared up over a family quarrel. Buondelmonte dei Buondelmonti, who was betrothed to a girl of the Amadei, jilted her for one of the Donati. When her kinsfolk were debating how best to avenge the slight, Mosca dei Lamberti said: "What's done is ended" (i.e. "stone dead hath no fellow"). Buondelmonte was accordingly murdered; the whole city took sides; and thenceforward Florence was distracted by the disputes of the rival factions. (See Introduction, p. 29.)

l. 134: *Bertrand de Born*: (*c.* 1140–1215), the warrior and troubadour, was lord of Hautefort (Altaforte) in Perigord. According to his Provençal biographers, he fomented the quarrel between Henry II of England and his son Prince Henry, "the Young King" (so-called because he was crowned during his father's lifetime). For Absalom and Achitophel, see 2 *Samuel* xv–xvii. Bertrand is decapitated because to part father and son is like severing the head from the body.

CANTO XXIX

THE STORY. *Dante lingers, expecting to see a kinsman of his in the Ninth Bowge; but Virgil says he has already passed by unnoticed. They cross the next bridge and descend into Bowge x, where the Falsifiers lie stricken with hideous diseases. Dante talks with an old friend, Capocchio.*

My eyes were grown so maudlin with the plight
    Of all these people racked with wounds and woe,
    They longed to linger weeping at the sight;

4   But Virgil said: "How now! Why dost thou grow
    Rooted to gaze? Why is thy vision drowned
    Among these smitten shades? Thou didst not so

7   At the other moats. Dost think that thou art bound
    To catalogue them all? Come, use thy wit;
    Consider, this fosse is twenty-two miles round,

10   And already the moon is underneath our feet;
    Short grows the time allowed, and on our way
    There's more to see than thou hast seen as yet."

13   "Hadst thou but waited," I began to say,
    "To find out what it was I was looking for,
    I think perhaps thou wouldst have let me stay."

16   My guide, however, had started on before,
    And I trailed after, making my reply
    And adding: "Somewhere on that rocky floor,

19   I think, among the throng that held my eye,
    A spirit of my own blood runs damnified,
    Weeping the guilt that there is priced so high."

22   "Let not thy mind," the master then replied,
    "Henceforth distract itself upon that fellow;
    Thou hast other things to think of – let him bide:

25   I saw him, close beneath the bridge's hollow,
    Pointing at thee, and threatening with bent fist,
    And heard him called by name Geri del Bello.

Just at that moment thou wast hard intent 28
 On him that dwelt in Altaforte; hence
 Thou didst not look his way, and so he went."

"Alas, dear Sir! his death by violence," 31
 Said I, "still unavenged by any of them
 Who shared the affront, has rankled to this sense

Of deep resentment; wherefore, as I deem, 34
 He went away and would not speak to me;
 And all the more for that, I pity him."

Thus we talked up the cliff, till presently 37
 The next moat's bottom came in sight, – or would
 Have come in sight had there been light to see.

There, from the crossing-span's high altitude, 40
 Malbowges' final cloister all appears
 Thrown open, with its sad lay-brotherhood;

And there, such arrowy shrieks, such lancing spears 43
 Of anguish, barbed with pity, pierced me through,
 I had to clamp my hands upon my ears.

Could all disease, all dog-day plagues that stew 46
 In Valdichiana's spitals, all fever-drench
 Drained from Maremma and Sardinia, spew

Their horrors all together in one trench – 49
 Like that, so this: suffering, and running sore
 Of gangrened limbs, and putrefying stench.

Down that last bank of the long cliff we bore, 52
 Still turning left; and now as I drew near,
 I saw more vividly to the very core

That pit wherein the High Lord's minister, 55
 Infallible Justice, dooms to pains condign
 The falsifiers she registers down here.

No sadder sight was seen, as I divine, – 58
 Even in Aegina, when wrath knew no term,
 But the whole people in that air malign

Sickened, and beasts, down to the littlest worm, 61
 Dropped dead, till in the end the ancient race
 Had to be born anew, as poets affirm,

64   From seed of ants – than in that dreadful place
         The sight of the spirits strewn through the dark valley,
         Heaped here, heaped there, enduring their distress.

67   This on the back, and that upon the belly
         One of another lay, while some crawled round
         The dismal road, all-fours, lethargically.

70   So step by step we went, nor uttered sound,
         To see and hear those sick souls in their pains,
         Who could not lift their bodies from the ground.

73   I saw two sitting, propped like a couple of pans
         Set to warm by the fireside, back to back,
         And blotched from head to foot with scabs and blains.

76   And I ne'er saw curry-comb plied by ostler's jack
         Or groom, in a frenzy because his master's waiting,
         Or because he is kept up late and wants to pack

79   Bedwards, to match the furious rasping and grating
         With which they curried their own hide with their nails,
         Maddened by the itch that still finds no abating.

82   The nail went stripping down the scurfy shales,
         Just as a scullion's knife will strip a bream,
         Or any other fish with great coarse scales.

85   "Thou that dost take thy finger-nails to trim
         Thy coat, and sometimes," thus my guide began
         To one of these, "for pincers usest them,

88   Tell us, so may thy claws outlast the span
         Of all eternity to do their task,
         Is any one here within a Latian man?"

91   "We who confront thee in this hideous mask
         Are Latians both," one answered in a wail,
         "But who art thou? and wherefore dost thou ask?"

94   "I am one who comes descending, vale by vale,
         To lead this living man," my guide averred,
         "And all my business is to show him Hell."

97   Their mutual propping broke; startled, they stirred
         And turned towards me trembling; others too
         Turned when they caught the echo of his word.

Then my kind master courteously withdrew 100
    To give me place: "Whate'er thou wilt," he said,
    "Ask them." And since he urged me so to do

I thus began: "So may your names not fade, 103
    In that first world, from human memory,
    But live for many suns, be not afraid

To tell me who and whence you both may be, 106
    Nor let your sad and shameful state prevent
    Your free unfolding of yourselves to me."

"I'm Aretine, and to the stake was sent 109
    By Alberto of Siena; yet," said one,
    "What caused my death caused not this punishment.

It's true I told the fool one day for fun: 112
    'I can take wings and fly,' and he – an ass
    Full of wild whims, with addled wits, or none –

Would have me teach him how; and just because 115
    I could not make him Daedalus, why, then
    He had me burned, by one who, more or less,

Fathered him; but to this last bowge of ten 118
    Unerring Minos doomed me for the art
    Alchemic, which I practised among men."

"Was ever race so frivolous of heart," 121
    Said I to the poet, "as the Sienese?
    I think they could give even the French a start

And a beating." Whereupon the second of these 124
    Leprous shades joined in: "Except, no doubt,
    Stricca, renowned for his economies,

And Niccolò, of course, who first found out 127
    How to make cloves a costly cult and passion
    In the garden where such seeds take root and sprout;

Oh – and except the club where Caccia d'Ascian 130
    Lost woods and vineyards, and the ingenious
    Abbagliato, like a man of fashion,

Displayed his wit. Wouldst know who backs thee thus 133
    Against Siena? Come, focus thy glance,
    Get my face clear; thou'lt not be at a loss

136   To know Capocchio's shadowy countenance,
          Transmuter of metals, alchemist, and – a feature
          Which, if I eye thee hard, thou wilt at once

139   Recall – a most consummate ape of nature."

THE IMAGES. *The Falsifiers.* The Tenth Bowge shows us the images
of those who falsified things, words, money, and persons. This
canto deals with the falsifiers of things, typified by the Alchemists
(transmuters of metals). They may be taken to figure every kind
of deceiver who tampers with the basic commodities by which
society lives – the adulterators of food and drugs, jerry-builders,
manufacturers of shoddy, and so forth – as well, of course, as the
baseness of the individual self consenting to such dishonesty.

The Valley of Disease. For the *allegory*, this is at one level the image of
the corrupt heart which acknowledges no obligation to keep faith
with its fellow-men; at another, it is the image of a diseased
society in the last stages of its mortal sickness and already necros-
ing. Every value it has is false; it alternates between a deadly
lethargy and a raving insanity. Malbowges began with the sale of
the sexual relationship, and went on to the sale of Church and
State; now, the very money is itself corrupted, every affirmation
has become perjury, and every identity a lie; no medium of ex-
change remains, and the "general bond of love and nature's tie"
(Canto XI. 56) is utterly dissolved.

NOTES. l. 9: *twenty-two miles round*: Various attempts have been
made to calculate the exact proportions of Malbowges from the
indications in this and the next canto; but I think it is best just to
bear in mind that Hell extends from a little below the Earth's surface to
its centre, and that the Great Barrier comes about half-way down; and
so leave imagination to fill in the details of this colossal scheme.

l. 10: *the moon is underneath our feet*: it is about 1 P.M.

l. 27: *Geri del Bello*: a cousin of Dante's father. He is said to have
delighted in making mischief, and to have been killed by a member
of the Sacchetti family, which he had set by the ears. The customary
vendetta for his death seems not to have been carried out by his kins-
men – or, at any rate, not before 1300.

l. 29: *him that dwelt in Altaforte*: Bertrand de Born.

ll. 47–9: *Valdichiana … Maremma and Sardinia*: All these districts

were reckoned extremely unhealthy, especially in summer; Valdi-
chiana (in Tuscany, between the mouths of the Chiana) and Mar-
emma being full of marshy and malarial swamps.

l. 59: *Aegina*: The story of the pestilence sent by Juno, and of how
Jupiter re-peopled the island by turning ants into men, is told by
Ovid. (*Metam.* vii. 523–657.)

l. 110: *said one*: The speaker is Griffolino d'Arezzo, a physicist, who,
by promising all kinds of miracles, extracted large sums of money
from a foolish young man, Albero, reputed to be the son of the
Bishop of Siena. His dupe eventually complained to the Bishop, who
had Griffolino burnt as a sorcerer. The offence which brings him to
the Tenth Bowge is, however, not alchemy considered as a magical
art (which would be punished in Bowge iv), but alchemy in its
more practical application – viz. the falsification of commodities.
(For Daedalus, see Canto XVII. 109, note.)

ll. 125 *sqq.*: *Except, no doubt, Stricca*: As in Canto XXI. 41, the
"except" is ironical. The four noblemen named all belonged to the
"Spendthrifts' Club" in Siena, of which Lano was also a member
(see Canto XIII. 115, note). Niccolò dei Salembeni specialized in the
invention of dishes prepared with costly spices.

l. 136: *Capocchio*: is said to have been a friend and fellow-student
of Dante's, and to be called an "ape of nature" on account of his
powers either as a draughtsman or as a mimic. If the latter, then his
saying, "If I eye thee hard", perhaps means that at this point he in-
dulged in some characteristic facial gesture which Dante could not
fail to recognize – he gave him, so to speak, a "George Robey look".

CANTO XXX

THE STORY. *The shades of Myrrha and Gianni Schicchi are pointed out by Griffolino. Dante becomes intent upon a quarrel between Adam of Brescia and Sinon of Troy, and earns a memorable rebuke from Virgil.*

When Juno was incensed for Semele,
 And wreaking vengeance on the Theban race,
 As her sharp strokes had shown repeatedly,

4 So fierce a madness seized on Athamas
 That, seeing his wife go with her two young sons
 One on each arm: "Spread nets, nets at the pass,

7 We'll take the lioness and the whelps at once!"
 He roared aloud; then, grasping in his wild
 And pitiless clutch one of those little ones,

10 Baby Learchus, as he crowed and smiled,
 He whirled him round and dashed him on a stone;
 She fled, and drowned herself with the other child.

13 And when, by Fortune's hostile hand o'erthrown,
 The towering pride of Troy fell to the ground,
 Kingdom and king together ruining down,

16 Sad Hecuba, forlorn and captive bound,
 After she'd seen Polyxena lie slain,
 After, poor hapless mother, she had found

19 Polydorus dead by the seashore, fell insane
 And howled like a dog, so fearfully distraught
 Was she, so wrenched out of her mind with pain.

22 Yet Theban or Trojan furies never wrought
 Such cruel frenzy, even in the maddened breast
 Of a brute, still less in any of human sort,

25 As I saw in two shades, naked, pale, possessed,
 Who ran, like a rutting boar that has made escape
 From the sty, biting and savaging all the rest.

28 One of them fell on Capocchio, catching his nape
 In its teeth, and dragging him prostrate, so that it made
 His belly on the rough rock-bottom scour and scrape.

The Aretine, left trembling, turned dismayed 31
  To me: "That's Gianni Schicchi, that hell-hound there;
  He's rabid, he bites whatever he sees," he said.

"So may thou 'scape the other's teeth, declare 34
  Its name," said I; "prithee be good enough –
  Quick! ere it dart away and disappear."

And he: "There doth the ancient spirit rove 37
  Of criminal Myrrha, who cast amorous eyes
  On her own father with unlawful love,

And in a borrowed frame and false disguise 40
  Went in to him to do a deed of shame;
  As he that fled but now, to win the prize

'Queen of the Stable', lent his own false frame 43
  To Buoso de' Donati, and made a will
  In legal form, and forged it in his name."

So when that rabid pair, on whom I still 46
  Kept my gaze fixed, had passed, I turned about
  To view those other spirits born for ill;

And saw one there whose shape was like a lute, 49
  Had but his legs, between the groin and haunch,
  Where the fork comes, been lopt off at the root.

The heavy dropsy, whose indigested bunch 52
  Of humours bloats the swollen frame within,
  Till the face bears no proportion to the paunch,

Puffed his parched lips apart, with stiffened skin 55
  Drawn tight, as the hectic gapes, one dry lip curled
  Upward by thirst, the other toward the chin.

"O you," said he, "that through this grisly world 58
  Walk free from punishment – I can't think why –
  Look now and hear; behold the torments hurled

On Master Adam! All that wealth could buy 61
  Was mine; and now, one drop of water fills
  My craving mind – one drop! O misery!

The little brooks that ripple from the hills 64
  Of the green Casentin to Arno river,
  Suppling their channels with their cooling rills,

67   Are in my eyes and in my ears for ever;
      And not for naught – their image dries me more
      Than the disease that wastes my face's favour.

70   Strict, searching justice balances my score:
      The very land I sinned in has been turned
      To account, to make my sighs more swiftly pour.

73   Romena's there, the city where I learned
      To falsify the Baptist's coin; up yonder,
      For the offence, I was condemned and burned.

76   But might I here see Guido or Alexander
      Damned, or their brother, I would not miss that sight
      For all the water in the fount of Branda.

79   One's here already, if those mad spirits are right
      Who circle all the track; but what's the good
      Of that to me, whose legs are tied so tight?

82   Were I but still so active that I could
      Drag myself only an inch in a hundred years,
      I'd be on the road by now, be sure I would,

85   To seek out from all these sufferers
      Disfigured and maimed, though it's half a mile across
      And eleven miles round at least, from all one hears.

88   They brought me into this gang of ruin and loss,
      They caused me coin the florins that brought me hither,
      Whose gold contained three carats by weight of dross."

91   Then I to him: "What shades lie there together
      Rolled in a heap on thy right – that abject pair
      Who smoke as a washed hand smokes in wintry weather?"

94   "When I tumbled into this coop I found them there,"
      Said he, "and they've never given a turn or kick,
      Nor will to all eternity, I dare swear.

97   Sinon of Troy is one, the lying Greek;
      One, the false wife who lyingly accused
      Joseph; their burning fever makes them reek."

100 Then, vexed belike to hear his name thus used
      Slightingly, one of those shadows seemed to come
      To life and fetched him a walloping blow, fist closed,

On the rigid belly, which thudded back like a drum;   103
   So Master Adam lammed him over the face
   With an arm as hard as his own, and hit him plumb.

"See now," said he, "though I cannot shift my place,   106
   Because my legs are heavy, yet if need be
   My arm is free, and I keep it ready, in case."

And he: "It was not so ready and not so free   109
   When they haled thee off to the fire; it was free to do
   Thy dirty job of coining – there I agree."

Then he of the dropsy: "Now thou speakest true;   112
   But when at Troy they called on thee to tell
   The truth, thy truthfulness was less in view."

"If I spoke false, thy coins were false as well;   115
   I uttered but one lie," quoth Sinon, "thou
   Hast uttered more than any fiend in hell."

"Perjurer, think of the horse, think of thy vow   118
   Forsworn," retorted the blown belly; "howl
   For grief to think the whole world knows it now."

"Howl for the thirst that cracks thy tongue, the foul   121
   Water that bloats thy paunch," the Greek replied,
   "To a hedge that walls thine eyes and hides thy jowl."

To whom the coiner: "Ay, thy mouth gapes wide   124
   As ever with evil words; if I feel thirst,
   And watery humours stuff me up inside,

Thou burnest, and thy head aches fit to burst;   127
   Hadst thou Narcissus' mirror there, we'd see
   Thee lap it up and need no prompting first."

I was all agog and listening eagerly,   130
   When the master said: "Yes, feast thine eyes; go on;
   A little more, and I shall quarrel with thee."

And when I heard him use that angry tone   133
   To me, I turned to him so on fire with shame,
   It comes over me still, though all these years have flown.

And like a man who dreams a dreadful dream,   136
   And dreams he would it were a dream indeed,
   Longing for that which is, with eager aim

139   As though 'twere not; so I, speechless to plead
            For pardon, pleaded all the while with him
            By my distress, and did not know I did.

142   "Less shame would wash away a greater crime
            Than thine has been"; so said my gentle guide;
            "Think no more of it; but another time,

145   Imagine I'm still standing at thy side
            Whenever Fortune, in thy wayfaring,
            Brings thee where people wrangle thus and chide;

148   It's vulgar to enjoy that kind of thing."

THE IMAGES. *The Falsifiers.* In this canto we have the images of im-
    personators (falsifiers of person), perjurers (falsifiers of words),
    and coiners (falsifiers of money).

NOTES. ll. 1 *sqq.*: *when Juno was incensed*, etc.: Semele, daughter of
Cadmus, king of Thebes, became by Jupiter the mother of Bacchus.
Among other acts of revenge upon the royal house, Juno sent a
homicidal madness upon Athamas, the husband of Semele's sister
Ino. (Ovid: *Metam.* iv. 512-30.)

    ll. 13 *sqq.*: *and when, by Fortune's hostile hand*, etc.: Hecuba was the
wife of Priam, king of Troy. After the fall of the city, she and her
daughter Polyxena were carried away captive to Greece. Having
seen Polyxena sacrificed at the tomb of Achilles, she found on the
shore the body of her son Polydorus, treacherously murdered by
Polymnestor, king of Thrace, to whom she had entrusted him for
safe keeping. (Ovid: *Metam.* xiii. 404-575.)

    l. 31: *the Aretine*: i.e. Griffolino.

    l. 32: *Gianni Schicchi*: a Florentine of the Cavalcanti family. When
Buoso Donati (see Canto XXV. 140, note) died, his son Simone was
haunted with the fear that he might have left a will restoring some of
the property he had unjustly acquired. Before making the death
known, he consulted Gianni Schicchi, who, being a very clever
mimic, offered to dress up as Buoso and dictate a new will in Simone's
favour. This he did, taking the opportunity to bequeath himself a
handsome legacy and the best mare in the stables.

    l. 38: *Myrrha*: The story of her crime is told by Ovid (*Metam.* x.
298 *sqq.*) (See Glossary.)

Commentaries

l. 42: *he that fled but now*: i.e. Gianni Schicchi; "Queen of the Stud" was the name of the mare.

l. 61: *Master Adam*: a native of Brescia who was employed by the Counts Guidi of Romena to counterfeit the gold florins of Florence. He was burnt in 1281. The coining was on a large scale, and the whole currency of Tuscany was seriously affected.

l. 65: *the green Casentin*: The Casentino is the beautiful hill district of the Upper Arno, where Romena, the castle of the Conti Guidi, was situated.

l. 74: *the Baptist's coin*: the Florentine florin bore the image of St John Baptist, patron saint of the city (see Canto XIII. 143, note), on one side and a lily-flower on the other.

l. 76: *Guido or Alexander ... or their brother* (Aghinolfo): i.e. the Conti Guidi.

l. 78: *the fount of Branda*: There was a famous fountain of this name at Siena; but Master Adam probably means the one at Romena.

l. 97: *Sinon of Troy*: the Greek spy, who, by a lying story backed up by the most solemn oaths, persuaded the Trojans to bring the Wooden Horse into Troy. (See Canto XXVI. 55, note.)

l. 98: *the false wife*: Potiphar's wife. (*Gen.* xxxix. 6–23.)

l. 128: *Narcissus' mirror*: water. Narcissus fell in love with his own reflection in a pool, and, pining away, was transformed into a flower.

l. 148: *vulgar*: The Italian word *basso* is rather stronger than the English "vulgar" – it means "base" as well; perhaps the most exact equivalent would be the colloquial use of "low".

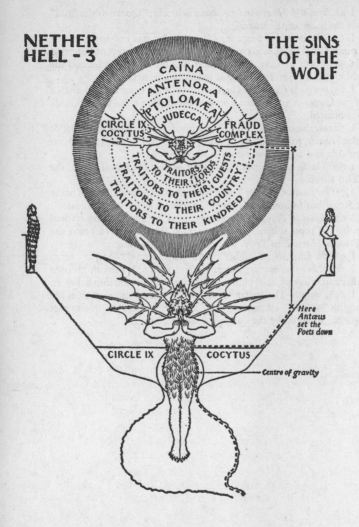

CAÏNA
ANTENORA
PTOLOMÆA
JUDECCA

CIRCLE IX
COCYTUS

FRAUD
COMPLEX

TRAITORS
TO THEIR LORDS
TRAITORS TO THEIR GUESTS
TRAITORS TO THEIR COUNTRY
TRAITORS TO THEIR KINDRED

Here
Antæus
set the
Poets down

CIRCLE IX   COCYTUS

Centre of gravity

CANTO XXXI

THE STORY. *Dante and Virgil now reach the Well at the bottom of the abyss, round which stand the Giants, visible from the waist up above its rim. They see Nimrod and Ephialtes, and are lowered over the edge of the Well by Antaeus.*

The self-same tongue that first had wounded me,
　　Bringing the scarlet blood to both my cheeks,
　　Thus to my sore applied the remedy;

Even so, Achilles' lance was wont to mix　　　　　　　4
　　Good gifts with ill, as erst his sire's had done,
　　Hurting and healing; so the old tale speaks.

We went our way, turning our backs upon　　　　　　7
　　That mournful vale, up by its girdling bound,
　　And silent paced across the bank of stone;

And less than day, and less than night, all round　　10
　　It gloomed; my eyes, strained forward on our course,
　　Saw little; but I heard a high horn sound

So loud, it made all thunder seem but hoarse;　　　13
　　Whereby to one sole spot my gaze was led,
　　Following the clamour backward to its source:

When Charlemayn, in rout and ruin red,　　　　　　16
　　Lost all the peerage of the holy war
　　The horn of Roland sounded not so dread.

And when I'd gazed that way a little more　　　　　19
　　I seemed to see a plump of tall towers looming;
　　"Master," said I, "what town lies on before?"

"Thou striv'st to see too far amid these glooming　　22
　　Shadows," said he: "this makes thy fancy err,
　　Concluding falsely from thy false assuming;

Full well shalt thou perceive, when thou art there,　　25
　　How strangely distance can delude the eye:
　　Therefore spur on thy steps the speedier."

But after that, he took me lovingly　　　　　　　　28
　　By the hand, and said: "Nay now, before we go,
　　I'll tell thee, lest the strange reality

265

31 Surprise thee out of measure; therefore know,
        These are not towers, but giants, set in a ring,
        And hid from the navel down in the well below."

34 And, just as when a mist is vanishing,
        Little by little the eye reshapes anew
        The outlines hid by the crowded vapouring,

37 So, as that thick, gross air we journeyed through,
        Little by little drawing nigh the well,
        My error left me, and my terror grew.

40 As Montereggion's ring-shaped citadel
        Has all its circling rampart crowned with towers,
        Even so, with half their bodies the horrible

43 Giants, whom Jove, when the thunder rolls and lowers,
        Threatens from heaven, girded the well's high rim,
        Turreting it – the tall and terrible powers.

46 Already I made out one huge face, the dim
        Shoulders and breast and part of the belly, and close
        Hung at his sides, both monstrous arms of him.

49 Nature in truth did wisely when she chose
        To leave off making such vast animals
        And let Mars lack executives like those;

52 If she repents not elephants or whales,
        Whoso looks subtly at the case will find
        How prudently her judgment trims the scales;

55 For where the instrument of thinking mind
        Is joined to strength and malice, man's defence
        Cannot avail to meet those powers combined.

58 As large and long his face seemed, to my sense,
        As Peter's Pine at Rome, and every bone
        Appeared to be proportionately immense,

61 So that the bank which aproned him from zone
        To foot, still showed so much, three Friesians
        Might vainly boast to lay a finger on

64 His hair; for from the place at which a man's
        Mantle is buckled, downward, you may call me
        Liar if he measured not fully thirty spans.

"*Rafel maı amech zabi almi*" 67
 The savage mouth began at once to howl,
 Such was the sweetest and the only psalm he

Could sing. "Stick to thy horn, thou stupid soul," 70
 My guide called up; "use that to vent thy breast
 When rage or other passions through thee roll.

Feel at thy neck and find the baldrick laced 73
 That girds it on thee; see, O spirit confused,
 The horn itself that hoops thy monstrous chest."

And then to me: "Himself he hath accused; 76
 That's Nimrod, by whose fault the gracious bands
 Of common speech throughout the world were loosed.

We'll waste no words, but leave him where he stands, 79
 For all speech is to him as is to all
 That jargon of his which no one understands."

So, turning to the left beside the wall, 82
 We went perhaps a cross-bow shot, to find
 A second giant, still more fierce and tall.

I do not know what master hand could bind 85
 Him thus, but there he stood, his left hand bound
 Fast down before him, and the right behind,

By an iron chain, which held him closely wound 88
 Down from the neck; and on the part displayed
 Above the brink the turns went five times round.

"So proud a spirit was this," my leader said, 91
 "He dared to match his strength against high Jove,
 And in this fashion his reward is paid.

Ephialtes is his name, who greatly strove 94
 When the giants made the gods tremble for fright;
 The arms he brandished then no longer move."

"Were it but possible, I wish my sight," 97
 Said I, "could once experience and take in
 Briareus' huge unmeasurable might."

"Not far from hence," he answered, "thou shalt win 100
 Sight of Antaeus, who speaks and wears no chain;
 And he shall bear us to the bottom of sin.

103   Very far off is he whom thou wouldst fain
            Behold; like this he's fettered, and doth look
            As this one looks, but twice as fierce again."

106   No terrible earthquake-trembling ever took
            And shook a tower so mightily as forthwith
            Huge Ephialtes in his fury shook;

109   And never had I been so afraid of death –
            For which no more was needed save the fear,
            But that I saw the chains, and dared draw breath.

112   So on we went; and presently drew near
            Antaeus; seven cloth-yards above the well,
            Without the head, his towering bulk rose sheer.

115   "Thou that of old within the fateful vale
            That made the name of Scipio ever-glorious,
            When Hannibal with all his host turned tail,

118   Didst ravish by thy prowess meritorious
            A thousand lions; thou whose aid, 'twould seem,
            Might well have made the sons of earth victorious

121   Hadst thou allied thee with thy brethren's team,
            Pray be not loth, but lower us to the deep,
            Where the great cold locks up Cocytus' stream.

124   Make us not go to Typhon; let not slip
            Thy chance to Tiryus; for this man can give
            That which is craved for here; curl not thy lip,

127   But stoop; for he's alive, and can retrieve
            Thy fame on earth, where he expects – so Grace
            Call him not early home – long years to live."

130   Thus spake the master; he, all eagerness,
            Stretched those enormous hands out to my guide
            Whence Hercules endured so great distress.

133   And when he felt them grasp him, Virgil cried
            To me: "Come here and let me take thee!" So
            He clasped me and made one bunch of us twined and tied.

136   As Carisenda looks, when one stands below
            On the leaning side, and watches a passing cloud
            Drift over against the slant of it, swimming slow,

Antaeus looked to me, as I watched him bowed   139
Ready to stoop; and that was a moment such
That I heartily wished we might travel another road.

But he set us lightly down in the deep whose clutch   142
Holds Judas and holds Lucifer pent fast;
Nor in that stooping posture lingered much,

But swung him up, as in a ship the mast.   145

THE IMAGES. *The Giants*. From the point of view of the *story*, it is easy to see that Dante placed the Giants here, not merely to furnish a means of transport from Malbowges to the depth of the Well, but, artistically, to provide a little light relief between the sickening horrors of the last bowges of Fraud Simple and the still greater, but wholly different, horrors of the pit of Treachery. But *allegorically*, what do they signify? In one sense they are images of Pride; the Giants who rebelled against Jove typify the pride of Satan who rebelled against God. But they may also, I think, be taken as the images of the blind forces which remain in the soul, and in society, when the "general bond of love" is dissolved and the "good of the intellect" wholly withdrawn, and when nothing remains but blocks of primitive mass-emotion, fit to be the "executives of Mars" and the tools of treachery. Nimrod is a braggart stupidity; Ephialtes, a senseless rage; Antaeus, a brainless vanity: one may call them the doom of nonsense, violence, and triviality, overtaking a civilization in which the whole natural order is abrogated.

NOTES. l. 4: *Achilles' lance*: Peleus, the father of Achilles, gave to his son a lance, whose wound could be healed only by sprinkling with rust from the lance-head itself. (See Ovid: *Remed. Amor.* 47–8; Chaucer, *Squire's Tale*, 231–2; Shakespeare, 2 *Hen. VI*. v. i, etc.)

l. 16: *Charlemayn*: When Charlemagne was returning from fighting the Saracens in Spain, his rearguard, led by his nephew Roland and the Twelve Peers, was betrayed to the enemy by Ganelon (see Canto XXXII. 122), and slaughtered at the Pass of Roncevaux in the Pyrenees. With almost his last breath, Roland blew his horn Olifant so loud that Charlemagne, eight miles away, heard it and returned to avenge his Peerage.

l. 40: *Montereggion*: A castle about six miles from Siena, surmounted by twelve turrets.

l. 59: *Peter's Pine*: A bronze image of a pine-tree, about 7½ ft. high, which, in Dante's time, stood under a canopy outside the old basilica of St Peter in Rome, but was later removed to the Vatican. Much ingenuity has been expended on calculating the height of the Giants; we may take them to average 50 or 60 ft.

l. 62: *Friesians*: The men of Friesland were celebrated for their immense stature.

l. 67: *Rafel maï amech zabi almi*: In view of Virgil's express warning (ll. 80–81), the strenuous efforts of commentators to make sense of this remark seem rather a waste of energy. My own impression, for what it is worth, is that if Dante did not make up this gibberish out of his own head, it may have been suggested to him by some conjuring book, for its diction and rhythm are curiously reminiscent of the garbled language of popular charms.

l. 77: *Nimrod*: "and the beginning of his kingdom was Babel" (*Gen.* x. 9–10). For the story of the building of Babel and the confusion of languages see *Genesis* xi. In making Nimrod a giant, Dante follows St Augustine. (*De Civ. Dei* xvi. 3.) He is given a horn because he was "a mighty hunter before the Lord".

l. 85: *what master hand*: cf. Canto xv. 11 and note.

l. 94: *Ephialtes*: son of Neptune (the sea); one of the giants who fought against the gods, threatening to pile Mount Ossa upon Olympus, and Mount Pelion upon Ossa. They were slain by Apollo.

l. 99: *Briareus*: son of Tellus (the earth), another giant who fought against the Olympians (*Aen.* x. 565 *sqq.*). According to Homer and Virgil, he had a hundred arms and fifty heads; but Dante seems here to have followed Statius, who (*Theb.* ii. 596) merely calls him "immense", and Lucan, who (*Phars.* iv. 596) refers to "fierce Briareus".

ll. 101–21: *Antaeus*: son of Neptune and Tellus – a giant who was invincible so long as he was in contact with his mother Earth. Hercules eventually overcame him by lifting him from the ground and squeezing him to death in mid-air (see l. 132 of this canto). Antaeus is left unchained because he was not one of the giants who fought against the gods. His exploit with the lions took place near Zama in Libya, where Hannibal was defeated by Scipio. Dante took all these details about Antaeus from Lucan's *Pharsalia* (iv. 593–660).

ll. 124–5: *Typhon ... Tityus*: two more of the sons of Tellus, who offended against Jupiter. All these earth-giants and sea-giants seem originally to have been personifications of elemental natural forces.

l. 136: *Carisenda*: a leaning tower at Bologna. When one stands beneath one of these towers and looks up, an optical illusion is produced as though it were about to fall upon one; and this illusion is strengthened if a cloud happens to be moving across in the opposite direction to the apparent movement.

CANTO XXXII

THE STORY. *The Ninth Circle is the frozen Lake of Cocytus, which fills the bottom of the Pit, and holds the souls of the Traitors. In the outermost region, Caïna, are the betrayers of their own kindred, plunged to the neck in ice; here Dante sees the Alberti brothers, and speaks with Camicion dei Pazzi. In the next, Antenora, he sees and lays violent hands on Bocca degli Abati, who names various other betrayers of their country; and a little further on he comes upon two other shades, frozen together in the same hole, one of whom is gnawing the head of the other.*

Had I but rhymes rugged and harsh and hoarse,
　　Fit for the hideous hole on which the weight
　　Of all those rocks grinds downward course by course,

I might press out my matter's juice complete;　　　　　4
　　As 'tis, I tremble lest the telling mar
　　The tale; for, truly, to describe the great

Fundament of the world is very far　　　　　　　　7
　　From being a task for idle wits at play,
　　Or infant tongues that pipe *mamma, papa.*

But may those heavenly ladies aid my lay　　　　　10
　　That helped Amphion wall high Thebes with stone,
　　Lest from the truth my wandering verses stray.

O well for you, dregs of damnation, thrown　　　　13
　　In that last sink which words are weak to tell,
　　Had you lived as sheep or goats in the world of the sun!

When we were down in the deep of the darkling well,　　16
　　Under the feet of the giant and yet more low,
　　And I still gazed up at the towering walls of Hell,

I heard it said: "Take heed how thou dost go,　　　19
　　For fear thy feet should trample as they pass
　　On the heads of the weary brotherhood of woe."

I turned and saw, stretched out before my face　　22
　　And 'neath my feet, a lake so bound with ice,
　　It did not look like water but like glass.

25   Danube in Austria never could disguise
         His wintry course beneath a shroud so thick
         As this, nor Tanaïs under frozen skies

28   Afar; if Pietrapan or Tambernic
         Had crashed full weight on it, the very rim
         Would not have given so much as even a creak.

31   And as with muzzles peeping from the stream
         The frogs sit croaking in the time of year
         When gleaning haunts the peasant-woman's dream,

34   So, wedged in ice to the point at which appear
         The hues of shame, livid, and with their teeth
         Chattering like storks, the dismal shades stood here.

37   Their heads were bowed toward the ice beneath,
         Their eyes attest their grief; their mouths proclaim
         The bitter airs that through that dungeon breathe.

40   My gaze roamed round awhile, and, when it came
         Back to my feet, found two shades so close pressed,
         The hair was mingled on the heads of them.

43   I said: "You two, thus cramponed breast to breast,
         Tell me who you are." They heaved their necks a-strain
         To see me; and as they stood with faces raised,

46   Their eyes, which were but inly wet till then,
         Gushed at the lids; at once the fierce frost blocked
         The tears between and sealed them shut again.

49   Never was wood to wood so rigid locked
         By clamps of iron; like butting goats they jarred
         Their heads together, by helpless fury rocked.

52   Then one who'd lost both ears from off his scarred
         Head with the cold, still keeping his face down,
         Cried out: "Why dost thou stare at us so hard?

55   Wouldst learn who those two are? Then be it known,
         They and their father Albert held the valley
         From which the waters of Bisenzio run;

58   Both of them issued from one mother's belly,
         Nor shalt thou find, search all Caïna through,
         Two shades more fit to stand here fixt in jelly;

Not him whose breast and shadow at one blow   61
    Were pierced together by the sword of Arthur,
    Not Focaccia, nor this other who

So blocks me with his head I see no farther,   64
    Called Sassol Mascheroni – if thou be
    Tuscan, thou know'st him; and I'll tell thee, rather

Than thou shouldst plague me for more speech with thee,   67
    I'm Camicion de' Pazzi, and I wait
    Till Carlin come to make excuse for me."

Then I saw thousand faces, and thousands yet,   70
    Made doggish with the cold; so that for dread
    I shudder, and always shall, whenever I set

Eyes on a frozen pool; and as we made   73
    Towards the centre where all weights down-weigh,
    And I was shivering in the eternal shade,

Whether 'twas will, fate, chance, I cannot say,   76
    But threading through the heads, I struck my heel
    Hard on a face that stood athwart my way.

"Why trample me? What for?" it clamoured shrill;   79
    "Art come to make the vengeance I endure
    For Montaperti more vindictive still?"

"Master!" I cried, "wait for me! I adjure   82
    Thee, wait! Then hurry me on as thou shalt choose;
    But I think I know who it is, and I must make sure."

The master stopped; and while the shade let loose   85
    Volleys of oaths: "Who art thou, cursing so
    And treating people to such foul abuse?"

Said I; and he: "Nay, who art thou, to go   88
    Through Antenora, kicking people's faces?
    Thou might'st be living, 'twas so shrewd a blow."

"Living I am," said I; "do thou sing praises   91
    For that; if thou seek fame, I'll give thee it,
    Writing thy name with other notable cases."

"All I demand is just the opposite;   94
    Be off, and pester me no more," he said;
    "To try such wheedling here shows little wit."

97   At that I grasped the scruff behind his head:
         "Thou'lt either tell thy name, or have thy hair
         Stripped from thy scalp," I panted, "shred by shred."

100   "Pluck it all out," said he; "I'll not declare
         My name, nor show my face, though thou insist
         And break my head a thousand times, I swear."

103   I'd got his hair twined tightly in my fist
         Already, and wrenched away a tuft or two,
         He yelping, head down, stubborn to resist,

106   When another called: "Hey, Bocca, what's to do?
         Don't thy jaws make enough infernal clatter
         But, what the devil! must thou start barking too?"

109   "There, that's enough," said I, "thou filthy traitor;
         Thou need'st not speak; but to thy shame I'll see
         The whole world hears true tidings of this matter."

112   "Away, and publish what thou wilt!" said he;
         "But prithee do not fail to advertise
         That chatterbox there, if thou from hence go free.

115   He wails the Frenchmen's *argent*, treason's price;
         'Him of Duera,' thou shalt say, 'right clear
         I saw, where sinners are preserved in ice.'

118   And if they should inquire who else was there,
         Close by thee's Beccaria, whose throat was cut
         By Florentines; Gianni de' Soldanier

121   Is somewhat further on, I fancy, put
         With Ganelon, and Tibbald, who undid
         Faenza's gates when sleeping eyes were shut."

124   And when we'd left him, in that icy bed,
         I saw two frozen together in one hole
         So that the one head capped the other head;

127   And as starved men tear bread, this tore the poll
         Of the one beneath, chewing with ravenous jaw,
         Where brain meets marrow, just beneath the skull.

130   With no more furious zest did Tydeus gnaw
         The scalp of Menalippus, than he ate
         The brain-pan and the other tissues raw.

"O thou that in such bestial wise dost sate   133
    Thy rage on him thou munchest, tell me why;
    On this condition," I said, "that if thy hate

Seem justified, I undertake that I,   136
    Knowing who you are, and knowing all his crime,
    Will see thee righted in the world on high,

Unless my tongue wither before the time."   139

THE IMAGES. *Cocytus.* Beneath the clamour, beneath the monoton-
ous circlings, beneath the fires of Hell, here at the centre of the
lost soul and the lost city, lie the silence and the rigidity and the
eternal frozen cold. It is perhaps the greatest image in the whole
Inferno. "Dante," says Charles Williams, "scatters phrases on the
difference of the place. It is treachery, but it is also … cruelty; the
traitor is cruel" (*The Figure of Beatrice*, p. 143). A cold and cruel
egotism, gradually striking inward till even the lingering passions
of hatred and destruction are frozen into immobility – that is the
final state of sin. The conception is, I think, Dante's own; although
the *Apocalypse of Paul* mentions a number of cold torments, these
are indiscriminately mingled with the torments by fire, and their
placing has no structural significance. (It is interesting, however,
that in the seventeenth century, the witches who claimed to have
had to do with Satan sometimes reported that he was ice-cold.)

    Cocytus, the "river of mourning", is the fourth of the great
infernal rivers. Caïna is named from Cain who slew his brother
(*Gen.* iv.); Antenora, from Antenor of Troy who, according to
medieval tradition, betrayed his city to the Greeks.

NOTES. l. 10: *those heavenly ladies*: The Muses. Amphion played so
bewitchingly upon the lyre that the stones of Mount Cithaeron were
drawn to hear him, and built themselves up into the walls of Thebes.

    l. 17: *under the feet of the giant and yet more low*: Antaeus, as we have
seen, was about 50–60 ft. high; therefore his feet cannot have been
more than 30 ft. or so below the edge of the well. The latter was,
however, "exceeding deep" (Canto XVIII. 5), and Dante here makes
it clear that they descended to a considerable depth below the feet of
the giant. We must suppose that there was, first, a sheer thirty-foot
drop, followed by a rather less steep descent which it was possible to
negotiate on foot (see sketch, p. 264). I get the impression that Dante

clambered down backwards, as one gets down a ladder; and consequently did not see where he had got to until Virgil's voice (l. 19) caused him to turn round (l. 22).

l. 27: *Tanais*: the Don.

l. 28: *Pietrapan or Tambernic*: Pietrapana: a corruption of Petra Apuana, a mountain in north-west Tuscany. Tambernic: either the *Frusta Gora*, near Tovarnicho, in Slavonia, or the Javornic in Carniola.

ll. 34–5: *to the point at which appear the hues of shame*: i.e. up to the neck.

l. 56: *they and their father Albert*: These are Napoleone and Alessandro degli Alberti, Counts of Mangona, who slew each other in a quarrel over their possessions in the valley of the river Bisenzio, a tributary of the Arno. One was a Guelf, the other a Ghibelline.

ll. 61–2: *him whose breast and shadow ... were pierced*: Mordred the traitor, who attempted to usurp the throne of Arthur. In their last fight, Arthur smote him so fiercely that when the lance was withdrawn the sun shone through the wound and broke the shadow of his body.

l. 63: *Focaccìa*: one of the Cancellieri family of Pistoia. He is said to have cut off the hand of one of his cousins and cut his uncle's throat, and thus to have started the family feud from which the Black and White Guelf factions had their origin.

l. 65: *Sassol Mascheroni*: One of the Toschi of Florence, who treacherously murdered his uncle's only son and seized the inheritance.

ll. 68–9: *Camicion de' Pazzi*: of Valdarno, murdered his kinsman Ubertino. *Carlino* dei Pazzi, another member of the family, was bribed by the Blacks to surrender the castle of Piantravigne, which he was holding for the Whites – and, having pocketed the bribe, sold it back to the Whites again. Camicion means that his own crimes will seem comparatively excusable beside that of Carlino (who is presumably destined for Antenora). It will be noticed that the shades of the Traitors, though inclined to be reticent about their own affairs, are only too eager to denounce each other, and pour out strings of names without even being asked. (Compare Bocca, ll. 113–23; and contrast, e.g. Farinata, Canto X. 118–20.)

ll. 73–4: *as we made towards the centre*: They are now entering Antenora (l. 89). There is no line of demarcation between the regions of Cocytus, but as we go on we find the sinners plunged more deeply in the ice.

l. 81: *Montaperti*: The speaker, Bocca degli Abati, was a Ghibelline; but in the Battle of Montaperti (see Canto X. 85, note) he fought on the Guelf side and, at the most critical moment, came treacherousl up behind the standard-bearer of the Florentine cavalry and cut off his hand, bringing down the standard and throwing the Florentines into a panic which lost them the day.

l. 90: *thou might'st be living*: i.e. the blow is heavier than the speaker can account for, as coming from another shade, which he supposes Dante to be.

ll. 97 *sqq.*: For the significance of Dante's ferocious behaviour, see Canto VIII. 45, note; treachery is cruel, and cruelty calls forth cruelty.

l. 114: *that chatterbox there*: Buoso da Duera; he was in command of the Ghibellines assembled to repel the French forces who were marching through Lombardy to link up with Charles of Anjou, and sold the passage of the Oglio to Guy de Montfort. Bocca uses the French word for money (*argent*) by way of rubbing in the accusation.

ll. 119–20: *Beccarìa*, ... *Gianni de' Soldanier*: see Glossary.

l. 122: *Ganelon*: see Canto XXXI. 16, note. *Tibbald*: one of the Zambrasi family of Faenza. He had a vendetta against the Lambertazzi, a Ghibelline Bolognese family who had taken refuge in Faenza, and in 1280 opened the gates of the city to the Bolognese Guelfs.

l. 130: *Tydeus*: king of Calydon, one of the "Seven against Thebes". Being himself mortally wounded by Menalippus, he yet killed his opponent, and, having ordered his head to be struck off, gnawed the scalp and tore out the brains. (Statius: *Theb.* viii. 740–63.)

CANTO XXXIII

THE STORY. *Having heard Count Ugolino's ghastly story of his death by famine, the Poets pass on to Ptolomaea, where Fra Alberigo is cheated by Dante into telling him about himself and Branca d'Oria and others who enjoy the terrible "privilege" of Ptolomaea.*

Lifting his mouth up from the horrid feast,
    The sinner wiped it on the hair that grew
    Atop the head whose rear he had laid waste;

4   Then he began: "Thou bid'st me to renew
    A grief so desperate that the thought alone,
    Before I voice it, cracks my heart in two.

7   Yet, if indeed my words, like seedlings sown,
    Shall fruit, to shame this traitor whom I tear,
    Then shalt thou see me speak and weep in one.

10   What man thou art, or what hath brought thee here
    I know not; but I judge thee Florentine,
    If I can trust the witness of my ear.

13   First learn our names: I was Count Ugolin,
    And he, Archbishop Roger; hearken well
    Wherefore I use him thus, this neighbour of mine.

16   That once I trusted him, and that I fell
    Into the snare that he contrived somehow,
    And so was seized and slain, I need not tell.

19   What thou canst not have learned, I'll tell thee now:
    How bitter cruel my death was; hear, and then,
    If he has done me injury, judge thou.

22   A narrow loophole in the dreadful den
    Called 'Famine' after me, and which, meseems,
    Shall be a dungeon yet for many men,

25   Had filtered through to me the pallid gleams
    Of many changing moons, before one night
    Unveiled the future to my haunted dreams.

28   I saw this man, a lord and master of might,
    Chasing the wolf and wolf-cubs on the hill
    Which shuts out Lucca from the Pisans' sight.

His hounds were savage, swift and keen of skill,
    And many a Sismund, Gualand and Lanfranc,
    Like huntsmen, rode before him to the kill.   31

I saw how father and sons wearied and sank
    After a short quick run; I saw the dread
    Sharp teeth that tore at bleeding throat and flank.   34

And waking early ere the dawn was red
    I heard my sons, who were with me, in their sleep
    Weeping aloud and crying out for bread.   37

Think what my heart misgave; and if thou keep
    From tears, thou art right cruel; if thou for this
    Weep not, at what then art thou wont to weep?   40

By now they'd waked; the hour at which our mess
    Was daily brought drew near; ill dreams had stirred
    Our hearts and filled us with unquietness.   43

Then at the foot of that grim tower I heard
    Men nailing up the gate, far down below;
    I gazed in my sons' eyes without a word;   46

I wept not; I seemed turned to stone all through;
    They wept; I heard my little Anselm say:
    'Father, what's come to thee? Why look'st thou so?'   49

I shed no tear, nor answered, all that day
    Nor the next night, until another sun
    Rose on the world. And when the first faint ray   52

Stole through into that dismal cell of stone,
    And eyeing those four faces I could see
    In every one the image of my own,   55

I gnawed at both my hands for misery;
    And they, who thought it was for hunger plain
    And simple, rose at once and said to me: 58

'O Father, it will give us much less pain
    If thou wilt feed on us; thy gift at birth
    Was this sad flesh, strip thou it off again.'   61

To spare them grief I calmed myself. Hard earth,
    Hadst thou no pity? couldst thou not gape wide?
    That day and next we all sat mute. The fourth,   64

67   Crept slowly in on us. Then Gaddo cried,
        And dropped down at my feet: 'My father, why
        Dost thou not help me?' So he said, and died.

70   As thou dost see me here, I saw him die,
        And one by one the other three died too,
        From the fifth day to the sixth. Already I

73   Was blind; I took to fumbling them over; two
        Long days I groped there, calling on the dead;
        Then famine did what sorrow could not do."

76   He ceased, and rolled his eyes asquint, and sped
        To plant his teeth, which, like a dog's, were strong
        Upon the bone, back in the wretched head.

79   O Pisa! scandal of all folk whose tongue
        In our fair country speaks the sound of *sì*,
        Since thy dull neighbours will not smite such wrong

82   With vengeance, move Gorgona from the sea,
        Caprara move, and dam up Arno's mouth,
        Till every living soul is drowned in thee!

85   For though Count Ugolin in very truth
        Betrayed thee of thy castles, it was crime
        To torture those poor children; tender youth,

88   O cruel city, Thebes of modern time,
        Made Hugh and Il Brigata innocent
        And the other two whose names are in my rhyme.

91   We passed; and found, as further on we went,
        A people fettered in the frost's rough grip,
        Flat on their backs, instead of forward bent.

94   There the mere weeping will not let them weep,
        For grief, which finds no outlet at the eyes,
        Turns inward to make anguish drive more deep;

97   For their first tears freeze to a lump of ice
        Which like a crystal mask fills all the space
        Beneath the brows and plugs the orifice.

100   And now, although, as from a calloused place,
        By reason of the cold that pinched me so,
        All feeling had departed from my face,

I felt as 'twere a wind begin to blow.　　　　　　103
　　Wherefore I said: "Master, what makes it move?
　　Is not all heat extinguished here below?"

"Thine eyes," said he, "shall answer soon enough;　106
　　We're coming to the place from which the blast
　　Pours down, and thou shalt see the cause thereof."

And one of the wretched whom the frost holds fast　109
　　Cried out: "O souls so wicked that of all
　　The posts of Hell you hold the very last,

Rend from my face this rigid corporal,　　　　　112
　　That I may vent my stuffed heart at my eyes
　　Once, though the tears refreeze before they fall."

Then I: "Tell me thy name: that is my price　　115
　　For help; and if I do not set thee free,
　　May I be sent to the bottom of the ice."

And he: "I am Friar Alberigo, he　　　　　　　118
　　Of the fruits of the ill garden; in this bed
　　Dates for my figs are given back to me."

"How now," said I, "art thou already dead?"　　121
　　And in reply: "Nay, how my body fares
　　In the upper world I do not know," he said.

"Such privilege this Ptolomaea bears　　　　　124
　　That oft the soul falls down here ere the day
　　When Atropos compels it with her shears.

And, if it will persuade thee take away　　　　127
　　These glazing tears by which my face is screened,
　　Know, when a soul has chosen to betray,

As I did, straight it's ousted by a fiend,　　　130
　　Who takes and rules the body till the full
　　Term of its years has circled to an end.

The soul drops down into this cistern-pool;　　133
　　Belike the shade wintering behind me here
　　Still has a body on earth – it's probable

Thou'lt know, if thou art new come down from there;　136
　　He is Ser Branca d' Oria; in this pit's
　　Cold storage he has lain this many a year."

139   "I think," said I, "that these are pure deceits,
     For Branca d' Oria has by no means died;
     He wears his clothes and sleeps and drinks and eats."

142   "Up in that moat where the Hellrakers bide,"
     He answered, "Michael Zanche'd not yet come
     To boil and bubble in the tarry tide

145   When this man left a devil in his room,
     In his flesh and that kinsman's flesh, whom he
     Joined with himself in treachery, and in doom.

148   And now, do thou stretch forth thy hand to me,
     Undo my eyes." And I undid them not,
     And churlishness to him was courtesy.

152   O Genoa, where hearts corrupt and rot,
     Lost to all decency! will no man hound
     Thy whole tribe from the earth and purge this blot?

154   For with Romagna's vilest spirit I found
     One of such rank deeds, such a Genoan,
     His soul bathes in Cocytus, while on ground

157   His body walks and seems a living man.

THE IMAGES. *Ugolin and Roger* are the last of those pairs of shades who image partnership in sin. In each case, only one of them speaks. Francesca speaks of the sharing of the sin, and offers excuses for Paolo along with herself. Ulysses ignores Diomede (partnership is lost). Ugolin justifies himself at Roger's expense (treachery can share nothing but a mutual hatred). There is a deliberate parallel between the Paolo-Francesca pair and the Ugolin-Roger pair: in both cases the lines that introduce their respective stories are drawn from the same passage of Virgil, and there are other, minor, correspondences. This is Dante's way of indicating that here in the ice of Cocytus we have the last state of the corruption of love; that every devouring passion, sexual or otherwise, that sets itself against the order of God and the City, bears in itself the seeds of treachery and a devouring passion of destruction.

Ptolomaea. This third region of Cocytus is probably named after Ptolemy, captain of Jericho, who invited Simon the High Priest and his sons to a banquet and there slew them (1*Maccabees* xvi).

Here lie the Traitors to Hospitality. They who denied the most primitive of human sanctities are now almost sealed off from humanity; they cannot even weep. And they are dead to humanity before they die; that which seems to live in them on earth is only a devil in human form – the man in them has withdrawn out of reach into the cold damnation.

NOTES. ll. 4–9: Compare with Canto v. 121–6, and both with *Aeneid* ii. 3, 10–13.

l. 13: *Count Ugolin*: Count Ugolino della Gherardesca and his grandson, Nino dei Visconti (whom we shall meet in *Purg.* viii), were respectively the heads of the two Guelf parties which in 1288 held power in Pisa. To get rid of Nino, Ugolino allied himself with the Archbishop, Ruggieri (Roger) degli Ubaldini. But as soon as Nino was driven out, the Archbishop, seeing the Guelfs thus weakened, turned on Ugolino and imprisoned him with four of his sons and grandsons in a tower subsequently named "the Tower of Famine". There they remained till March 1289, when the Archbishop ordered the tower to be locked and the keys thrown into the river. (Dante's word (*chiavar*), however, probably means "nail up" – a sound more alarming to the prisoners.) After eight days the tower was opened and all the victims found dead of starvation.

l. 29: *the wolf and wolf-cubs*: i.e. Ugolino and his children. *The hill that shuts out Lucca* is the Monte di San Giuliano, half-way between Pisa and Lucca.

l. 32: *Sismund, Gualand and Lanfranc*: Ghibelline families of Pisa.

l. 34: *father and sons*: Actually, the youths imprisoned with Ugolino were his own two youngest sons, Gaddo and Uguccione (Hugh), and his two grandsons, Nino (surnamed *il Brigata*) and Anselm. All except Anselm were young men rather than "children" or "boys" as Dante represents them. Anselm was 15.

ll. 72–3: *already I was blind*: "from grief", say some commentators; but Dante knew, I think, that one of the effects of starvation is to produce blindness.

l. 75: *then famine did what sorrow could not do*: i.e. kill him.

l. 80: *speaks the sound of si*: i.e. all who speak Italian. The various romance-languages were distinguished by the word used for "Yes", that of Northern France being the *langue d'oïl* (*oui*); that of Southern France, the *langue d'oc*; that of Italy, the *lingua di si*.

ll. 82–3: *Gorgona ... Caprara*: These two islands near the mouth of the Arno then belonged to Pisa.

ll. 85–6: *in very truth betrayed thee of thy castles*: Ugolino was accused of treachery in ceding certain Pisan strongholds to the Florentines and Lucchese. Others think he had no choice but to do so; Dante's words are ambiguous, but in any case Ugolino's treacherous conspiracy with Ruggieri against Nino, by which he betrayed both his party and his city, would have sufficed to bring him to Antenora.

l. 91: *as further on we went*: They are now passing into Ptolomaea.

l. 105: *is not all heat extinguished*: Dante knows that winds are caused by differences of temperature in the atmosphere, and wants to know how, in this region of absolute cold, there can be wind without heat. Virgil replies that he will see the cause of it later on. (Canto XXXIV. 46–51.)

l. 110: *O souls so wicked*: The speaker thinks that Dante and Virgil are damned souls going down to the Circle of Judecca.

l. 117: *to the bottom of the ice*: Treachery calls forth treachery; Dante knows that he *is* going to the bottom – though not in the sense the shade supposes.

ll. 118-20; *Friar Alberigo*: a "Jovial Friar" of the Manfredi family of Faenza. His younger brother, Manfred, struck him in the face in the course of a dispute. Alberigo pretended to forgive and forget, and later on invited Manfred and one of his sons to a dinner. When it was time for the dessert he called out: "Bring on the fruit!" This was the signal for armed servants to rush in and kill Manfred and his son. The "fruit of the ill garden" is probably an allusion to this. "To receive dates for one's figs" is a Tuscan expression meaning "to get back one's own with interest", "to be given tit for tat".

l. 126: *Atropos*: the Fate who cuts the thread of life.

l. 137: *Ser Branca d' Oria*: a Ghibelline of Genoa, who invited his father-in-law, Michael Zanche (see Canto XXII. 88), to a banquet and there, with the help of a nephew, murdered him. Dante says that Zanche had not yet reached the Bowge of the Barrators before the traitor's body had been taken over by a devil and his soul fallen to Ptolomaea – i.e. he was damned in the moment of committing – or perhaps even of assenting to – the treachery.

l. 146: *that kinsman*: i.e. the nephew.

l. 149: *and I undid them not*: The chorus of indignant comment about Dante's behaviour becomes so loud at this point that I feel obliged to repeat that it arises from a misunderstanding of the *allegory*, and once more refer to Canto VIII. 45, note.

CANTO XXXIV

THE STORY. *After passing over the region of Judecca, where the Traitors to their Lords are wholly immersed in the ice, the Poets see Dis (Satan) devouring the shades of Judas, Brutus, and Cassius. They clamber along his body until, passing through the centre of the Earth, they emerge into a rocky cavern. From here they follow the stream of Lethe upwards until it brings them out on the island of Mount Purgatory in the Antipodes.*

"*Vexilla regis prodeunt inferni*
    Encountering us; canst thou distinguish him,
    Look forward," said the master, "as we journey."

As, when a thick mist breathes, or when the rim   4
    Of night creeps up across our hemisphere,
    A turning windmill looms in the distance dim,

I thought I saw a shadowy mass appear;   7
    Then shrank behind my leader from the blast,
    Because there was no other cabin here.

I stood (with fear I write it) where at last   10
    The shades, quite covered by the frozen sheet,
    Gleamed through the ice like straws in crystal glassed;

Some lie at length and others stand in it,   13
    This one upon his head, and that upright,
    Another like a bow bent face to feet.

And when we had come so far that it seemed right   16
    To my dear master, he should let me see
    That creature fairest once of the sons of light,

He moved him from before me and halted me,   19
    And said: "Behold now Dis! behold the place
    Where thou must steel thy soul with constancy."

How cold I grew, how faint with fearfulness,   22
    Ask me not, Reader; I shall not waste breath
    Telling what words are powerless to express;

This was not life, and yet it was not death;   25
    If thou hast wit to think how I might fare
    Bereft of both, let fancy aid thy faith.

28   The Emperor of the sorrowful realm was there,
            Out of the girding ice he stood breast-high,
            And to his arm alone the giants were

31   Less comparable than to a giant I;
            Judge then how huge the stature of the whole
            That to so huge a part bears symmetry.

34   If he was once as fair as now he's foul,
            And dared outface his Maker in rebellion,
            Well may he be the fount of all our dole.

37   And marvel 'twas, out-marvelling a million,
            When I beheld three faces in his head;
            The one in front was scarlet like vermilion;

40   And two, mid-centred on the shoulders, made
            Union with this, and each with either fellow
            Knit at the crest, in triune junction wed.

43   The right was of a hue 'twixt white and yellow;
            The left was coloured like the men who dwell
            Where Nile runs down from source to sandy shallow.

46   From under each sprang two great wings that well
            Befitted such a monstrous bird as that;
            I ne'er saw ship with such a spread of sail.

49   Plumeless and like the pinions of a bat
            Their fashion was; and as they flapped and whipped
            Three winds went rushing over the icy flat

52   And froze up all Cocytus; and he wept
            From his six eyes, and down his triple chin
            Runnels of tears and bloody slaver dripped.

55   Each mouth devoured a sinner clenched within,
            Frayed by the fangs like flax beneath a brake;
            Three at a time he tortured them for sin.

58   But all the bites the one in front might take
            Were nothing to the claws that flayed his hide
            And sometimes stripped his back to the last flake.

61   "That wretch up there whom keenest pangs divide
            Is Judas called Iscariot," said my lord,
            "His head within, his jerking legs outside;

As for the pair whose heads hang hitherward: 64
  From the black mouth the limbs of Brutus sprawl –
  See how he writhes and utters never a word;

And strong-thewed Cassius is his fellow-thrall.   67
  But come; for night is rising on the world
  Once more; we must depart; we have seen all."

Then, as he bade, about his neck I curled   70
  My arms and clasped him. And he spied the time
  And place; and when the wings were wide unfurled

Set him upon the shaggy flanks to climb,   73
  And thus from shag to shag descended down
  'Twixt matted hair and crusts of frozen rime.

And when we had come to where the huge thigh-bone   76
  Rides in its socket at the haunch's swell,
  My guide, with labour and great exertion,

Turned head to where his feet had been, and fell   79
  To hoisting himself up upon the hair,
  So that I thought us mounting back to Hell.

"Hold fast to me, for by so steep a stair,"   82
  My master said, panting like one forspent,
  "Needs must we quit this realm of all despair."

At length, emerging through a rocky vent,   85
  He perched me sitting on the rim of the cup
  And crawled out after, heedful how he went.

I raised my eyes, thinking to see the top   88
  Of Lucifer, as I had left him last;
  But only saw his great legs sticking up.

And if I stood dumbfounded and aghast,   91
  Let those thick-witted gentry judge and say,
  Who do not see what point it was I'd passed.

"Up on thy legs!" the master said; "the way   94
  Is long, the road rough going for the feet,
  And at mid-terce already stands the day."

The place we stood in was by no means fit   97
  For a king's palace, but a natural prison,
  With a vile floor, and very badly lit.

100 "One moment, sir," said I, when I had risen;
     "Before I pluck myself from the Abyss,
     Lighten my darkness with a word in season.

103 Kindly explain; what's happened to the ice?
     What's turned him upside-down? or in an hour
     Thus whirled the sun from dusk to dawning skies?"

106 "Thou think'st," he said, "thou standest as before
     Yon side the centre, where I grasped the hair
     Of the ill Worm that pierces the world's core.

109 So long as I descended, thou wast there;
     But when I turned, then was the point passed by
     Toward which all weight bears down from everywhere.

112 The other hemisphere doth o'er thee lie –
     Antipodal to that which land roofs in,
     And under whose meridian came to die

115 The Man born sinless and who did no sin;
     Thou hast thy feet upon a little sphere
     Of whose far side Judecca forms the skin.

118 When it is evening there, it's morning here;
     And he whose pelt our ladder was, stands still
     Fixt in the self-same place, and does not stir.

121 This side the world from out high Heaven he fell;
     The land which here stood forth fled back dismayed,
     Pulling the sea upon her like a veil,

124 And sought our hemisphere; with equal dread,
     Belike, that peak of earth which still is found
     This side, rushed up, and so this void was made."

127 There is a place low down there underground,
     As far from Belzebub as his tomb's deep,
     Not known to sight, but only by the sound

130 Of a small stream which trickles down the steep,
     Hollowing its channel, where with gentle fall
     And devious course its wandering waters creep.

133 By that hid way my guide and I withal,
     Back to the lit world from the darkened dens
     Toiled upward, caring for no rest at all,

He first, I following; till my straining sense   136
  Glimpsed the bright burden of the heavenly cars
  Through a round hole; by this we climbed, and thence

Came forth, to look once more upon the stars.   139

THE IMAGES. *Judecca*. The region of the Traitors to sworn alle-
giance is called Judecca after Judas, who betrayed Our Lord.
Here, cut off from every contact and every means of expression,
those who committed the final treason lie wholly submerged.

Judas, Brutus and Cassius. Judas, obviously enough, is the image of
the betrayal of God. To us, with our minds dominated by Shake-
speare and by "democratic" ideas, the presence here of Brutus and
Cassius needs some explanation. To understand it, we must get
rid of all political notions in the narrow sense. We should notice,
first, that Dante's attitude to Julius Caesar is ambivalent. *Person-
ally*, as a pagan, Julius is in Limbo (Canto IV. 123). *Politically*, his
rise to power involved the making of civil war, and Curio, who
advised him to cross the Rubicon, is in the Eighth Circle of Hell
(Canto XXVIII. 97–102 and note). But, although Julius was never
actually Emperor, he was the founder of the Roman Empire, and
by his function, therefore, he images that institution which, in
Dante's view (see Introduction, p. 45), was divinely appointed to
govern the world. Thus Brutus and Cassius, by their breach of
sworn allegiance to Caesar, were Traitors to the Empire, i.e. to
World-order. Consequently, just as Judas figures treason against
God, so Brutus and Cassius figure treason against Man-in-Society;
or we may say that we have here the images of treason against the
Divine and the Secular government of the world.

Dis, so Virgil calls him; Dis, or Pluto, being the name of the King
of the Classical Underworld. But to Dante he is Satan or Lucifer
or Beelzebub – or, as we say, the Devil. "He can see it now – that
which monotonously resents and repels, that which despairs. ...
Milton imagined Satan, but an active Satan; this is beyond it, this
is passive except for its longing. Shakespeare imagined treachery;
this is treachery raised to an infinite cannibalism. Treachery gnaws
treachery, and so inevitably. It is the imagination of the freezing
of every conception, an experience of which neither life nor death
can know, and which is yet quite certain, if it is willed." (Charles
Williams: *The Figure of Beatrice*, p. 144.)

289

NOTES. l. 1: *Vexilla regis prodeunt inferni*: "The banners of the King of Hell go forth". This, with the addition of the word *inferni* (of Hell), is the first line of the Latin hymn which we know best as "The royal banners forward go".

l. 28: *fairest once of the sons of light*: referring to Satan's original status as one of the brightest of the Cherubim.

l. 28: *the Emperor*: "Dante uses the word with the full meaning of its perversion" (Charles Williams). In Canto II, he refers to God as "the Emperor of the Imperium on high"; this is the Emperor of the realm below, who gives his name to the "sorrowful City". (Canto VIII. 68.)

l. 38: *three faces*: The three faces, red, yellow, and black, are thought to suggest Satan's dominion over the three races of the world: the red, the European (the race of Japhet); the yellow, the Asiatic (the race of Shem); the black, the African (the race of Ham). But they are also, undoubtedly, a blasphemous anti-type of the Blessed Trinity: Hatred, Ignorance, Impotence as against Love, Wisdom, Power.

l. 46: *from under each sprang two great wings*: Satan was a fallen cherub, and retains, in a hideous and perverted form, the six wings which belong to his original rank.

ll. 51-2: *three winds ... and froze up all Cocytus*: see Canto XXXIII. 103-108.

l. 68: *night is rising on the world*: it is about 6 P.M.

l. 74: *from shag to shag descended*: Satan's body is shaggy like that of a satyr, according to a well-known medieval convention. The poets clamber down him, feet-first, as one descends a ladder, working their way through the points where the thick pelt prevents the ice from adhering close to the surface of his body. (We must remember the enormous height of Satan – somewhere about 1000 or 1500 ft. at a rough calculation.)

l. 79: *turned head to ... feet*, etc.: They have been descending feet-first; now they turn themselves topsy-turvy and go *up* again, head-first.

l. 93: *what point it was I'd passed*: Since Dante proceeds to take the sting out of "thick-witted" by admitting that he himself was completely bewildered, we may perhaps, without offence, explain that the "point" was the centre of gravity, which was situated precisely at Satan's navel. The sketch on p. 264 will make all these geographical complexities clear.

l. 96: *mid-terce*: Terce, the first of the four canonical divisions of the day, lasted from sunrise (6 A.M. at the equinox) till 9 A.M.; mid-terce would therefore be about 7.30 A.M.

Commentaries

l. 103: *Kindly explain:* Dante wants to know (1) why Satan is apparently upside-down; (2) how it is that, having started their descent of Satan about 6 P.M., they have, after about an hour and a half of climbing, apparently arrived at the following morning. Virgil explains that (1) having passed the centre, they are now in the Southern Hemisphere, so that "up" and "down" are reversed, and (2) they are now going by southern time, so that day and night are reversed. Purgatory stands on the opposite meridian to Jerusalem; therefore Purgatory time is twelve hours behind Jerusalem time; i.e. it is now 7.30 A.M. on Holy Saturday, all over again. (See note on Chronology, p. 296.)

l. 108: *the ill Worm:* Satan. At the centre of the Earth is a little sphere (see l. 116, and look at the sketch, p. 264), and Satan's body is run through this, like a knitting-needle through an orange, with his head out at one end and his legs at the other.

l. 113: *that which land roofs in:* the Northern Hemisphere, which, according to St Augustine and most medieval geographers, contained all the land in the world.

l. 114: *under whose meridian:* the meridian of Jerusalem, where Christ ("the Man born sinless') was crucified.

ll. 116–17: *a little sphere*, etc.: See Sketch, p. 264.

ll. 121 *sqq.*: *This side the world:* i.e. the southern side. When Satan fell from Heaven, two things happened. (1) The dry land, which until then had occupied the Southern Hemisphere, fled in horror from before him, and fetched up in the Northern Hemisphere; while the ocean poured in from all sides to fill the gap. (2) The inner bowels of the Earth, to avoid contact with him, rushed upwards towards the south, and there formed the island and mountain at the top of which was the Earthly Paradise, ready for the reception of Man, and which, after Hell's Harrowing became Mount Purgatory. This, according to Dante, is the only land in the Southern Hemisphere. The hollow thus left in the middle of the Earth is the core of Hell, together with the space in which Dante and Virgil are now standing – the "tomb" of Satan. From this a winding passage leads up to the surface of the Antipodes. By this passage the river Lethe descends, and up it the poets now make their way.

l. 130: *a small stream:* This is Lethe, the river of oblivion, whose springs are in the Earthly Paradise. They are moving against it – i.e. towards recollection.

DANTE'S UNIVERSE

In the fourteenth century, all astronomical calculations were made upon the hypothesis that the Earth was to be regarded as a fixed point at the centre of the universe. This was the Ptolemaic system of astronomy, which was used by everyone until Copernicus discovered that celestial phenomena could be much more simply described and calculated by considering the Sun to be at rest in the centre of the Solar System, with the Earth and the other planets (accompanied by their satellites) revolving about him and rotating upon their own axes.

Ptolemaic astronomy is, however, quite easy to understand if we only remember that, in this system, the *apparent* motions of the heavenly bodies are assumed to be their *real* motions. Indeed, whenever we speak of "moonrise" or of the "low winter sun", we are still using the Ptolemaic system.

The heavenly motions with which readers of the *Comedy* will be most concerned are five:

1. The apparent movement of all the heavenly bodies from east to west about the Earth every 24 hours. We describe this by saying that the real movement is that of the Earth rotating upon her own axis from west to east. The medieval astronomers described it as a real movement of the whole Heavens about an axis passing through the centre of the Earth, whose extremities were the North and South celestial poles.

2. The apparent annual movement of the Sun from west to east among the signs of the Zodiac. We account for this by the Earth's annual revolution about the Sun, so that, as she moves, we observe the Sun against a different background of stars every month (just as, in a moving train, we see a church spire in the foreground change its position with reference to objects on the horizon). The medieval astronomers accounted for it by saying that the Sun had a proper motion of its own, from west to east – i.e. backwards against the diurnal motion of the Heavens (like the motion of a man walking upward upon the down-side of a moving staircase).

3. The apparent spiral movement by which the Sun's path across the sky rises higher towards the pole each day from the winter to the summer solstice and then descends again, so that the days

are longer in summer than in winter. We explain this by saying that the axis of the Earth is inclined to her orbit; the medieval astronomers, by saying that the ecliptic (the Sun's path along the Zodiac) was inclined to the pole of the Heavens.

4. The complicated movements of the planets, which, in their apparent annual motion round the Earth from west to east, seem sometimes to move faster and sometimes to lag behind, or go backwards. This we explain by saying that, since the Earth is also moving round the Sun in the same direction as the planets, but all at different speeds, these apparent changes of direction are due to changes in our own point of view. The medieval astronomers, taking the Earth's position as their fixed point, found that, as seen from that point, each planet had two kinds of proper motion, apart from the 24-hour movement east to west, which they shared with the rest of the Heavens. (a) Like the Sun, it described a "great cycle" about the Earth from west to east; (b) as it went, it described a small cycle, or "epicycle", revolving about a point upon the "great cycle": that is to say, it moved like a point upon the rim of a travelling wheel, which moves forward in the upper half of its revolution and backwards in the lower half, while being continually carried forward in the direction in which the vehicle is travelling. The epicycles, besides explaining the apparent acceleration and retardation of planetary movement, also explained why the planets are nearer to the Earth at some times than at others – thus, if you imagine the travelling wheel to be spinning horizontally, any point on its rim will alternately approach and recede from you as it spins. In the case of the outer planets (Mars, Jupiter, and Saturn), the great cycle corresponds to the planets' own movement round the Sun, and the epicycle to ours; in the case of the inner planets (Mercury and Venus), it is the other way round. (The Sun itself has no epicycle.)

5. The slow swaying movement, like that of a top coming to rest, known as the "precession of the equinoxes", which causes the equinoxes to recede gradually along the ecliptic, so that each year they find the Sun a trifle less advanced on his apparent path through the Zodiac than he was the year before. We call this a movement of the Earth's axis with respect to the Fixed Stars; the medieval astronomers described it as a movement of the Fixed Stars with respect to the pole of the Heavens. (The movement is extremely slow – it will take nearly 26,000 years for the equinoxes to move back through the whole circle of the

Zodiac. Already, however, by Dante's time the equinoxes had moved back so far that the *signs* of the Zodiac no longer coincided with the *constellations* of the Zodiac from which the early astronomers had named them. Dante, however, ignores this discrepancy and always treats the *sign* and the *constellation* as being identical.)

All the planets, including the Sun and Moon, were considered as being carried round the Earth upon a series of transparent and concentric globes, known as the "celestial spheres". (It is these which Dante, considering only that section of them which actually contains the planet, frequently refers to as "*rote*", the heavenly "wheels".) We thus have seven planetary spheres enclosing the Earth (like those "nests" of ivory balls, one within the other, made by Chinese craftsmen). These are, counting from the Earth outwards, the spheres of the Moon, Mercury, Venus, the Sun, Mars, Jupiter, and Saturn. (Uranus, Neptune, and the belt of asteroids between Mars and Jupiter had, of course, not yet been discovered.) Beyond these seven is the sphere of the Fixed Stars, and beyond that the sphere of the Primum Mobile (First Mover), which carries no heavenly bodies, but imparts motion to all the rest. Since all the planetary spheres perform their daily revolution in the same time (24 hours), their speed increases with their distance from the Earth (as the rim of a wheel revolves faster than the hub); the speed of the Primum Mobile, says Dante, cannot itself be measured, for from this sphere time and spaces themselves take their measurement. Beyond all nine spheres lies the Tenth Heaven, or Empyrean, the true abode of God and of His saints, it has neither position nor velocity nor movement nor duration: it is eternal and infinite, and to it all space-time measurements are wholly irrelevant and meaningless. The idea that "the Middle Ages" believed in a localized, temporal, and material Heaven is entirely false; intelligent Christians no more believed such a thing then than they do now.

It is well to remind ourselves that, apart from incidental inaccuracies of observation and measurement due to a lack of instruments of precision, the Ptolemaic view of the universe is neither more true nor more false than our own: it is merely another way of describing the same phenomena. Its truth, however, is of a different kind from ours. The difference is like that between a realistic perspective drawing and a map. In the one, all the geometrical facts are falsified; the lines which we know to be parallel are made to meet; it is a faithful presentation of what we actually see. In the other, all the geometrical facts are adhered to, but the view presented is one we can never see so long as we keep our feet on the earth. The first picture corresponds to our observation; the second is reached by inference.

Although, of course, the "machinery" of the rotating spheres with their deferents and epicycles bears no closer relation to objective fact than do models of the atom made of little rotating balls, yet, *as seen from the Earth*, the movements of the heavenly bodies do trace precisely such patterns as the medieval astronomers described. We find it more convenient to take an imaginary stand at some point *outside* the Solar System and describe the motions from there, so that we can see the whole arrangement laid out as on a plan. For many practical purposes, however, we still use the Ptolemaic vocabulary, turning on our car-lights half an hour after "sunset", and not after "solar horizon-rise", and orientating ourselves at night by that "heavenly pole" which is only the reflection of the Earth's pole and by no means the central pole of the cosmos, if it has one. The Ptolemaic universe is the universe we recognize, as we recognize a photograph or picture of the house in which we live. It is inferior to the Copernican in that its mathematics, even when corrected by modern knowledge, would be too complicated for ready calcula-tion; but it is superior as a description of what the Heavens have to show us, because it is a direct transcript of the observed phenomena.

CHRONOLOGY

THE action of the *Divine Comedy* takes place at Eastertide in the year 1300, and lasts just a week. It is on the night of Maundy Thursday that Dante finds himself astray in the Dark Wood, and on the evening of Good Friday that, after a day spent in vainly endeavouring to scale the Mountain, he meets Virgil and begins his journey through Hell, Purgatory, and Heaven. By the evening of Holy Saturday, the two poets have reached the bottom of Hell at the dead centre of the earth. The greater part of the next twenty-four hours is occupied in climbing the long tunnel which brings them to the surface again at the foot of Mount Purgatory on the other side of the globe, where they arrive at the time corresponding to sunset in our hemisphere, which is, of course, sunrise over there.

Dante does not say whether Purgatory time is to be reckoned as being twelve hours ahead of our time or twelve hours behind, but I think the latter reckoning gives the better symbolical results. In that case, the twenty-four hours taken to climb up from the centre to the Antipodes would cover Holy Saturday (over again in the other hemisphere) and the following night; and the first dawn seen by Dante when he emerged from Hell at the foot of Mount Purgatory would be that of Easter Sunday. This would make the period of the "descent into Hell" coincide exactly with that of our Lord's burial in the grave; so that the soul, "dying to sin", is "buried with Christ" on the Good Friday evening and rises with Him in the dawn of Easter Day; and I cannot but think that Dante had this signification in mind when he dated the opening of his poem so precisely.

According to this chronology, then, Dante, after spending three days and three nights in the ascent of Mount Purgatory and passing six hours in the Earthly Paradise at the top of it, is taken up into the Heavenly Paradise at noon on the Wednesday after Easter. He then rises successively through the ten spheres, all the time going round the world with Wednesday, until, as he passes over the meridian of Jerusalem, the day changes to Thursday. At sunset on Thursday (by our time) he attains the height of the Empyrean, and the visionary journey ends.

HOUR OF THE EARTHQUAKE

HERE I have ventured to differ from the best authorities, ancient and modern, who are almost unanimous in putting the time of the earthquake at noon, and, consequently, that of the poets' interview with Malcoda (Belzecue) at 7 A.M. This argument is based on the fact that Dante wrote in the *Convivio*, "And this is made manifest to us by the hour of His death, for He willed to make that conformable to His life, wherefore Luke says that it was about the sixth hour when He died, that is to say, the culmination of the day." (Meaning, that as Christ ended His life at the middle point of man's mortal span, i.e. about His thirty-fifth year, so also He died at the middle point of the day.) (*Conv.* IV. xxiii. 103–110.)

Allowing full weight to this, I still find it impossible to believe that Dante can have ignored the *unanimous and explicit testimony of all three synoptists* that the last cry from the Cross, followed by the earthquake and the rending of the veil, took place *at the ninth hour*. Nor do I feel that any real contradiction is involved.

I think that Dante looked upon the death of Christ as a single act, occupying three hours in the performance. At noon the "great darkness" descended and Incarnate God entered into death. At the ninth hour the act was completed and the earth quaked. The earthquake, that is to say, marked, not the entry into death, but the entry into Hell, and the breaking open of the gate on which, since then, "no bars remain for ever".

Accordingly, I have made the conference with the demons take place at 10 A.M. The chief objection to this interpretation is that it crams the long and complicated action in Bowges vi, vii, viii, and ix into three hours, while leaving an unnecessarily long time for getting from Bowge iv to Bowge v. On the other hand, Dante seems to imply that the distance between these two bowges was a long one, during which there was leisure for a good deal of conversation "whereof my Comedy cares not to tell". If, with Dr Wicksteed, we start by assuming that the exact time of full moon coincided with sunrise on the morning of Good Friday, the *other* interpretation allows only about eight minutes for the passage between the two bowges, the incident of Bottaio, and the parley with the demons (T. C. *Inf.* pp. 396–7). Neither arrangement is wholly satisfactory; but we may note that in the previous three hours or so (4 A.M. to 6.52 A.M.) are comprised (1) the descent to the Seventh Circle and the journey through the semi-circumference of Ring i, (2) the passage through Ring ii, and (3) Ring iii, (4) the descent of the Great Barrier, in "slow spirals" on Geryon's back, (5) the crossing of Bowge i, and (6) Bowge ii, (7) the descent into Bowge iii, and (8) the arrival at and stay upon the bridge over Bowge iv; so that, compared with this, three hours may appear ample for the adventures between the Sixth and Ninth Bowges. (If, with some commentators, we take 6.15 and not 6.52 as the time of quitting Bowge iv, then 7 A.M. does not seem unreasonably early for the interview with Belzecue, but the passage from the Sixth Circle to the Fourth Bowge is accomplished at still more lightning speed.)

In view of the nightmare distances traversed, it would seem absurd to insist on any great exactness in the matter of miles per hour. I have therefore, after careful consideration, and with a due sense of my own temerity, decided to bring Dante into line with the Evangelists and time the Earthquake for the Ninth Hour.

The confusion in the minds of the early commentators on this point probably arises from the fact that the bell for Nones was rung and the Office said at the *beginning* of the period, i.e. at noon; but *Convivio* IV. xxiii. 140–60 shows Dante to have understood perfectly well that the Canonical division of Nones covered the whole three hours from noon to 3 P.M.

GLOSSARY OF PROPER NAMES

THIS list contains all the names of persons and places mentioned in the *Inferno*, with an indication of all the passages in which they occur. If sufficient information about them has already been given in the "IMAGES" or "NOTES", I have merely inserted the relevant reference; if not, I have included a brief description or explanation here. All references are given by Canto and Line (not by page); if the actual name is not mentioned in Dante's text, the reference relates to the line which identifies the person or place in question. Names of actual inhabitants, or places forming part of the geography, of Dante's Three Kingdoms are shown in capital letters, thus: BEATRICE; STYX; names of persons and places which are merely referred to in the text or notes are shown in italic type, thus: *Nisus*; *Arno*.

Where the English form of the name differs from the classical or Italian form, the form used in the English text is given first, followed by the original or more correct form in brackets, thus: GALEN (Claudius Galenus), *Caieta* (Gaeta).

For the Italian personages the main entry will be found sometimes under the Christian name and sometimes under the family name, according to which is the more familiar, or figures the more prominently in the poem; but a cross-reference is given in every case. Thus, information about FARINATA DEGLI UBERTI will be found under FARINATA, with a cross-reference under UBERTI; but information about JACOPO RUSTICUCCI will be found under RUSTICUCCI, with a cross-reference under JACOPO.

N.B. Both here and in the notes, the myths and stories of antiquity are given as they were known in Dante's day, i.e. in versions that are frequently post-classical and, by modern standards of scholarship, garbled and debased. One god or hero is often confused with another who happened to have a similar name or attributes; the Greek legends in particular have, since the time of Homer, suffered many alterations and additions in passing through the hands of generation after generation of Greek and Latin story-tellers. Here and there I have pointed out a few of the more flagrant corruptions, but for the most part I have been content to tell the tale as it was known to Dante.

Glossary

ABATI, BOCCA DEGLI: see BOCCA DEGLI ABATI.

ABATI, BUOSO DEGLI: see BUOSO DEGLI ABATI.

Abbagliato: the nickname means "Muddlehead"; the spendthrift so called has been identified with a certain Bartolommeo di Rainieri dei Folchacchieri, a Sienese official who held various important posts between 1277 and 1300: but the identification is not certain. (XXXIX. 132.)

ABEL: son of Adam. (IV. 56.)

ABRAHAM: the Patriarch. (IV. 58.)

Absalom: prince of Israel. (XXVIII. 136 and *note* to XXVIII. 134.)

ACCORSO, FRANCIS OF (Francesco d'): Florentine lawyer (1225–93), who lectured at Oxford and Bologna. (XV. 109).

ACHERON: river of Hell. (III. 78 and Images to III; XIV. 116.)

ACHILLES: Greek warrior, the hero of the *Iliad*. He was the son of Peleus by the Nereid Thetis. According to Homer, he was killed at the siege of Troy (*q.v.*); but a later tradition, which Dante follows, tells that he fell in love with Polyxena, daughter of King Priam of Troy, and was promised her hand on condition that he should join the Trojans. Deceived by this promise, he ventured unarmed into a Trojan temple and was there assassinated by Paris. (V. 65; XII. 71; XXVI. 62 and *note* to XXVI. 55; XXXI. 4 and *note*.)

Achitophel: the Gilonite. (XXVIII. 138 and *note* to XXVIII. 134.)

Acquacheta: river of Italy; the old name for the upper reaches of the Montone (see map, p. 173). (XVI. 97 and *note* to XVI. 95.)

Acre: city of Palestine. (XXVII. 89 and *note*.)

ADAM: father of mankind. (III. 116; IV. 55.)

ADAM OF BRESCIA, MASTER: counterfeiter. (XXX. 61 and *note*.)

Adige: river of Italy. (XII. 5 and *note*.)

Aegina: island off the coast of Greece, in the Saronic Gulf between Attica and Argolis. (XXIX. 59 and *note*.)

AENEAS: a Trojan prince, son of Anchises by the goddess Venus; the hero of Virgil's *Aeneid*. Troy having fallen, he escapes with his father, his young son Ascanius, and a number of followers, his wife Creusa having been lost in the confusion. He is told by the Penates (household gods), whose images he has piously brought away with him, that his destiny is to settle in Italy. After many wanderings by sea, in the course of which Anchises dies, his fleet is wrecked by the spite of Juno, but Aeneas with seven of his ships is saved by Neptune and brought to the coast of Africa. Here the Trojans are hospitably received by Dido, queen of Carthage, who, breaking her oath of fidelity to her dead husband, Sychaeus, falls in love with Aeneas, and, when he again sails for Italy at the bidding of Mercury, kills herself.

Aeneas lands in Sicily, celebrates the funeral games of Anchises, and leaves some of his followers to found a colony there. The rest sail on and visit Cumae; here, guided by the Sibyl, Aeneas makes the descent into Hades, where he sees the punishment of the wicked and the placid after-life of the virtuous. Among the latter he meets Anchises, and learns from him that he is destined to be the ancestor of the Roman people, who are to possess the empire of the world. (This is the famous Book VI of the *Aeneid*, from which Dante derived so much of the geography and machinery of his *Inferno*.) Aeneas then sails up the mouth of the Tiber and lands in Latium; here the fulfilment of an oracle shows that the Trojans have reached their destined goal. Latinus, the king of the country, welcomes Aeneas and offers him the hand of his daughter Lavinia, previously betrothed to Turnus, prince of the Rutuli. Juno, with the aid of the Fury Alecto, stirs up war between the Trojans and the Latins, and after a number of engagements, in which allies are called in on both sides, the Rutulians are routed. Turnus challenges Aeneas to single combat; and Juno at length comes to an agreement with Jupiter that Aeneas shall be the victor, on condition that Latium shall keep its own name. Thus in Aeneas and Lavinia the Trojan and Latian lines are united and the way is open for the foundation of the city and empire of Rome. (II. 32; IV. 122; XXVI. 93.)

Aesop: Greek fabulist. (XXIII. 4 and *note*.)

AGHINOLFO DA ROMENA: see ROMENA, AGHINOLFO DA.

AGNEL (Agnello) DEI BRUNELLESCHI: Ghibelline nobleman of Florence. He is said to have begun as a child by stealing from his parents, and when grown up to have got into people's houses, disguised as an old beggar. (XXV. 68.)

Alard (Érard) *de Valéry*: constable of Champagne (*c.* 1200–1277). He accompanied St Louis (Louis IX of France) on his crusading expeditions of 1248 and 1265; and on his way home in 1268 he passed through Italy and there assisted Charles of Anjou to win the Battle of Tagliacozzo. In 1270 he accompanied St Louis to the East for the third time, and after his death returned to France, where he died in great honour at the age of about 77. (XXVIII. 18 and *note* to XXVIII. 17.)

ALBERIGO: Friar, of the Manfredi family. (XXXIII. 118 and *note*.)

Albero of Siena: (XXIX. 110 and *note*).

Alberti, Alberto degli: count of Mangara. (XXXII. 56 and *note*.)

ALBERTI, ALESSANDRO, and NAPOLEONE DEGLI: sons of Alberto degli Alberti. (XXXII. 56 and *note*.)

Alberto degli Alberti: see *Alberti, Alberto degli*.

Glossary

ALDOBRANDI, TEGGHIAIO: a Florentine Guelf nobleman of the Adi-
mari family. He was spokesman of the Guelf nobles who, with
Guido Guerra (*q.v.*) at their head, advised against the disastrous
expedition against Siena which ended in the defeat of the Floren-
tines at Montaperti (1260) (see Introd., p. 30). (VI. 78; XVI. 41 *sqq.*
and *note*.)

ALECTO: see FURIES.

ALESSANDRO DEGLI ALBERTI: see ALBERTI, ALESSANDRO DEGLI.

ALESSIO INTERMINEI: see INTERMINEI, ALESSIO.

ALEXANDER: (1) Alexander the Great, king of Macedonia and
conqueror of Asia (356–323 B.C.). Having subdued Greece, he
crossed the Hellespont, vanquished Darius the Persian at the
Battles of Granicus and Issus, and took most of the cities of Phoe-
nicia. He next received the submission of Egypt and founded
Alexandria; and thence marched into Mesopotamia, where he
decisively overcame the Persians at the Battle of Arbela (331 B.C.).
After taking Babylon, Susa, and Persepolis and subduing the
Northern provinces of Asia, he invaded India, crossing the Urdas
and advancing as far as the Hydaspes. He intended to conquer
Arabia, subjugate Italy, Carthage, and the West and so become
master of the world; but died of a fever at Babylon at the age of
32. (XII. 107, or the ref. may be to Alexander of Pherae or Jeru-
salem; XIV. 31.)

(2) Alexander of Pherae – Tagus of Thessaly (reigned 369–367
B.C.). His rule was tyrannical; the historian Diodorus Siculus
relates that he sewed his victims into the skins of beasts and had
them mangled by fierce hounds; Plutarch, that he had them buried
alive. (XII. 107, if the ref. is not to Alexander the Great or Alex-
ander of Jerusalem.)

(3) Alexander Jannaeus, king of the Jews (103–76 B.C.), son
of Hyrcanus, who waged war on his own subjects with great
butchery. Thought by some commentators to be the tyrant
referred to by Dante. (XII. 107.)

N.B. The fact that in the *Convivio* Dante mentions Alexander
the Great as an example of munificence has made some writers
think that the tyrant mentioned in XII. 107 must be some other
Alexander; but Orosius (*q.v.*), on whom Dante relied for much of
his history, calls Alexander the Great "insatiable of human blood",
and "a whirlpool of miseries and most ferocious whirlwind for
the whole Orient", and, having said that he "oppressed the world
by the sword for 12 years", winds up with a long diatribe about
the ruin and wretchedness wrought by his violence and cruelty.
It is therefore almost certain that he is the tyrant intended.

Glossary

Alexander (Alessandro) *da Romena*: see *Romena, Alexander da.*

ALI IBN ABU TALEB: nephew of and successor to Mahomet (*q.v.*). (XXVIII. 32 and *note*.)

ALICHINO: see HELLKIN.

ALIGHIERI, DANTE: see DANTE ALIGHIERI.

Almayn (Germany): (XX. 61.)

Alps: mountains. (XIV. 30; XX. 62.)

Altaforte (Hautefort): castle in the Limousin district of France near Périgueux, belonging to Bertrand de Born (*q.v.*). (XXIX. 29.)

AMPHIARAÜS: one of the seven kings who fought against Thebes (XX. 34 and *note*.)

Amphion: in class. myth., son of Zeus and Antiope. (XXXII. 11 and *note*.)

ANASTASIUS II, POPE: (X. 8 and *note*.)

ANAXAGORAS: Ionian philosopher (500–428 B.C.). He rejected the materialist explanation of the universe, and held that mind or intelligence (*nous*) was the cause of all things. (IV. 137.)

Anchises: father of Aeneas (*q.v.*). (I. 74.)

ANDREA DEI MOZZI: see MOZZI, ANDREA DEI.

ANGEL: see HEAVENLY MESSENGER.

ANGELS, BLACK: (XXIII. 131).

Angiolello da Calignano: nobleman of Fano. (XXVIII. 77 and *note*.)

ANNAS: High Priest of Israel, father-in-law to Caiaphas. (XXIII. 122.)

Anselm (Anselmuccio): grandson of Count Ugolino della Gherardesca. (XXXIII. 50 and *note* to XXXIII. 34.)

ANTAEUS: giant. (XXXI. 101 and *note*.)

ANTENORA: region of Hell. (XXXII. 89 and Images to XXXII.)

Apennine, Mount: (XX. 65 and see map, p. 173).

Apennines: mountain-range in Italy. (XVI. 96.)

Apulia: region of S.E. Italy. (XXVIII. 9.)

    Apulian: (XXVIII. 16.)

Aquarius: see *Zodiac.*

AQUINAS, ST THOMAS (Tommaso d' Aquino) (1225 or 7–1274): the greatest of the scholastic theologians, the "Common Doctor" of the Church, whose great work in systematizing Christian Doctrine according to Aristotelian philosophic method dominated the thought of the Middle Ages, and is still officially accepted as fundamental to the exposition of Catholic theology.

    Born at Rocca Sicca in Campania, the son of the Count of Aquino; entered the Dominican Order at the age of 17; studied under Albertus Magnus of Cologne; debated in Paris, 1245; taught in Cologne, 1248; Doctor of Theology (Sorbonne), 1257; lectured in Paris, Rome, Bologna, etc.; wrote exhaustive commentaries on the Works of Aristotle, and many theological works, including the *Summa contra Gentiles* (dealing with the principles of natural religion) and the monumental *Summa Theologica* – usually referred to briefly as the *Summa* – a complete systematization of Christian theology; died at Fossa Nuova, near Terracina, on the way to attend the Council of Lyons in 1274; canonized, 1323 (two years after Dante's death).

The work of St Thomas in "baptizing" secular philosophy into the Christian faith, and so reconciling reason with revelation, was of incalculable value, especially at that period, when the rediscovery of classical learning and literature was threatening to disturb people's minds by the apparent dilemma of having to choose between the two. St Thomas maintained and demonstrated that the knowledge that God exists could be arrived at by the reason, and that revelation, although transcending reason, at no time contradicted it.

Dante studied the works of St Thomas closely, and the theological structure of the *Comedy* owes more to him than to any other single theologian, although the poet supplemented his teaching by that of many other authorities, and did not hesitate to differ from him, now and again, in points of detail. References to relevant passages from St Thomas will be found from time to time in the *notes*.

Dante places St Thomas in Paradise, in the Heaven of the Sun, among the Doctors of the Church (*Para*. x–xiii). *Notes, passim*.)

Arabia: *Arabian*. (XXIV. 106.)

Arachne: daughter of Idmon of Colophon in Lydia, was rash enough to challenge the goddess Athene (Minerva) to a weaving competition and to produce a web of such unsurpassable beauty that the jealous goddess tore it to pieces. Arachne hanged herself in despair; but Athene changed the rope to a cobweb and Arachne to a spider. (XVII. 18.)

Arbia: river near Siena. (See Introd., p. 30 and X. 32, *note*). (X. 86.)

Arethusa: in class. myth., a nymph who, being pursued by the river-god Alpheus, was changed by Artemis (Diana) to a fountain. (XXV. 98.)

Arezzo: city of Italy, in the S.E. of Tuscany; the Aretines were strongly Ghibelline and in continual feud with the Florentines (see Introd., p. 30).

    Aretine(s): (XXII. 5; XXIX. 109; XXX. 31).

Glossary

AREZZO, GRIFFOLINO D': see GRIFFOLINO D' AREZZO.

ARGENTI, FILIPPO: Florentine knight. (VIII. 61 and *note*.)

Argo: men of – (*gente Argolica*) – either (1) men of Argos (Greece), or (2) possibly, the crew of the ship Argo in which Jason brought back the Golden Fleece (see JASON). (XXVIII. 84 and *note*.)

Ariadne: sister of Theseus (*q.v.*). (XII. 19.)

Aries: see *Zodiac*.

ARISTOTLE: the great Athenian philosopher, founder of the Peripatetic School (384–322 B.C.). He was Plato's most brilliant pupil, but later diverged considerably from his master's teaching. His works were rediscovered and translated in the Middle Ages (largely through the work of the Arabian scholars), and became enormously influential. The work of St Thomas Aquinas incorporated the Aristotelian system of philosophy into Catholic theology. All Western philosophy derives ultimately from the twin Platonic and Aristotelian traditions.

The works of Aristotle were voluminous, and covered every branch of learning known in his day: Dialectics and Logic (*The Organon*); Philosophy (the *Physics* and other works on natural science; the *Metaphysics*; 2 treatises on *Mathematics*); Politics (the *Ethics*, the *Politics*, the *Economics*); Art (the *Poetics*, the *Rhetoric*). Only the major works are mentioned in this list, but there are many others.

For Aristotle, human thought proceeds by abstraction from the data provided by the senses; i.e. investigation into the nature of being starts from the observation of individual things sensibly existing. It is in this feature that his philosophy contrasts most forcibly with the Platonic idealism, for which (especially in its later developments) the world of existence is only the shadow of the world of essences. Aristotle analyses the individual existent into Matter (undifferentiated "stuff") and Form (structural organization), and the process by which a thing comes to attain its proper end (to be what it was intended to be) into the passage from Potentiality to Actuality. Neither Form nor Matter has any real existence by itself – every individual existent being a Form-Matter complex. The soul of the individual man is the "form" of the human body, both soul and body being thus considered as essential parts of the actualized personality. It is obvious that this concept lends itself readily to incorporation into orthodox Christian doctrine (e.g. of the sanctity of the material universe, sacramentalism, and the Resurrection of the Body) as opposed to the Gnostic doctrines of the inherent evil of matter derived from the Neo-Platonists. God is "the unmoved Mover", source of all change, motion, and process – a definition which has left its mark on Thomist theology.

Dante was well acquainted with all the works of Aristotle that were available in Latin translation in his time, and refers to them many times. (IV. 131: VI. 106; (*Ethics*) XI. 80; (*Physics*) XI. 101.)

Arles: city in the S. of France at the mouth of the Rhone. (IX. 112 and *note*.)

Arno: river of Italy. (XIII. 146; XV. 113; XXIII. 95; XXX. 65; XXXIII. 83.)

ARRIGO: probably Oderigo Fifanti, a Florentine Ghibelline, one of the murderers of Buondelmonte (see Introd., p. 29 and XXVIII. 106, *note*). (VI. 80.)

Arsenal: in Venice. (XXI. 7 and *note*.)

ARUNS: Etruscan augur. (XX. 46 and *note*.)

Asciano, Caccia d': see *Caccia d'Asciano*.

ASDENTE: soothsayer of Parma. (XX. 118.)

Athamas: husband to Ino, the sister of Semele (*q.v.*) and daughter of Cadmus, king of Thebes. (XXX. 4 *sqq.* and *note* to XXX. 1.)

Athens, Duke of: see Theseus.

Atropos: see *Fates*. (XXXIII. 126.)

ATTILA: king, or chieftain, of the Huns (433–53). Called the Scourge of God for his atrocities. He made himself master of all the peoples of Germany and Scythia, and with his hordes overran Illyria, Thrace, Macedon, Greece, etc. In 451 he invaded Gaul, but was checked by Theodoric and finally routed by Thorismond the Goth. The following year he descended upon Italy, devastating Aquileia, Milan, Padua, and other places. Temporarily restrained by Pope Leo I, he was preparing for a fresh invasion when he died, or was murdered, in the following year. (XII. 135; XIII. 149 (where he is confused with Totila (*q.v.*)) and *note*.)

Augustus: (as Imperial title denoting the Emperor Frederick II). (XIII. 68.)

Augustus Caesar: see CAESAR.

Austria: (XXXII. 25).

Aventine, Mount (Monte Aventino): one of the Seven Hills of Rome, legendary site of the Cave of Cacus (*q.v.*). (XXV. 26.)

AVERROES (Ibn Roshd): Arabian physician and philosopher. His famous commentary on Aristotle, translated into Latin, had a wide vogue in the Middle Ages, and did much to revive the study of Aristotelian philosophy. He taught a pantheistic doctrine of Universal Reason, and denied the immortality of the individual soul. He was born at Cordova and died at Morocco (1126–98). (IV. 144.)

Glossary

AVICEN (Avicenna): Arabian physician and philosopher (980–1037), wrote commentaries on Aristotle and Galen (*q.v.*). (IV. 143.)

AZZOLINO (or Ezzelino) III DA ROMANO (1194–1259): a Ghibelline noble, son-in-law of the Emperor Frederick II and Imperial Vicar in the Marca Trivigiana. He was notorious for his cruelty, and especially for a hideous massacre of the citizens of Padua. (XII. 109; *note* to XIII. 115.)

Babel: (1) Babylon in Asia; city of Babylonia, ruled over anciently by Ninus (*q.v.*); apparently confused by Dante with

(2) Babylon in Egypt, ruled over in Middle Ages by the Soldan; identified by medieval writers with

(3) Babel, city mentioned in *Gen.* xi (see NIMROD). (V. 54.)

Babylon: see *Babel*.

Bacchiglione: river of Italy, in Venetia, on which Vicenza stands. (XV. 113.)

Bacchus: in Greek myth. god of wine, "Bacchus' city" is Thebes. (XX. 59.)

BAPTIST: see JOHN BAPTIST, ST.

BARBARICCIA: see BARBIGER.

BARBIGER (Barbariccia): demon. (XXI. 120; XXII. 28, 59, 145.)

BEATRICE: daughter of Folco Portinari, born in Florence, 1266. In the *Vita Nuova* (*New Life*) Dante says that he first saw and fell in love with her when she was 8 years and 4 months old and he was nearly 9. She was married to Simone dei Bardi, and died in 1290 (see Introd., pp. 23 *sqq.* and The Greater Images, p. 67. (II. 53 *sqq.*; X. 131; XII. 88; XV. 89.)

BECCARIA, TESAURO DEI: of Pavia, Abbot of Vallombrosa and Legate in Florence of Pope Alexander IV. He was accused by the Florentine Guelfs of intriguing against them after the expulsion of the Ghibellines in 1258, and was beheaded the same year. (XXXII. 119.)

BECCHI, GIOVANNI BUIAMONTE DEI: see BUIAMONTI, GIOVANNI.

BELLO, GERI DEL: see GERI (Ruggieri) DEL BELLO.

BELZEBUB (Beelzebub): see DEVIL. (XXXIV. 128.)

BELZECUE (Malacoda): demon. (XXI. 76, 79.)

Benaco (Lake Garda): (XX. 63 *sqq.* and see map, p. 173).

Benedetto, San: see *Benedict's, St*.

Benedict's, St (San Benedetto in Alpe): Monastery on the upper reaches of the Acquacheta (*q.v.*). (XVI. 101, 102, *note*.)

Bergamo: Bergamese. (XX. 71.)

BERTRAND DE BORN: lord of Hautefort (Altaforte), soldier and troubadour. (XXVIII. 134 and *note*; XXIX. 29.)

Glossary

Bisenzio; river of Italy, tributary of the Arno. (XXXII. 57.)

BOCCA DEGLI ABATI: Florentine traitor. (XXXII. 106 and *note* to XXXII. 79.)

Bologna: city of Italy, in the Romagna (see map, p. 173). (XVIII. 58 XXIII. 104, 143.)

BONATTI, GUY (Guido): astrologer of Forlì. (XX. 118.)

BONIFACE VIII: Pope (Benedict Caietan) (*c.* 1217–1303; Pope, 1294–1303) (see Introd., pp. 34 *sqq.*). (XV. 112; XIX. 53 and *note*; XXVII. 70, 85.)

Bonturo Dati: head of the popular party in Lucca. Notorious for his barratry. Benvenuto da Imola says that he "controlled the whole commune, and promoted or excluded from office whomever he chose". He was eventually (1314) expelled from Lucca and fled to Florence, where he died. (XXI. 41.)

BORN, BERTRAND DE: see BERTRAND DE BORN.

BORSIER (E), GUILLIM (Guglielmo): according to the old commentators, this Florentine was originally a purse-maker, who gave up his trade in order to "go into society", where he made himself useful by arranging marriages, treaties of peace and alliance, etc., between noble families. Boccaccio, who tells a story about him in the *Decameron* (Day i, Novel 8), describes him as worthy, witty, and respected. (XVI. 70.)

BOTTAIO, MARTINO: alderman of Lucca. (XXI. 35 and *note*.)

BRANCA D' ORIA: of Genoa. (XXXIII. 137 and *note*; XXII. 88, *note*.)

Branda, Fountain of: in Siena, or, more probably, Romena. (XXX. 78.)

Brenta: river of Italy. (XV. 7.)

Brescia: city of Italy (see map, p. 173). (XX. 69.)
    Brescians: (XX. 71).

BRESCIA, MASTER ADAM OF: see ADAM OF BRESCIA.

BRIAREUS: giant. (XXXI. 99 and *note*.)

Brigata: see *Nino della Gherardesca*.

Brigata Spendereccia: see *Spendthrift's Club*.

Bruges: city of Flanders. (XV. 5.)

BRUNELLESCHI, AGNELLO DEI: see AGNEL DEI BRUNELLESCHI.

BRUNETTO LATINI: Florentine politician and man of learning. (XV. 30 *sqq.* and *note* and see Introd. p. 31.)

BRUTUS: (1) Lucius Junius: aroused the Roman people to overthrow Tarquinius Superbus, whose son Sextus had outraged Lucretia, the wife of his cousin L. Tarquinius Collatinus (510 B.C.). (IV. 127.)

    (2) Marcus Junius (85–42 B.C.): son of M. Brutus the Tribune and Servilia, half-sister of Cato of Utica. Trained by his uncle Cato in the principles of the aristocratic party, when the civil war broke out in 49 B.C., he joined Pompey, although the latter had

put his father to death. After the Battle of Pharsalia in 48 B.C., Julius Caesar not only pardoned him but raised him to high favour, making him governor of Cisalpine Gaul (46 B.C.) and praetor (44 B.C.), and promising him the governorship of Macedonia. Persuaded, however, by Cassius (*q.v.*), he took part in the conspiracy to murder Caesar in the hope of re-establishing the Republic (Ides of March, 44 B.C.). After Caesar's death, he took possession of Macedonia, and was joined by Cassius, who commanded in Syria. In 42 B.C. their united forces were defeated by Octavian (afterwards Augustus) Caesar and Mark Antony at the Battle of Philippi, and Brutus committed suicide. (XXXIV. 65.)

BUIAMONTE, GIOVANNI: a notorious usurer, whose family were lords of Torre Becchi in the territory of Florence, and bore arms: *or*, 3 *becchi* (goats, or possibly eagles' beaks) *sable*. Giovanni was living in Florence in 1300, but is said to have died later in great poverty. (XVII. 72 and *note* to XVII. 55.)

Bulicame: spring near Viterbo. (XIV. 79 and *note*.)

BUOSO DA DUERA: see DUERA, BUOSO DA.

BUOSO DEGLI ABATI: Florentine nobleman, of whom nothing is known except that the old commentator Lana and Dante's son Pietro identify him as the "Buoso" mentioned in the Bowge of the Thieves; others say the ref. is to Buoso dei Donati (*q.v.*). (XXV. 140 and *note* to XXV. 35–6.)

BUOSO DEI DONATI: of the great Florentine family to which belonged Corso dei Donati, the Black Guelf leader, and Dante's wife, Gemma (see Introd., pp. 32, 38). (XXX. 44 and *note* to XXX. 32.) He is perhaps also the Buoso mentioned in XXV. 140 (see *note* to XXV. 35–6).

Caccia d'Ascian(o): Sienese spendthrift. (XXIX. 130.)

CACCIANEMICO, VENEDICO: Guelf nobleman of Bologna. (XVIII. 49–50 and *note*.)

CACUS: monster (according to Dante a centaur). (XXV. 25 and *note*.)

CADMUS: in class. myth., son of Agenor, king of Phoenicia. Jupiter in the form of a white bull carried away his sister Europa; and Cadmus, going in search of her, became the founder of Thebes (q.v.). Having killed a dragon sacred to Mars, he was changed into a serpent. (XXV. 98.)

CAESAR: (1) Caius Julius, Dictator of Rome (100–44 B.C.) – son of C. Julius Caesar the praetor, he liked to claim descent from the Trojan hero Aeneas (*q.v.*), founder of Rome. A brilliant general, and strong adherent of the democratic party, he was made Consul, 59 B.C.; his conquest of Gaul (59–51 B.C.) made him the idol of the people and the army. His rival, Pompey, jealous of his rising power, joined the aristocratic party and headed an armed opposition against him; but Julius, crossing the river Rubicon which separated his own province from Italy, marched upon Rome, and being everywhere received with acclamation, made himself master of all Italy (49 B.C.). After defeating Pompey's adherents in Spain, he crossed over into Greece and decisively overthrew Pompey at the Battle of Pharsalia (48 B.C.). He was made Dictator and, after a period of further military triumphs, was offered the kingship; this, however, he reluctantly refused, for fear of offending the people. On the Ides of March, 44 B.C., he was assassinated in the Capitol by a band of conspirators, led by Brutus and Cassius. His successor Augustus (*q.v.*) was the first Roman Emperor, and the name Caesar became part of the Imperial title. (I. 70; IV. 123; XXVIII. 97; see also Images to XXXIV.)

(2) Caesar Augustus (Caius Julius Caesar Octavianus): 1st Roman Emperor (63 B.C.–A.D. 14). He was the great nephew of Julius Caesar and adopted by him as his heir. After the assassination of Julius, he assumed the name of Caesar, and became, with Lepidus and Mark Antony, one of the triumvirs who took over the government of the Republic. He gradually gathered all the great offices of state into his own hands, and in 32 B.C. he accepted the title of Imperator. The defeat of Antony at Actium (31 B.C.) and the death of Lepidus (12 B.C.) left him in fact and in name sole master of the Roman Empire. The epithet "Augustus", conferred on him by the Senate in 27 B.C., was borne by his successors as part of the Imperial title. The "Augustan age" was marked by a brilliant flowering of Latin literary genius.

Caesar (as Imperial title denoting the Emperor Frederick II). (XIII. 65.)

CAGNAZZO: see HARROWHOUND.

Cahors: city of France. (XI. 50 and *note*.)

CAIAPHAS: High Priest of Israel, who condemned Christ. (XXIII. 115 *sqq*. and Images to XXIII.)

Caieta (Gaeta): (XXVI. 92 and *note*).

Cain (with Thornbush): the Man in the Moon. (XX. 124 and *note*.)

CAÏNA: a region of Hell. (V. 107 and *note*; XXXII. 59 *sqq*. and Images to XXXII. 59.)

CALCABRINA: see HACKLESPUR.

Calchas: augur who accompanied the Greeks to the siege of Troy. (XX. 111.)

Calignano, Angiolello da: see *Angiolello da Calignano*.

CAMICION DEI PAZZI: of Valdarno. (XXXII. 68 and *note*.)

CAMILLA: a warrior-maiden vowed to the service of Diana. She assisted Turnus (*q.v.*) against Aeneas, and after killing many Trojans was slain by Aruns. (I. 108; IV. 124.)

Camonica, Val: valley in Lombardy (XX. 66.)

Campaldino: Battle of. (XXII. 1 and *note*; see Introd., p. 31.)

CANCELLIERI, FOCACCÌA DEGLI: see FOCACCÌA DEGLI CANCELLIERI.

CAPANEUS: one of the "Seven against Thebes". (XIV. 63, also *note* to XIV. 51 and Images to XIV; XXV. 15.)

CAPOCCHIO: the name, or nickname, means "Blockhead": the family name of this counterfeiter is not known; nor is it certain whether he was a Florentine or a Sienese. (XXIX. 136; XXX. 28.)

Caprara (Capraia): island near the mouth of the Arno. (XXXIII. 83 and *note* to XXXIII. 82.)

Caprona: fortress of Pisa. (XXI. 95 and *note*; see also Introd., p. 31.)

Carisenda (Garisenda): leaning tower at Bologna. (XXXI. 136 and *note*.)

CARLIN(O) DEI PAZZI: of Valdarno. (XXXII. 69 and *note*.)

Carrara: town and hills in Italy (Tuscany). (XX. 48 *sqq.*)

Casalodi, Alberto di: (XX. 95 and *note*.)

Casentin(o): district of Tuscany. (XXX. 65 and *note*.)

Cassero, Guido del: see *Guido del Cassero*.

CASSIUS (Caius Cassius Longinus): Roman statesman and general. After distinguishing himself as a soldier in the campaigns against the Parthians (53–51 B.C.) he returned to Rome. In 49 B.C. he was tribune of the plebs, but when the civil war broke out, he joined the aristocratic party and fled from Rome with Pompey, whose fleet he commanded in 48 B.C. After the Battle of Pharsalia he went to the Hellespont and, accidentally falling in with Julius Caesar, surrendered to him. Caesar not only pardoned him but made him praetor and promised him the governorship of Syria. Cassius, however, repaid this generosity by heading a conspiracy to murder Caesar, and persuading M. Brutus (*q.v.*) to join it. After Caesar's death (Ides of March, 44 B.C.) he claimed the governorship of Syria according to Caesar's promise, although the Senate had given it to Dolabella. He defeated Dolabella and, after plundering Syria and Asia, joined Brutus in Macedonia in opposition to Octavian (Augustus) Caesar and Mark Antony. At the Battle of Philippi (42 B.C.) Cassius was defeated by Antony and took his own life. (XXXIV. 67.)

CATALANO DEI MALAVOLTI, FRA: *podestà* of Florence. (XXIII. 104, 114.)

CATO OF UTICA (Marcus Porcius Cato the Younger): Roman statesman (95–46 B.C.). A strict republican of the old school, nurtured in the Stoic philosophy, he at first opposed both Caesar and Pompey, but when the civil war broke out (see CAESAR, JULIUS), found himself obliged to take sides with the latter. After the Battle of Pharsalia he escaped into Africa and, after a terrible march across the desert, joined forces with Metellus Scipio, who had the command of Pompey's African forces. Caesar defeated Scipio at the Battle of Thapsus, and Cato, rather than make terms with the victor, committed suicide. He became for the Romans the typical example of Stoic virtue. In the *Purgatorio*, Dante makes him guardian of the approach to Mt. Purgatory. (XIV. 15 and *note*.)

Cattolica, La: town of Italy on the Adriatic. (XXVIII. 80 and *note* to XXVIII. 77.)

Caurus: N.W. wind. (XI. 114.)

CAVALCANTI, CAVALCANTE DEI: father of Guido Cavalcanti. (X. 53 and *note*.)

CAVALCANTI, FRANCESCO GUERCIO DEI: Florentine nobleman, mentioned by Dante as a thief; murdered by the people of Gaville (*q.v.*). (XXV. 151 and *note*.)

CAVALCANTI, GUIDO DEI: son of Cavalcante dei Cavalcanti, was born between 1250 and 1259. Dante, who calls him "the first of my friends", says that their friendship began when Guido wrote a reply to one of his sonnets, and it was with him that Dante went to the famous party where Beatrice mocked at him (Introd., p. 27). Like Dante, he belonged to the younger school of poets, who wrote in the "sweet new style – *il dolce stil nuovo*" and, like his father, was an "Epicurean". Guido was a White Guelf, and his marriage to the daughter of the Ghibelline Farinata degli Uberti was one of the alliances frequently arranged in the hope of reconciling the two parties. He died in August 1300 (Introd. p. 34 and *note*). (X. 63 and *note*.)

Cecina: river of Italy. (XIII. 8 and *note*.)

CELESTINE V, POPE: (III. 59 and *note*; XXVII. 103 and *note*; XXVII. 105.)

CENTAURS: in Homer, an ancient and savage race, inhabiting Mt. Pelion in Thessaly; represented in later legend as monsters, half-horse, half-man. (XII. 55 *sqq.* and *note*, and Images to XII.)

Ceperan(o): pass of. (XXXVIII. 16 and *note*.)

CERBERUS: the three-headed hound of Hell. (VI. 13 *sqq.* and Images to VI; IX. 98 and *note*.)

CERVIA: town near Ravenna. (XXVII. 42 and *note* to XXVII. 40.)

CESNA: town of N. Italy on the Savio. (XXVII. 52 and *note*.)

CEUTA: city in Morocco, on the peninsula which forms the S. side of the Straits of Gibraltar. (XXVI. 110.)

Glossary

CHARLEMAYN (Charlemagne): emperor of the West (742–814), son of Pépin le Bref, king of the Franks; received the Imperial Crown from Pope Leo III, Christmas Day, 800. As a defender of the Christian faith in two wars against heretics and Saracens, he was canonized in 1165. Dante places him in Mars, the Heaven of the Warriors (*Para.* xviii. 43). His wars and his Twelve Peers, of whom his nephew Roland and Roland's friend Oliver are the best known, became legendary and were celebrated in the early *chansons de geste* and many later epics. (XXXI. 16.)

CHARLES I: king of Naples and Sicily, count of Anjou and Provence, son of Louis VIII of France and Blanche of Castile (1220–1284). Invited by Pope Urban IV to assume the crown of Naples, and urged by Pope Clement IV to take possession of the kingdom, he entered Italy in 1265, was crowned King of Sicily and Apulia in 1265, and defeated Manfred at Benevento in 1266. The Sicilians, revolting against French rule, invited Conradin (son of the Emperor Conrad IV) to expel him. He defeated Conradin at Tagliacozzo in 1268, but in 1282 the Sicilian "underground movement" (surreptitiously aided, as was believed, by Pope Nicholas III and others) broke out into open insurrection, ending in a fearful massacre of the French (the "Sicilian Vespers") and the end of their rule in Sicily. Charles died in 1284, while trying to regain the kingdom. He appears in person in the *Comedy* on the lower slopes of Purgatory. (XIX. 99 and *note*; see also Introd., p. 25.)

CHARON: ferryman of Hell (Acheron). (III. 83 *sqq.* and Images.)

Charybdis: In the *Odyssey*, the ship of Ulysses (Odysseus) has to pass through a narrow strait between rocks which are inhabited respectively by two sea-monsters: Scylla, who devours the sailors with her teeth, and Charybdis, who thrice a day sucks down the sea into a fearful whirlpool and thrice spews it up again. In later legend, both Scylla and Charybdis are women, changed into these shapes for having wittingly or unwittingly offended the gods. Ovid (*Metam.* xiii. 749 *sqq.*) tells the story of Scylla, and locates the perilous passage between Scylla and Charybdis in the Straits of Messina. (VII. 23.)

CHERUBS, BLACK: (XXVII. 114).

Chiana, Val di: see *Valdichiana*.

Chiarentana: mountain of Italy. (XV. 9 and *note* to XV. 4.)

CHIRON: Centaur. (XII. 63 *sqq.* and *note*.)

CHRIST: The name of Christ is never spoken in Hell. He is, however, referred to by various periphrases:
    my Lord (by Beatrice). (II. 73.)

the high Wisdom (inscription on Hell-gate). (III. 6.)

One coming in majesty (by Virgil). (IV. 53.)

the Enemy Power (by Virgil). (VI. 96.)

He ... who seized from Dis the mighty prey (by Virgil). (XII. 38.)

our Lord (by Dante). (XIX. 92.)

(the) Spouse (of the Church) (by Dante). (XIX. 111.)

the Man born sinless and who did no sin (by Virgil). (XXXIV. 115.)

CIACCO: Florentine citizen. (XI. 52 and *note*.)

CIAMPOLO (or Gian Polo): barrator, from Navarre. (XXII. 44 *sqq*.)

CIANFA DEI DONATI: Florentine nobleman, said to have been a cattle-thief and shop-breaker. (XXV. 43, 49 *sqq*.)

Cicero (Marcus Tullius): Roman orator (106–43 B.C.). Author of various rhetorical and philosophical works. His discourses on *Friendship* (*de Amicitia*) and *Old Age* (*de Senectute*) were well known to Dante, and the arrangement of sins in the *Inferno* is partly derived from his essay *On Duty* (*de Officiis*). (IV. 140; Images to XI.)

Circe: the sorceress. (XXVI. 91 and *note*.)

CIRATTO: see GUTTLEHOG.

CLEMENT V (Bertrand de Got): Pope, 1305–14. It was he who, under pressure from Philip the Fair, transferred the Holy See to Avignon, where it remained from 1309 to 1377. (XIX. 83.)

CLEOPATRA: queen of Egypt (68–30 B.C.): mistress of (*a*) Julius Caesar, (*b*) Mark Antony. When Antony's defeat by Octavius (Augustus) Caesar was followed by his suicide, she killed herself by the bite of an asp. (V. 63.)

COCYTUS: Circle and River of Hell. (XIV. 119, 120; XXXI. 123; XXXIII. 156; XXXIV. 52.)

Colchis: ancient country of Asia, below the Caucasus, between Iberia and the Euxine (Black Sea). (XVIII. 87 and *note*.)

Cologne: city of Germany, on the Rhine. (XXIII. 63.)

Colonna (Colonnesi): a great Roman family, with whom Pope Boniface VIII had a feud for many years, and against whom he actually proclaimed a crusade. In 1297, Sciarra Colonna having robbed the Papal treasury, Boniface deprived his uncles, the Cardinals Jacopo and Pietro, of their dignities, excommunicated them and their whole house, and destroyed their palaces. The Colonnesi retired to their fortresses at Palestrina and Nepi. The Pope, having taken Nepi, proceeded, on the advice of Guido da Montefeltro, to procure the surrender of Palestrina and the submission of the Colonnesi by promising a full amnesty; which promise he treacherously broke. The Colonnesi rebelled again, were again excommunicated; and in 1303, it was Sciarra Colonna who, on behalf of Philip the Fair of France, made Boniface a prisoner at Anagni (Introd., p. 33). The Pope's feud against the Colonna family is alluded to in *Inf.* xxvii. 86 *sqq.*; and his capture at Anagni (Alagna) by Sciarra Colonna and Guillaume de Nogaret (the "living thieves") in *Purg.* xx. 90.

CONSTANTINE THE GREAT: Emperor of Rome (A.D. 272–337; Emperor, 306), son of the Emperor Constantius Chlorus. During his campaign against Maxentius, in 312, he is said to have seen a shining cross in the heavens, with the words "*In hoc signo vinces*" – "in this sign thou shalt conquer". He defeated Maxentius near Rome, embraced Christianity, and so became the first Christian Emperor. Later, he transferred the seat of Empire from Rome to Byzantium. It was Constantine who convened the great Council of Nicaea, which gave its name to the Nicene Creed. For the legend of the "Donation of Constantine" see *note* to XIX. 115. Dante places Constantine in the Heaven of Jupiter, among the spirits of the Just. (*Para.* xx. 55–57; *Inf.* xix. 115; xxvii. 94 and *note*.)

CORNELIA: daughter of Scipio Africanus the Elder; wife of Tiberius Semptonius Gracchus (*fl.* 169 B.C.), and mother of the two famous Tribunes Tiberius and Caius. She is celebrated as a model Roman matron of the old school, who brought up her sons in the utmost rectitude; after her death, the people of Rome erected a statue to her, inscribed: "The Mother of the Gracchi". (IV. 128.)

CORNETAN RINIER: see RINIER DA CORNETO.

Corveto: town of Italy. (XIII. 8 and *note*.)

Corybants: priests of Cybele or Rhea in Phrygia, who celebrated her worship with enthusiastic dances, to the sound of drum and cymbal and loud and frenzied cries. (XIV. 102.)

Crete: island in the Mediterranean, the fabled birthplace of Jove. Many legends are told about its semi-mythical King Minos, who reigned in Crete before the time of the Trojan War. (See *Minos, Minotaur, Daedalus*, etc. See also *Saturn*.) (XII. 13 and *note*; XIV. 95 *sqq.* and *note*.)

Cronos: Greek deity and legendary king of Crete (see *Saturn*).

CURIO (Caius Scribonius Curio): Tribune of the Plebs, 50 B.C. Originally an adherent of Pompey, he was bought over by Caesar; and fled from Rome to join him when he was proclaimed an enemy of the Republic (see CAESAR, JULIUS). Dante, following Lucan, makes Curio responsible for advising Caesar to cross the

Rubicon and march upon Rome. Curio was later made propraetor of Sicily; after expelling Cato, he made an expedition to Africa and was defeated and killed by Juba. (XXVIII. 101 and *notes* to XXVIII. 93, 98.)

Cyprus: island of the Mediterranean. (XXVIII. 83.)

Daedalus: the cunning artificer who, in classical legend, lived in Crete and made the image of a heifer for Pasiphaë, the labyrinth in which Minos kept the Minotaur, and wings for himself and his son Icarus. (XII. 13, *note*; XVII. 109, *note*; XXIX. 116.)

Damietta: city of Egypt. (XIV. 104 and *note*.)

DANTE ALIGHIERI: poet. Born in Florence in Tuscany, May–June 1265, son of Alighiero Alighieri, and his first wife Bella (family name uncertain). Baptized at church of San Giovanni Battista (St John Baptist).

First meeting with Beatrice Portinari (*q.v.*), May 1274. Fought on the Guelf side at Campaldino, 11 June 1289. Enrolled in Apothecaries' Guild, 1295 or 1296. Spoke in *Consiglio dei Centi*, 1296. Ambassador to San Gemignano, 1299.

Married, not later than 1298, Gemma Donati, by whom he had issue: Pietro, Jacopo, Giovanni (?), Antonia (?), Beatrice.

Elected to priorate to serve 15 June to 15 August 1300. Said to have been sent with embassy to Pope Boniface VIII, October 1301. Exiled from Florence with White Guelfs: 1st Decree, 27 January 1302; 2nd Decree, 10 March 1302. Joined Ghibelline party, but appears to have left them *c.* 1304, and taken refuge with Bartolommeo della Scala at Verona.

Lived a wandering life of which little record remains. With the Malaspini family, 1306–7; said to have visited Paris about this time; in Italy (probably as guest of Guido Novello), 1310–11, when he wrote letters in the Imperial cause to the Florentines and to the Emperor Henry VII. Excluded from decree of pardon the same year; 3rd Decree of exile (including his sons Pietro and Jacopo) published 6 November 1315. Refused to return to Florence under amnesty of 1316.

After visiting Verona again as guest of Can Grande della Scala, went to live at Ravenna, under the protection of Guido Novello, with his banished sons and his daughter Beatrice. Sent on embassy to Venice, July 1321. Died of fever on his return to Ravenna, 14 September 1321.

Works (dates conjectural, but order pretty certainly established): *La Vita Nuova* (*The New Life*), probably between 1292 and 1295; *Il Canzoniere* (*Song-book*), collection of lyrics of various dates;

Il Convivio (*The Banquet*), *c.* 1307–1309 (unfinished); *De Vulgari Eloquentia* (*Of Writing in the Vulgar Tongue*), probably about the same time as *Il Convivio* (unfinished); *De Monarchia* (*Of Monarchy*), probably about 1311; various *Letters* (chiefly political) in Latin; two Latin *Eclogues* addressed to Giovanni del Virgilio, 1319; a scientific treatise, *Quaestio de Aqua et Terra*, of which the authenticity has been much disputed. A number of other minor works have been attributed to him from time to time.

The *Commedia* (the word "Divina" is not part of Dante's own title for the work) is thought by some to have been begun before Dante's exile, and Boccaccio states that the first draft of it was in Latin. As we have it, however, the *Inferno* cannot have been completed before 1314. The *Purgatorio* seems to have been partly or wholly written by 1319; some place its completion before 1312. Of the *Paradiso*, the twenty-seventh canto cannot have been written before 1316, and the poem was apparently finished only a short time before the author's death in 1321.

DANUBE: river. (XXXII. 25.)

Dati, Bonturo: see *Bonturo Dati*.

DAVID: king of Israel. (IV. 58; XXVIII. 136 and *note* to XXVIII. 134.)

Deïanira: wife of Hercules. (XII. 67 and *note*.)

Deïdamia: in class. myth., daughter of Lycomedes, king of Scyros. (XXVI. 62 and *note* to XXVI. 55.)

DEMOCRITUS: "the laughing Philosopher", so-called from his cheerful outlook; born and lived at Abdera in Thrace (*c.* 460–361 B.C.). He taught that the universe was founded by the chance – i.e. mechanistic (as opposed to the purposive) – combination of atoms. (IV. 136.)

DEVIL: the Devil is referred to by various names in the *Comedy*, according to the speaker:

    (1) BELZEBUB (by Dante). (XXXIV. 127.)

    (2) DIS (by Virgil). (VIII. 68; XI. 65; XII. 39; XXXIV. 20.)

    (3) LUCIFER (by Dante). (XXXI. 143; XXXIV. 89.)

    (4) SATAN (by Pluto). (VII. 1.)

    See also under DIS.

DIDO: queen of Carthage (see AENEAS). (V. 61, 85.)

DIOGENES: the famous Greek cynic philosopher (*c.* 412–323 B.C.), who lived ascetically in a tub, preaching the practical virtues and despising all bookish theory, arts, and civilized amenities. (IV. 135.)

DIOMEDE (Diomedes): in class. myth., king of Argos, son of Tydeus and Deiphyle; one of the Greek heroes who fought against Troy. (XXVI. 56 and *note*.)

DIONYSIUS: tyrant of Sicily:
    (1) the Elder (430–367 B.C.).
    (2) the Younger, son of the above (reigned 367–343 B.C.).
    Both of these tyrants were notorious for their cruelty, and either
    or both may be intended by Dante. (XII. 107.)

DIOSCORIDES: Greek physician; probably of second century A.D.;
author of a *Materia Medica* which described the qualities and
virtues of all plants, minerals, etc., then used in medicine. (IV. 138.)

DIS: in ancient mythology, the Underworld (Hades) itself, and also
the god or king of the Underworld (otherwise called Pluto). He
was the son of Cronos and Rhea, and brother of Zeus (Jupiter);
his queen was Proserpine (*q.v.*). In the *Comedy*, the classical name
"Dis" is used by Virgil for Satan. (XI. 65; XII. 39; XXXIV. 20.)

DIS, CITY OF: the fortified city moated by the river Styx and en-
closing the whole of Nether Hell. (VIII. 68 *sqq.* and Images to
VIII; VIII. 130; XII. 39.)

DOLCINO, FRA: schismatic. (XXVIII. 56 and *note*.)

DONATI, BUOSO DEI: see BUOSO DEI DONATI.

DONATI, CIANFA DEI: see CIANFA DEI DONATI.

DRAGHIGNAZZO: see DRAGONEL.

DRAGONEL (Draghignazzo): demon. (XXI. 121; XXII. 73.)

DUERA, BUOSO DA: Ghibelline traitor. (XXXII. 116 and *note* to XXXII.
114.)

ELECTRA: in class. myth., daughter of Atlas and Pleione, and by
Italian tradition, wife of the Italian king Corythus. She was the
mother by Jupiter of Dardanus, the mythical founder of Troy and
ancestor of the Trojan race; consequently, in Dante's eyes, she
counts as a Trojan, and is placed among the Trojan heroes in
Limbo. According to one story, she and her 6 sisters were raised
to the stars (the cluster of the Pleiades) and Electra lost her bright-
ness for grief at the fall of Troy. (IV. 121.)

Elijah: prophet of Israel, who was taken up to Heaven in a fiery
chariot (2 *Kings* ii. 11). (XXVI. 34.)

Elisha: prophet of Israel. (XXVI. 35 and *note*.)

EMPEDOCLES: Greek philosopher, born in Sicily (*fl. c.* 444 B.C.);
famous as a psychologist and student of nature. He first estab-
lished the number of the 4 elements (earth, water, air, fire) from
which all material bodies were, for many centuries, held to be
compounded. (IV. 137.)

EPHIALTES: giant. (XXXI. 94 and *note*.)

EPICURE (Epicurus): Greek philosopher (342–270 B.C.), founder of a
famous school at Athens. He looked upon earthly happiness as the

end and aim of all human endeavour, and has often been regarded (quite unjustly) as preaching a philosophy of mere hedonism. He believed that all knowledge was relative, being based upon impressions derived from the senses, and that the gods, existing apart in a realm of pure happiness, had no influence upon human affairs; in his own time he thus incurred the charge of atheism. The belief that the soul dies with the body seems to be implicit, rather than explicit in his teaching, though it is made explicit in his follower and interpreter Lucretius. (X. 14.)

Erichtho: a witch, whose necromantic powers provide a sensational incident in Lucan's *Pharsalia* (VI. 507 *sqq*.). There seems to be no foundation for Dante's story of her having called up the shade of Virgil. (IX. 23.)

ERIDANUS: in *Aen.* vi, a river flowing through the Elysian Fields; probably to be identified with the "goodly rivulet" of *Inf.* iv. 108.

ERINYES: the Greek name of the Furies. (IX. 45; see FURIES.)

ESTE, OBIZZO D': see OBIZZO D' ESTE.

Eteocles: in class. myth., son of Oedipus. (XXVI. 54 and *note*.)

Ethiope (Ethiopia): (XXIV. 69).

Etna, Mt.: see *Mongibel*.

EUCLID: the famous mathematician; lived at Alexandria (323–283 B.C.). Besides the Elements of Geometry with which his name is so firmly associated, he wrote treatises on Music, Optics, etc. (IV. 142.)

Euryalus: a companion of Aeneas (see *Nisus*). (I. 107.)

EURYPYLUS: Greek augur who accompanied Agamemnon to the siege of Troy.

In the *Aeneid*, Eurypylus is associated with Calchas only in Sinon of Troy's lying story (cf. *Inf.* XXX. 97, *note*), where the two augurs are said to have declared that the gods demanded a human sacrifice before the Greeks could depart from Troy (*Aen.* ii. 108–29); he is not there mentioned (as Dante seems to imply) in connexion with prophesying the right moment for the Greek fleet to sail to Troy from Aulis. It is possible that Dante has confused the two occasions. On the other hand, Virgil is only made to assert that the two augurs were in fact associated at Aulis (which he might do independently of the poem) and to add – with that vagueness which occasionally comes over authors – "my sublime tragedy sings of him by that name (*così*) somewhere or other (*in alcun loco*)", which is quite true. (XX. 112.)

EZZELINO III DA ROMANO: see AZZOLINO.

Faenza: town of Italy, on the Lamone, between Forlì and Imola, near Bologna. (XXVII. 49 and *note*; XXVII. 50; XXXII. 123.)

Glossary

Famine, Tower of (Torre della Fame): this tower stood in the Piazza degli Anziani at Pisa; it is said to have been destroyed in 1655. (XXXIII. 23.)

Fano: town of Italy, on the Adriatic coast. (XXVIII. 77.)

FARFAREL (Farfarello): demon. (XXI. 123; XXII. 94.)

FARINATA DEGLI UBERTI: Ghibelline leader of Florence (VI. 78; X. 32 *sqq.* and *note*; see also Introd., p. 30.)

Fates: in Greek and Roman mythology, the deities who preside over the destinies of mankind. According to the Greek poet Hesiod, there were three Fates, later distinguished as: Clotho, who span the thread of a man's life; Lachesis, who wove it on the loom; and Atropos, who cut it at death. (IX. 97; (Atropos) XXXIII. 126.)

Feltro: (query: geographical name). (I. 105 and *note*.)

Fiesole: town of Italy, near Florence. (XV. 62 *sqq.* and *note*.)

FILIPPO ARGENTI: see ARGENTI, FILIPPO.

Fishes (Pisces): see *Zodiac*.

Flanders: (XV.4).

Florence: in Italy, on the river Arno, chief city of Tuscany, and birthplace of Dante. (For history see Introd., pp. 29 *sqq.*) (VI. 49 *sqq.*; VI. 61; X. 92; XIII. 143 *sqq.* and *note*; XVI. 75; XXIV. 144; XXVI. 1.)

Florence: denunciation of (XXVI. 1 *sqq.*).

  Florentines: (VI. 61; VIII. 62; XVII. 70; XXXII. 120; XXXIII. 11).

Focara: headland on the Adriatic coast between Fano and La Cattolica; the rounding of the headland was made so dangerous by violent squalls that there was a proverbial saying: "God preserve you from a wind of Focara". (XXVIII. 90 and *note* to XXVIII. 77.)

FOCACCÌA DEGLI CANCELLIERI: reputed originator of the feud between the Black and White Guelfs of Pistoia. Dante, by implication, places him in Caïna. (XXXII. 63 and *note*.)

Forlì: town of Italy (see map, p. 173). (XVI. 98; XXVII. 43.)

Fortune: see *Luck*.

France, Philip IV of: see *Philip the Fair*.

FRANCESCA DA RIMINI: wife to Gianciotto da Verruchio, and lover of his brother Paolo. (V. 116 *sqq.* and *note* to V. 88.)

FRANCESCO D' ACCORSO: see ACCORSO, FRANCIS OF.

FRANCESCO GUERCIO DEI CAVALCANTI: see CAVALCANTI, FRANCESCO GUERCIO DEI.

FRANCIS, ST, OF ASSISI (Francesco Bernadone) (1182–1226): son of a rich wool merchant, he lived the usual pleasant life of a young man of means until, after a severe illness at the age of 25, he experienced a change of heart and vowed himself to the life of religion. Publicly renouncing all his worldly goods, and stripping off even his clothes, he made himself "the Bridegroom of

Poverty". Later, he founded the order of the Cordeliers, who, in accordance with Christ's injunction (*Matt.* x. 9, 10; *Mark* vi. 8, 9; *Luke* ix. 3, 4), possessed no money, went barefoot, and wore only a single garment, girt with a cord. The Order, called Friars Minor (Frati Minori) in token of humility, was sanctioned by Pope Innocent III; and in 1212 made its home in and about the little church of the Portiuncula, near Assisi, presented to it by the Benedictines. In 1219 Francis went to Egypt in a vain attempt to convert the Sultan; and returning in 1221 founded the Tertiary Order of Franciscans, for penitents of both sexes, who, while still living in the world, wish to live a dedicated life and keep the Rule of the Order in a form adapted to their condition. (Some think that Dante may have been a tertiary of the Order – see *note* on the "rope girdle" XVI. Images). In 1223 the Order was confirmed by a Bull of Pope Honorius III. In 1224 Francis had a vision in which he received the "Stigmata" (marks of Christ's wounds) in his hands, feet, and side. He died, at Assisi, at the age of 45 (4 Oct. 1226), and in 1228 was canonized by Pope Gregory IX.

In the *Paradiso* Dante puts the story of St Francis and of his Order in the mouth of St Thomas Aquinas; and later sees Francis himself among the ranks of the Blessed in the Empyrean. (XXVII. 112.)

Franciscans: see *Friars Minor*.

FREDERICK II: Emperor (1194–1250) (see Introd., p. 25). (X. 119; XIII. 58; XXIII. 66 and *note*.)

French: (XXIX. 123).

Friars, Jovial: see *Jovial Friars*.

Friars Minor: (Franciscans) see FRANCIS, ST. (XXIII. 3.)

Friesians: natives of Friesland, a N. province of Holland. (XXXI. 62.)

FUCCI, VANNI: see VANNI FUCCI.

FURIES (Gk. Erinyes): the avenging deities of class. myth.; usually represented as women stained with blood and with snakes for hair. In the later writers their number is given as three: Alecto, Megaera, and Tisiphone. (IX. 38 *sqq.* and Images to IX.; XXX. 22.)

Gaddo (? contr. of Gherardo) *della Gherardesca*: son of Count Ugolino. (XXX. 67 and *note* to XXXIII. 34.)

Gaeta: see *Gaieta*.

GALEN (Claudius Galenus): Greek physician and highly skilled anatomist (131–c. 201). His comprehensive account of the medical knowledge of his time remained authoritative for many centuries. (IV. 142.)

GALIGAI, PUCCIO DEI ("Limping Puccio"): see PUCCIO DEI GALIGAI.

Galleot (Galehalt or Galehaut: Lat. Galeottus): (V. 137 and *note*.)

Glossary

Gallura: province of Sardinia. (XXII. 82 and *note* to XXII. 81.)

GANELON: father-in-law of Charlemagne's nephew Roland. (XXXII. 122; see also *note* to XXXI. 16.)

Garda: Italian town on S.E. shore of Lake Garda. (XX. 66.)

Gardingo: quarter of Florence near the Palazzo Vecchio, site of the present Piazza di San Firenze. (XXIII. 108 and *note*.)

Garisenda: see *Carisenda*.

Gaville: village in the Arno Valley. (XXV. 151 and *note*.)

Genius: invoked by Dante. (II. 7.)

Genoa: (XXXIII. 151.)

    Genoan: (XXXIII. 155).

GERI (Ruggieri) DEL BELLO: son of Bello degli Alighieri, who was brother to Dante's grandfather Bellincione; he was therefore first cousin to Dante's father and first cousin once removed to Dante himself. (XXIX. 27 and *note*.)

Germans: (XVII. 22).

GERYON: monster of Hell (see Images to XVII.) (XVII. 97 (desc. XVI. 131 *sqq*.); XVII. 1 *sqq*.; XVIII. 19.)

Gherardesca: *Anselm(uccio) della* – see *Anselm*.

    Gaddo della – see *Gaddo*.

    Hugh (*Uguccione*) *della* – see *Hugh*.

    Nino il Brigata della – see *Nino*.

GHERARDESCA, UGOLIN(O) DELLA: see UGOLIN(O) DELLA GHERARDESCA.

GHISOLA (or Ghisolabella): sister to Venedico Caccianemico. (XVIII. 56.)

GIANFIGLIAZZI: a Florentine family of the Black Guelf party, notorious for their usury in Dante's time and later. Their arms were: *or*, a lion *az*. (XVII. 59 and *note* to XVII. 55.)

GIANNI SCHICCHI: Florentine of the Cavalcanti family. (XXX. 32 and *note*.)

GIANNI DEI SOLDANIER: see SOLDANIER, GIANNI DEI.

GIANTS: according to Homer, were a huge and savage race in Trinacia, destroyed on account of insolence towards the gods; according to Hesiod, they sprang from the blood of Ouranos (Lat. Uranus, the sky), falling upon Ge (Lat. Tellus, the earth). Later poets confuse them with the Titans (*q.v.*) and say that they rebelled against Zeus (Jupiter) and attempted to storm Olympus. Dante, in placing the Giants round the edge of the infernal Well, seems to have the later legend in mind. (XXXI. 32, 43 *sqq*.)

Giordano, Monte: hill in Rome. (XVIII. 33 and *note*.)

GIOVANNI BUIAMONTE: see BUIAMONTE, GIOVANNI.

GOMITA, FRA: Judge of Gallura in Sardinia. (XXII. 81 and *note*.)

Glossary

GORGON: according to the Greek poet Hesiod, there were three
Gorgons: Stheno, Euryale, and Medusa. All were hideous winged
monsters, with human faces and brazen claws, and with living
serpents for hair. Only Medusa was mortal, for she had at first
been a human maiden, who was changed into a Gorgon because
she had offended the goddess Athene (Minerva). Her face was so
horrible that it turned the beholder to stone, but she was at
length killed by Perseus, who looked, not at her, but at her
reflection in the shield lent him by Athene. Statues of Athene
usually show the Gorgon's head on her shield or breast-plate.
(IX. 56 and Images to IX.)

Gorgona: island near mouth of the Arno. (XXXIII. 82 and *note*.)

Governo (Governolo): town in Italy (see map, p. 173). (XX. 76.)

GRABBERSNITCH (Graffiacane): demon. (XXI. 122; XXII. 34.)

GRAFFIACANE: see GRABBERSNITCH.

Greyhound (Il Veltro): (I. 101 and *note*.)

GRIFFOLINO D' AREZZO: alchemist. (XXIX. 110 and *note*.)

Gualand(i): Ghibelline family of Pisa. (XXXIII. 32.)

Gualdrada: daughter of the distinguished Florentine citizen Ballin-
cione Berti dei Ravignoni mentioned by Dante in *Para.* xv and
xvi. The story went that the Emperor Otho IV was so greatly
impressed by her discreet modesty, as well as her beauty and
manners, that he arranged for her marriage to a young nobleman
called Guido Beisangue, giving him as her dowry a great territory
in the Alps and the Casentino, of which he made him Count
(Count Guido the Elder). One of their sons was the father of
Guido Guerra. (XVI. 37.)

GUERRA, GUIDO: grandson of "the good Gualdrada" (*q.v.*). A
Guelf Florentine nobleman, who in 1255 commanded the army
that expelled the Ghibellines from Arezzo. After the Battle
of Montaperti (Introd., p. 30) he was banished from Florence
with other leading Guelfs, including Dante's father. In 1266
he was made Imperial Vicar of Tuscany; he died in 1272. (XVI.
38 *sqq.*)

Guidi, Conti: great Lombard family, with possessions in Tuscany and
Romagna; their castle was in Romena. Dante mentions several of
them in the *Inferno*. (See *Guido Guerra* and *Romena, Aghinolfo,
Alexander, Guido da*.)

GUIDO CAVALCANTI: see CAVALCANTI.

Guido da Romena: see *Romena, Guido da*.

Guido del Cassero: nobleman of Fano. (XXVIII. 77 and *note*.)

GUIDO GUERRA: see GUERRA, GUIDO.

GUILLIM BORSIER(E): see BORSIER(E), GUILLIM.

GUISCARD, ROBERT: Duke of Apulia and Calabria (*c.* 1015–85); born at Hauteville in Normandy; one of the 12 sons of Tancred. A military adventurer, he took a prominent part in the warfare against the Greeks and Saracens in the S. of Italy, and is placed by Dante in the Heaven of Mars, along with Godfrey of Bouillon and other Christian warriors (*Para.* xviii. 48). (XXVIII. 14.)

GUTTLEHOG (Ciriatto): demon. (XXI. 122; XXII. 55.)

GUY (Guido) BONATTI: see BONATTI, GUY.

GUY DE MONTFORT: see MONTFORT, GUY DE.

HACKLESPUR (Calcabrina) : demon. (XXI. 105; XXII. 133.)

Hannibal: Carthaginian general (247–*c.* 183 B.C.), son of Hamilcar Barca; the great adversary of Rome. Having overrun Spain, he entered Italy and, in the 2nd Punic War, defeated the Romans at the Battles of Lake Trasimene (217 B.C.) and Cannae (216 B.C.) (cf. XXVIII. 11, *note*). He was eventually defeated by Scipio Africanus the Great (*q.v.*) and killed himself to avoid capture. (XXXI. 117.)

HARPIES: originally personifications of the storm-winds, the Harpies are described by Hesiod the Greek poet as beautiful winged maidens; but in later myth they become hideous twy-formed monsters. Virgil (*Aen.* iii. 210) makes them inhabit the islands called the Strophades in the Ionian Sea. (XIII. 10 *sqq.* and Images to XIII; XIII. 101.)

HARROWHOUND (Cagnazzo): demon. (XXI. 119; XXII. 106.)

HEAVENLY MESSENGER: this mysterious and terrible figure has been variously identified. Some argue from his lack of radiance that he cannot be an angel, and suggest that he is Mercury, or even Aeneas (!); forgetting that, in Hell, the Divine Glory can appear only as darkness and terror. It seems clear, however, from VIII. 126–30 and IX. 85–6, that he enters from beyond Hell-gate and is sent from Heaven, and that Dante intends him for an angel and for an image of Divine Revelation. (IX. 71 *sqq.* and Images to IX.)

HECTOR: son of Priam, king of Troy, chief of the Trojan heroes in the *Iliad*. He was killed by Achilles. (iv. 122.)

Hecuba: wife of Priam, king of Troy. (XXX. 16 and *note* to XXX. 13.)

HELEN (of Troy): see PARIS, AENEAS.

HELLKIN (Alichino): demon. (XXI. 118; XXII. 112, 139.)

HELLRAKERS (Malebranche = Evil-Claws): guardian demons of the Fifth Bowge. (XXI. 37; XXII. 100; XXIII. 23; XXXIII. 142.)

Henry, Prince: son of Richard Duke of Cornwall and nephew to Henry III of England. (XII. 120 and *note*.)

Glossary

Henry, Prince of England: "The Young King" – son of Henry II. (XXVIII. 135 and *note* to XXVIII. 134.)

HERACLITUS: of Ephesus; Greek philosopher, *fl. c.* 513 B.C. Sometimes called "the weeping philosopher". He considered fire to be the primary form of matter, and that all things are in a continual flux of becoming and perishing. (IV. 138.)

Hercules (Gk. Heracles): in class. myth., a demi-god, renowned for his enormous strength; the son of Zeus by Alcmene, the wife of Amphitryon. Of the famous twelve Labours which he had to perform in the service of King Eurystheus, two are alluded to in the *Inferno*: the capture of the Oxen of Geryon (*q.v.*) which the Monster Cacus stole from him as he was driving them back (XXV. 25 *sqq.* and *note*), and the carrying off of Cerberus from Hades (VI. 18 and Images; IX. 98 and *note*). After his death at the hand of his wife Deïanira (XII. 67 and *note*) he was taken up to Olympus and became one of the Immortals. He was also honoured with a constellation, which lies beneath the head of the Dragon, between the Lyre and the Crown. (XXV. 33; XXVI. 107; XXXI. 132; and *note* to XXXI. 101–21.)

Hercules, Pillars of: see *Pillars of Hercules*.

HIPPOCRATES: greatest of all physicians of antiquity, was born and practised in the Island of Cos, whose medical school he made famous (460–*c.* 357 B.C.). His writings show him to have been a superb diagnostician, and his name survives to-day in the phrase "the Hippocratic fascia" to denote the facial signs, as he observed them, of approaching death, and in the "Hippocratic oath" which prescribes the ethical duty of physician to patient. (IV. 143.)

HOMER: the great epic poet of Greece, probably *fl. c.* 9th or 10th century B.C., author of the *Iliad* (siege of Troy) and the *Odyssey* (wanderings of Odysseus or Ulysses). He is said to have been blind; seven cities dispute the honour of being his birthplace. Dante knew no Greek, and in his day no Latin translation of Homer seems to have been available. He knew the poems only by reputation and by a few fragments quoted by Aristotle and Horace. (IV. 85 *sqq.*)

HORACE (Quintus Horatius Flaccus): Latin poet (65–8 B.C.). His poems are lyrical, satirical, and critical (*Odes, Satires, Epistles, Art of Poetry*), and his outlook that of a cultured man of the world. Born in Apulia, he was educated and lived in Rome, until he earned enough to retire to a small Sabine farm in Ustica. (IV. 89.)

Hugh (Uguccione) della Gherardesca: son of Count Ugolino. (XXXIII. 89 and *note* to XXXIII. 34.)

Hypsipyle: in Greek myth., daughter of Thoas, king of Lemnos. (XVIII. 91 and *note* on XVIII. 88.)

Icarus: son of Daedalus. (XVII. 109 and *note*.)

Ida, Mount: in Crete. (XIV. 97.)

Ilium: see *Troy*.

Imola: town of Italy, on the Santerno. (XXVII. 49 and *note*.)

Ind (India): (XIV. 32.)

Ino: wife of Athamas and sister to Semele (*q.v.*), daughter of Cadmus, king of Thebes. (XXX. 5 *sqq.* and *note* to XXX. 1.)

INTERMINEI, ALESSIO: of Lucca. (XVIII. 122 and *note*.)

ISCARIOT, JUDAS: see JUDAS ISCARIOT.

ISRAEL (Jacob): the Patriarch. (IV. 59.)

Italy: Dante refers several times to "Italy", but never uses the word "Italian" for its inhabitants collectively (see *note* to XXII. 65). (I, 106; IX. 114; XX. 61; XXVIII. 71.)

JACOB: the Patriarch – see ISRAEL.

JACOMO DI SANT' ANDREA: see SANT' ANDREA, JACOMO DI.

JACOPO RUSTICUCCI: see RUSTICUCCI, JACOPO.

Janiculum: one of the "seven hills" of Rome. (XVIII. 33 and *note*.)

JASON: Greek hero. (XVIII. 86 and *note*.)

Jason: High Priest of Israel. (XIX. 85 and *note*.)

Jehoshaphat, Valley of: in Palestine.. (X. 11 and *note*.)

Jews: (XXIII. 123; XXVII. 87.)

JOHN BAPTIST, ST: Patron Saint of Florence. (XIII. 143 and *note*; XXX. 74.)

John Baptist, St: Church of, in Florence. (XIX. 7 and *note*.)

JOHN, ST: the Divine. (XIX. 106.)

Joseph: son of the Patriarch Jacob. (XXX. 99.)

JOVE (Jupiter): Roman deity identified with the Greek Zeus, the son of Cronos and Rhea, "father of gods and men" and chief of the Olympian deities. His spouse was Juno (Gk. Hera), and his weapon the thunderbolt. (XIV. 52; XXXI. 43, 92.)

Jovial Friars (Frati Gaudenti): (XXIII. 103 and *note*.)

Jubilee: in the Christian Church, a period of remission from the penal consequences of sin; first instituted by Pope Boniface VIII, who, in 1300, issued a bull granting plenary indulgence to all pilgrims visiting Rome in that year, on condition of confession, penitence, and prescribed attendance at St Peter's. (As first instituted, ordinary Jubilees were to have been held every hundredth year; the period was subsequently reduced to 50 and later to 25 years, and the conditions of pilgrimage altered.) The name is taken from the Hebrew institution, for which see *Lev*. XXV. (XVIII. 29.)

JUDAS ISCARIOT: the disciple who betrayed Christ. (IX. 27; XXXI. 143; XXXIV. 62.)

JUDECCA: region of Hell. (XXXIV. 117 and Images to XXXIV.)

JULIA: daughter of Julius Caesar and wife of Pompey. (IV. 127.)

JULIUS CAESAR: see CAESAR, JULIUS.

Juno (Gk. Hera): the goddess wife of Jupiter. She was the enemy of the Thebans, on account of Semele (*q.v.*), and of the Trojans, on account of the judgment of Paris (*q.v.*). (XXX. 1 and *note.*)

Jupiter: see JOVE.

Laertes: father of Ulysses (*q.v.*). (XXVI. 95.)

LAMBERTI, MOSCA DEI: see MOSCA DEI LAMBERTI.

Lamone: river of Italy (see map, p. 173). (XXVII. 49 and *note* to XXVII. 50.)

Lancelot: the greatest knight of Arthur's court, the lover of Queen Guinevere. (V. 128 and *note.*)

LANDOLO, LODERINGO DI: see LODERINGO DI LANDOLO.

Lanfranc(hi): Ghibelline family of Pisa. (XXXIII. 32.)

LANO (of Siena): (XIII. 115 and *note.*)

Lateran: palace in Rome; in Dante's time the usual residence of the Popes. The palaces of the Colonna family were in the same district. (XXVII. 86.)

Latian(s) (Latino, Latini): Dante's name for the inhabitants of Italy, especially of Lower Italy (anc. Latium). (XXII. 65; XXVII. 26, 33; XXIX. 90, 92.)

LATINI, BRUNETTO: see BRUNETTO LATINI.

LATINUS: king of Latium (see AENEAS). (IV. 125.)

LAVINIA: daughter of Latinus (see AENEAS). (IV. 126.)

Learchus: infant son of Athamas and Ino (see *Semele*). (XXX. 10.)

Lemnos: island in the Aegean. (XVIII. 88 and *note.*)

LETHE: river of the Earthly Paradise. (XIV. 130 *sqq.* and *note*; XXXIV. 130 and *note.*)

LIBBICOCCO: see LIBBICOCK.

LIBBICOCK (Libbicocco): demon. (XXI. 121; XXII. 70.)

Libya, Libyan: desert in N. Africa. (XXIV. 85.)

LINUS: mythical Greek poet. (IV. 140.)

Livy (Titus Livius): Roman historian (57 B.C.–A.D. 17). Born at Padua, he passed most of his life at Rome, where, under the patronage of Augustus Caesar, he wrote his great *History of Rome* (from the landing of Aeneas to the death of Drusus in 9 B.C.) in 142 books. Of these, the greater part were lost before Dante's time, but we still possess 35, together with epitomes of most of the rest. Dante frequently uses and quotes Livy's authority, though he sometimes attributes to Livy statements which are actually to be found in Orosius (*q.v.*). (XXVIII. 12.)

Glossary

LODERINGO DI LANDOLO, FRA: *podestà* of Florence. (XXIII. 105 and *note*.)

Logodor(o): province of Sardinia. (XXII. 89.)

Lombardy: northern part of Italy between the Alps and the Po, and bounded by Venice to the E. and Piedmont to the W. (I. 68; XXVII. 20.)

    Lombards: (XXII. 99).

LUCAN (M. Annaeus Lucanus): Roman poet (A.D. 39–65). Born at Cordova, he was educated at Rome and lived there until, having joined the conspiracy of Piso against the Emperor Nero, he was condemned to death and committed suicide. His epic, *Pharsalia*, which tells of the struggle between Caesar and Pompey, was extensively drawn upon by Dante. (IV. 90; XXV. 93.)

Lucca: town and province of Italy. (XVIII. 123; (St Zita) XXI. 38; XXXIII. 30).

LUCIFER: see DEVIL.

Luck (or *Fortune*): (II. 61; VII. 53, discourse on; VII. 73 *sqq.* and *note*; XV. 93, 95; XXX. 13).

LUCRECE (Lucretia): wife of Lucius Tarquinius Collatinus. Having been outraged by Tarquin, the son of Tarquinius Superbus (*q.v.*), she stabbed herself, calling upon Collatinus to avenge her. (IV. 127.)

LUCY (St) (Lucìa): She is traditionally associated with the especial gifts of the Holy Ghost; and it is possible that in the "Three Blessed Ladies" (Mary, Lucy, and Beatrice) who interest themselves in Dante's salvation, we are to see an analogue of the Holy Trinity of Father, Son, and Spirit – or, in St Hilary's phrase, Basis, Image, and Gift – Mary, the absolute Theotokos, corresponding to the Basis; Beatrice, the derived God-bearer, to the Image; Lucy, the bond and messenger between them, to the Gift. (II. 97 and Images to II.)

Luna (Luni): city of Italy, near Carrara. (XX. 47 and *note*.)

Lunigiana: see *Valdimagra*.

Macra, Val di: see *Valdimagra*.

MAHOMET (Mohammed) (*c.* 570–632): born at Mecca; founder of the Mohammedan religion (Islam). About the age of 40 he saw a vision of the Angel Gabriel, commanding him to teach the true religion, and proclaimed himself as the Prophet (*c.* 610). He gathered many converts about him, but, having aroused the enmity of the people of Mecca, he was obliged to flee to Medina, 16 July 622 – the date from which the Mohammedans reckon the beginning of their Era (Hegira). He became ruler of the city, proclaimed war upon the enemies of Islam, conquered Mecca in

Glossary

630, and was thereafter recognized as prophet and chief over all the country between the Euphrates and the Red Sea.

His teaching was much influenced by the later Jewish Scriptures, and he professed a deep reverence for Jesus, calling Him "the greatest prophet of God, after himself".

After Mohammed's death, without surviving male issue, the caliphate was held successively by three of his companions, until, after the murder of the last of these in 656, it was claimed by the Prophet's nephew, Ali ibn abu Taleb. Disputes over his right to succeed divided the Mohammedans into two sects, the Sunnites and the Fatimites (represented in modern times by the Turks and the Persians).

Dante, in accordance with medieval opinion, regards Mohammed as a Christian schismatic; and accordingly places both him and Ali in the Circle of the Sowers of Discord. (XXVIII. 31 *sqq.*)

Mainardo Pagano: lord of Faenza. (XXVII. 50 and *note*.)

Majorca: island of the Mediterranean. (XXVIII. 83.)

MALACODA: see BELZECUE.

Malaspina, Moroëllo: Lord of Lunigiana. (XXIV. 145–6 and *note* to XXIV. 142.)

Malatesta \
Malatestino } of Rimini: Black Guelf noblemen. (XXVII. 46, *note*; XXVIII. 81, 85; and *note* to XXVIII. 77.)

MALAVOLTI, CATALANO DEI: see CATALANO DEI MALAVOLTI.

MALBOWGES (It. Malebolge): region of Hell. (XVIII. 2 *sqq.* and *note*.)

MALEBRANCHE: see HELLRAKERS.

MANTO: prophetess, daughter of Tiresias. (XX. 55 *sqq.*)

Mantua (Mantova): city in N. Italy, birthplace of Virgil. (I. 69; XX. 93.)

Mantuan(s): (I. 69; II. 58).

Marcabò: castle in the territory of Ravenna, hear the mouths of the Po, at E. extremity of Lombardy. (XXVIII. 75.)

MARCIA: wife of Cato of Utica (*q.v.*). After she had borne three children to Cato, he ceded her, as an act of friendship, to Q. Hortensius; after whose death she returned to Cato at her own request. In the *Convivio*, Dante makes of this story an allegory of the return of the soul to God (IV. 28). Marcia is mentioned again in *Purg*. i. (IV. 128.)

Maremma: malarious and swampy district along the coast of Tuscany (XXV. 19; XXIX. 48.)

Mars: God of War – ancient patron of Florence. (XIII. 144 and *note* to XIII. 143; XXIV. 145; XXXI. 51.)

MARTINO BOTTAIO: see BOTTAIO, MARTINO.

MARY, B. V.: (II. 94 and *note*).

Glossary

MASCHERONI, SASSOL: Florentine. (XXXII. 65 and *note*.)

Matthias, St: (XIX. 96).

Medea: in Greek myth., daughter of Aietes, king of Colchis. (XVIII. 96 and *note* to XVIII. 36.)

MEDICINA, PIER DA: Bolognese nobleman of the Biancucci family. (XXVIII. 76 and *note*.)

MEDUSA THE GORGON: (see GORGON). (IX. 52, 56 and Images to IX.)

MEGAERA: see FURIES.

Memory (Mnemosyne): Mother of the Muses (*q.v.*); invoked by Dante. (II. 8 and *note*.)

Menalippus (or Melanippus): Theban warrior. (XXXII. 131 and *note* to XXXII. 130.)

Michael, Saint: the Archangel, chief of the angelic host. (VII. 12 and *note*.)

MICHAEL SCOTT: see SCOTT, MICHAEL.

MICHAEL ZANCHE: see ZANCHE, MICHAEL.

Mincio: river of Italy (see map, p. 173). (XX. 76.)

MINOS: in class. myth., the legendary king of Crete, who after death became a judge in the Underworld. (V. 5 *sqq.* and *note*; XX. 36; XXVII. 124; XXIX. 119.)

MINOTAUR: offspring of Pasiphaë and the Bull. (XII. 13 *sqq.* and *note*; and Images to XII.)

MOHAMMED: see MAHOMET.

Mongibel(lo): Mt. Etna, the fabled site of Vulcan's smithy. (XIV. 56.)

Montagna dei Parcitati: Ghibelline nobleman of Rimini. (XXVII. 47 and *note*.)

Montaperti: village near Siena in Tuscany, site of the defeat of the Florentine Guelfs by the Ghibellines, 4 September 1260. (X. 85; XXXII. 81 and *note*; and Introd., p. 30.)

Monte di San Giuliano: hill between Pisa and Lucca. (XXXIII. 29 and *note*.)

MONTEFELTRO, GUIDO DA (1223–98): the great Ghibelline leader. Villani calls him "the wisest and subtlest man of war of his time in all Italy". In 1274 he took command of the Ghibellines of Bologna and Romagna, and after defeating the Guelfs in two pitched battles and capturing various towns, he successfully defended Forlì against the French troops sent by Pope Martin IV (1282). In 1285, however, Forlì, together with most of Romagna, made terms with the Pope, and Guido was driven out. In 1280 he made his submission to the Church and was banished to Piedmont, but later returned, and went to Pisa to put himself at the head of the Ghibellines there, who celebrated his arrival by the murder of Count Ugolino (XXXIII.). He was excommunicated for defying the ban, but after some years was again reconciled with the Church, and in 1298 entered the Franciscan Order. The story of how he advised Pope Boniface VIII to subdue the fortress of Palestrina by treachery (XXVII.) is found in Villani. He died at the age of 75 in the Franciscan monastery at Assisi (or, according to others, at Ancona.) His son, Buonconte, was killed in 1289 while fighting on the Ghibelline side at the Battle of Campaldino, in which Dante fought on the Guelf side (Introd., p. 30); Buonconte's account of his own death forms one of the most beautiful passages in the *Purgatorio*. (XXVII. 29, *note*.)

Montereggione: castle near Siena. (XXXI. 40 and *note*.)

Monte Veso: peak of the Alps in Piedmont; source of the Montone (Acquacheta) (see map, p. 173). (XVI. 95.)

MONTFORT, GUY DE: son of Simon de Montfort who led the rebellion of the English barons against Henry III and was killed at Evesham by Prince Edward (afterwards Edward I). Guy de Montfort later became Vicar-General of Tuscany, and, to avenge his father's death, assassinated Henry III's nephew at Viterbo. (XII. 119 and 120 and *note*.)

Montone: river of Italy (see *Acquacheta*).

MORDRED: King Arthur's son (by Queen Morgawse of Orkney), who betrayed his father. Dante mentions him as being worthy of a place in the circle of Caïna, and, by implication, places him there. (XXXII. 61 and *note*.)

Morocco: in N. Africa. (XXVI. 103.)

Moroëllo Malaspina: see *Malaspina, Moroëllo*.

MOSCA DEI LAMBERTI: Florentine nobleman. (VI. 80; XXVIII. 106 and *note*.)

MOSES: the Law-Giver of Israel. (IV. 57.)

Moslems: (XXVII. 87.)

MOZZI, ANDREA DEI: Bishop of Florence (on the Arno) from 1287 to 1295. His levity, stupidity, and unnatural vices caused so much scandal there that Pope Boniface VIII translated him to the see of Vicenza on the Bacchiglione, where he died in 1296. (XV. 112.)

Muses: the nine Muses, inspirers and patronesses of the Arts, dwelt upon Mt. Parnassus, of which, according to Dante, one peak (Nyssa) was dedicated to them, and the other (Cyrrha to Apollo (see *Para*. i. 13–18). They were said to be the daughters of Zeus (Jupiter) and Mnemosyne (Memory). (II. 7; XXXII. 10.)

MYRRHA: daughter of Cinyras, king of Cyprus. Having conceived an incestuous passion for her own father, she persuaded her aged nurse to bring her to his bed, disguised and under a false name, while her mother Cenchreis was away attending a festival of

Ceres. When the king discovered who she was, he drew his sword to kill her, but she fled into Arabia and was changed into a myrtle-tree; and from her trunk was born Adonis. (XXX. 38.)

NAPOLEONE DEGLI ALBERTI: see ALBERTI, NAPOLEONE DEGLI.

Narcissus: beautiful youth of class. myth. (XXX. 128 and *note*.)

Nasidius: Roman soldier mentioned in Lucan's *Pharsalia*. (XXV. 95 and *note* to XXV. 94.)

Navarre: kingdom in the Pyrenees. (XXII. 121.)

    Navarrese: (XXII. 121).

Neptune: in Roman myth., god of the sea. (XXVIII. 82.)

NESSUS: Centaur. (XII. 67 *sqq*. and *note*.)

Nicolò dei Salimbeni: Sienese spendthrift. (XXIX. 127.)

NICHOLAS III: Giovanni Gaetani Orsini (Pope, 1277–80). (XIX. 70 and *note*.)

Nile: river of Egypt. (XXXIV. 45.)

NIMROD: Biblical king. (XXXI. 77 and *note*.)

Nino (Ugolino) il Brigata: grandson of Count Ugolino della Gherardesca. (XXXIII. 89 and *note* to XXXIII. 34.)

Ninus: a warrior king, who with his wife Semiramis (*q.v.*) is said to have founded the Assyrian empire of Nineveh (*c.* 2182 B.C.) and conquered the greater part of Asia. Dante's reference to his having "ruled in the land the Soldan now rules over" suggests that *either* Dante confused Babylon in Assyria with Babylon in Egypt, *or* there was a tradition that Ninus had conquered Egypt. (V. 59.)

Nisus: a companion of Aeneas. He and Euryalus were killed in a night attack against the Rutulian camp (*Aen.* ix. 176–450). (I.107.)

NOAH: the Patriarch. (IV. 56.)

Novara: town in N.E. of Piedmont, near Milan. (XXVIII. 59.)

    Novarese: (XXXVIII. 59).

OBIZZO II D'ESTE: Marquis of Ferrara (1264–93) – a Guelf nobleman, who assisted the army of Charles of Anjou to cross the river Po in the campaign against Manfred. His reputation for cruelty and vice may have been exaggerated by Ghibelline chroniclers, and the story of his murder by his own son is sometimes denied. (XII. 111; XVIII. 56.)

Ordelaffi, Sinibaldo degli: see *Sinibaldo degli Ordelaffi*.

ORIA, BRANCA D': see BRANCA D' ORIA.

OROSIUS, PAULUS (Paolo Orosio): Spanish priest and historian of the fifth century A.D. His chief work, the *Historiarum adversus Paganos vii Libri*, usually known as the *Ormista*, a history of the world from the Creation to A.D. 417, was written as a companion to St

Augustine's *City of God*, and is based on Livy, Justin, Tacitus, Suetonius, and other Roman historians. It was a favourite historical text-book in the Middle Ages, and Dante was indebted to it for many points, e.g. in the *Inferno*, the story of Semiramis (v. 54–60), the character of Alexander the Great (XII. 107), and, in all probability, the account, quoted from Livy, of the Battle of Cannae (XXVIII. 10–11). In the *Paradise*, Dante places Orosius in the Heaven of the Sun, among the Doctors of the Church.

ORPHEUS: mythical Greek poet and musician; one of the Argonauts (see JASON). (IV. 140.)

Orsini: illustrious Roman family, to which Pope Nicholas III (*q.v.*) belonged. Alluded to in XIX. 70–71 (*see note*).

OTTAVIANO DEGLI UBALDINI; see UBALDINI, OTTAVIANO DEGLI.

OVID (Publius Ovidius Naso): Roman poet (43 B.C.–A.D. 18). Of his numerous works the best known, and the one of which Dante made most use, is the *Metamorphoses*, a collection of legends narrating the transformations of human beings into other shapes, knit into a connected story from the Creation to the time of Julius Caesar. (IV. 90; XXV. 97.)

Padua: town of Italy, in Venetia.

    Paduans: (XV. 7; XVII. 71).

Pagano, Mainardo: see *Mainardo Pagano*.

Palestrina (Penestrino): fortress of the Colonna family (see *Colonna*). (XXVII. 102 and *note*.)

Palladium: statue of Pallas (Minerva). (XXVI. 63 and *note* to XXVI. 55.)

PAOLO DA RIMINI: lover of Francesca da Rimini. (V. 101 and *note* to v. 88.)

Parcitate, Montagna dei: see *Montagna dei Parcitate*.

PARIS: son of King Priam of Troy. He was invited to award the prize of beauty (a golden apple) between Juno, Minerva, and Venus. Juno offered him riches and Minerva conquest, but Venus promised him the love of the most beautiful woman in the world, so he gave the apple to her. Aided by Venus, he carried off the beautiful Helen, wife of King Menelaus of Sparta, and took her to Troy. After a ten years' siege, in the course of which Paris was killed, the Greeks, under Agamemnon, took and sacked Troy and recovered Helen. (V. 67.)

Paul, St: (II. 28 and *note*; II. 32).

PAZZI, CAMICION DEI: see CAMICION DEI PAZZI.

PAZZI, CARLIN(O) DEI: see CARLIN(O) DEI PAZZI.

PAZZIAN RINIER: see RINIER DEI PAZZI.

Peleus: father of Achilles. (XXXI. 5 and *note* to XXXI. 4.)

Glossary

Penelope: wife of Ulysses (*q.v.*). (XXVI. 96.)

PENTHESILEA: queen of the Amazons, who assisted the Trojans after Hector's death, but was killed by Achilles. (IV. 124.)

Perillus: maker of the "Bull of Phalaris". (XXVII. 7 and *note*.)

Peschiera: fortress at the S. end of Lake Benaco (Garda) (see map, p. 173). (XX. 70.)

PETER, ST: (II. 24; XIX. 91, 94).

Peter's Gate, St: the gate, guarded by the Angel of Repentance, by which redeemed souls are admitted to Purgatory (see *Purg.* IX). (I. 134.)

Peter's Pine: bronze image in Rome. (XXXI. 59 and *note*.)

Phaeton (Gk. Phaethon): son of Phoebus. (XVII. 107 and *note*.)

Phalaris: tyrant of Sicily, brazen bull of. (XXVII. 7 and *note*.)

Pharisees: (XXIII. 116); "the modern P." (XXVII. 85.)

Philip the Fair (Philippe Le Bel): Philip IV of France (1285–1314). (XIX. 87 and *note* to XIX. 85.)

PHLEGETHON: river of Hell. (XII. 47 *sqq.* and Images to XII; XIV. 116 XIV. 131.)

Phlegra: Battle of. (XIV. 58 and *note*.)

PHLEGYAS: ferryman of Hell (Styx). (VIII. 19 and Images to VIII.)

PHOLUS: Centaur. (XII 72 and *note*.)

Photinus: deacon of Thessalonica. (XI. 9 and *note*.)

Piceno: field of. (XXIV. 148 and *note* to XXIV. 142.)

PIER DA MEDICINA: see MEDICINA, PIER DA.

PIER DELLE VIGNE: see VIGNE, PIER DELLA.

Pietrapan(a): prob. Petra Apuana; mountain in N.W. Tuscany. (XXXII. 28.)

Pillars of Hercules: the two heights – Mt. Abyla in Morocco and Mt. Calpe (Gibraltar) in Spain – which stand one on either side of the Straits of Gibraltar and were supposed to mark the "sunset" and the western limit of the habitable world. In class. myth., the two mountains were originally one, which was broken in two by Hercules. (XXVI. 108 and *note*.)

Pinamonte dei Buonaccorsi: (XX. 96 and *note* to XX. 95).

Pisa: (XXXIII. 79).

 Pisans: (XXXIII. 30).

Pisces: see *Zodiac*.

Pistoia: town in Tuscany, about 22 miles from Florence. (XXIV.126 and *note*; XXV. 10; see also Introd., p. 33.)

PLATO: the great Athenian philosopher (pupil of Socrates and founder of the Academic School (*c.* 428–347 B.C.). Although his *Dialogues* had not, for the most part, been translated into Latin by the beginning of the fourteenth century, so that Dante was directly acquainted only with the *Timaeus*, yet through the writings of the Neo–Platonists, Platonic thought had had a profound influence from very early days upon the development of Christian philosophy.

Of especial importance is the Platonic doctrine of "Ideas" – the eternal archetypes or universal patterns in the Divine Mind, conceived as the "most real existences", of which particular and material things are only, as it were, the types and shadows. Thus in contrast with Aristotelianism, Platonism is concerned with the world of essence rather than with that of experience.

The *Timaeus* is a mystical and figurative account of the creation of the world by God the Artificer ("the Demiurge"); the Cosmos is "made in his image", the imperfection of all actually existing things being attributed to the inherent limitations of matter. This line of thought, while not in itself irreconcilable with Christian orthodoxy, was developed by later writers, under Oriental influence, so as to lead to the conception that matter was in itself not only finite but actually evil, and so to the Gnostic and Dualist theory that the material creation was the work of the Devil. (This heresy Dante specifically repudiates.) The Neo–Platonic doctrine of the (active) "Divine Mind", proceeding from the "One" who is the ultimate Being beyond Mind, was on the one hand taken up into the Christian doctrine of the First and Second Persons of the Trinity, while on the other it was expanded into various Gnostic heresies of a Godhead declining by successive and subordinate "emanations" into materiality. In its orthodox form, it appears in the Fourth Gospel, the Nicene Creed, and the theology of St Augustine and his followers; so that Platonism has thus been – perhaps less explicitly but quite as firmly as Aristotelianism – incorporated into the body of Christian philosophy. (IV. 139.)

PLUTO: god of riches and of the underworld. (VI. 115 and *note*; VII. 2.)

Po: river of N. Italy (see map, p. 173). (V. 98; XX. 78.)

Pola: town in N. Italy. (IX. 113 and *note* to IX. 112.)

Polenta: castle near Forlì in Romagna, which gave its name to the great Guelf family who were, in Dante's time, "lords of Ravenna". (XXVII. 40–41 and *note*.)

Polydorus: son of Priam, king of Troy and Hecuba. (XXX. 19 and *note* to XXX. 13.)

Polyxena: daughter of Priam, king of Troy and Hecuba. (XXX. 17 and *note* to XXX. 13.)

POTIPHAR'S WIFE: who falsely accused Joseph. (XXX. 98.)

Prato, Cardinal Nicholas of: (XXVI. 9 and *note*).

PRISCIAN (Priscianus Caesariensis): famous Latin grammarian, born at Caesaraea in Cappadocia in the sixth century A.D. (XV. 110.)

PROSERPINE (Gk. Persephone): in Greek and Roman myth., the daughter of Ceres (Gk. Demeter), the Earth-Mother. She was stolen away by Dis (Pluto) while gathering flowers in the vale of Enna, in Sicily, and carried off to be his queen in Hades. She is identified with the Moon, as being one of the manifestations of the "Triple Goddess" Hecate – Luna in Heaven, Diana on earth, and Proserpine in Hades. (IX. 44 and *note*; X. 80.)

PTOLEMY (Claudius Ptolemaeus): the famous mathematician, astronomer, and geographer, *fl.* at Alexandria in the second century. For his geocentric astronomy, which held the field until displaced in the sixteenth century by that of Copernicus, which placed the Sun in the centre of the Solar System, see Appendix on *Dante's Universe*, p. 292. (IV. 142.)

PTOLOMAEA: region of Hell. (XXXIII. 124 and Images to XXXIII.)

PUCCIO DEI GALIGAI: called "SCIANCATO" ("Limping Puccio"): Florentine nobleman, of whom little seems to be known except that Dante classes him among the thieves. (XXV. 48.)

PURGATORY, Mount: (see Greater Images, p. 86). Seen by Ulysses on his last voyage. (XXVI. 133.)

PYRRHUS: (1) son of Achilles, who killed Priam, king of Troy, and sacrificed Polyxena (*q.v.*); Virgil emphasizes his cruelty (*Aen.* ii. 469 *sqq.*). (XII. 134, or the ref. may be to P. of Epirus.)
(2) King of Epirus, fabled descendant of the above (318–272 B.C.) who was a fierce enemy to Rome. (XII. 134, if the ref. is not to P., son of Achilles.)

Quarnaro (Bay of): on the Adriatic. (IX. 113 and *note* to IX. 112.)

RACHEL: wife of the Patriarch Jacob and mother of Joseph and Benjamin (*Gen.* xxix *sqq.*). (II. 102 and *note*; iv. 60.)

Ram (Aries): see *Zodiac*.

Ravenna: town on the sea-coast of Italy, near the mouth of the Po (see map, p. 173); the birthplace of Francesca da Rimini. (V. 97 and V. 88 *note*; XXVII. 40.)

Red Sea: (XXIV. 90).

Reno: river of Italy. (XVIII. 61 and map, p. 173.)

Rhea: wife of Saturn and mother of Jupiter. (XIV. 100 and *note*.)

Rhone: river of France. (IX. 112 and *note*.)

RIMINI, FRANCESCA DA: see FRANCESCA DA RIMINI.

Rimini, house of: (XXVII. 48 and *note* XXVII. 46).

RIMINI, PAOLO DA: see PAOLO DA RIMINI.

RINALDO DEI SCROVEGNI: see SCROVEGNI, RINALDO DEI.

Glossary

RINIER DA CORNETO: a robber-baron of Dante's own day, who had his hold near Corneto in the Maremma district. (XII. 138.)

RINIER DEI PAZZI: a robber-baron, of the Pazzi family, contemporary with Dante. He infested the country between Florence and Arezzo, and is said to have made a speciality of despoiling prelates. Excommunicated in 1269 by Pope Clement IV. (XII. 138.)

ROBERT GUISCARD: see GUISCARD, ROBERT.

ROGER (Ruggieri) DEGLI UBALDINI: Archbishop of Pisa (1278–95), nephew of the Cardinal Ottaviano degli Ubaldini mentioned in *Inf.* x. 120. (XXXIII. 14 and *note* to XXXIII. 13.)

ROLAND (Orlando): nephew of Charlemayn (*q.v.*). He was an historical personage, but little is known of him beyond the many legends and poetical traditions that have clustered about his name. Dante places him in Mars, the Heaven of the Warriors (*Para.* xviii. 43). (XXXI. 18 and *note* to XXI. 16.)

Romagna: province of Italy, lying between Bologna and the Adriatic. (XXVII. 37; XXXIII. 154.)

Romagnols: (XXVII. 28).

ROMANO, AZZOLINO DA: see AZZOLINO.

Rome: (I. 71; II. 20; XIV. 105; XXXI. 59).

Romans: (XV. 77; XVIII. 28; XXVI. 60).

Romena: village in the Casentino district. (XXX. 73 and *note*.)

ROMENA,
AGHINOLFO DA   } members of the Conti Guidi family, who in-
Romena,   duced Adam of Brescia to falsify the currency.
Alexander   Dante implies that one of them was already
(Alessandro) da in Hell at the time of his vision – probably
Guido da   Aghinolfo, who died 1300. (XXX. 76–77.)

RUBICANT (Rubicante): demon. (XXI. 123; XXII. 40.)

RUSTICUCCI, JACOPO: a Florentine Guelf of humble origin, but of great wealth and liberality, and a distinguished statesman. The evil temper of his wife, which obliged him to separate himself from her, is said to have driven him into the vice for which he is punished. (VI. 79; XVI. 44 *sqq.*; and *note* to XVI. 37.)

Sabellus: Roman soldier mentioned in Lucan's *Pharsalia*. (XXV. 95 and *note* to XXV. 94.)

Sacred Face: holy image venerated at Lucca. (XXI. 48.)

St John (Baptist): Church of, in Florence (see *John Baptist, St*).

St Peter's: Cathedral, in Rome. (XVIII. 32.)

ST THOMAS AQUINAS: see AQUINAS, ST THOMAS.

ST ZITA: patron saint of Lucca, and by transference the city itself. (XXI. 38.)

Glossary

SALADIN (Salah-ed-din Yussuf ibn Ayub): Sultan of Egypt and Syria (1137–93); the famous Moslem hero of the Third Crusade. (IV. 129.)

Salimbeni $\left\{ \begin{matrix} Niccolò \\ Stricca \end{matrix} \right\}$ dei: see $\left\{ \begin{matrix} Niccolò \\ Stricca \end{matrix} \right\}$ dei Salimbeni.

Salse: place of execution near Bologna. (XVIII. 51, note.)

San Benedetto: monastery of (see Benedict's, St).

SANHEDRIM: members of, who condemned Christ. (XXIII. 122.)

SANT' ANDREA, JACOMO DELLA CAPELLA DI: of Padua. (XIII. 133 and note to XIII. 115.)

Sant' Angelo: Castle and Bridge of, in Rome. (XVIII. 32 and note.)

Santerno: river of Italy (see map, p. 173). (XXVII. 49 and note to XVII. 50.)

Sardi, Island of: see Sardinia.

Sardinia: (XXII. 90; XXVI. 104; XXIX. 48).

SASSOL MASCHERONI: see MASCHERONI, SASSOL.

SATAN: see DEVIL.

Saturn: an ancient Roman deity, whose early history is extremely obscure. Whence his name derived, or what he was originally the god of, nobody knows. At some point, however, he became identified by the Romans with the Greek deity Cronos, so that the whole Cronos-myth became attached to him. He was thus said to have been the father, by Rhea, of Jupiter (Gk. Zeus) and of various other Olympian deities, and to have been overthrown by his own children and cast out of Olympus. Since Zeus-Jupiter was fabled to have been born in Crete (probably by a further identification with some native Cretan god), the connexion with Crete was extended to Saturn also; so that by the time we get to Servius, the commentator of Virgil (*fl. c.* A.D. 400), we find him writing in a note on *Aen.* viii. 319: "for Saturn was king of Crete, and was overthrown in war by his son Jupiter. And fleeing hence, he was hospitably received by Janus, who was then reigning in Italy." According to Latin tradition, Saturn eventually became king of Italy, where he introduced civilization and agriculture, so that the "great Saturnian reign" took its place in legend at Italy's "golden age". This mixture of personalities and places is characteristic of the confusion in which the ancient myths became involved in post-classical and medieval times; Dante is no doubt relying on Servius when he speaks of "Crete, under whose king the world was once chaste". (XIV. 95–6 and *note*; XIV. 100 and *note*.)

Savena: river of Italy (see map, p. 173). (XVIII. 86 and note.)

Savio: river of Italy (see map, p. 173). (XXVII. 52 and note.)

SCARAMALLION (Scarmiglione): demon. (XXI. 105.)

Glossary

SCARMIGLIONE: see SCARAMALLION.

SCHICCHI, GIANNI: see GIANNI SCHICCHI.

SCIANCATO, PUCCIO ("Limping Puccio"): see PUCCIO DEI CALIGAI.

Scipio (Publius Cornelius Scipio Africanus Major). Roman general, (234–c. 183 B.C.); fought against Hannibal at Cannae (cf. XXVIII. 11, *note*); was appointed to the command of the army in Spain, captured New Carthage (Cartagena) (210 B.C.) and drove the Carthaginians out of Spain; crossed into Africa and there gained a decisive victory over Hannibal at the Battle of Zama (202 B.C.). For these services he earned the title Africanus. After being twice consul, and serving in the war against Antiochus the Great, he was accused of accepting bribes, and eventually left Rome and died in exile. (XXXI. 116.)

SCOTT, MICHAEL: Scottish philosopher and magician. (XX. 116 and *note*.)

SCROVEGNI, RINALDO DEI: member of a Paduan family notorious for their usury, whose arms were: *arg.*, a pregnant sow *az*. Rinaldo is said to have died with the words on his lips: "Give me the keys of my strong-box so that no one may get my money". (XVII. 64, and *note* to XVII. 55.)

Semele: daughter of Cadmus, king of Thebes, who became, by Jupiter, the mother of Bacchus. In revenge, Juno, disguised as Semele's old nurse, persuaded her to ask Jupiter to show himself to her in his divine splendour as the god of thunder, whereupon Semele was struck by lightning and burnt to ashes. Juno also revenged herself on Semele's three sisters: Ino (*q.v.*), Agave, and Autonoe. (XXX. 1 and *note*.)

SEMIRAMIS: wife and successor to Ninus (*q.v.*), renowned for her beauty and bravery; said to have built Babylon in Asia with its famous Hanging Gardens, and the great tomb of Ninus in Nineveh. The many mythical elements in her story, and the legends told of her lasciviousness, suggest that she may originally have been a Syrian goddess of love (Astarte). (V. 58.)

SENECA, LUCIUS ANNAEUS: Roman philosopher and tragic poet (4 B.C.–A.D. 65). He was tutor to the Emperor Nero, under whom he acquired great wealth and administrative power; but being accused of complicity in Piso's conspiracy, he committed suicide. He wrote various treatises on ethics, philosophy, and natural science, together with a number of tragedies on the Greek model. Dante, however, like many people of his time, supposed that the plays and the treatises were written by two different Senecas; and is careful to make it clear that the one he puts with the other philosophers in Limbo is "Seneca the Moralist". (IV. 141.)

Serchio: river near Lucca. (XXI. 49.)

Seville: city of the S. coast of Spain. (XX. 126; XXVI. 111.)

SEXTUS POMPEIUS: son of Pompey the Great; a sea pirate mentioned by Lucan (*Phars*. vi. 420–22); defeated by Caesar at Munda 45 B.C. (XII. 134.)

Sicily: island in the Mediterranean, divided from Italy by the Straits of Messina (see *Charybdis*). (XII. 108.)
    Sicilian: (XXVII. 7.)

Siena: city of N. Italy, in Tuscany; stronghold of the Ghibelline party. (XXIX. 109, 134.)
    Sienese: (XXIX. 122).

Siena, Albero of: see *Albero of Siena*.

SILVESTER I: Pope (314–35). (XIX. 117 and *note* to XIX. 115; XXVII. 95 and *note* to XXVII. 94.)

Silvius: first king of Alba Longa; son of Aeneas by Lavina, daughter of Latinus, according to Virgil (*Aen*. vi. 763), though he is usually described as the son of Ascanius and grandson of Aeneas (*q.v.*). (II. 13, 32.)

SIMON MAGUS: the magician. (XIX. 1 and *note*.)

Sinibaldo degli Ordelaffi: (XXVII. 45 and *note* to XXVII. 43).

SINON OF TROY: (XXX. 97 and *note*).

Sismund(i): Ghibelline family of Pisa. (XXXIII. 32.)

SOCRATES: Athenian philosopher (*c*. 469–399 B.C.), famous for the method of argument which proceeds by question and answer so framed as to elicit from the opponents an admission of the confusions and self-contradictions which their opinions involve (the "Socratic Dialectic"). He held that all vice was ignorance, and that rightly to understand virtue would enable men to live virtuously. Accused of blasphemy against the gods and of perverting the morals of the young, he was condemned to death by drinking hemlock. He is best known to us in the "Socratic Dialogues" of his disciple Plato, who inherited the spirit of his philosophy. (IV. 134.)

Sodom: a "city of the plain", near the Dead Sea, destroyed by fire from heaven because of the notorious vice of its inhabitants (*Gen*. xix). (XI. 50.)

Sol (the Sun): (XXIV. 2).

Soldan (Sultan): the, of Egypt, was also called in Dante's time the "Sultan of Babylon" – hence, by a confusion between the two Babylons, Dante refers to the kingdom of Semiramis as the "land the Soldan rules over". (V. 60 and *note*.)

    The Soldan mentioned by Guido da Montefeltro is El-Melik El-Mansoor La'geen (1296–99). (XXVII. 90.)

Glossary

SOLDANIER, GIANNI DEI: he was a Ghibelline, but when, in 1266, after the defeat of Manfred at Benevento, the Guelfs rebelled against Guido Novello and the Ghibelline nobles, he put himself at their head in opposition to his own party. (XXXII. 120.)

Soracte (in Dante, Siratti: now corrupted into S. Oreste): mountain near Rome, on which stand the church and monastery of San Silvestro (see SILVESTER, POPE) and the town of Soratte.

Spain: (XXVI. 103).

Spendthrifts' Club (Brigata Spendereccia): in Siena. (See *notes* to XIII. 115; XXIX. 125.)

Stricca (? dei Giovanni dei Salimbeni): of Siena. The identity of this young spendthrift is not certain. Some think he was the Stricca of the Salimbeni family who was *podestà* of Bologna in 1276 and 1286, and brother to the Niccolò mentioned in XXIX. 127; others think he was of the Tolomei family, others of the Morescotti.

Strophades: islands (see HARPIES).

STYX: river of Hell. (VII 106 and Images VIII; IX. 81; XIV. 116.)

Sychaeus: husband of Dido, queen of Carthage (see AENEAS). (V. 62.)

Tagliacozzo: Battle of. (XXVIII. 17 and *note*.)

Tambernic, Mt.: not certainly identified. (XXXII. 28 and *note*.)

Tanaïs: river (the Don). (XXXII. 27.)

Tarquin (Tarquinius Superbus): king of Rome, notorious for his tyranny and cruelty; banished by decree of the people at the instance of L. Junius Brutus (*q.v.*), 510 B.C. (IV. 126.)

Tartars: (XVII. 16).

TEGGHIAI(O) ALDOBRANDI: see ALDOBRANDI, TEGGHIAIO.

Telemachus: son of Ulysses (*q.v.*). (XXVI. 94.)

Teobaldo II: of Navarre (see *Tibbald*).

TESAURO DEI BECCARÌA: see BECCARÌA, TESAURO DEI.

THAÏS: the harlot; character from play by Terence. (XVIII. 133 and *note*.)

THALES: Ionic philosopher, astronomer, and mathematician; one of the "Seven Sages" (*c.* 636–*c.* 546 B.C.). (IV. 135.)

Thames: river of England. (XII. 121.)

Thebes: city of Boeotia, celebrated in many classical myths and legends, to several of which Dante alludes in the *Inferno*. Its walls were fabled to have built themselves to the music of the great musician Amphion; it was the birthplace of the prophet Tiresias and one of the cities which claimed to be the birthplace of Bacchus. It was the scene, among other episodes of vengeance and horror, of the tragic story of Oedipus and the consequent war of the

"Seven against Thebes", and of the infanticidal madness of Athamas. (XIV. 69 and *note* to XIV. 51; XX. 59; XXVI. 52 *sqq.* and *note*; XXXII. 11 and *note*; XXXIII. 88.)

    Thebans: (XX. 33; XXV. 15; XXX. 2 *sqq.* and *note*.)

Theseus: legendary king (or, as Dante calls him, "Duke") of Athens. Greek hero, son of Aegeus, king of Athens and of Aethra, daughter of Pittheus, king of Troezen. Among his many exploits are the slaying of various robbers and monsters, and in particular of the Minotaur, his war against the Amazons, and his attempt to carry off Persephone (Proserpine) from Hades. (IX. 53 and *note*; XII. 17 and XII. 13 *note*.)

Thibaut V: count of Champagne (see *Tibbald*).

THOMAS AQUINAS, ST: see AQUINAS, THOMAS.

TIBBALD (Tebaldello or Tribaldello dei Zambrasi): of Faenza. (XXXII. 122 and *note*.)

Tibbald (Theobald or Teobaldo II): Count Thibaut V of Champagne, king of Navarre. (XXII. 52 and *note*.)

Tiber: river on which Rome stands. (XXVII. 30.)

TIRESIAS: Theban soothsayer. (XX. 40 and *note*.)

TISIPHONE: see FURIES.

Titans: in class. myth., the children of Ouranos (Lat. Uranus, the sky) and Ge (Lat. Tellus, the earth), who rebelled against their father and set Cronos, one of their number, on the throne of Heaven. They were eventually overthrown by Zeus (Jupiter), the son of Cronos (Saturn), and his sister-wife Rhea (XIV. 100, *note*). Their rebellion was confused, by later writers, with that of the GIANTS (*q.v.*).

TITYUS: giant. (XXXI. 125 and *note*.)

TOPPO: ford and Battle of. (XIII. 121 and *note* to XIII. 115.)

Totila: the Hun – confused by Dante with ATTILA (*q.v.*). (XIII. 149 *note*.)

Trent: city of Italy (see map, p. 173). (XII. 5 and *note*; XX. 68.)

TRISTRAM (of Lyonesse): knight of Arthurian legend, the lover of Iseult the Fair, wife to King Mark of Cornwall. According to the version of the story which Dante is probably following, Mark surprised him with the queen and killed him. (V. 67.)

Troy (or Ilium; Gk. Ilion): ancient coast-town in Asia Minor, taken and sacked by the Greeks under Agamemnon, after 10 years' siege for the recovery of Helen (see PARIS). The siege is described in Homer's *Iliad*, and the sack in Virgil's *Aeneid* (*q.v.*). (I. 74–5; XXX. 14, 22, 97, 113.)

    Trojans: (IV. 22; XIII. 11; XVIII. 10 and *note*; XXVIII. 10 and *note*).

TROY, SINON OF: see SINON OF TROY.

TULLY: see CICERO, MARCUS TULLIUS.

Turks: (XVII. 16).

Turnus: prince of the Rutuli, in Latium; killed in fighting against Aeneas, to whom King Latinus (q.v.) had given in marriage his daughter Lavinia, previously promised to Turnus (*Aen.* viii–xii). (I. 107.)

Tuscany: that district of Italy which lies, for the most part, between the Apennines and the Mediterranean, extending roughly from the Gulf of Genoa in the N. to Orbitello in the S. It is watered by the Arno, and Dante's birthplace, Florence, was its chief city. Many Tuscan towns are mentioned in the *Comedy*, and on two occasions the spirits in Hell recognize Dante by his Tuscan speech. (XXIV. 122; XXVIII. 108.)

   Tuscans: (X. 22; XXII. 99; XXIII. 76, 91; XXXII. 66).

Tydeus: king of Chalydon. (XXXII. 130 and *note*.)

TYPHON (or Typhoeus): giant. (XXXI. 124 and *note*.)

Tyrol: (XX. 62).

UBALDINI, OTTAVIANO (Cardinal, 1210–73): a violent Ghibelline, who exulted loudly over the issue of the Battle of Montaperti (see X. 32, *note*), and was rebuked by another cardinal with the words: "If he knew the upshot of this Florentine war, he would not be so merry about it. The vanquished will triumph victoriously, and will not be lost eternally." (X. 120.)

UBALDINI, RUGGIERI DEGLI: see ROGER (Ruggieri) DEGLI UBALDINI.

UBBRIACHI: a Florentine family, notorious for their usury about Dante's time; their arms were: *gu.*, a goose *arg.* (XVII. 61 and *note* to XVII. 55.)

UBERTI, FARINATA DEGLI: see FARINATA.

UGOLIN(O) DELLA GHERARDESCA: Count, of Pisa. (XXXIII. 13 and *note*.)

ULYSSES (Odysseus): Prince of Ithaca; hero of Greek mythology, renowned for his cunning. He was in the army of Agamemnon at the siege of Troy (*note*, XXVI. 55); his exploits there are recounted in Homer's *Iliad*, and his long wanderings before he reached home, in the *Odyssey*. The name of his "old father" (XXVI. 95) was Laertes, and that of his son, Telemachus. During his absence his wife Penelope was courted by many suitors, whom she kept quiet by promising to marry one of them as soon as she had finished the web she was weaving; but every night she unravelled what she had woven during the day. When Ulysses returned, he killed all the suitors with the bow which none but he could bend. Homer gives no account of his death; other poets

say he was killed by Telegonus, the son he bore to the enchantress
Circe (XXVI. 91 and *note*). Dante's account appears to be his own
invention. (XXVI. 55 *sqq.* and *notes* to XXVI. 55, 83.)

Urbino: town of Italy, in Romagna. (XXVII. 30.)

Ursa Major: see *Wain*.

Val Camonica: see *Camonica, Val*.

Valdichiana: the valley of the Chiana, in Tuscany, notorious for its
malarial and unhealthy climate. (XXIX. 47.)

Valdimagra (Val di Macra): valley of the R. Macra, in Lunigiana, a
district in the N.W. of Tuscany ruled over in Dante's time by the
Malaspina family. (XXIV. 145 and *note* to XXIV. 142.)

Valéry, Alard de: see *Alard de Valéry*.

VANNI (Giovanni) FUCCI: thief from Pistoia. (XXIV. 125 *sqq.* and
note.)

VENEDICO CACCIANEMICO: see CACCIANEMICO, VENEDICO.

Venice: city of Italy. (XXI. 7 and *note*.)

Vercelli: town of Italy, at W. extremity of Lombardy. (XXVIII. 75.)

Verona: city of Italy, in Venetia. (XV. 22 and *note* to XV. 121 (see
map, p. 173); XX. 68.)

Verrucchio: castle and village near Rimini, seat of the Malatesta
family. (XXVII. 46 and *note*.)

Veso, Monte: see *Monte Veso*.

VIGNE, PIER DELLE: (XIII. 58 *sqq.* and *note*).

VIRGIL (P. Vergilius Maro): Roman poet (70–19 B.C.). Born at
Andes, near Mantua. His great epic, the *Aeneid*, tells the story of
Aeneas, and celebrates the origins of the Roman people and
empire (see AENEAS). Author also of the *Georgics* and of the
Eclogues, one of which (*Ec.* iv.) looks forward to the birth of a
Wonder-Child who should restore the Golden Age, and was held
in the Middle Ages to be an unconscious prophecy of Christ
(*Purg.* xxii. 64–81). In medieval legend, V. had the reputation of
being a White Magician. In the *Divine Comedy* he is the image of
Human Wisdom; he guides Dante through Hell and accompanies
him through Purgatory. First meeting with Dante, I. 62; recog-
nized by him, I. 79; visited by Beatrice, II. 53; his place in
Limbo, IV. 39; his companions there, IV. 67 *sqq.*; his "words of
power", III. 95, V. 23, VII. 11, XXI. 83; his conjuration of the spirits,
XXVI. 79; prophecy of Greyhound, I. 101 *sqq.*; discourse on
Luck, VII. 73 *sqq.*; on arrangement of Hell, XI. 16 *sqq.*; on origin
of infernal rivers, XIV. 94 *sqq.*; on origin of Mantua, XX. 61,
sqq.; opposed at gates of Dis, VIII. 112 *sqq.*; deceived by demons,
XXI. 106 *sqq.*; carries Dante in his arms, XIX. 34 *sqq.*, 124 *sqq.*,

XXIII. 37 *sqq.*, XXXIV. 70; explains fall of Satan and geography of Antipodes, XXXIV. 106; and *passim*.

VITALIANO DEI VITALIANI: member of a Paduan family who, about Dante's time, were notorious for their usury and lived near the houses of the Scrovegni family. (XVII. 68 and *note* to XVII. 55.)

Vulcan: in class. myth., the blacksmith of the gods. (XIV. 52 and *note*.)

Wain (the Plough, or Great Bear: Ursa Major): N. Polar constellation. (XI. 114.)

Water-Carrier (Aquarius): see *Zodiac*.

Wissant: town of Flanders. (XV. 4.)

Young King (*il re giovane*): see Henry, Prince of England.

ZAMBRASI, TEOBALDO DEI: see TIBBALD DEI ZAMBRASI.

ZANCHE, MICHAEL: Vicar of Logodoro in Sardinia. (XXII. 88 and *note*; XXXIII. 143.)

ZENO: Greek philosopher, founder of the Stoic school; born in Cyprus, he taught at Athens in the porch (stoa) which gave its name to his philosophy. Dates unknown, but said to have been still living 260 B.C. (IV. 135.)

Zodiac, signs of:

> *Aquarius* (the Water-Carrier): (Sun in Aq. mid-Jan. to mid-Feb.) (XXIV. 2, *note*.)
>
> *Aries* (the Ram): (Sun in A. mid-Mar. to mid.-Apr.) (I. 37 and *note*.)
>
> *Pisces* (the Fishes): (Sun in P. mid-Feb. to mid-Mar.) (XI. 113 and *note*.)

BOOKS TO READ

BOOKS about Dante are almost as innumerable as books about Shakespeare, and, like them, range from the vast and erudite to the trivial and tendentious. Here are a few titles which will be of help to the ordinary reader; they are all of modest size and price, though it is impossible to say whether they are all in print at the moment.

DANTE'S WORKS: Temple Classics edition (Dent) (6 vols.). This contains text and prose translation, on opposite pages, of the *Commedia* (3 vols.) and the *Vita Nuova* and *Canzoniere* (1 vol.) for those who would like to read Dante in his own language. The other two vols. contain the *Convivio* and the *Latin Works* in English.

PAGET TOYNBEE: *The Life of Dante* (Methuen).

DEAN CHURCH: *Essay on Dante* in the vol. entitled *Dante and S. Anselm* of the "New Universal Library" (Routledge) – admirable for historical background and literary appreciation.

P. H. WICKSTEED: *From Vita Nuova to Paradiso* (Manchester University Press). This traces the development of Dante's political and religious thought, and is an invaluable introduction to the theological significance of the *Comedy*.

CHARLES WILLIAMS: *The Figure of Beatrice* (Faber) – a beautiful and illuminating guide to the allegory, though a little difficult in places for those who are not accustomed to this writer's intensely individual approach to religion and poetry.

For those who would like to know something of Dante's literary friends and predecessors there is D. G. ROSETTI: *Poems and Translations* (Everyman), which contains verse-translations of many contemporary Italian poets, together with a translation of the *Vita Nuova*.

The sport of tracking Dante back to his sources may be enjoyably embarked upon with the aid, for a start, of the Bible, the *Apocryphal New Testament*, Virgil's *Aeneid*, Ovid's *Metamorphoses*, Statius' *Thebaïd*, Lucan's *Pharsalia*, and (if philosophy and theology are found attractive) Aristotle's *Nicomachean Ethics* and the *Summa Theologica* of St Thomas Aquinas. All these works are obtainable in translation; but people who read Latin should remember that for Dante "the Bible" means the Vulgate.

MORE ABOUT PENGUINS
AND PELICANS

For further information about books available from Penguins please write to Dept EP, Penguin Books Ltd, Harmondsworth, Middlesex UB7 0DA.

In the U.S.A.: For a complete list of books available from Penguins in the United States write to Dept CS, Penguin Books, 625 Madison Avenue, New York, New York 10022.

In Canada: For a complete list of books available from Penguins in Canada write to Penguin Books Canada Ltd, 2801 John Street, Markham, Ontario L3R 1B4.

In Australia: For a complete list of books available from Penguins in Australia write to the Marketing Department, Penguin Books Australia Ltd, P.O. Box 257, Ringwood, Victoria 3134.

In New Zealand: For a complete list of books available from Penguins in New Zealand write to the Marketing Department, Penguin Books (N.Z.) Ltd, P.O. Box 4019, Auckland 10.

DANTE
THE DIVINE COMEDY

II: PURGATORY
Translated by Dorothy L. Sayers

III: PARADISE
Translated by Dorothy L. Sayers and Barbara Reynolds

'We shall never see the like again, where Dante is concerned' –
Twentieth Century

'The translation is brilliantly successful' –
The Times Literary Supplement

No previous translator has succeeded in following so closely not only the metre and rhyme of the original, but the subtle variations of rhythm by which Dante expresses his changing moods; and the press comments which greeted the first two volumes were outstanding. When Dorothy Sayers died in 1957 she had translated nearly two-thirds of *Paradise* and so was almost in sight of completing her translation of the whole of *The Divine Comedy*. *Paradise* has now been completed by her friend Barbara Reynolds of Cambridge University, who has drawn on the experience of eleven years' discussion with Dorothy Sayers about Dante. Here, then, in a clear and straightforward translation with accompanying introductions and commentaries, is the greatest poem of the Middle Ages, available to thousands of new readers.

Also available
LA VITA NUOVA